MARKETING COMMUNICATIONS

To my mother, Una

'... to free the breath from its restless tides ...'

MARKETING COMMUNICATIONS

An Integrated Approach

P R SMITH

KOGAN
PAGE

Disclaimer

The masculine pronoun has been used throughout this book. This stems from a desire to avoid ugly and cumbersome language, and no discrimination, prejudice or bias is intended.

First published in 1993
Reprinted 1993
Reprinted 1994 (twice)
Reprinted with revisions 1995
Reprinted 1996

Kogan Page Limited
120 Pentonville Road
London N1 9JN

© P R Smith, 1993

British Library Cataloguing in Publication Data

A CIP record for this book is available from the British Library.

ISBN 0 7494 0775 1

Typeset by Books Unlimited (Nottm), Mansfield NG19 7QZ
Printed in England by Clays Ltd, St Ives plc

CONTENTS

WITHDRAWN

PART 1 BACKGROUND TO THE COMMUNICATIONS PROCESS

PART 2 THE MARKETING COMMUNICATION TOOLS

FOREWORD

Marketing communications must become more integrated! Whether you are a businessperson determined to obtain the maximum effectiveness from a limited promotional budget or a student coming to grips with all the different promotional elements in a marketing mix, it is important to make sense of the total process. It will only be possible to do so if marketing communications is seen as an integrated process. Although the logic of an integrated approach is obvious, it is not easy to achieve either theoretically or practically. Despite this inherent difficulty, Paul Smith's book demonstrates the potential of an integrated approach to marketing commucations.

Advertising has dominated much of promotional thinking and teaching, partly because it is the promotional form which is most obvious to us every day, and partly because it often accounts for the largest proportion of the promotional budget. Increasingly, however, below the line activities have become more important. Sales promotions have a vigorous role to play; direct marketing has grown strongly and public relations has become increasingly a separate discipline with its own agencies and its own academic courses. Internal marketing, the art of persuading an organisation's own employees to adopt a marketing orientation, is still in its infancy. All these separate elements must be integrated together.

However, the academic world has not yet provided a sufficiently strong theoretical framework either to support a totally integrated approach to the study of marketing communications, or to assist practitioners in making sound decisions on the division of the promotional budget. This is not to underestimate the valuable work already carried out in the field of consumer behaviour and organisational behaviour which rightly underpins promotional decisions.

The words 'marketing communications' are themselves neither well known nor well understood. The number of people with the title 'Marketing Communications Manager', although growing, is still very limited. In my experience in Britain, it is academics who are more comfortable with the term but I understand that in America 'marketing communications' is a preferred term among marketing practitioners. Whatever the exact situation, the lack of clarity only adds weight to my proposition that marketing communications must become more integrated and better understood academically and in business.

By integrated I mean that all the various elements of promotion devoted to informing, persuading or inducing action, from a range of target audiences, must be studied, analysed, planned and implemented in a coordinated and effective manner. This is an extremely difficult process. It presupposes that all the elements are individually understood and that their effects can reasonably be predicted.

At last we have a text by a European author which provides a comprehensive framework to enable the reader to better understand the individual contribution and the collective combination of each of the elements of the mix, including the important personal selling element.

In my role as Senior Examiner of the Chartered Institute of Marketing, in Marketing Communications, I intend to encourage this integrated approach. I am also adopting

it in my responsibilities as director of a full service agency and in my teaching responsibilities. I therefore commend the integrated approach to marketing communications
to the reader whether they be a student coming to grips with the subject or a practitioner aiming to obtain maximum effectiveness from a limited promotional budget.

Alan Pulford, Senior Examiner,
Marketing Communications,
Chartered Institute of Marketing,
The Manchester Metropolitan University
April 1993

ACKNOWLEDGEMENTS

Many friends, colleagues and business connections helped in the development of the material in this book. My thanks are extended to:

Jim Addison, CPM Sales Promotions
Joe Agius, McGregor Cory
Jacqueline Aldridge, Welbeck Golin/Harris
Nigel Baker, MS Surveys
Ross Barr, BMP DDB
Derek Bowden, Zenith Media
Ann Brunton, Welbeck Golin/Harris
Quentin Bell, The Quentin Bell Organisation
Kevin Browne, Bartle Bogle Hegarty
Sheila Clarke, PI Design Consultants
Caroline Crawford, ASA
Julian Cummins, Avista
John Farrell, IMP
Terry Forshaw, The Direct Marketing Centre
Les Geary, Nissan Motor (GB)
Karen Haig, Handel Communications
Robin Halsall, CPM Field Marketing
Margery Hancock, BJM
Ed Haynes, Logistics Data Systems International
Nick Hewison, Nestle Rowntree
Shirley Horn, Hewlett Packard
Michael Ingram, The Ingram Company
Kirsten Jenson, RSCG Conran Design
Stephen Jupp, Consumer Focus
Tim Lofts, Euro RSCG Direct
Simon Mahoney, SMP
Mike Maguire, Procter and Gamble
Les Maher, MFI
David Marshall, Shell UK
Paul Martin, Prudential
Ian Maynard, RSCG Euro
Harry McDermott, Exhibition Surveys
Karina Mellinger, CACI
James Murphy, Ogilvy and Mather
David Poole, DP&A
Alan Pulford, Manchester Metropolitan University
Simon Redman, Esso UK
Bill Reed, Canning International Management Development

Keith Roberts, PIMS
Bruno Rumano
Judith Seycombe, Media Week
Emma Simmons, Sedgwick Europe
Philip Spratt-Callaghan
Rex Sweetman, Muscutt Sweetman
Alan Topalian, Alto Design
Linda Wallace, Colgate Palmolive
Geoff Wicken, TGI
Andy Wilson, Independent Television Commission
Mike Wilson, BMP DDB Needham
Gerald Witing, Waitrose
Ze Zook Kale Dot 7 Communication

Thanks also to my marketing colleagues, both past and present, at the London Guild-hall University: Jeremy Baker, Ute Bradley, Andy Inglis, Syd Lowe, Owen Palmer, Mark Wronski and, in particular, to Chris Berry, with whom I have had the pleasure of sharing an office for some nine fascinating years. Constant inspiration from my brother, Rory, and the brothers Mullarkey, not to mention my ever patient wife, Beverley, who managed to entertain, educate and love our three children as I hid in my study for the last couple of years.

HOW TO USE THIS BOOK

This book should not be read from cover to cover but rather it should be used as a reference when addressing a particular aspect of marketing communications. The integrated nature of the subject does, however, refer the reader to other chapters and sections which are relevant to the particular area of interest. The anecdotal style, examples, cases, questions, key points and sections have been carefully structured so that the reader can dip into an area of interest, absorb the information and cross-refer if required. This allows the reader to extract specific answers quickly and easily. This book is designed to entertain as well as inform and so it is hoped that when dipping into a particular area, the reader will be lured into reading more.

Part 1 gives a general introduction to marketing, the marketing communications mix, theories of communication and buyer behaviour. This first part of the book continues to build a background to marketing communications by looking at what marketing research can and cannot provide, how to work with agencies and consultancies of all types, understanding the media, moving with the changing business environment and finally, international marketing communications. Part 2 covers specific marketing communication tools which marketing professionals have to manage at some time or other. These include selling and sales management; advertising; sales promotion; direct marketing; publicity and public relations; sponsorship; exhibitions; corporate identity and corporate image; packaging; merchandising; and finally the most potent of all the marketing communication tools, word of mouth.

The short cases at the end of each chapter in Part 2 (and at the end of Chapter 2 in Part 1) have been carefully selected to show a range of different types and sizes of organisations using various communications tools across a range of different industries and markets. Materials are drawn from both individuals (with marketing communications budgets of only £130) and organisations (with budgets of £1.4 billion). In this way, the book should prove useful to anyone interested, or working, in marketing.

The reader will discover that all of the communication tools can and should integrate with each other (as shown in Figure 0.2). It is therefore sometimes difficult to separate and categorise an activity as being one type of tool or another. For example, direct marketing and sales promotions should probably be called 'direct promotions' since they both more than likely involve each other. The chapters are not listed in order of importance. Selling and sales management is not always included in a marketing communications budget but the salesforce is a potent form of communication and generally they (or the sales manager) report to the marketing manager. In fact it has been put to the top of the list because all the other chapters thereafter tend to lead into each other.

The successful application of the marketing communications mix is helped by an understanding of communication theory and buyer behaviour theory. Marketing research can provide some practical and specific answers to the questions which the theories generate. This provides the building blocks for the marketing communications plan, which draws upon an understanding of how agencies operate and how

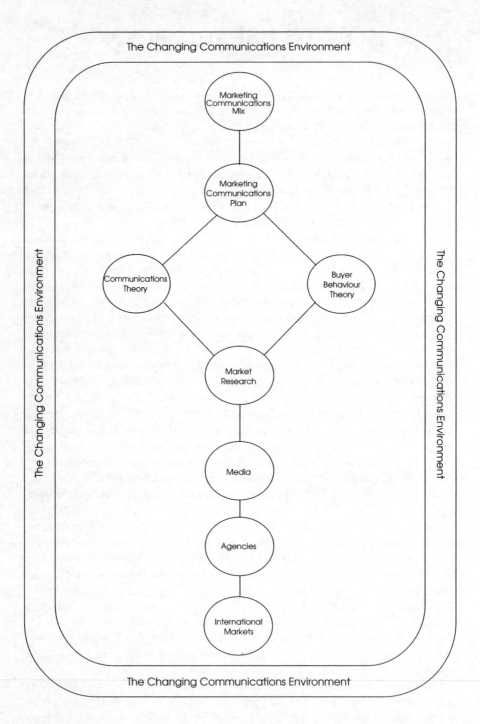

Figure 0.1 Part One: Background to the communications process

Figure 0.2 Part Two: The web of marketing communications mix

different media work. The details of the plan are worked out within the, sometimes complex but always integrated, web of the marketing communications mix (see figure 0.2). The changing marketing communications environment and international opportunities/threats constantly affect the whole marketing communications mix.

Different organisations allocate the same communication tools to different departments/budgets, eg exhibitions may be seen to be part of public relations, although the sales team will man the stand and benefit from extra sales. Sponsorship is considered by some to be an extension of advertising while others consider it to be quite separate. Regardless of classification, each tool integrates in reality with many others.

PART ONE

BACKGROUND TO THE COMMUNICATIONS PROCESS

1

THE MARKETING COMMUNICATIONS MIX

INTRODUCTION TO MARKETING

Before looking at the marketing communications mix we will consider briefly marketing and the marketing mix. A simple dictionary definition of marketing reveals:

Marketing n. the business of moving goods from the producer to the consumer

'Goods' can be taken to mean goods or services. The Chartered Institute of Marketing in the UK define marketing as:

'The management process responsible for identifying, anticipating and satisfying customer requirements profitably.'

A few years ago the American Marketing Association spent a lot of time and effort considering the appropriateness and accuracy of their definition of marketing. Their new definition incorporated one major change — they took 'profit' out, possibly because it excluded the vast armies of marketing professionals who work for charities and other non-profit-making organisations. Perhaps the UK definition could replace 'profitably' with 'efficiently', or, 'in a way that meets the organisation's goals'?

A simpler definition is '*marketing is the selling of goods that don't come back to people that do*'. 'Goods that don't come back' emphasises the importance of matching the promise (made by, say, the advertising or the packaging) with the reality of the product's or service's *quality*, ie the level of quality should match that which is advertised. In the long term it does not pay to cheat the customer. *Real marketing success depends on repeat business* and that is where 'people that do come back' embraces the customer's '*lifetime value*' concept (see 'Direct Marketing', Chapter 13). Customers do not buy just one can of beans, one car, or one photocopying machine. They buy thousands of cans of beans, dozens of cars and dozens of photocopiers during their 'lifetime'. There the marketing challenge lies — attracting and retaining customers efficiently. A move away from the 'one-off sale syndrome' allows marketing horizons to broaden.

The tinned catfood market in the UK is huge. To put it in perspective, imagine, if you can, the entire Albert Hall filled from ceiling to floor in catfood. Remove the shell of the building like a giant jelly mould, to leave a quivering mountain of foul smelling, jellied meat and you have a lucid picture of the amount of food that cats in this country munch their way through every two months — amazing when you consider that only 23 per cent of homes in the UK have a cat.
(Source: Ivan Pollard, Media Planning Director, BMP DDB Needham)

The four Ps

One conceptual framework which helps to structure the approach to each marketing challenge is what Jerome McCarthy called the *marketing mix*, or the *four Ps*. These four ingredients (product, price, place/distribution and promotion/communication) can be mixed together in an infinite number of ways. It is the combination of these components, and a *fifth 'P'*, 'people' (customers, competition and employees), which are the basic building blocks of a marketing programme.

A poor quality product or service generally says more than any amount of advertising (see Chapter 20). Price is used by many buyers as an indicator of quality. The place of purchase also communicates, eg an item purchased in Harrods has a different perceived value to an item purchased in Woolworths. The fourth P, promotion, has its own mix of communication tools, which are sometimes called the promotions mix or the communications mix. This mix includes every communications tool which is available to the organisation. As Frank Jefkins says, '...marketing communications mean what it says (sic). It consists of every form of communication relevant to marketing.' The relation of the communications mix to the marketing mix is shown in Figure 1.1.

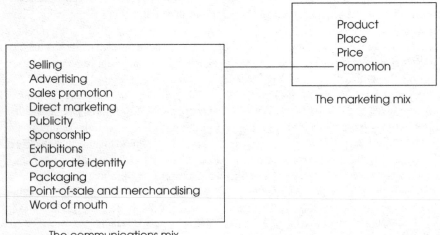

The communications mix
(the promotions mix)

Figure 1.1 The relation of the communications mix to the marketing mix

The marketing communications mix

The marketing communication tools consist of:

1) Selling
2) Advertising
3) Sales promotion
4) Direct marketing
5) Publicity (and public relations)
6) Sponsorship
7) Exhibitions
8) Corporate identity
9) Packaging
10) Point-of-Sale and merchandising
11) Word of mouth

This list is not in any order of priority since different industries lay different emphasis on certain communication tools, eg an FMCG (fast moving consumer good — such as a tin of beans) manufacturer may consider advertising, packaging, sales promotion and point-of-sale to be the most important tools while a heavy industrial machine manufacturer may lay emphasis on selling, exhibitions and word of mouth to be the most important set of communications tools. The second part of this book devotes a chapter to each of the communication tools listed in the communications mix. The next couple of paragraphs clarify and explain the interpretation and categorisation of the marketing communications mix since many marketing professionals interpret or categorise them differently.

Direct marketing draws on and integrates with advertising and sales promotion. Direct marketing includes direct response advertisements. Chapter 13 focuses on direct mail and telemarketing/telesales. Publicity means positive editorial coverage in the media; it is not meant to include 'bad press'. It does include stunts or events as well as certain other techniques included in Chapter 12, 'Public Relations'.

The marketing communications mix should, in one way, include employees and customers as 'word of mouth' can be very effective communicators among their own networks. Their salaries and wages are not part of the communications budget but they are worth including in some of the communications activities which enhance the word-of-mouth process (see Chapter 20). Although selling is all about communicating, some companies choose to leave selling and sales management out of the communications budget and put the salesforce into their distribution plan instead. This makes sense since one of the salesforce's main responsibilities is to service existing distribution channels and penetrate new channels. However, since face-to-face selling is a potent and expensive marketing communications tool (on a cost per thousand contacts basis) it is clearly included in the marketing communications mix.

Above the Line and Below the Line

'Above the line' refers to advertising. 'Below the line' basically refers to any other communications tool other than the salesforce (which does not fall into either category). Traditionally, below the line refers to sales promotion and public relations. Above the line advertising means any advertising which has to pay for the space it uses, eg TV, press, print, cinema or radio space, all of which cost money. Advertising agencies used to separate activities to above and below the line because the agencies earned commission on above the line advertising and fees only on below the line activities. The line is eroding as many agencies are moving away from commission-based earnings to fee-based earnings. The line is also somewhat vague since some professionals see direct marketing as 'through the line'. In addition, advertorial (advertising that looks like editorial) is sometimes paid for out of a PR budget (below the line) since it is written through the eyes of a journalist as opposed to an advertising copywriter, yet it is paid-for space which is bought like advertising space (above the line).

Push and pull strategies

Different blends of the marketing communications mix are required for two different marketing strategies. A 'push strategy' is dependent on a strong salesforce supported by trade promotions which serve to 'push' the product hard into the distribution channels and on to the distributors' shelves. It is all about distribution penetration. A 'pull strategy' is more concerned with pulling the customers into the store/distributor and motivating them to 'pull' the product off the shelf. This requires an investment in advertising to create customer demand. Many retailers today want to be assured that a brand has comprehensive marketing support, eg advertising. In effect the 'pull' helps the 'push' since the advertising reassures the retailer that the stocks will move and this, in turn, makes the salesperson's 'push' that bit easier.

Two of the biggest and most successful FMCG companies, Lever Brothers and Procter and Gamble, have different basic strategies here. Philip Kotler reports that Lever Brothers emphasise a push strategy, while Procter and Gamble prefer a pull strategy. Both companies appear to enjoy success despite their different strategies.

Pushing and pulling is not enough

A well-planned and carefully executed marketing communications programme cannot, on its own, guarantee success. This is dependent on a balanced marketing mix. A great advertisement may succeed in getting people to go out and ask for a particular product but the overall plan fails if, say, the place is wrong. Too much 'pull' and not enough 'push'. Perhaps less investment in advertising ('pull') and more investment in sales training ('push') or simply more direct investment in distribution (new delivery vehicles, more drivers, better serviced vans, bigger stocks, smaller minimum orders, quicker deliveries, etc) might enable the right goods to get to the right place at the right time. If the goods are not there when they are needed then *the success of advertising fails*. Similarly, the promotion and the place might work to bring a potential customer close to buying a particular product but the price might just put the product out of reach.

Finally, the product (or service) must match the promise made through the communications mix if long-term success (repeat sales) is to be achieved. A customer only buys a bad product once. This means that difficult investment decisions have to be made in areas often outside the marketing manager's control, eg product quality programme, product design progamme, new product development programme, production equipment, staff motivation, customer care programmes and so on. Constable and McCormack's 1987 management forecast indicated that tomorrow's organisations will be leaner and flatter. This means that tomorrow's managers will be multi-skilled. Even those managers who are not directly involved in marketing will require an overall integrated marketing perspective, as they will have to balance financial decisions along with production, quality, human resource and marketing decisions. Perhaps more boardrooms will display proud pictures of the organisation's products, services and employees?

THE INTEGRATED COMMUNICATIONS MIX

Each element of the communications mix should *integrate with other tools* of the communications mix so that a unified message is consistently reinforced in a cost effective manner.

Some major *advertising campaigns are supported by PR* activity. In fact many advertisements have press launches not for the product but for the advertisement itself. Thus publicity and advertising can work together to create a bigger impact in a cost effective way. Press launches and photo opportunities were seized upon by the political parties whenever they released a new advertisement during the 1992 UK election. Many poster advertisements were officially unveiled by celebrities or senior politicians. The free media coverage (editorial coverage) which followed was often greater than the coverage which the paid-for advertising generated, ie more people saw the publicity (editorial coverage) about the advertisement than subsequently saw the advertisement only. Here, *below the line supports above the line activity.*

Sales promotions are often tied in with or supported by advertising or PR or both. It is no use having a great sales promotion campaign if no one hears about it in the first place. Again, instead of the product being advertised, it is the sales promotion which is advertised. Here, *above the line supports the below the line activity.* There are publicity opportunities which public relations professionals can exploit if they are briefed and integrated into the overall programme at an early enough stage. Some sales promotions get national coverage without any above the line support. Pears Soap annual contest gains national coverage every year purely through carefully planned below the line (public relations) activities. In this case, *below the line activities are integrated with other below the line activities.*

British Airways launched a sensational sales promotion when they announced free flights to anywhere in the world. The sales promotion was so newsworthy it hardly needed any advertising by the time the public relations people had maximised the editorial opportunities. The *sales promotion also helped to build a database* for future direct mail activities. Many direct response advertisements (with coupons or toll-free telephone numbers) offer an incentive, premium, gift or sales promotion. The term, '*direct promotion*' succinctly combines direct marketing with sales promotion. Fully integrated *hybrid marketing systems* are looked at in more detail in Chapter 13.

Many *FMCG* (fast-moving consumer goods such as groceries) sales promotions are also promoted on the product's *pack* itself (on-pack promotion). A new pack or new sales promotion usually has to be brought to the attention of the retailer by the *sales-force*. They need to be fully briefed and sometimes they need new *literature* to leave with the retail buyers. In addition, new *point-of-sale* materials may be required to display and promote the sales promotion inside a retail outlet. A modified pack (carrying the on-pack promotion) has to be designed and produced. This means new stocks and so a properly co-ordinated team has to be briefed and ready to move into sometimes several hundred outlets within, say, 24 hours. This is generally too big a job for the regular salesforce so it is sometimes supplemented by a *team of merchandisers* or *field marketing team*.

Integrated Cost Effectiveness

Any communication tool should integrate with and draw on as many other communication tools as possible in order to maximise cost effectiveness and reinforce a consistent image. Photography, design and printing of advertisements, sales promotion leaflets, new packs, point of sale, press packs, direct mail leaflets, sales literature, etc can, for example, be co-ordinated by choosing and briefing the same service supplier whether a photographer, designer or printer. This can save time and money and simultaneously keep the communications mix integrated. This may not always be possible eg some photographs may be suitable for inclusion in the pack design but not suitable for inclusion in a press pack. However, the photographer can of course be briefed to cover both requirements. Even this is not always possible since, for example, some designers may only specialise (or be really experts in), say, packaging or direct mail leaflets.

Alternatively, sometimes different people handle different aspects — an in-house marketing or advertising department may prefer an *à la carte* approach by working with several agencies or consultants on different promotional aspects. In fact, some organisations avoid giving one agency all their promotional work for fear of it all having the same 'look'. That is fine as long as first, an integrated approach is considered, and secondly, a bigger budget (and more time) is available since many potential cost savings are lost (eg pack photography that could have been used in a mail shot or blown up for a backdrop to an exhibition stand). Careful planning creates *marketing communications synergy* which reinforces a consistent message or image in a cost effective manner.

Intensive marketing communications

Buying models (see page 70, Chapter 4) are helpful when considering how to plug all the communication gaps or channels which lead to a buyer's mind. By identifying the stages a buyer goes through and all the possible communication channels, it is possible to force a product or service into the mind of a buyer (if the resources are available). Hopefully, what is forced in is accepted and perceived to be pleasant rather than resented and rejected. A major soft drinks manufacturer once tested this idea in a European town. There was blanket local advertising supported by street bands, free samples, free gifts, new point-of-sale material in every CTN (confectioner, tobacconist and newsagent). Even extra vending machines and street stalls were placed strategically to maximise the consumer's opportunity to sample and buy the brand. The consumer could not avoid the brand. Every route to the consumer's mind was filled.

The term *'share of mind'* is an awesome piece of marketing jargon. It effectively means how many minds you can get an organisation, or its brand, into. Share of mind can be bought by increasing the marketing communications spend. Many companies obviously want to keep their brands in the front of the buyer's mind (*'front of mind awareness'*). This obviously depends on the quality and frequency of advertising and other marketing communication tools compared to a competitor's communications. *'Share of voice'* refers to the share of advertising spend against the total market spend on advertising. Of course it isn't all plain sailing since first, most companies have limited resources and, second, there is a phenomenon called 'competition'. They may be trying to use the same communication channels.

Can you ignore Euro Disney?

Can you ignore EuroDisney? Has it forced its way into your mind? Readers with children will know what this means. Interestingly, EuroDisney's initial promotional mix appears to be all below the line publicity, while sponsors pay Disney for the privilege of promoting Disney on breakfast TV, on breakfast cereal boxes, in restaurants, in petrol stations and so on. Most of the avenues to the minds of the target audience are filled with the Disney message. It will be interesting to see how long Disney can maintain this high profile.

THE MARKETING COMMUNICATIONS BUDGET

How much should be spent on the marketing communications mix? How much is really needed? Half of it is wasted but which half? How much is spent on each particular communication tool is a separate question which is addressed in 'mixing the mix' (page 25).

Most organisations agree that there are four basic approaches to building a communications budget. These will be discussed in the next paragraph. What most organisations do not agree on, however, is the name of the budget. Few call it an advertising budget since much more than advertising is required to survive in today's communication jungle. Many organisations call it an A & P budget (advertising and promotion). In their worldwide analysis of the breakdown of marketing budgets, the research group Profit Impact of Marketing Strategy (PIMS) use the word 'promotion' to cover sales promotion, public relations, direct mail and exhibitions, but not salesforce. Others call it a MARKOM (marketing communications) budget. Although it is a key communication tool, salesforce costs are often not included in the MARKOM budget. Some companies suggest that if the salesforce costs are included then the result is a full-blown marketing budget per se. To turn this into a full-blown marketing plan the other three Ps (product, price, promotion), market review, and controls have to be built in.

Whatever the name and whatever the components, here are the four main approaches to developing, appropriating or setting aside resources for marketing communications:

1) Affordable
2) Objective and task
3) Competitive parity
4) Percentage of sales

1) The affordable approach is the antithesis of marketing because of its production oriented approach. After calculating gross margins and determining required net profits, whatever is left after all other costs and expenses is allocated towards the marketing communications budget. This residual approach relegates marketing to the bottom of the business functions.

2) The objective and task approach takes the opposite view. Determine what needs to be done and calculate the funds required. This requires specific objectives and detailed tasks which need to be completed to achieve these objectives, eg create a certain level of awareness or achieve a certain number of enquiries, etc. When each task is fully costed they are added up to give the total marketing communications budget. This approach seems ideal, but a manager has to be able to give a detailed justification. The proposed budget will be checked against previous years' percentage of sales (see below) and against the competition's percentage of sales.

3) Competitive parity basically uses the competition as a yardstick. It is a sort of 'if they spend more we spend more' scenario. If, on the other hand, they spend less, then there is an opportunity to reduce the spend or maintain it and seize the initiative. Some companies do actually use this approach when calculating 'share of voice' to ensure that customers get as many, or more, opportunities to hear their company's message rather than the competition's. Most figures are historical but can, if monitored during a year, indicate future spending patterns (eg a continuing increase suggests bigger budgets next year). See 'Marketing Intelligence and Information System' (page 104, Chapter 5).

4) The percentage of sales method is, arguably, everyone's favourite because it is the easiest to calculate. It can be used on forecasted or historical figures. An agreed percentage, say, 5 per cent is allocated against the sales figure, say, £10 million to give a budget of £500,000. Estimates suggest that the consumer products and services range from 3 per cent to 30 per cent while industrial products and services range from 0 per cent to 5 per cent (these figures exclude any allowance for the salesforce, ie sales have a separate budget). Problems arise when sales are falling and the percentage figure is calculated on the reduced sales figure. This may be the very time when more, not less, promotional expenditure is required. In a sense, this method views promotion as a result rather than as a cause of sales.

Past experience

Many companies know historically what is required to sustain a given business from year to year. They test their way to finding out what sales impact a bigger or lesser spend will have in order to optimise profit return. They also have data to tell them what impact a new competitor or higher competitor spending will have on their own business. There are some software packages which help to calculate the optimum spend in advertising. In reality a little of each method is used with different companies emphasising one particular approach over another. There are arbitrary influences which affect the final budget allocation. These are often emotionally charged and seemingly psychologically attached to the status quo, eg 'We've always advertised on television'. Some promotional budgets have to be justified in terms of *return on investment*, eg 'Why not invest the money in a new plant or equipment instead of advertising?' As discussed in 'Pay by Results' (see page 115, Chapter 6), there are difficulties in isolating the direct effect of promotions. Nevertheless, it is a useful discipline to try to justify the spend in terms of profit generated over size of expenditure/investment. Some agencies sit down with their clients at the end of each year and review the effectiveness of the campaigns by asking 'Was the advertising worth the money spent?' or 'What was the return on investment?'. Advertising agency BMP DDB Needham calculated the return on investment from its award-winning campaign for the National Dairy Council (see pages 212–15 , Chapter 11, for an insight into how the campaign was created) as follows: the campaign stimulated the sales of an extra 145 million bottles of milk (delivered by the milkman) which generated a profit of £17.5 million against an investment (advertising expenditure) of £5 million giving a 250% return on investment.

Recession Cutbacks?

It is interesting to note that the giant worldwide Unilever company allocate over 10 per cent of turnover to advertising and promotion, which gives them a global A & P spend of £2.37 billion. In 1991, in the teeth of a recession, Unilever increased its advertising spend by 9 per cent.
(Source: M & M Europe, October 1992)

SPLITTING THE BUDGET/MIXING THE MIX

Should more be spent on sales promotions than advertising? What would happen if a company switched all press, print and TV advertising over to direct mail? Or spent half on advertising, and half on sales promotion and excluded publicity? Almost every promotional activity involves sacrificing something else.

Advertising is still seen by many in the UK as the most effective way to nurture a brand's image over the long haul whereas sales promotion tends to be seen as shorter-term, tactical, temporary sales boosters (although there are exceptions). Professor Ehrenberg's Pan-European sales promotion research claimed sales promotions had basically no positive effect on brand building, brand loyalty and repeat purchase patterns. This is not surprising since the research focused mostly on price promotions (money-off, discounts etc). Price discounts dilute the brand franchise or the quality images of the brand. Endorsing this obvious logic, International Business News reported a change in the communications mix in American companies in September 1991:

Many giant consumer good companies are saddled with huge levels of debt so, in category after category, brand managers are scrambling to boost quarterly sales instead of investing in image advertising to nurture brands for the long haul. To increase sales, they are *shifting marketing dollars from ads to promotions* such as coupons, contests or sweepstakes and because most promotions are placed locally companies are shifting dollars from national to local media. Many experts believe that such strategies — carried to an extreme — run the *risk of damaging valuable brand franchises* that enable marketers to price their products at a premium.

PIMS research states that *companies relying more on sales promotion than on advertising are, on average, far less profitable* than those that adopt the opposite approach.

Despite all this, some surveys show UK sales promotion taking the biggest share of the communications cake, followed by advertising, while public relations has enjoyed the strongest growth. This is shown in Table 1.1.

Table 1.1 The size and growth of some marketing service sectors

The UK Mix	1991 Size £ Billion	1981 Size £ Billion	Source
Sales promotion	9.0	3.5	Campaign & ISP
Advertising	8.8	2.7	ISBA
Public relations	0.7	0.1	IPR/PRCA
Direct marketing	0.9	0.3	ISBA
Exhibitions	0.9	0.2	ISBA

Carefully chosen sales promotions can of course enhance and reinforce the brand image. These consumer franchise building promotions are looked at in more detail in Chapter 12. There are always exceptions to the rule where some consumer companies do not advertise or run sales promotions. For example, Body Shop do not advertise, but instead lay emphasis on good public relations, merchandising, customer care and direct marketing.

European idiosyncrasies

National differences complicate life for the Pan-European marketing manager since local idiosyncrasies demand local mixes. According to the Pan-European Marketing Communications Report (1990), the Germans, for example, spend more on advertising than the British, but far less on sales promotion. The Spanish, on the other hand, invest heavily in design and exhibitions while the French invest heavily in public relations. There is some guidance on how to balance the communications mix (in mostly FMCG markets in both Europe and North America). This is shown in the PIMS research data referred to in the third key factor influencing the optimum marketing communications mix — market structure. We will first consider all the four key factors affecting the optimum communications mix.

The key factors influencing the optimum mix

Factors which affect how the marketing communications mix should be balanced, apportioned or mixed include:

1) The response required (objectives)
2) Type of product or service
3) Market structure (share, growth and concentration)
4) The resources available

The response required

As mentioned in 'Outline Marketing Communications Plan' (page 34, Chapter 2), clearly defined objectives help to drive the marketing communications strategy and ultimately identify the optimum mix of communications tools. For example, building awareness requires advertising and PR while brand switching requires some kind of integrated sales promotion campaign.

Figure 1.2 shows the general effectiveness of various communications tools at various stages in the communications process (AIDA is fully explained in Chapter 5). Clearly defined objectives identify the response required from the audience which, in turn, helps the marketer to select the optimum mix of communication tools.

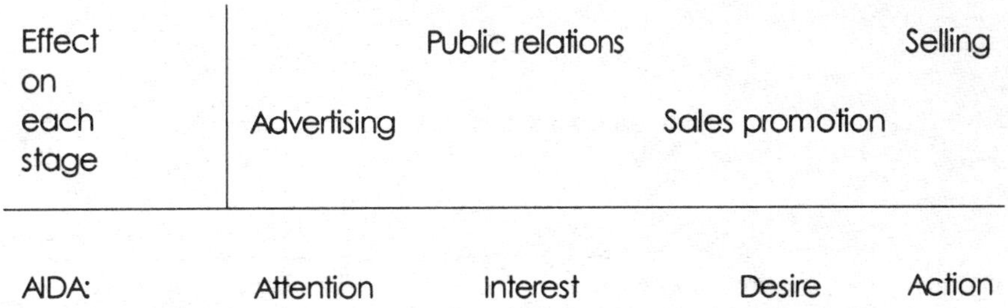

Effect on each stage			
	Public relations		Selling
	Advertising	Sales promotion	

| AIDA: | Attention | Interest | Desire | Action |

Figure 1.2 The effect of various communication tools

Advertising and publicity lend themselves towards creating awareness while sales promotion and selling are more action oriented or more sales oriented. This may change because as much as 70 per cent of US press advertisements have a direct response mechanism built in, eg a toll-free number coupon for more information or a free test drive, etc.

Type of product or service

FMCG brands need a lot of advertising and little personal selling compared with industrial goods, which need little advertising and a lot of personal selling. Figure 1.3 illustrates this.

Organisations also use other communication tools, as shown in figure 1.4.

The PIMS 1992 database reveals the following average marketing communications mix for both consumer and industrial markets (Table 1.2). This is not necessarily the

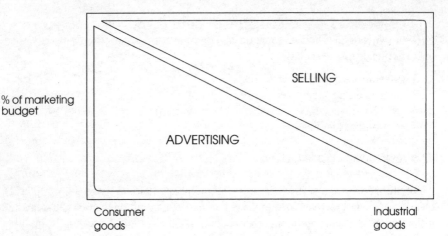

Figure 1.3 Type of product or service and the communications mix

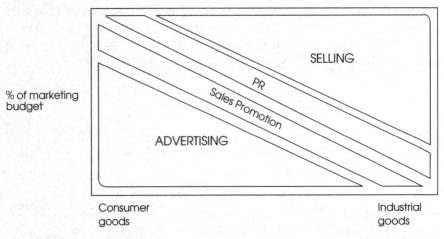

Figure 1.4 Type of product or service and the communications mix

optimum mix but can, in a sense, be seen as the accumulated wisdom of winners and losers.

Table 1.2 Average communications mix for consumer and industrial markets

	% of marketing budget	
	Consumer markets	**Industrial markets**
Advertising	25	3
Sales promotions	33	7
Other	10	20
Salesforce	32	70

Source: PIMS 1992

This clearly demonstrates how industrial companies spend a large proportion of their marketing communications budget on very well-trained and well-paid sales teams whereas consumer/FMCG products spend the bulk of their marketing budgets on advertising and sales promotion (A & P).

Market structure (share, growth and concentration)

PIMS international business consultancy collates and analyses worldwide FMCG marketing communications mixes across North America and Europe. This research has lead them to conclude that:

A company's profits are affected by, among other things, how it mixes its communications mix. It is not so much the size of the budget but more the allocation of that budget among different communication tools (ie the mixing of the mix) which affects profits.

The optimum communications mix can be determined by an individual company's relative market share, the growth of the market itself and whether the market is concentrated in the hands of a few key players or fragmented among many players. Here are five specific findings:

1) Good profitability depends on the mix of advertising and promotion. It does not depend on the total marketing spend, either in absolute terms or relative to competitors.
2) Gaining market share depends on the sum of the two amounts — advertising and promotion.
3) Market share rank determines the optimum mix of advertising and promotion. For example, the market leader should spend 70 per cent or more of its marketing budget above the line (advertising). The optimum amount of advertising for number two and three brands lies between 50 per cent and 70 per cent of the marketing budget (with the balance being spent below the line). The fourth place brand, by contrast, would actually lose money by employing the same strategy. *Low share businesses with high advertising, on average, lose money* in their attempt to play the big boy's turf. The optimum above the line allocation here is between 30 per cent and 50 per cent of the marketing budget.

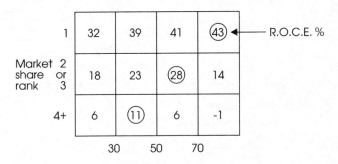

(Source: PIMS FMCG database)

Figure 1.5 Maximising profits by matching the mix with market share

The PIMS figures use one measure of profit known as ROCE (return on capital employed) or profit expressed as a percentage of everything tied up in (or invested in) the business. In the long term the percentage of profit returned from the business (and its investment) should be more than the bank rate. Otherwise the business might consider selling itself (realise its assets) and invest the funds realised in a bank so that it could earn a higher percentage return .

Figure 1.5 shows average profitability/return on capital employed (over a four year period) resulting from different mixes and brand ranks (1 = market leader, 4 = 4th place, etc). The highest ROCE is circled in each row. The bottom row shows how tough life is for the smaller brands (with smaller market share). The best they can do is earn 11 per cent ROCE, probably less than their cost of capital. They can even lose money (–1 per cent ROCE) if they use the worst mix (eg. advertising gets 70 per cent of the communications mix). The best mix for these low market share brands is around 40:60 (advertising : advertising + promotion). As mentioned, the optimum mix for the number one brand shows advertising taking 75 per cent or more of the mix.

4) Advertise in declining markets, promote in growth markets. This suggests that heavy advertising can wait until a market is bigger and the consumer matures. In the interim (during the growth stages), sales promotions can stimulate consumer trial. During the decline stages, the survivors will be the well-advertised brands.

As you can see from Figure 1.6, maximum profits during the decline stage appear where the advertising proportion of the mix is increased. Sluggish and declining markets need brand maintenance (advertising). As Keith Roberts of PIMS says:

Advertise in declining markets, promote in growth markets... The underlying

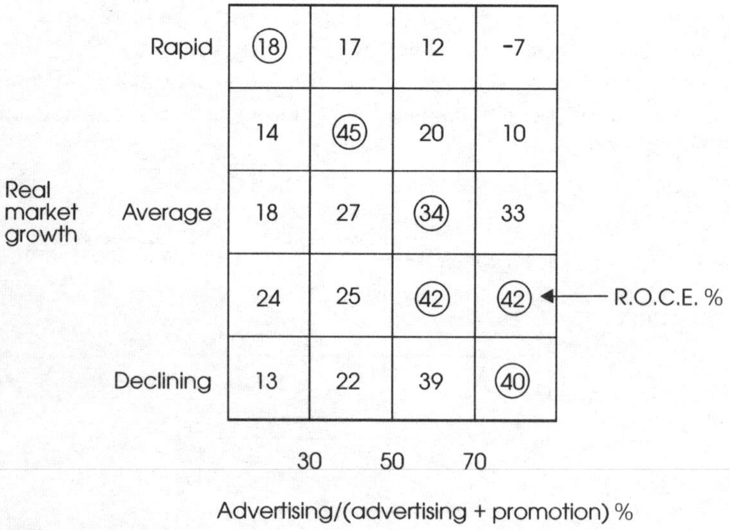

(Source: PIMS FMCC database)

Figure 1.6 Maximising profits by matching the mix with market growth

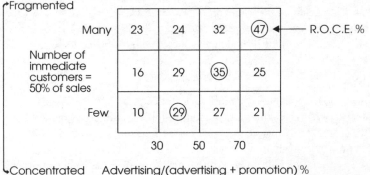

(Source: PIMS FMCG database)

Figure 1.7 Maximising profits by matching the mix with market concentration

explanation seems to be that competition is very different in a boom. Dozens of entrants jostle for leadership, and brand franchises don't count for much with inexperienced consumers. Marketers must be single-minded about getting their product on the shelf and stimulating consumer trial: they do not need to advertise. Advertising can wait until the market is bigger and consumers more mature.

5) As markets concentrate, reduce the proportion of advertising expenditure. Many markets today are concentrating as buyers get bigger and gain more buying power. Inevitably concentrated markets with a few powerful buyers means lower profits as the buyers exert their buying power.

   As Figure 1.7 shows, optimum profits in fragmented markets emerge when advertising takes almost 85 per cent of the marketing communications budget. Optimum profits in more concentrated markets emerge when less emphasis is placed on advertising, ie around 45 per cent.

Resources Available

Products in organisations with a portfolio of different products or services may have to compete internally for a limited supply of resources. Specific allocation of resources to products may depend on the overall balance of the product range or portfolio, with some products requiring more money proportionately (high growth markets) than other products (say, low growth brand dominant markets).

The *three key resources*, the *three Ms*, men/women, money (budgets) and minutes (time) are limited in supply. Money is invariably a limited resource. Time is also a limited resource. The management of time affects the organisation's overall performance since firstly, time management is vital in any kind of project management, and secondly, good time management improves an individual's performance. Stress, health, time management and job performance are generally linked.

Minutes and men are linked. How much management time can be allocated to each communication tool? Some departments say that they don't have the time to start researching, testing and learning about alternative marketing communication tools. How many organisations that do not use direct marketing have reviewed the feasibility of introducing database marketing (see 'Database Marketing', page 254, Chapter 13)? How many staff can be delegated to various tasks? Are some tasks more time consuming than others? Can some be handled by junior staff? Who has to be involved at every stage?

As Dan O'Donoghue, joint CEO of Publicis says:

> In the 1980s, some marketing directors started to believe the Thatcherite theory that ads could solve everything ... some people would be spending 50 per cent of their time with creative directors rather than sticking to their knitting ... it's the more cautious marketers, who kept to more classical marketing strategies, who have emerged strongly. Advertising shouldn't really occupy more than about 5 per cent of a marketing director's time.

Some of the larger FMCG companies do see advertising as the key element, so much so that they call brand managers, 'advertising managers'. These kinds of companies would like the managers to devote half of their time to the constant monitoring, refining and developing of advertising campaigns, but time pressures prevail and therefore often restrict their total devotion to the advertising process. In reality, less than 50 per cent of the time is spent on advertising campaigns.

A large FMCG company with agencies, consultants and experts has a different approach to a medium- or small-sized company with only a secretary to help the sales and marketing manager. There is no simple answer here.

Time and money can be saved and the impact of marketing communications increased if the various activities are planned and integrated in advance. Planning or scheduling various activities allows time to build a better picture, and gain a better understanding by putting the jigsaw of communication tools together to seize any overlapping opportunities which may emerge (eg a video news release, can be produced along with a TV or cinema advertisement — see page 287, Chapter 14). The planning process helps to give a clearer vision of where the organisation is going. Good plans take the stress out of work. Planning also saves money since it is possible to get alternative quotes and shop around for the best deal when buying services. Expensive rush rates or overnight rates can be avoided by planning and scheduling. Advance order discounts can sometimes be taken if, say, a printer is given a couple of months' notice.

There is no one, single, exact, perfect communications mix. Several guidelines have been discussed, but there is no substitute for experience, particularly when it is enriched by constant 'testing and measuring' in the continual search for better performance from the marketing communications mix.

Equipped with these communications mix guidelines, how should a marketing communications plan be written? What must it include? The next chapter builds a framework for a marketing communications plan so that the reader can start to develop his or her own plan.

Key Points from Chapter 1:
1) Integrate all elements
2) Make time to plan ahead

Further reading

Arnold, W `Meet the brand man', *Media and Marketing Europe*, October 1992

Constable, J and McCormack, R (1987) *The Making of British Managers*, British Institute of Management/Confederation of British Industry, London

Ehrenberg, A Hammond, K and Goodhardt, G (1991) *The After Effects of Large Consumer Promotions*, London Business School, London

Jefkins, F (1990) *Modern Marketing Communications*, Blackie, Glasgow

Kotler, P (1988) *Marketing Management Analysis, Planning, Implementation and Control*, 6th edition, Prentice Hall, Englewood Cliffs, New Jersey

Media & Marketing Europe (1992) EMAP Business Publications, London, October, pp34-37

Pan-European Marketing Report, *Marketing*, 8 November 1990

Profit Impact of Marketing Strategy (PIMS) (1992), PIMSLetter Number 50, London

`The campaign report' (1991), *Campaign*, 19 April 1991

McDonald, M (1992) *The Marketing Planner*, Butterworth-Heinemann, Oxford

Further contacts

CAM Foundation, Communications Advertising and Marketing Education Foundation, Abford House, 15 Wilton Road, London SW1V 1NJ. Tel: 0171-828 7506

Chartered Institute of Marketing, Moor Hall, Cookham, Maidenhead, Berkshire SL6 9QH. Tel: 01628 524922

Incorporated Society of British Advertisers, 44 Hertford Street, London W1Y 8AE. Tel: 0171-499 7502

Institute of Public Relations, The Old Trading House, 15 Northburgh Street, London EC1V OPR. Tel: 0171-253 5151.

Institute of Sales and Marketing Management, National Westminster House, 31 Upper George Street, Luton, Bedfordshire LU1 2RD. Tel: 01582 411130

Institute of Sales Promotion, Arena House, 66–68 Pentonville Road, London N1 9HS. Tel: 0171-837 5340

Marketing Society, St Georges House, 3-5 Pepys Road, London SW20 8NJ. Tel: 0181-879 3464

Public Relations Consultants Association, Willow House, Willow Place, Victoria, London SW1P 1JH. Tel: 0171-233 6026

2

THE MARKETING COMMUNICATIONS PLAN

OUTLINE MARKETING COMMUNICATIONS PLAN

The outline marketing communications plan develops a system of reviews, goals, strategies, tactics and resources which come together in a sensible and systematic manner. The *SOSTT + 4Ms* acronym gives a focus or direction to all the individual elements of the communications/promotions mix:

- **S**ituation (where are we now?)
- **O**bjectives (where do we want to go?)
- **S**trategy (how do we get there?)
- **T**actics (details of strategy)
- **T**argets (segmentation and target markets)
  +
- **M**en (men and women required to do the above)
- **M**oney (budgets)
- **M**inutes (time-scale)
- **M**easurement (monitor effectiveness)

There is no single, standard outline for a plan but any marketing communications plan should include SOSTT + 4Ms. It is more of a checklist than a sequence of planning activities since some companies, for example, start with target markets, analyse the situation and then develop strategies and tactics. The Prudential example on page 41 shows how analysing the target market's state of mind actually helps to determine the communication objectives and, ultimately, drive the creative execution of the advertisements themselves.

Three of the Ms (men, money and minutes) are the three key resources required to achieve the objectives. Men means professional men and women skilled and capable of handling specific activities. Some can be drawn from within the organisation, others have to be brought in from an agency or consultancy or recruited as full-time members of staff.

Page 394 shows the profile of the kind of professional marketing people which Colgate Palmolive like to recruit. Many organisations may not have this calibre of person, or if they do, they may be kept so busy that they cannot do any additional tasks. Is it worth asking over-busy people to give half their attention to a project or ask under-qualified and under-utilised people to have a go? Perhaps the marketing communications task is too important to be casual? There is no doubt about the importance and limited supply of the human resource.

SOSTT + 4Ms can be used in different ways, eg to build an overall marketing plan, a marketing communications plan, or a project plan for a particular communication tool (an advertising campaign, say). It can even be used as a guide to brief an agency or consultant. The amount of detailed information will obviously be constrained by confidentiality and the strategic importance of the information.

A further description of SOSTT + 4Ms is as follows:

- Situation
  - (a) Company — sales and market share trends, summary strengths and weaknesses.
  - (b) Product/service range — features, benefits and USPs, product positioning.
  - (c) Market, structure and growth, opportunities and threats, target markets and competition.
- Objectives   Short, medium and long term
  - (a) Marketing objectives
  - (b) Communication objectives
- Strategy   How the objectives will be achieved. This can be a summary of the communications mix and sometimes includes the marketing mix (no tactical details here).
- Tactics   The detailed activities of strategy. The detailed planning of how, when and where various marketing activities (communication tools) occur.
- Targets   Segmentation and target marketing — who, what, where, when, how and why do the target customers buy or not buy? These questions must be answered before any strategy or tactics can be developed.

  + 4Ms

- Men   Men and women — who is responsible for what? Are there enough suitably experienced men and women in-house to handle various projects? Have they got the spare capacity to take on extra tasks? Are outside agencies needed, or should extra permanent staff be recruited?
- Money   Budget — what will it cost? Is it affordable? Is it good value for money? Should the money be spent elsewhere? Does the budget include research to measure the effectiveness of various other activities? Is there an allowance for contingencies?
- Minutes   Time-scale and deadlines for each stage of each activity (proposals, concept development, concept testing, regional testing, national roll-out, European launch, etc).

• *M*easurement Monitoring the results of all activities helps the marketing manager to understand what works well and what is not worth repeating in the next campaign. Clearly defined and specific objectives provide yardsticks for measurement. The monitored results also help the manager to make realistic forecasts and ultimately to build better marketing communications plans in the future.

Note: There are an infinite number of strategic and tactical options available, ranging from the bizarre, to radical change or minor modification of previous strategies and tactics, through to the easy option of do nothing. These options can be assessed and the best ones selected before developing any specific strategies or tactics.

SITUATION

The situation covers all the basic information already outlined. It also gives a review of the performance during the most recent period, identifying any trends. It can involve the marketing mix, ie price levels compared to competition, distribution networks, product quality, strengths and weaknesses of both the product and the organisation, and the opportunities and threats relevant to the product or organisation (SWOT). It certainly should include an explanation of the product's *'positioning'*. This means how the product is perceived in the minds of the target market. Lucozade was positioned as a sick child's drink until the marketing people saw a bigger opportunity and repositioned it as a healthy adults drink. *'Perceptual maps'* plot where different brands and product types are positioned on certain criteria as shown in Figure 2.1.

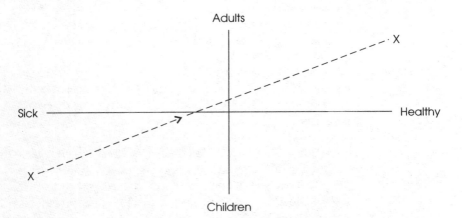

Figure 2.1 A perceptual map showing Lucozade's image repositioning

OBJECTIVES

After analysing the situation through secondary and primary sources (see Chapter 5) a clear picture of where you are emerges. The next step is to define as specifically as possible where you want to be. Ideally *objectives should be quantified* in terms of success or failure criteria. Time-scales should also be clearly defined. Clearly defined objectives make the management task of control much easier. Drawing up objectives for the first time is a difficult task. In future years, the previous year's objectives and corresponding results will help to make the planning job a little easier as everyone has a better idea of what is realistic and what is not.

Establishing clear objectives is necessary to give a clear focus to the organisation or division. Clear objectives also give direction to subsequent creative efforts. Some marketing managers and agencies break objectives into many different types. Our approach uses just two — marketing objectives and communications objectives.

Marketing objectives

Typical marketing objectives refer to sales, market share, distribution penetration, launching a number of new products and so on. For example, marketing objectives might be:

- To increase unit *sales* of product/brand X by 10 per cent over the next 12 months.
- To increase *market share* by 5 per cent over the next 12 months.
- To generate 500 *new enquiries* each month.
- To increase *distribution penetration* from 25 per cent to 50 per cent within twelve months.
- To establish a *network of distributors* covering Germany, France, Holland and Italy during the first six months, followed by Switzerland, Austria, Belgium and Luxembourg, in the second six months.

It is worth noting that not all marketing objectives are growth oriented. In Denmark, electricity boards no longer pride themselves on how much electricity they sell but how little.

Communications objectives

These typically refer to how the communications should affect the mind of the target audience, eg generate awareness, attitudes, interest or trial. Again, these tend to be most useful when quantified. *DAGMAR* (defining advertising goals for measuring advertising responses) and *AIDA* (attention, interest, desire and action) provide yardsticks for communication objectives by trying to separate the various mental stages a buyer goes through before buying. These response hierarchy models are discussed in `Buyer Behaviour Theory', Chapter 4.

The mental stages suggested by DAGMAR and AIDA are as follows:

DAGMAR	AIDA
Unawareness	
Awareness	Attention
Comprehension	Interest
Conviction	Desire
Action	Action

Examples of communications objectives might be:

- To *increase awareness* from 35 per cent to 50 per cent within eight weeks of the campaign launch among 25–45 year old ABC1 women (see Appendix 3, page 50 for a full breakdown of the ABC1 socio-economic groupings).
- To *position* the product or service as the chunkiest chocolate bar on the market within 12 month period among 70 per cent of heavy chocolate users.
- To *reposition* Guinness from an old, unfashionable older man's drink to a fashionable younger person's drink over two years among all 25–45 year old male drinkers.
- To maintain Fairy Liquid as the *preferred brand* (or number one) brand of washing up liquid among 50 per cent of UK housewives.
- To *include* Bulgarian wines in the *repertoire* of possible wine purchases among 20 per cent of ABC1 wine buyers within 12 months.
- To support the *launch* of a new shop by generating 50 per cent awareness in the immediate community one week before the launch.
- To *announce* a sale and create 70 per cent *awareness* one day before the sale starts.

STRATEGY

Having assessed the situation (where you are now) and determined the objectives (where you want to be), a strategy can now be devised to take you there. The strategy is an overview of how to get there. It embraces a major objective and explains briefly how it will be achieved. Tactics are details, while strategy is, in a sense, a summary of all the details. An example for an FMCG product, eg beans, might be:

Reposition the brand with a new TV advertising campaign highlighting the benefits of the newly designed, ozone friendly pack. The expanded salesforce will introduce the new pack to the trade during February through a series of exhibitions followed up by blanket sales calls to 90 per cent of retailers throughout Europe.

TACTICS

With the situation analysed, objectives clearly defined and the overall strategy agreed, the implementation details and tactics can now be ironed out. Prioritising objectives and drawing on previous knowledge gained from constant measurement make the tactical stage easier to manage. For example, if building awareness is the key objective then a TV advertising campaign might be planned, or if brand switching is the priority then vouchers or some form of sales promotion may be the starting point for the detailed tactical activity. /

Table 2.1 presents a bird's eye view or a summary of the timing and expenditure of a range of tactical communication tools which might be used by the FMCG company.

Table 2.1 Summary marketing communications plan

	J	F	M	A	M	J	J	A	S	O	N	D	£
New pack design	x												50K
New pack launch		xx											30K
TV advertising										x	x	xx	880K
Trade advertising	xx	x	x										13K
Trade exhibitions	x x												20K
Consumer exhibitions										xx	xx		35K
Promotional gifts	xx									xx	xx	xx	5K
Editorial publicity	x x									xx	xx	x	20K
Sponsorship							xx			xx			40K
Direct mail					xx	xx	xx						45K
Telesales follow-up						xx	xx	xx					22K
Contingencies													40K

1994 Total expenditure (excluding the sales force)   £1.2M
K = £(000)

The details of each activity, including schedules, costings and concepts, etc form the bulk of the marketing communications plan. The target market is clearly identified in each activity. The three key resources, men, money and minutes are also built into each of the tactical activities. The fourth and final M, measurement, is also built in so that some form of control can be exercised and any necessary changes made before the end of each activity's scheduled programme.

The previous example is somewhat simplified since, firstly, it addresses only a single product or service, and secondly, the time horizon is limited to a 12 month period. The plan becomes more complex when a range or portfolio of products/services has to be planned and co-ordinated over, say, a three year period. Malcolm McDonald's *The Marketing Planner* provides various sets of forms, sample plans and explanations for a complete marketing plan (as opposed to the one year, single product marketing communications approach taken here).

The 'Gold Heart' minicase at the end of this chapter summarises how a real marketing communications plan comes together for a non-profit-making organisation, The Variety Club.

TARGET MARKETS

Target marketing involves the division of a large market into smaller market segments. Each segment has its own distinct needs and/or its patterns of response to varying marketing mixes. The most attractive segments are targeted according to the organisation's resources. Attractive target markets are those that will generally be more profitable, eg segments located closer to the organisation, heavy users of a particular product or service etc. Targeting reduces wastage of resources (eg money spent on mass advertising) and, ultimately, it increases sales since better prospect customers are contacted. *Segmentation and target marketing are absolutely fundamental approaches to marketing.* Some communication channels are more wasteful than others, eg TV, but the Target Group Index (TGI) (see Chapter 5) index helps to identify what kind of brands people buy, papers they read, programmes they watch, etc).

As mass markets fragment and splinter into mini markets or segments, there is less requirement for mass marketing and mass communications. Chapter 13, 'Direct Marketing', explains how product differentiation and market fragmentation occur.

Consumer segments

Segmenting markets into groups of buyers and targeting those groups which are more likely to be the best customers is absolutely vital if marketing communications are to be both effective and efficient. Markets can be broken into segments using many different criteria. Here are some typical consumer criteria:

• *Demographics:*

    a) Age — see figures in Appendix 1.
    b) Sex — see figures in Appendix 1.
    c) Family life cycle — see SAGACITY in Appendix 2.
    d) Job Type — see socio-economic grouping in Appendix 3.

• *Geodemographics:*

    Geographic location, type of neighbourhood and demographic data — see ACORN types in Appendix 4 and also page 51 of Chapter 5.

• *Psychographics:*

    a) Lifestyle — see TGI data on page 95 Chapter 5.
    b) Attitudes, beliefs and intentions (as above).
    c) Benefits sought — see the 'toothpaste test' on page 68.

The target draught Guinness buyer might be 'the independent-minded drinker, aged 25–35'. In reality, all the target customers rarely fall neatly into one single segment, eg 70 per cent of the *Sun* newspaper's customers might be C2DEs and 30 per cent ABC1s (see Appendix 3 for a full expanation of the ABC1 C2DE social grades).

There is, however, usually a core target made up of heavy users or easily convertible prospects. Lyons Tetley's Quickbrew tea is targeted at aged 35+ (core C1C2D) women. Some markets have several people involved in the decision-making (decision-making units). For example, the advertising campaign promoting Shell's free miniture classic sports car collection was aimed at ABC1 fathers aged between 25–64 with children aged 3–9 ... and within all this they also had to ensure high coverage of high mileage drivers (heavy users). Other markets have customers who drift into the market place and then out again as in the case of financial services (see below).

Floating Targets

Other markets have a floating percentage who move in and out of the market. For example, less than 1 per cent of the population buy any financial service in any one month.

And to the remaining 99 per cent financial services, particularly insurance, are dull and off-putting subjects they would rather not think about. With such a small number of consumers in the market at any one time there is clearly little point talking about specific product benefits. Instead the role of advertising is to ensure the Prudential is on the candidate list when people do have a need for a particular service.

(Source: Media Week Awards 1992)

Industrial segments

In industrial markets and business to business markets, segmentation criteria are different but none the less absolutely vital. The Hewlett Packard minicase at the end of Chapter 14 shows that their target market (for a particular promotional activity) was 'executive directors responsible for long-term investments and the management of change'. This was further refined into two target markets: (a) directors and board level management in companies with £10–£50 million turnover; (b) directors, board level managers plus information technology management plus financial management in companies with over £50 million turnover.

Here are some commonly used segmentation criteria for industrial markets:

- Type of company (Standard industrial code — SIC)
- Size of company
- Structure of company (autocratic vs centralised)
- Location/geographic area
- Heavy or light users
- Existing suppliers
- Benefits sought
- Title or position of key decision-makers

Most airlines target at least two different segments on each plane: the business traveller and the leisure traveller. These segments can be further segmented, eg the business traveller may be divided into Club Class, Executive Class and so on. These can be further divided into different benefit segments, eg those that want a fast check-in, those that want frequent flights, those that want top class in-flight service, those that want a reasonable price, those that want 'seamless travel' (connections for the next flight, cars and hotels all done for them) etc. Most travellers want all of these benefits but they usually consider some benefits to be more important than others, so much so that they choose one airline over another because of a particular key benefit. If this type of flier proves to be significant in number then it is a valid segment (see other criteria for valid segments below). The organisation then decides if it has the resources and sustainable advantages suitable to target this segment.

To continue the airline example, Transavia airlines segmented various companies who might have had some sort of connection with Holland (and therefore might have had a need for Transavia air service) into five different target groups of business fliers and travel agents. As shown in Figure 2.2, a different communications strategy was developed for each segment. A gift/food hamper and a boxed presentation was delivered personally by the sales manager to those accounts (customers) which warranted this kind of attention (resources). Lighter users had a smaller mailing. Top travel agents got a boxed mailing, while other travel agents just got a mailing.

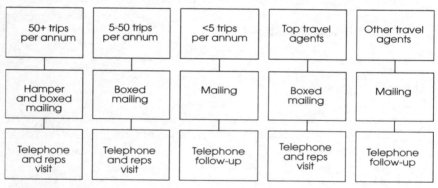

(Source: Stevens, M (1991))

Figure 2.2 Business traveller segments and communication mixes

Ideally, segments should satisfy the following criteria:

1) *Measurable*

   Is it quantifiable? Can buyers that fall into this category or segment be identified?

2) *Substantial*

   How many buyers fall into this segment?
   Is there a sufficient number of buyers in the segment to warrant special attention and targeting?

3) *Accessible*

   Can this group be contacted? Can they be isolated or separated from other non-targeted markets? Are there specific media and distribution channels that provide access to them?

4) *Relevant*

The benefits of the product or service being offered must be relevant to the target. There is no point picking measurable, accessible and substantial segments if they have no interest in what is being offered in the first place.

Know your own customers

Knowing the ideal customer's profile is fundamental to success. Some database companies actually carry out *'profiling'* or an analysis of an organisation's own customers into groups with distinctive profiles. This helps target the appropriate message through the appropriate medium.

Who knows who or why they buy from us?

A few years ago a comparative study of British and foreign-owned companies revealed that:

47 per cent of British and 40 per cent of American companies (vs 13 per cent of Japanese) acknowledged that they were unclear about the type of customers in the market and what their needs were.

(Source: Doyle, Saunders and Wright (1987)).

A Rembrandt probably would not sell (even for £50) in the wrong target market, whereas in the right target market it would fetch several million pounds. Some segments are obvious. Cat food is bought by cat owners. Petrol is bought by motorists and heavy-duty cranes are bought by both large construction companies and leasing companies. Other segments are less obvious. Expensive cars are bought by both high income groups, while cheaper cars are bought by high income groups (as a second or third car) and low income groups. Who are the heavy users, eg who are the 9 per cent of the UK adult population who drink 65 per cent of the lager consumed? Who are the buyers? Gift boxes of chocolates are bought for ladies by men. Who are the deciders? Cola drinkers may tend to be young but who does the buying, who makes the decision, who influences and who pays? This is where segmentation focuses on the *'Decision-making unit'* (DMU).

The DMU is made up of influencers, advisers, deciders, users, buyers and payers. It applies to all types of markets (industrial, consumer, products and services). A baby's pram may be used by mother and child, bought by the mother and father, influenced by the mother-in-law, and decided by the whole family. Similarly, the purchase of a new photocopier may have been instigated by the secretary who keeps complaining to her boss about the machine breaking down. The end user may be several secretaries, the decider may be the financial director, the buyer may be the organisation's professional buyer, or the managing director. In some organisations the DMU may be a committee. In other organisations there is a central decision-maker or there may be a decentralised approach with each branch/region making their own decisions. The *SPADE* acronym helps to identify some of the different members of the decision-making unit:

Starter
Payer
Adviser
Decider
End User

The DMU can consist of several people or committees, or it can sometimes be just one person. There is one other influential member of a business to business or industrial DMU, and that is the 'gatekeeper' who acts as a screen which sorts out unsolicited sales pitches from more important incoming communications. The gatekeeper is often a secretary or personal assistant who may decide whether to interrupt a manager with a phone call or allow a direct mail shot to land on the manager's desk.

Global segments

An Englishman living in a fashionable apartment in London's Knightsbridge area has more in common with an American living in an expensive apartment overlooking New York's Central Park than he has with another Englishman living in some drab South London suburb.

Segments do not always have to be localised or defined on a geographic basis. Values, attitudes and lifestyles (VALS) can be used to identify *cross-cultural common characteristics*. For example, the advertising agency Horner Collis and Kirwan identify the four main European psychographic segments as follows:

1) Modern materialists — 117 million
2) New radicals — 50 million (concerned with change and reform)
3) Get what you deserve — 110 million (more conservative and resistant to change)
4) Bygones — 83 million (oldest, most moralistic group threatened by consumerism)

Global idiosyncracies complicate the supposedly simple global segments. Chapter 9 looks at the international arena in more detail.

MEASUREMENT

Ideally, the marketing communications plan should have a system of measurement built in so that improvements can be made in the future. The plan should provide a system of measurement which gives feedback to help plan the next campaign or series of activities. It is also possible to assess the effectiveness of what one plans to do by testing an advertisement, a promotion or a direct mail shot before rolling out on a larger scale. In addition to well-defined objectives (which facilitate monitoring and measurement) some resources have to be allocated to measurement to ensure that the effectiveness of various communications tools and tactics does, in the end, actually get measured.

SHORT CASE: GOLD HEART DAY

The short cases at the end of each chapter in Part 2 focus on a particular element of the marketing communications mix while also demonstrating the importance of an integrated approach. They are drawn from a wide variety of industrial and consumer products and services. A short case on marketing communications planning has been added to the end of this chapter to show how the outline plan actually comes together, in this case, for the Variety Club's Gold Heart Day.

Situation

The Variety Club is a well-known international children's charity whose mission is to raise funds to help sick, disabled and disadvantaged children, regardless of race, colour or creed. Its members, called 'Barkers' — including many celebrities — give all their time and efforts free. Overheads are kept low. In fact, well over 90p in every £1 goes to help the children directly. The public, however, tended to see the Variety Club as showbiz rather than a charity. A major new fund-raising event was needed to focus the public's attention on the work of the charity. The solution was Gold Heart Day. This would be an annual fund raising event culminating on Valentine's Day, 14 February — a day associated with love and care — on which members of the public would be able to show they cared by purchasing and wearing their heart on their sleeve.

Objectives

*   To increase awareness of the plight of sick, disabled and disadvantaged children in the UK and the work of the Variety Club in trying to help them.
*   To maximise funds raised (minimum £1 million) and build commercial partnerships.

- To develop a promotional format capable of adoption and adaptation in all other Variety Clubs worldwide.

Strategy

To develop an annual fund-raising event, Gold Heart Day, by generating massive media coverage, with considerable retail and trade participation opportunities, thereby increasing awareness of the plight of the children, and the Variety Club's efforts to help them.

Tactics

- A full communication programme was developed (see Table 2.1 on page 47).
- The Gold Hearts were made available to the public at a number of major high street retailers including Tesco, Mothercare, Texas Homecare, W H Smith and the Sainsbury's Staff Association (in year 2, McDonald's, Index, Forte Hotels, The National and Provincial Building Society and the National Federation of Retail Newsagents were added to the founder partners).
- A strong corporate identity was created and point-of-sale materials including posters, showcards and collection boxes (easily tailorable to each partner) were supplied to help the in-store display at each retail/distribution point.
- A full PR campaign was planned.
- A series of three 30 second TV ads were produced free of charge and broadcast nationally via Channel 4 and Thames TV. Wherever possible TV airtime costs were sponsored. Michael Caine, Patricia Hodge and Suzi Quatro gave their time free.
- A 7 inch 'Heart on my sleeve' single was rewritten by Gallagher and Lyle and released.

Targets

Primarily, male and female adults living in towns and cities throughout the UK. Secondarily, men, women and children of all ages, living across the UK.

Men

A committee of around 60 Variety Club members, together with head office staff, undertook all aspects of the promotion under the direction of co-chairmen John and Marsha Ratcliff. The Ingram Company handled the logo, designs, print material and all promotional work other than the extensive PR programme, which was handled by Lynne Franks PR. Much assistance and tremendous staff support was also provided by all the participant retailers.

Money

Each heart cost about 15p (1992) and sold for a minimum of £1. Eighty-five pence per heart goes back to the Variety Club. The vast majority of print is donated free, saving thousands of pounds. The commercial value of the TV ads might have been £100k or more.

Minutes

The first Gold Heart Day was planned in a tight time-frame of September 1990 to launch in January 1991. Gold hearts had to be sourced, including a multi-way competitive pitch, manufactured and distributed to hundreds of retail sites. The design, print and distribution of all the supporting point-of-sale materials had similar deadlines. Subsequent Gold Heart Days are now worked on all year round by the committee.

Measurement

- Year 1 (1991) sold out (target: 1 million gold hearts).
- Year 2 (1992) sold out (target: 3 million gold hearts).
- Year 3 (1993)* (target: 5 million gold hearts).
- In addition, hundreds of thousands were sold around the world.

(* unknown at time of writing.)

Table 2.1 summarises the plan.

	1990				1991												1992			Approx
	S	O	N	D	J	F	M	A	M	J	J	A	S	O	N	D	J	F	M	£
Concept, designs, heart production, partner liaison	X	X	X	X								X	X	X	X	X				10K
Heart distri.				X	X	X									X	X	X	X		-10K
Forward partner planning							X	X	X	X	X	X	X	X	X	X				-
TV Sponsorship drive				X	X							X	X	X	X	X				10K
PR				X	X	X	X									X	X	X	X	25K
Promotions & in-store					X	X											X	X		Partner Costs
TV Airtime					X	X											X	X		100K

Table 2.1 Summary of the Gold Heart Day plan

Key Points from Chapter 2:
1) There are many different approaches to marketing plans but certain key factors have to be included.
2) SOSTT + 4Ms cover the key points.

APPENDIX 1

UK population distribution by age and sex

RESIDENT POPULATION

	1980 '000	1980 %	1985 '000	1985 %	1990 '000	1990 %
England	46,787	83.1	47,112	83.2	47,837	83.3
Wales	2,816	5.0	2,812	5.0	2,881	5.0
Scotland	5,194	9.2	5,137	9.1	5,102	8.9
GB	54,797	97.3	55,061	97.2	55,821	97.2
N. Ireland	1,533	2.7	1,558	2.8	1,589	2.8
UK	56,330	100.0	56,618	100.0	57,411	100.0

Sources: OPCS; General Register Offices for Scotland and Northern Ireland.

Notes: Figures may not add due to rounding. 1991 figures unavailable at press date.

RESIDENT POPULATION OF GB BY SEX & AGE: ESTIMATE MID-1990

Years of age	Total '000	Males '000	Males %	Females '000	Females %
0– 4	3,706	1,898	7.0	1,808	6.3
5– 9	3,516	1,802	6.6	1,714	6.0
10–14	3,302	1,697	6.2	1,605	5.6
15–24	8,204	4,191	15.4	4,013	14.0
25–34	8,571	4,324	15.9	4,246	14.9
35–44	7,699	3,852	14.1	3,847	13.5
45–54	6,335	3,166	11.6	3,169	11.1
55–64	5,695	2,779	10.2	2,916	10.2
65+	8,793	3,523	12.9	5,271	18.4
Total	**55,821**	**27,232**	**100.0**	**28,589**	**100.0**

Of the resident population of Great Britain 48.8% are males and 51.2% are females.

Sources: OPCS; General Register Offices for Scotland and Northern Ireland.

Notes: Figures may not add due to rounding. 1991 figures unavailable at press date.

PROJECTED POPULATION OF GREAT BRITAIN AT MID-YEAR

		1989 Base	1991	1996	2006	2016
Home population	millions	55.7	56.0	56.8	58.1	58.8
	index	100.0	100.6	102.1	104.3	105.6
Sex distribution	males %	48.7	48.8	49.0	49.2	49.4
	females %	51.3	51.2	51.0	50.8	50.6
Age distribution	0– 4 %	6.6	6.7	6.8	6.2	6.1
	5–14 %	12.1	12.3	12.8	13.3	12.1
	15–29 %	23.3	22.5	20.0	18.6	19.8
	30–44 %	20.7	21.1	21.7	21.3	17.7
	45–64 %	21.5	21.6	22.9	24.9	26.7
	65+ %	15.7	15.8	15.8	15.7	17.7

Source: 1989 Population projections by the Government Actuaries Department.

APPENDIX 2

UK population distribution by life cycle and job type

The basic thesis of the SAGACITY grouping is that people have different aspirations and behaviour patterns as they go through their life cycle.
Four main stages of the life cycle are defined which are sub-divided by income and occupation groups:

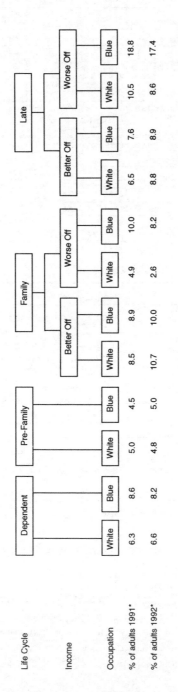

Life Cycle	Dependent		Pre-Family		Family				Late			
Income					Better Off		Worse Off		Better Off		Worse Off	
Occupation	White	Blue	White	Blue	White	Blue	White	Blue	White	Blue	White	Blue
% of adults 1991*	6.3	8.6	5.0	4.5	8.5	8.9	4.9	10.0	6.5	7.6	10.5	18.8
% of adults 1992*	6.6	8.2	4.8	5.0	10.7	10.0	2.6	8.2	8.8	8.9	8.6	17.4

Definitions of life cycle stages
Dependent   -   Mainly under 24s, living at home or full-time student.
Pre-family   -   Under 35s, who have established their own household but have no children.
Family   -   Housewives and heads of household, under 65, with one or more children in the household.
Late   -   Includes all adults whose children have left home or who are over 35 and childless.

Definitions of occupation groups
White   -   Head of household is in the ABC1 occupation group
Blue   -   Head of household is in the C2DE occupation group

* Year to June

Source: RSL - Research Services Ltd

APPENDIX 3

UK population distribution by socio-economic group

DISTRIBUTION OF THE POPULATION BY SOCIAL GRADE

Social Grade	All Adults 15+		Men		Women		Main Shoppers* (Female)	
	'000's	%	'000's	%	'000's	%	'000's	%
A	1,307	2.9	673	3.1	634	2.7	542	2.8
B	6,799	15.0	3,432	15.7	3,366	14.4	2,787	14.4
C1	10,970	24.2	5,007	22.9	5,963	25.5	4,993	25.8
C2	12,278	27.1	6,443	29.5	5,835	24.9	4,773	24.7
D	7,939	17.5	3,946	18.1	3,993	17.0	3,195	16.5
E	5,958	13.2	2,330	10.7	3,628	15.5	3,066	15.8
Total	45,250	100.0	21,832	100.0	23,418	100.0	19,355	100.0

Note: These social grades are based on grades of head of household.

*Main shoppers are identified as those who personally select half or more of the items bought for their household from supermarkets and food shops. This member may be male or female:

	'000	%
Female main shopper	19,355	71.7
Male main shopper	7,627	28.3
All main shoppers	26,982	100.0

Source: National Readership Survey, July 1991 – June 1992.

NRS SOCIAL GRADE DEFINITIONS*

Social Grade	Social Status	Occupation
A	Upper middle class	Higher managerial, administrative or professional.
B	Middle class	Intermediate managerial, administrative or professional.
C1	Lower middle class	Supervisory or clerical, and junior managerial, administrative or professional.
C2	Skilled working class	Skilled manual workers.
D	Working class	Semi and unskilled manual workers.
E	Those at lowest level of subsistence	State pensioners or widows (no other earner), casual or lowest-grade workers.

* These are the standard social grade classifications using definitions agreed between Research Services Ltd., and JICNARS. A JICNARS publication "Social Grading on the National Readership Survey" and National Readership Survey Appendix E describes the definitions and methodology used.

Source: National Readership Survey.

APPENDIX 4

UK population distribution by residential neighbourhood (ACORN)

Geodemographic classification systems, such as CACI's ACORN system, give marketers a scientific link between geography and demographics. Geodemographics can identify the consumer demographics for a given location and, conversely, can show the geographic profile of a particular consumer characteristic.

ACORN classifies consumers into varying socio-economic Types, according to the

The CACI ACORN Classification

ACORN TYPES

CACI

CACI Ltd, CACI House, Kensington Village, Avonmore Road, London W14 8TS
Tel: (071) 602 6000

CACI Ltd, 4 Hanover Street, Edinburgh EH2 2EH
Tel: (031) 225 2666   Fax: (031) 225 2677

INFORMATION SERVICES

- **A1** Agricultural Villages — 2.6% of GB Population
- **A2** Areas of Farms and Smallholdings — GB Population

- **B3** Post-War Functional Private Housing — 4.4% of GB Population
- **B4** Modern Private Housing, Young Families — 1.8% of GB Population
- **B5** Established Private Family Housing — 4.0% of GB Population
- **B6** New Detached Houses, Young Families — 1.7% of GB Population
- **B7** Transient Workforces, Living at their Place of Work — 0.3% of GB Population

- **C8** Mixed Owner-Occupied and Council Estates — 3.5% of GB Population
- **C9** Small Town Centres and Flats above Shops — 4.3% of GB Population
- **C10** Villages with Non-Farm Employment — 4.9% of GB Population
- **C11** Older Private Housing, Skilled Workers — 5.5% of GB Population

- **D12** Unmodernised Terraces, Older People — 2.4% of GB Population
- **D13** Older Terraces, Lower Income Families — 1.6% of GB Population
- **D14** Tenement Flats — 0.4% of GB Population

- **E15** Council Estates, Older Workers — 5.5% of GB Population
- **E16** Recent Council Estates — 2.8% of GB Population
- **E17** Better Council Estates, Younger Workers — 5.0% of GB Population
- **E18** Small Council Houses, Often Scottish — 1.9% of GB Population

- **F19** Low Rise Estates in Industrial Towns — 4.6% of GB Population
- **F20** Inter-War Council Estates — 2.8% of GB Population
- **F21** Council Housing, Elderly People — 1.4% of GB Population

- **G22** New Council Estates — 2.0% of GB Population
- **G23** Council Estates, Higher Unemployment — 3.0% of GB Population
- **G24** Council Estates with Aging Population — 1.5% of GB Population
- **G25** Council Estates with Some New Home Owners — 0.6% of GB Population

- **H26** Multi-Occupied Older Housing — 0.4% of GB Population
- **H27** Cosmopolitan Owner-Occupied Terraces — 1.0% of GB Population
- **H28** Multi-Let Housing in Cosmopolitan Areas — 0.7% of GB Population
- **H29** Better-Off Council Areas — 1.7% of GB Population

- **I30** High Status Inner City Areas — 0.7% of GB Population
- **I31** Multi-Let Big Old Houses and Flats — 1.0% of GB Population
- **I32** Furnished Flats, Mostly Single People — 0.5% of GB Population

- **J33** Inter-War Semis, White Collar — 5.7% of GB Population
- **J34** Spacious Inter-War Semis, Big Gardens — 6.0% of GB Population
- **J35** Villages with Wealthy Commuters — 2.9% of GB Population
- **J36** Detached Houses — 2.3% of GB Population

- **K37** Private Houses Well-Off — 2.3% of GB Population
- **K38** Private Flats Single People — 1.5% of GB Population

J36   Detached Houses, Exclusive Suburbs

Of all the 38 ACORN Types, J36 is the one with the highest status, whether measured by car ownership, or by the proportion of professional or managerial workers.

These, therefore, are areas of large detached houses, in mature grounds, in locations of choice landscape value, such as Esher and Solihull.

Most of these areas were developed in the 1930s so that this Type attracts mostly the older professional with school age or grown-up children. Younger families are seldom able to afford the house prices and those who can are more likely to prefer more modern executive estates.

Low unemployment and very affluent lifestyles predominate. In fact the high earnings in this Type are spent on a variety of goods producing some of the highest relative levels of consumption recorded in the various categories.

People in the J36 Type, for example, are three types more likely than average to own a car which costs over £10,000 (although rarely spending money on DIY maintenance for their cars), five times more likely to be in an earnings bracket of over £40,000 pa and four times more likely to own credit cards other than Access and Visa.

Purchases of golf clubs in the last year would indicate an extremely high popularity for the sport in this Type. As might be expected, electrical appliances and durables such as video cameras and deep freezes are popular purchases. Preferred groceries include fresh fruit, ice cream, wines, ground coffee, mineral waters and yoghurt.

Copyright CACI Limited 1992, All Rights reserved

---

sort of residential area in which they live. ACORN is built around the premise that people who live in similar neighbourhoods are likely to have similar behaviourial, purchasing and lifestyle habits.

The ACORN system provides the critical link between target markets and their consumption patterns with geographical areas. Its geodemographic application enables marketers and planners to understand in detail the nature of their markets and the potential for their products and services. It is this detail which means that marketing strategies can be planned for absolute minimum wastage and greatest potential sales.

Acorn Profile Report

CACI LTD AREA: GB BASE: ALL GB		1992 population			
		1992 pop	%	BASE %	INDEX
	ACORN Groups				
A	Agricultural Areas	1808289	3.3	3.3	100
B	Modern Family Housing, Higher Incomes	9729155	17.7	17.7	100
C	Older Housing of Intermediate Status	9853739	18.0	18.0	100
D	Older Terraced Housing	2278829	4.2	4.2	100

E	Council Estates – Category I	7244456	13.2	13.2	100
F	Council Estates – Category II	4780317	8.7	8.7	100
G	Council Estates – Category III	3786994	6.9	6.9	100
H	Mixed Inner Metropolitan Areas	2084520	3.8	3.8	100
I	High Status Non-family Areas	2236048	4.1	4.1	100
J	Affluent Suburban Housing	8667293	15.8	15.8	100
K	Better-off Retirement Areas	2079121	3.8	3.8	100
	ACORN Types				
A1	Agricultural Villages	1412501	2.6	2.6	100
A2	Areas of Farms and Smallholdings	395788	0.7	0.7	100
B3	Post-war Functional Private Housing	2421013	4.4	4.4	100
B4	Modern Private Housing, Young Families	2025081	3.7	3.7	100
B5	Established Private Family Housing	3324090	6.1	6.1	100
B6	New Detached Houses, Young Families	1593510	2.9	2.9	100
B7	Military Bases	365461	0.7	0.7	100
C8	Mixed Owner-occupied and Council Estates	1917117	3.5	3.5	100
C9	Small Town Centres and Flats above Shops	2256713	4.1	4.1	100
C10	Villages with Non-farm Employment	2669426	4.9	4.9	100
C11	Older Private Housing, Skilled Workers	3010483	5.5	5.5	100
D12	Unmodernised Terraces, Older People	1340565	2.4	2.4	100
D13	Older Terraces, Lower Income Families	740773	1.4	1.4	100
D14	Tenement Flats Lacking Amenities	197491	0.4	0.4	100
E15	Council Estates, Well-off Older Workers	1885525	3.4	3.4	100
E16	Recent Council Estates	1570548	2.9	2.9	100
E17	Better Council Estates, Younger Workers	2752924	5.0	5.0	100
E18	Small Council Houses, often Scottish	1035459	1.9	1.9	100
F19	Low Rise Estates in Industrial Towns	2495409	4.6	4.6	100
F20	Inter-war Council Estates, Older People	1545665	2.8	2.8	100
F21	Council Housing, Elderly People	739243	1.3	1.3	100
G22	New Council Estates in Inner Cities	1066907	1.9	1.9	100
G23	Overspill Estates, Higher Unemployment	1605080	2.9	2.9	100
G24	Council Estates with Some Overcrowding	813935	1.5	1.5	100
G25	Council Estates with Greatest Hardship	301072	0.5	0.5	100
H26	Multi-occupied Older Housing	201147	0.4	0.4	100
H27	Cosmopolitan Owner-occupied Terraces	572500	1.0	1.0	100
H28	Multi-let Housing in Cosmopolitan Areas	384880	0.7	0.7	100

H29	Better-off Cosmopolitan Areas	925993	1.7	1.7	100
I30	High Status Non-family Areas	1137812	2.1	2.1	100
I31	Multi-let Big Old Houses and Flats	817869	1.5	1.5	100
I32	Furnished Flats, Mostly Single People	280367	0.5	0.5	100
J33	Inter-war Semis, White Collar Workers	3114205	5.7	5.7	100
J34	Spacious Inter-war Semis, Big Gardens	2740714	5.0	5.0	100
J35	Villages with Wealthy Older Commuters	1563183	2.9	2.9	100
J36	Detached Houses, Exclusive Suburbs	1249191	2.3	2.3	100
K37	Private Houses, Well-off Older Residents	1246536	2.3	2.3	100
K38	Private Flats, Older Single People	832585	1.5	1.5	100
U39	Unclassified	292598	0.5	0.5	100
	Area Total	54841359	100.0	100.0	

Note: These are projected figures taken from the 1981 census.

Source: © CACI Limited, 1992. All rights reserved. ACORN is the service mark of CACI Limited. From OPCS data Crown Copyright.

Further reading

Doyle, P Saunders, J and Wright, L (1987) 'A comparative study of US and Japanese marketing strategies in the British market', Warwick University Report

Media Week Awards (1992), *Media Week*, London

McDonald, M (1992) *The Marketing Planner*, Butterworth-Heinemann, Oxford

Smith, P R (1985) 'The who what why of industrial segmentation' (parts 1 and 2), *The Industrial Marketing Digest*, Spring and Summer 1985

Stevens, M (1991) *The Handbook of Telemarketing*, Kogan Page, London

Westwood, J (1990) *The Marketing Plan*, Kogan Page, London

3

THEORIES OF COMMUNICATION

COMMUNICATIONS THEORY

A dictionary definition of 'communications' is as follows:

> communication n. 1. a transmitting 2. a) giving or *exchange of information*, etc. by talk, writing b) the information so given 3. a means of communicating 4. the science of transmitting information. (My italics)

What is interesting is the exchange of information. Communication is not a one-way flow of information. Talking at or to someone does not imply successful communication. This only occurs when the receiver actually receives the message which the sender intended to send. Message rejection, misinterpretation and misunderstanding are the opposite of effective communication.

Millions die from ineffective communications

There is evidence that a mistake in translating a message sent by the Japanese government near the end of World War II may have triggered the bombing of Hiroshima, and thus ushered in atomic warfare. The word 'mokusatsu' used by Japan in response to the US surrender ultimatum was translated by Domei as 'ignore', instead of its correct meaning, 'withhold comment until a decision has been made'.

(Source: Cutlip, Center and Broom (1985))

The above is an extreme and tragic example of communications gone wrong. *Communication errors* in marketing generally do not cost lives but can, if allowed to continue unchecked, *cost market share*, company survival and jobs. On the other hand, good marketing communications help an organisation to thrive by getting its messages across in a focused and cost effective way.

Good marketing communications is *not as simple as it may appear*. Even David Ogilvy, the advertising guru, was once reported to have used the word 'obsolete' in an advertisement only to discover that (at the time) 43 per cent of US women had no idea what it meant. The delicacy and difficulty of creating effective communications to target audiences can be explained by Douglas Smallbone's analogy of radio communication.

The Human Radio

'Given good transmitting conditions and receiver and transmitter tuned to the same wavelength, perfect reception can be effected.'

(Source: Smallbone, D (1969))

Perfect transmitting conditions might exist if there was no noise (extraneous factors which distract or distort the message such as other advertisements, poor reception, a flashing light, a door bell, an ambulance, etc). Without noise perfect transmitting conditions would exist. In reality, there is almost always noise so perfect transmitting conditions do not exist. Cinemas may be the exception, where a captive audience is in an attentive state and receptive to, say, a well produced X-rated advertisement. But even when the target audience is seemingly tuned in (watching, listening or looking at a particular organisation's package, promotion, advertisment, etc) they may not be on the same wavelength because of the hidden internal psychological processes which may be reshaping or distorting the message to suit the audience's own method of interpretation.

The human receiver is in fact equipped with five distinct means of receiving messages or information or marketing communications — the five senses of hearing, sight, touch, taste and smell. Marketing communication tools can address many senses simultaneously (eg packaging).

Non-verbal and non-symbolic communications

Although verbal and visual communications gain a lot of conscious attention, there are *non-verbal and non-symbolic* ways of communicating such as space, time and kinetics. Crowded areas, or lack of *space*, send messages to the brain which, in turn, can stimulate a different set of thoughts and a different behavioural response. The opposite is also true: a spacious office or living room conveys a message of wealth or power. Look how different stores use space to convey different images. In western cultures the use of *time* creates images, eg a busy but organised person gives an impression of authority. 'Thanks for your time' immediately conveys a respect for and an appreciation of a seemingly important person's time. A busy diary can project an image of importance. 'I can squeeze you in on Friday at...' implies seniority in the relationship. In the UK, the term 'window' is starting to be used for free time or space in a busy diary. Some advertisements sell products and services primarily on time-saving/convenience benefits. In fact, banks are really time machines which allow an individual to move forward in time by buying, say, a house which would not normally be affordable for thirty years. Finally, *kinetics* communicate. Gestures and movements send messages. Even the simple, swift clicking of a briefcase, entering or leaving a room or closing or not closing a door can communicate. Most of all, body language and facial gestures are powerful communicators. An understanding of body language allows an individual to learn more about what another person is really feeling. A smile, for example, communicates immediately, effectively and directly.

Semiotics

The field of semiotics (or semiology) opens up a rich discussion of how symbols and signs are used in communications, particularly advertising. Audiences often unconsciously perceive images stimulated by certain symbols.

Engel, Warshaw and Kinnear (1991) demonstrate how Lever Brothers fabric softener, Snuggles, uses a cuddly teddy bear in its advertising.

Carol Moog, advertising consultant and psychologist, says that: the bear is

> an ancient symbol of aggression, but when you create a teddy bear, you provide a softer, nurturant side to that aggression. As a symbol of tamed aggression, the teddy bear is the perfect image for a fabric softener that tames the rough of clothing.

The user symbolises the product

Engel, Warshaw and Kinnear comment:

> The key point here is that if marketing communicators are not aware of the subtle meanings of symbols, then they are liable to communicate the wrong message.

Miss Moog's advice to Pierre Cardin on their men's fragrance advertisement, which was designed to show men who are `aggressive and in control' splashing fragrance, was accepted but rejected! Miss Moog saw `cologne gushing out of a phallic shaped bottle' creating a conflict of images since it `symbolised male ejaculation and lack of control'. Pierre Cardin acknowledged that she probably was right but decided to keep the shot as it was `a beautiful product shot plus it encourages men to use our fragrance liberally.'

Rutger Hauer's black clothes and blond hair in the Guinness Genius advertisements symbolise the pint of Guinness itself. See Chapter 11 for more on the Guinness Genius campaign (see previous page).

COMMUNICATION MODELS

No simple diagram can reflect all the nuances and complexities of the communication process. This section considers some basic theories and models.

A single-step communication model

There are three fundamental elements in communication, the sender (or source), the message and the receiver as shown in Figure 3.1.

Figure 3.1 A simple communication model

This basic model assumes that the sender is active, the receiver is inactive or passive and the message is comprehended properly. In reality this is rarely the case. Chapter 5, `Buyer Behaviour', demonstrates how we see what we want to see and not necessarily what is sent. An understanding of the target receiver or audience helps to identify what is important to the audience and how symbols, signs and language are interpreted. The message is `dressed up' or coded in an appropriate way, sent through a media channel and, if it gets through all the other noise, finally decoded by the receiver. Guinness advertisements basically ask their target audience to drink Guinness, but they are very carefully coded. For example, `It's not easy being a dolphin' were the only words uttered in one of their television advertisements. The audience decodes the message (correctly or incorrectly) and ultimately rejects, accepts, stores or decides whether to drink Guinness or not. Amidst the careful coding and decoding there is noise, the extraneous factors which distract or distort the coded message such

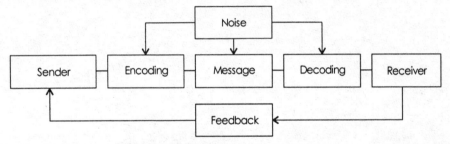

Figure 3.2 The communication process

as other advertisements, poor reception, a flashing light, a door bell, an ambulance siren, etc. Figure 3.2 demonstrates this.

The sender monitors feedback (eg whether the receiver changes his or her behaviour, facial expression, beliefs or attitudes) so that the message (and/or the channel in which it is sent) can be modified or changed. With so many other advertisements out there, it is easy to understand why so little communication actually gets through and works on the target market.

Mass communications

Despite the attractions of one-to-one marketing (see Chapter 13, `Direct Marketing'), mass communications such as television advertising is still considered attractive because it can reach a large audience quickly and cheaply (when comparing the cost per thousand individuals contacted — see page 264 Chapter 13). Much of this kind of mass advertising is ignored or distorted by an individual's information processing system. However, there is usually, within the mass audience, a percentage who are either actively looking for the particular product type or who are in a receptive state for this type of message (see the financial services example on page 41 of Chapter 2). Mass communication is therefore of interest to many marketing communicators. It is not a single-step process as it was considered to be in the early mass communication model shown in Figure 3.3.

Figure 3.3 Single-step communication model

This kind of inaccurate model of mass communication suggests that the sender has the potential to influence an unthinking and non-interacting crowd. Audiences (receivers) are active in that they process information selectively and often in a distorted manner (we see what we want to see). Receivers also talk to each other. Opinion leaders can be key players in the communications process as shown in the next two-step model in Figure 3.4.

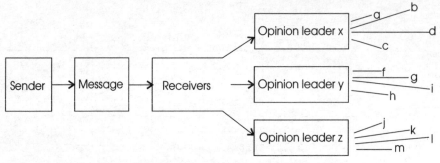

Figure 3.4 Two-step communication model

Two-step communication model

Katz and Lazarsfeld's two-step hypothesis (1955) helped to reduce fears of mass indoctrination by an all-powerful media. It also assumed mass messages filtered through opinion leaders to the mass audience.

Multi-step communication model (a)

Communication is in fact a multifaceted, multi-step and multi-directional process. Opinion leaders talk to each other. Opinion leaders talk to their listeners. Listeners talk to each other and subsequently feedback to opinion leaders, as shown in Figure 3.5. Some listeners/readers receive the message directly.

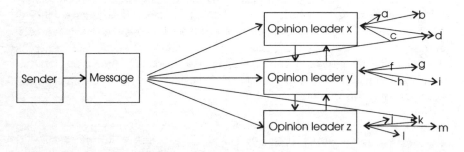

Figure 3.5 Multi-step communication model (a)

Multi-step communication model (b)

Noise, channels and feedback can be added to the multi-step model to make it more realistic, as shown in Figure 3.6.

The process of communicating with groups is fascinating. Group roles (leaders, opinion formers/leaders and followers) group norms and group attitudes are considered in 'Group Influence' (page 83, Chapter 4) and 'Social Change' (page 155, Chapter 8). In fact, all the intervening psychological variables can be added into the communications models to show how perception, selection, motivation, learning, attitudes

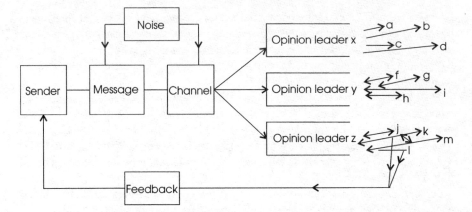

Figure 3.6 Multi-step communication model (b)

and group roles all affect the communication process. The intervening variables and some more complex models of buyer behaviour are also considered in more detail in Chapter 4.

Individuals do talk to each other, particularly when sharing personal product experiences. In fact, dissatisfied customers tell up to another 11 people about their bad experience, whereas satisfied customers tell only three or four. As marketing guru Philip Kotler says, 'bad news travels faster than good news.' Although this is not in the realm of mass communications, it does demonstrate how everything an organisation does communicates something to someone somewhere. Chapter 20 looks at this whole process in a lot more detail. Suffice to say, at this stage, that many advertisers use teaser, surreal and puzzle advertising (by sending incomplete or obscure messages) to arouse involvement and discussion among target audiences.

Understanding multi-phase communication

Here is how an understanding of multi-phase communication helps many advertisers to communicate directly to the mass (through the mass media) and indirectly through opinion leaders, style leaders, innovators, early adopters, influential individuals and opinion formers.

Advertisers recognise that in each market there are smaller target markets of opinion leaders who influence other members in the market place. Major brands can maintain their credibility by talking (advertising) specifically to these leaders as well as talking to the mass through other media channels (sometimes with messages tailored for the two groups). Whether advertising hi-fi, fashion, tennis rackets or social issues, multi-step communications can be employed.

In the world of fashion, the leaders are called '*style leaders*'. Even cult fashion products can be mass marketed by carefully splitting the messages between style leaders and the mass. While the leaders want to set themselves apart from the rest, the mass market consciously and/or unconsciously look to the leaders for suggestions about what to buy. The difficulty lies with success — as the mass market buys more the leaders lose interest unless they are reinforced with brand values that preserve the brand's credibility among the cognoscenti. This is important because if the leaders move away today, the mass sales will eventually start falling away next year or the year after. So, in addition to the mass advertising, some brands use small audience, targeted, opinion-leader media to send the 'right' messages to reinforce the leaders' relationship with the brand.

Hi-fi trendsetters need a different kind of advertising than just colour supplements with glossy brand images. These *'innovators and early adopters'* read additional magazines and look for more detailed technical information in music magazines or specialist hi-fi magazines, buyers guides, etc. Less knowledgeable buyers often refer to a friend who is a bit of a music buff (innovator or adopter) for an opinion on a brand of hi-fi before deciding to buy.

Just getting the product into the hands of the opinion leaders can help a brand competing in a large market. American marketing guru Philip Kotler suggests that special offers to opinion formers can work wonders:

> A new tennis racquet may be offered initially to members of the high school tennis teams at a special low price. The company would hope that these star high school tennis players (or *influential individuals*) would 'talk up' their new racquet to other high schoolers.

An understanding of multi-phase communication processes can contribute something to the development of social issue campaigns like AIDS. The initial stages of the campaign were temporarily restricted by inaccurate editorial coverage. Some tabloid *journalists* were feeding conflicting messages to the same mass which the advertising was addressing. The factual advertising was switched into the press so that *opinion formers* (journalists) could not write any more conflicting and inaccurate reports.

The power of *influential individuals* and *influential organisations* can be seen in industrial markets also. An entire industry may follow a well-respected and highly successful company which makes an early decision to buy. Expert sales teams focus on these kinds of companies initially. Marketers in consumer markets can also focus on the people who are the first to buy new ideas. Better information today can provide a focused approach through database marketing (see Chapter 13, page 245) while the imagery used can reflect the lifestyles, attitudes and aspirations of these 'innovators/early adopters' of fresh ideas.

Who are these 'early adopters' of new products and services? Are they different from the other potential customers in the same market? How do they 'adopt' new products or services? Is there a particular type of process through which they pass? The final section of this chapter provides some answers.

Adoption model

Several different hierarchical message models are considered in Chapter 4. The adoption model (Rogers 1962) is one of these. As shown in Figure 3.7, it attempts to map the mental process through which an individual passes on his journey towards purchasing, and ultimately adopting (or regularly purchasing), a new product or service.

This somewhat simplistic hierarchical model is nevertheless useful for identifying firstly, communication objectives and secondly, the appropriate communication tools.

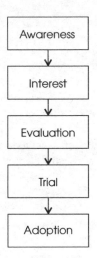

Figure 3.7 Adoption model

For example, television advertising may create awareness while a well-trained salesman or expertly designed brochure may help the individual in the evaluation stage. In
reality, the process is not simply hierarchical. Some individuals move directly from
awareness to trial while others loop backwards from the later stages by never actually
getting around to trying the new idea, subsequently forgetting it and then having to go
through being made aware of it again.

Rogers was also interested in how a new idea spreads or diffuses through a social
system or market. He defined diffusion as 'the spread of a new idea from its source of
invention or creation to its ultimate users or adopters'. Several groups who moved
towards adoption — at different rates — were identified. The first group to try a new
product were called 'innovators'. They represent approximately two and a half per
cent of all of the buyers who will eventually adopt the new product. Their profile was
different than those who were last to try a new idea (the laggards). Opinion leader
characteristics were part of the innovators. The key to the market is to identify, isolate
and target resources at the innovators and early adopters rather than everyone (84 per
cent will not buy the product until they see the innovators and early adopters with it
first). The early adopters are the second group to adopt a new idea (they represent 13.5
per cent of the total market), followed by the 'early majority' (34 per cent), the 'late
majority' (34 per cent) and the 'laggards' (16 per cent).

Each group has a different profile encompassing income, attitudes, social integration, etc. Innovators are venturesome, socially mobile and they like to try things that
are new. The early adopters tend to be opinion leaders who carefully adopt new ideas
early. The early majority adopt earlier than the majority of the market and they are
even more careful, almost deliberate, in their buying process. The late majority only
adopt after they have seen the majority of people try it. They tend to be sceptical. The
laggards are self-explanatory — tradition-bound and the last to adopt.

Adapting the Adoption Process

Although it is not a new product, Guinness have adapted the adoption process. They researched the 'adoption process' for a pint of Guinness because high increases in consumption among young session-drinkers resulting from the previous Guinness campaign were not sustained. This begged the question: 'How does one adopt a pint of Guinness?' How many pints, sessions or weeks does it take before becoming a regular, fully converted, loyal Guinness drinker? The answers to these questions were carefully collected before the commencement of the current Genius campaign (see Chapter 11).

Many of the previously discussed models offer some insight into the communication process but, almost invariably, they distort or oversimplify the process of communication. Chapter 4 draws on some of the communication models discussed here and looks at buying models, the buying process and the intervening psychological variables. How do we buy? Why do we buy? What influences our choices? Are there unconscious motives playing havoc with our day-to-day shopping behaviour? The next chapter attempts to look inside the customer's mind and answer some of these questions.

Key Points from Chapter 3:
1) Communication involves a two-way flow of information.
2) Communication theories can be applied to practical marketing situations.

Further reading

Cutlip, S Center, A and Broom, G (1985), *Effective Public Relations*, 6th edition, Prentice Hall International, Englewood Cliffs, New Jersey

Engel, J Warshaw, M and Kinnear, T (1991), *Promotional Strategy: Managing the marketing Communications Process*, 7th edition, Irwin, Homewood, Illinois

Katz, E and Lazarfield, P (1955) *Personal Influence: The Part Played by People in the Flow of Mass Communications*, New York Free Press, New York

Kotler, P (1988) *Marketing Management Analysis, Planning, Implementation and Control*, 6th edition, Prentice Hall, Englewood Cliffs, New Jersey

Rogers, E (1962) *Diffusions of Innovations*, New York Free Press, New York

Smallbone, D (1969) *The Practice of Marketing*, Staples Press, London

Tuck, M (1976) *How Do We Choose: a Study in Consumer Behaviour*, Methuen, London

4

BUYER BEHAVIOUR THEORY

INTRODUCTION

The first step in formulating a marketing communications strategy is to identify, analyse and ultimately understand the target market and its buying behaviour. This chapter considers some of the theories and models which the marketing professional can use to help to communicate with and influence the buyer at various stages before, during and after purchasing. Buying behaviour is often more complex than it appears. Individuals are generally not very predictable but, in the aggregate, groups of customers (or percentages of markets) can be more predictable.

Whether in the industrial or consumer market, or whether they are buying products or services, buyers respond in different ways to the barrage of marketing communications which are constantly aimed at them. Theoretical frameworks borrowed from psychology, sociology, social psychology, cultural anthropology and economics are now added to by both commercial and academic market research into consumer and industrial buyer behaviour. All of this contributes to a better understanding of buyer behaviour. It is this understanding that helps to reveal what kind of marketing communications work better than others.

This chapter can only provide an outline of the vast amount of work written in this area. The complex burger buyer example below is used to open up some of the types of question that need to be considered. The chapter then looks at types of purchases, the buying process (including some buying models) and eventually briefly considers how the 'intervening variables' of perception, motivation, learning, memory, attitudes, beliefs, personality and group influence can influence the communication process and, ultimately, buying behaviour.

THREE KEY QUESTIONS

There are three key groups of questions which have to be answered before any marketing communications can be carried out:

1) *Who is the buyer* (target market/s and decision-making units)?
2) *Why do they buy* (or not buy) a particular brand or product?

3) *How, when and where do they buy?*

The second question, 'Why do they buy?' is the most difficult to answer. It requires *qualitative* rather than *quantitative* data (which generally answers the other questions). Products and services are bought for a range of different reasons or benefits, some conscious, others unconscious, some rational, others emotional. Many buyers buy for a mixture of reasons. Consider a simple hamburger.

THE COMPLEX BURGER BUYER

Why buy a burger? The answer might be as simple as 'because I was hungry — so I bought a Big Mac'. The real reason, however, may be quite different. Perhaps the buyer was in a receptive state for food because of the time of the day. In the same way that a stimulus such as a bell for Pavlov's dog (see 'Learning' page 78) can cause a dog to salivate, the highly visible yellow McDonald's logo can possibly act as a stimulus to the customer to remind him of food and arouse feelings of hunger — even salivation. Perhaps the yellow logo also acts as a *cue* by triggering memories of the happy advertising images which are learned and stored in memory banks?

A teenage burger buyer may prefer McDonald's because friends hang out there and it feels nice to be in with the in-crowd (Maslow's need to be accepted or loved, see 'Motivation' on page 82). Maybe the friendly image and the quick service simultaneously satisfy two basic needs — love and hunger? Many convenience purchases today are, in fact, purchasing time, ie buying a time-saving product or service releases free time to do something else, to satisfy another need. It is likely that many buyers have different reasons with different orders of importance. Different segments can seek different benefits (benefit segmentation, see page 40). But why don't they go into a Wimpy restaurant or a fish and chip shop instead of a McDonald's?

Choice is often influenced by familiarity with the brand, or sometimes the level of trust in a brand name. Familiarity can be generated by actual experience and/or increased awareness boosted by advertising. If one brand can get into the front of an individual's mind ('*front of mind awareness*') through advertising etc, then it will stand a better chance of being chosen in a simple buying situation like this, unless, of course, the buyer has a *preferred set* of fast food restaurants which specifically exclude a particular brand. In this case the buyer is usually prepared to search a little harder (even cross the road) before satisfying the aroused need.

The choice of another group of burger buyers can be determined by simply location — offering the right goods or services in the right place at the right time at the right prices. Assuming this is all supported by the right image (eg clean and friendly, nutritious, fast service, socially responsible, etc), then the marketing mix has succeeded in capturing this segment of non-loyal burger buyers who have no strong preferred set of fast food outlets.

More health-conscious buyers may prefer a nice warm cup of soup. Why? What motivates them? Health? A desire to live longer? A fear of death? A desire to be fit, stay slim, look good (esteem) or just feel healthy/feel good (self-actualisation, see Maslow page 82)? Or perhaps it's cheaper than a burger? Or is it because everyone else in the office recommends the local delicatessen's soup (pressure to conform to group norms, desire to be accepted by a group — again, the need to be loved)?

There are other possibilities which lie in the dark depths of our vast information storage chambers, otherwise known as our unconscious. For example, in the 1950s Vance Packard suggested that

> the deepest roots of our liking for warm, nutritious and plentiful soup may lie in the comfortable and secure unconscious prenatal sensations of being surrounded by the amniotic fluid in our mother's womb.

Impulse buying and repeat purchasing of low-cost fast food obviously differs from the buying behaviour involved in the purchase of, say, a new compact disc system, a house, a holiday or a fleet of new cars for the company. It is likely that more 'information search' will occur than in the simple stimulus-response buying model (McDonald's yellow logo stimulates the senses and arouses hunger, which generates the response — buy a Big Mac). Regular low-cost purchases are known as 'routinised response behaviour' and therefore have a different buying process than a high-cost, high-risk, irregular purchase, which is known as a 'high-involvement purchase'. Some basic buying models help to explain the different types of purchases and the types of buying process involved. These will be considered further in this chapter, but first let us consider why buyers buy.

WHY DO THEY BUY?

Marketing people really do need to know the reasons why buyers buy. There appears to be a host of conscious and unconscious reasons underlying why people buy what they buy. Some reasons are more important than others to a particular segment or group of buyers. Some of these reasons are rational and some are emotional. The split between the two is called the 'emotional/rational dichotomy'. This quagmire of complex reasons is not restricted to consumer purchasing but also to hard-nosed professional buying behaviour. The bottom line is that marketing managers have to constantly ask this question: 'Why are they buying or not buying my products or services?'. The answers are not static, one-off pieces of research findings but a constant flow of information. Reasons change, people change, markets change, competition and technology change. A valid reason for buying a particular product yesterday may become obsolete tomorrow. Likewise, an apparently irrelevant feature yesterday may become a key reason for buying tomorrow.

A company executive might buy one brand of a computer rather than another simply because of a distant fear of being fired. Even an apparently simple product like toothpaste presents a complex web of reasons for buying. The toothpaste manufacturers respond by supplying different images of different benefits of different types of toothpaste to different segments who have different reasons (needs or motives) for brushing their teeth. The following toothpaste test explains.

The Toothpaste Test

Why do you buy toothpaste? 'To keep teeth clean.' 'To stop cavities and visits to dentist.' 'To keep a full set of beautiful shining teeth.' Some people will admit that 'it is habit' or that 'my parents taught me always to...' All of these answers suggest different benefits that different groups or segments want from their toothpaste and so the toothpaste suppliers oblige by positioning certain brands as those that deliver a particular benefit. But when do you brush your teeth? First thing in the morning? If people were serious about seeking the above benefits they would carry a small portable brush and use it after each meal. Why do most people brush first thing in the morning? To avoid bad breath (which destroys one's confidence). Yet many people do not like admitting it. The real reason is often hidden below the surface.

The Colgate 'ring of confidence' was one of the UK's best-known toothpaste advertisements. It was basically selling a tube of social confidence. This need to be accepted is relatively obvious although not always admitted initially. There are, however, deeper feelings, emotions, memories, moods, thoughts, beliefs and attitudes locked up inside the dark depths of our unconscious. Sigmund Freud suggested that the mind was like an iceberg in so far as the tip represents the conscious part of the mind while the greater submerged part is the unconscious. Even long since forgotten childhood experiences can affect buying behaviour, including hard-nosed American industrial buyers (see 'Mommy's Never Coming Back', page 93, Chapter 5). Some theories of motivation are discussed further in this chapter (page 80).

In the UK many organisations use in-depth research, eg Guinness carry out in-depth research to tap into drinkers' deeply ingrained feelings about the product. Individuals are asked to express their, often unconscious, feelings through clay modelling, picture completion and cartoon completion techniques. This kind of research has revealed that people associate natural goodness and quasi-mystical qualities with the brand. The section on motivation (page 80) looks at in-depth feelings.

TYPES OF BUYING SITUATION

The amount of time and effort which a buyer is prepared to put into any particular purchase depends on the level of expenditure, the frequency of purchase and the perceived risk involved. Relatively larger expenditure usually warrants greater deliberation during search and evaluation phases. In consumer markets this buying process is classified as '*extensive problem solving*' (EPS) if the buyer has no previous product experience and the purchase is infrequent, expensive and/or risky. The situation is different where the buyer has some knowledge and experience of, and familiarity with, a particular product or service. This is called '*limited problem solving*' (LPS). In the case of strong brand loyalty for an habitually purchased product '*routinised response behaviour*' (RRB) can be identified by the repeat brand purchasing of convenience products like baked beans. The buyer chooses quickly and has a *low involvement* with the purchase. EPS requires *high involvement* from the buyer, which means that the buyer spends time and effort before actually deciding to buy a particular product or brand. This can be complicated by further advisers and influencers who form part of the '*decision-making unit*' or DMU (see below). LPS obviously requires lower levels of involvement than EPS but more than RRB.

Industrial buying is even more clearly influenced by decision-making units, particularly when the purchase is considered large, infrequent and risky. Like consumer buying, types of purchase situation also vary in industrial markets. A '*new task*' buying situation means what it says — the organisation has no experience of the product or service and is buying it for the first time. A '*modified rebuy*' situation is where the industrial buyer has some experience of the product or service, while a '*straight rebuy*' is where the buyer, or purchasing department, buys on a regular basis.

DECISION MAKING UNITS

As mentioned previously, there are often several individuals involved in any one person's decision to purchase either consumer or industrial products and services. The choice of a family car may be influenced by parents, children, aunts, uncles, neighbours, friends, the Automobile Association and so on. Each may play a different role in the buying process. Similarly, the purchase of a new factory machine may have been instigated by a safety inspector, selected by a team of engineers, supervisors, shop steward, production manager, agreed by the board, bought or ordered by the purchasing director and paid for by the financial director or company secretary.

PAGES is a simple acronym which helps to build a marketing communications DMU checklist:

Purchaser (orders the goods or services)
Adviser (those that are knowledgeable in the field)
Gatekeeper (secretaries, receptionists and assistants who want to protect their bosses
        from being besieged by marketing messages)
End user (sometimes called 'the customer')
Starter (instigator or initiator)

The actual decision-maker and the payer (cheque authoriser) may, in fact, be added to the above 'PAGES'.

MODELS OF BUYER BEHAVIOUR

There are many different models which attempt to model the buyer's behaviour. Figure 4.1 shows how a buyer in either an EPS (extensive problem solving) or LPS (limited problem solving) situation moves through the purchasing cycle or purchasing continuum. The basic model can also be borrowed and used in industrial markets also. It highlight some of the stages through which a potential buyer passes. Sources and channels of information plus buying criteria can also be identified, which, in turn, provide a checklist for the marketing plan.

The buying process

We can demonstrate this simple buying model by considering, say, the purchase of a new compact disc player. Somewhere somebody or something tells you that you need a CD. This is known as problem recognition, which is followed by 'information search'. This may involve ads and editorial in magazines, visits to stores, discussion among friends, etc. Next comes evaluation. Leaflets, catalogues, ads and discussions are amassed and a set of criteria is further refined. This may include size, shape, colour, delivery, guarantee, etc. Performance is really difficult to assess since few can read sound graphs let alone decipher a good sound in a shop full of other speakers. Finally, a decision is made to choose a particular model. It isn't over yet. The chosen

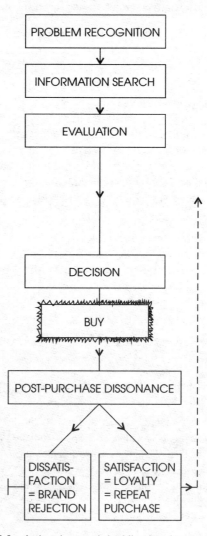

Figure 4.1 A simple model of the buying process

brand may be out of stock (in which case the communications mix has worked but the marketing mix has failed since distribution has not got the product on the shelf). Another brand is eventually purchased. This is when waves of worry, doubt or 'post-purchase dissonance' come. This may be addressed by reassuring the buyer (with a congratulatory note, additional advertising, after-sales service and, most of all, a product or service that lives up to the promise made in the advertising). And if the product matches the promise then both repeat business and word-of-mouth referrals are more likely over the longer run.

This simple buying model shown in Figure 4.1 serves as a useful checklist to see whether you are filling in all the communication gaps in the buying process. The model should not be hierarchical since in reality there are loops, eg between information and evaluation as the buyer learns about new criteria not previously considered.

Stage	AIDA	Lavidge & Steiner	Adoption	DAGMAR	Howard & Sheth (excerpt)
Cognitive	Attention	Awareness ↓ Knowledge ↓	Awareness ↓	Unawareness ↓ Awareness ↓ Comprehension ↓	Attention ↓ Comprehension ↓
Affective	Interest ↓ Desire ↓	Liking ↓ Preference ↓ Conviction ↓	Interest ↓ Evaluation ↓ Trial ↓	Conviction ↓	Attitude ↓ Intention ↓
Behaviour	Action	Purchase	Adoption	Action	Purchase
	E K Strong (1925)	L & S (1961)	E M Rogers (1961)	R H Colley (1961)	H & S* (1969)

*The Howard and Sheth excerpt is taken from the full model shown on page 75.

Figure 4.2 Communication models

This model is more relevant for a high-involvement purchase whether extensive problem solving (consumer) or new task (industrial). A routinised response situation, like buying a beer, would not involve this lengthy deliberation.

Response hierarchy models

Although the ultimate objective for most marketing managers is to build repeat purchasing, there are many stages in between creating problem recognition or need arousal and purchase. The communication models in Figure 4.2 show what are thought to be the sequence of mental stages through which a buyer passes on his journey towards a purchase.

These models are sometimes called '*message models*' or '*response hierarchy models*' since they help to prioritise the communication objectives by determining whether a cognitive, affective or behavioural response is required, ie whether the organisation wants to create awareness in the target audience's mind, or to change an attitude, or to act in some way (buy, vote, participate, etc). (See 'Attitudes' on page 82 for a more detailed explanation of cognitive, affective and behavioural/conative elements of an attitude.) Message models are helpful but not conclusive since 1) not all buyers go through all stages 2) the stages do not necessarily occur in a hierarchical sequence and 3) impulse purchases contract the process.

Although repeat purchase (loyal behaviour) is the ultimate marketing goal, a PR campaign, advertisement or sales promotion may have a tactical objective focusing on a particular stage in the above models, eg increasing awareness, changing an attitude, generating trial, etc.

These hierarchical communication models identify the stages through which buyers generally pass. An understanding of these stages helps to plan appropriate marketing communications. DAGMAR (Defining Advertising Goals and Measuring Advertising Results) was created to encourage measurable objectives for each stage of the communications continuum.

Some of the stages can sometimes occur simultaneously and/or instantaneously, as in the case of an impulse purchase. Buyers can also avoid moving in a straight line or hierarchy of stages when making a more considered purchase (extended problem solving). For example, during the evaluation stage a potential buyer may go back to the information stage to obtain more information before making a decision to buy.

Ideally, these models should allow for these and other loops caused by '*message decay*' (or forgetting), changes in attitudes, competitive distractions, etc. The models also ignore the mind's 'intervening variables', some of which are identified in both the '*personal variable models*' of Fishbein et al (page 74) and the '*complex models*' of Howard and Sheth, and Engel, Kollatt and Blackwell (1978). The complex models, do, in fact, allow for both loops and the complexities of the intervening variables (see page 75).

Three types of model, 'black box', 'personal variable' and 'complex', will now be considered briefly. Black box models consider external variables that act as stimuli (such as price, shops, merchandise, advertisements, promotions and the social environment including families and friends) and responses such as sales. Personal variable models focus on some of the internal psychological variables such as attitudes and beliefs. The complex models attempt to include both the internal and external variables in one grand model. To some this proves impossible. As Gordan Foxall (1992) points out: 'No one model can capture human nature in its entirety; nor can a handful of theoretical perspectives embrace the scope of human interaction'.

Black box models

The behaviourist school of psychology concentrates on how people respond to stimuli. It is not concerned with the complex range of internal and external factors which affect the behaviour. The complexities of the mind are left locked up in a '*black box*'. The resulting *stimulus-response models* ignore the complexities of the mind (including the intervening variables such as perception, motivation, attitudes, etc) and focus on the input or stimulus) eg advertising, and the output, eg purchase behaviour. A classical approach to stimulus-response models is considered in 'Learning' on page 78. Figure 4.3 shows a black box model.

Figure 4.3 Black box model

As Williams (1989) says: 'Black box models treat the individual and his physiological and psychological make-up as an impenetrable black box.' Only the inputs and outputs are measured. Any internal mental processes (the intervening processes) which cannot be measured are ignored. The model below shows some examples of 'input' and 'output'.

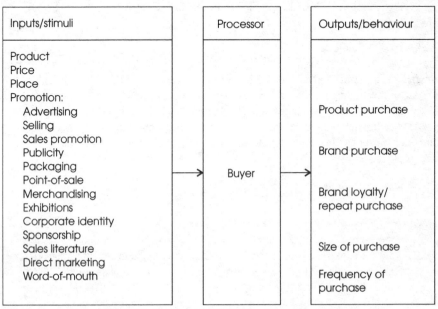

Inputs/stimuli	Processor	Outputs/behaviour

Product
Price
Place
Promotion:
  Advertising
  Selling
  Sales promotion
  Publicity
  Packaging
  Point-of-sale
  Merchandising
  Exhibitions
  Corporate identity
  Sponsorship
  Sales literature
  Direct marketing
  Word-of-mouth
	Buyer	Product purchase
		
		Brand purchase
		
		Brand loyalty/
		repeat purchase
		
		Size of purchase
		
		Frequency of
		purchase

Figure 4.4 An enlarged black box model

The black box approach considers only the inputs and outputs. Careful analysis under controlled tests (using reasonably sophisticated computer models) can reveal the optimum price, the optimum level of advertising and so on.

Personal variable models

These models take a glimpse inside the black box of the mind. The models only involve a few personal variables such as beliefs, attitudes and intentions. These kinds of model are sometimes used within more complex models. Three types of personal variable models, `linear additive', `threshold' and `trade-off' are briefly considered below.

Linear additive models

Linear additive models like that of *Fishbein* are based on the number of attributes which a particular product or service has, multiplied by the score each attribute is perceived to have, multiplied by the weighting which each attribute is deemed to have. This model opens up attitudes by indicating which attributes are considered to be important to the customer and how each attribute is scored by the customer. Attitudes are not always translated into purchasing behaviour. Even intentions are not always translated into action. Nevertheless, marketing strategies can be built around changing beliefs about attributes, and altering their evaluation or scores.

Threshold models

Most purchases have cut-off points or thresholds beyond which the buyer will not venture. It may be price or some particular feature which a product or service must have (or must not have in the case of some environmentally damaging ingredients) if it is to be considered at all. Here, the buyer has a selection process which screens and accepts those products or services within the threshold for either further analysis or immediate purchase. Those beyond the threshold are rejected and will not be considered any further.

Trade-off models

Buyers generally have a wide array of choices, many with different types and amounts of attributes. A trade-off occurs when the buyer accepts a product which is lacking in one attribute but strong in another. A sort of compensatory mechanism emerges. When buying a car, engine size and price can be traded off against each other, eg a bigger engine means a worse price (higher price). A number of combinations of price and engine size can be researched to find the value or `utility' for different prices and engine sizes.

Complex models

The cognitive school attempts to open the lid and look inside the mind's black box. Here, more complex buying models, like that of Howard and Sheth (1969), try to incorporate into the hierarchical communication models the intervening variables of perception, motivation, learning, memory, attitudes, beliefs, group influence, etc; in fact, almost everything inside the mind.

Howard and Sheth

A simplified version of Howard and Sheth's complex model divides the black box into perceptual constructs, and learning constructs as shown in Figure 4.5. The exogenous variables are external to this model and they include personality traits, social class, financial status, the social/organisational setting and even the importance of the purchase to the individual.

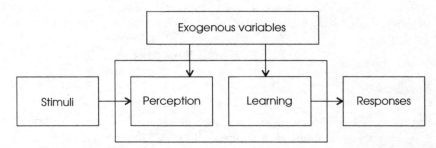

Figure 4.5 A simplified version of Howard and Sheth's model

The complete complex model in Figure 4.6 includes perception, learning, attitudes and motivation. Stimulus ambiguity implies inadequate information to make a decision. Perceptual bias (see 'Perception', page 76) basically means that there is a certain amount of distortion in the way that an individual perceives a stimulus.

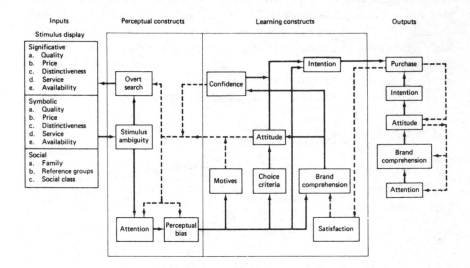

Source: Howard, J and Sheth, JN (1969)
© Copyright (1969) John Wiley & Sons. Reprinted by permission of John Wiley & Sons Inc.

Figure 4.6 The complete Howard and Sheth model

This complex model has, however, been criticised for its lack of clear definition of the relationship between some of the variables and a lack of distinction between the endogenous variables (within the model) and exogenous variables (external to the model). The model is, for many readers, difficult to understand and for many practitioners, impossible to use. Nevertheless it does provide a useful insight into the possible workings of the mind.

The remainder of this chapter looks at some of the influencing variables such as perception, learning, motivation, values, attitudes and life styles and considers how an understanding of them helps to make more effective marketing communications.

THE INTERVENING VARIABLES

Perception

Perception means the way stimuli, such as commercial messages, advertisements, packaging, shops, uniforms, etc are interpreted. Messages and images are not always perceived in the manner intended by the advertiser. As Chisnall (1984) says; `Our perceptual system has a tendency to organise, modify and distort information reaching it.' Perception is selective . We see what we want to see.

The Smoker

Here's a simple test. Ask a smoker to recall exactly what the health warning says on the side of their packet of cigarettes. Few will be able to tell you the exact words. This is because we all selectively screen out messages or stimuli which may cause discomfort, tension or `cognitive dissonance'. Imagine that the smoker allows the message (warning) to be perceived. This will cause discomfort every time a cigarette is taken since the box will give the smoker an unpleasant message. In order to reduce this tension, the smoker has two options: a) change behaviour (stopping smoking) or b) screen out the message and continue the behaviour (smoking).

Many stimuli are *screened out* by the perceptual system, which, it is estimated, is

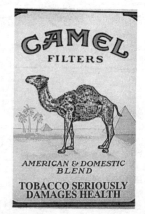

Many smokers screen out negative messages

hit by between 500 and 1500 different advertisements a day. The next example shows how preferences and motivations affect perception.

The Football Match

A striker is clean through with only the goalkeeper to beat when out of nowhere a defender slides in and makes a tackle. Fifteen thousand people applaud the 'great tackle' while the opposing 15,000 fans, having received exactly the same information (the tackle), scream at the referee and demand that he gives a penalty to the attacking side. We see what we want to see. We like to organise, modify and distort the information or messages that come to us.

Before perception occurs, attention has to be gained by, say, the advertiser. As Williams (1989) says, interests, needs and motives determine 'not only what will arouse attention, but also what will hold it'. For example, advertisements for a new house are ignored by the mass population. But there is a sector of the population who are actively looking for a house. This sector has a need for a new house and it is therefore receptive to any of these advertisements. Individuals from this sector positively select information relevant to their needs. This is known as '*selective attention*'.

There are also certain physical properties which increase the likelihood of a message gaining attention: intensity and size; position; sound; colour; contrast; and movement (eyes are involuntarily attracted to movement because of the body's instinctive defence mechanism). Given that an individual's attention is constantly called upon by new stimuli, repetition can enhance the likelihood of a message getting through. Novelty can also be used to jar expectations and grab attention.

Perceived differences in brands are not necessarily dependent on real product differences (in either function or form). As Chisnall (1984) says: 'Consumers evaluate products against the background of their experiences, expectations and associations. Perception is seldom an objective, scientific assessment of the comparative values of competing brands'.

An understanding of the way our perceptual system organises information has helped some brand advertisers to exploit perceptual systems through an understanding of *Gestalt* psychology. Gestalt means 'total figuration'. One of the four basic perceptual organising techniques from the Gestalt school is '*closure*'. An individual strives to make sense of incomplete messages by filling in the gaps or shaping the image so that it can fit comfortably into his cognitive set or (set of knowledge). Marlboro's 'MARL' advertisements and Kit-Kat's 'Kit' advertisments play on the need to fill in these gaps. This may happen so fast that the viewer is not aware of what is going on inside his head. Effectively, the mind momentarily becomes the medium since the complete image is only visible inside our head while the external advertisement only shows the incomplete image. In a sense, a giant billboard inside our forehead is switched on by an incomplete stimulus. The natural perceptual tendency towards 'closure' completes the advertisement's image inside the audience's mind.

Perception is also inextricably linked with past experiences, motivation, beliefs, attitudes and the ability to learn.

Learning

Marketers obviously want customers to learn about firstly, the existence of their brand or company, and secondly, the merits of their particular brands. A knowledge of the learning process is therefore useful in understanding how customers acquire, store, and retrieve messages about products, brands and companies. How are attitudes about companies, products and brands developed (or learned)? Advertising and sales promotions can help customers learn in different ways (see *'classical' and 'operant' conditioning* below). In addition, how many times (*frequency*) should an advertisement be shown before it is remembered or, alternatively, before it causes irritation? Should it be repeated regularly once a week for a year ('drip' strategy) or concentrated into 12 times a week for four weeks only ('burst' strategy). Differing levels of intelligence, memory capacity, motivations, perceptual systems, associations and rewards (reinforcement) affect the learning process.

> ### The Party
>
> When introduced to someone at a party, do you ever forget their name? An inability to learn and remember names can create embarrassment. Perhaps the host should increase the frequency of the branding process by repeating the individual's name three times during the introduction? Or would this be irritating? Perhaps it would be better if the individual's name was inserted in a 'drip' strategy rather than a 'burst' strategy ie occasionally the host will pass by and casually drop the individual's name into the conversation and move on.

Connectionist learning theories

Simple *'connectionist theory'* suggests that associations can be made between messages, or stimuli, and responses. Hence the term, 'stimulus-response' model. In the late 1890s, the Russian physiologist Ivan Pavlov demonstrated how *'classical conditioning'* or involuntary conditioning worked on dogs. By regularly ringing a bell before presenting food to a dog, it learned to associate (or connect) the bell with food. After a period of conditioning the dog would salivate (respond) upon hearing the bell (stimulus) without any food arriving. As Williams (1989) says: 'It is the idea of association that underlines the concept of branding in modern marketing'. Constant repetition can build associations between needs, products and brands, eg if you are thinking of beans, think Heinz: 'Beanz Meanz Heinz'.

'Operant conditioning', on the other hand, is voluntary in so far as the participant actively searches for solutions. The *'Skinner box'* was devised by America's Dr Skinner during the 1930s. By placing a hungry rat in a box where food only arrived once the rat pressed a lever, Skinner observed that the rat would search, investigate and,

eventually, press the lever accidentally. Food then arrived. Over a period of time the rat, when aroused by the hunger motive, learned to press the lever for food. An association or connection was made between the lever pressing and the drive to satisfy the hunger need. This approach to building associations through voluntary participation suggests that sales promotions can actively invite the buyer to participate, be rewarded, and eventually connect a particular product or service with a particular stimulated need.

Stimuli-responses

Connectionist theories of learning highlight the importance of firstly, timing, and secondly, frequency of marketing communications. The establishment of a connection or association between a stimulus and a response is fundamental to the conditioning process. Advertising jingles, pictures and even smells are some of the stimuli which can arouse emotional or behavioural responses. Some people feel good when they hear the Coca Cola jingle `I'd like to teach the world to sing...', others are aroused and excited when they hear the sound of a sports commentator's voice with crowd sound effects in the background. McDonald's large, highly-visible yellow `M' logo can trigger a response, particularly if an individual is involved in goal-oriented behaviour (is hungry and is ready to consider eating food). Could this yellow logo be the equivalent of Pavlov's bell? Do some humans salivate just at the sight of the logo? Certainly the release of certain aromas can stimulate immediate responses. For example as customers leave the pub and walk down the street they are often greeted by a wafting smell of frying chips, which can stimulate or arouse the need for food, and lead to an immediate purchase.

A UK travel operator, Next Island, is using perfume impregnation in its packaged holiday brochure. `What does a holiday smell like?' Their brochures have the smell of coconut suntan oil to help to conjure up associations, connections, memories and feelings of sun, sea and holiday-time.

Reinforcement and *reward* enhance the learning process. In other words, good quality products and services reward the buyer every time. This consistent level of quality reinforces the brand's positive relationship with the buyer. On the other hand, if the quality is poor, there is no reward (response does not satisfy the need) and the response (to buy a particular brand or visit a particular shop) will not be repeated.

Positive reinforcement helps the learning process (or helps the buyer to remember the brand or shop). It is possible to `unlearn' or forget (`message decay'), so many advertisers seek to remind customers of their products, their names and their benefits. Some advertisements seek to remind the buyer what a good choice they have already made by frequently repeating their messages. The connectionist approach ignores all the other complex and influential variables involved in learning and, ultimately, buying. Arguably, it oversimplifies a complex process.

Packaging design can also act as a cue to arouse momentarily the happy images conveyed in the previously seen and unconsciously stored advertising images. This is where a `pack shot' of the product/pack in the advertisement (usually at the end) aids recall of the brand, the advertisement and its image when the consumer is shopping or just browsing along shelves full of different brands.

Every brand's manager would like to have their brand chosen automatically every time. Some brands achieve this through an unconsciously learned response. How? By building a presence through frequency of advertising and maximum shelf facings (amount of units displayed on shelves — see Chapter 19) and, most importantly, supplying an appropriate level of *reinforcement* (an appropriate level of *quality* in the product or service itself). Chapter 20 emphasises the importance of quality in the long-term repeat buying success strategies of today and tomorrow.

Cognitive learning

Cognitive learning focuses on what happens in between the stimulus and response. It embraces the intervening mental processes.

Insight, meaning, perception, knowledge and problem-solving are all considered relevant concepts. Cognitive learning is not dependent on 'trial and error'. It depends on an ability to think, sometimes conceptually, and to perceive relationships and 'what if' scenarios. It is not dependent on an immediate reward to reinforce the learning process; in fact, *'latent learning'* occurs in the absence of reward and without any immediate action. Of course , an individual has to be suitably motivated to achieve this kind of learning. The next intervening variable — motivation — will now be considered.

Motivation

Motivation is defined as the drive to satisfy a need. Some motives are socially learned (eg wanting to get married) and others are instinctive (eg wanting to eat when hungry). Many motives are unconscious but active in that they influence every-day buying behaviour. Brands carry covert messages which are fleetingly understood at a subconscious level. As the Market Research Society says in its 1986 conference paper, 'It is often this deeper meaning which is what is exchanged for money. These deep underlying feelings are often the real reason why people buy products or services'.

Sigmund Freud suggested that an individual is motivated by conscious and unconscious forces. His psychoanalytical approach broke the personality into the id (instinctive drives and urges, eg eat food, grab food), the ego (the social learning process which allows the individual to interact with the environment, eg ask politely for food or pay for food) and the super-ego, which provides a conscience or ethical/moral referee between the id and the ego. Freud suggested that 'all actions are the results of antecedent conditions' (see how childhood experiences might affect industrial buying behaviour some 30 or 40 years later in 'Mommy's Never Coming Back', page 93, Chapter 5). Occasionally, these unconscious stirrings manifest themselves in dreams, responses to ambiguous stimuli and slips of the tongue (Freudian slips).

Clinical psychology uses thematic apperception tests, Rorschach tests and word association tests to help them to analyse the underlying and sometimes unconscious personality traits and motivations of an individual. In-depth market researchers (*qualitative researchers*) use metaphors, picture completion and montages in an attempt to throw the interviewee's ego off guard and dip into the real underlying feelings which interviewees find difficult both to become aware of and express in an articulate manner.

In the 1950s Vance Packard was concerned about how *in-depth researchers* like Dr Ernest Dichter were attempting to extract buyers' unconscious feelings, aspirations and motivations, which were then subtly reflected through advertising imagery, which in turn manipulated buyers unconsciously. Although discredited by some and criticised by others, Dichter's *Handbook of Consumer Motivations* (1964) is an extremely thought-provoking and entertaining read.

Here are some other well-known in-depth research findings from the 1950s which supposedly reveal the deep underlying motivations which drive certain forms of behaviour, including buying behaviour:

- A woman is very serious when she bakes a cake because unconsciously she is going through the act of birth.
- Soon after the initial trial period housewives who used a new improved cake-mix (no egg needed, just add water) stopped buying it. The new improved cake mix provoked a sense of guilt as the cooking role of the housewife was reduced.
- A man buys a convertible as a substitute mistress.
- Smoking represents an infantile pleasure of sucking.
- Men want their cigars to be odoriferous in order to prove that they (the men) are masculine.
- Shaving for some men is the daily act of cutting off this symbol of manliness (stubble). It is therefore a kind of daily castration.

This all appears to be too American and is arguably outdated now. Man is a rational animal and is not concerned with such psycho-analytic interpretations of every-day, ordinary and, supposedly, commonsense behaviour. Consider the close shave below.

A Close Shave?

I have a simple test that I use in lectures with different groups. I pose a question and ask for male respondents only. The question is 'How many of you find shaving a hassle?' Usually a unanimous show of hands emerges. 'How many of you would like to be able to dispense with the aggravation of shaving?' Slightly fewer hands emerge. 'Well, here is a cream that will solve your problem. This cream closes your hair follicles so that hair will never grow there again. It is medically approved and cleared for a market launch next year. Who would like to try some right now?' All the hands are gone. The question 'Why not?' is usually answered faintly with 'Freedom to choose to have a beard later in life and so on.' Or is there something deeper here? Dichter would have said 'yes'.

Abraham Maslow's hierarchy of needs (1954) provides a simple but useful explanation of the way an individual's needs work. Essentially, he showed that one is driven or motivated initially to satisfy the lower level needs and then, when satisfied, move up to the next level of need. This theory also implies that motivation can be cyclical in so far as buying a house may be motivated initially by the lower level survival needs and subsequently by the higher level need of esteem. Figure 4.7 shows Maslow's hierarchy of needs.

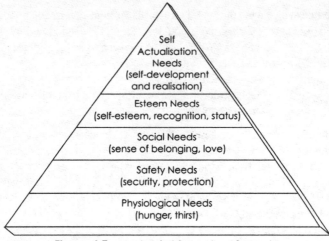

Figure 4.7 Maslow's hierarchy of needs

Cars transport people from A to B. Sometimes the need to buy a car is a basic survival need (eg to get to work, to earn money to buy food). Sometimes it can provide a cocoon (or shelter) from the mass of bodies scrambling for the public transport system. Sometimes it can provide freedom to explore the countryside, visit friends, do what you want (self-actualise). Cars can also act as status symbols (esteem). Some cars position their benefits (power, speed, safety, environmental, etc) so that they dominate the ad and appeal to the predominant need of a particular segment. Page 81 refers to Dichter's `substitute mistress car'.

Different people (or groups of people) extract different benefits from the same product. Some people want to drive a Porsche because it gives them power; others because they see it a symbol of success (good for the ego and esteem); others just want the thrill of driving very fast (self-actualisation), as in the case of the driver's last wish in Nevil Shute's *On the Beach*; others again may simply want a very fast reliable car which allows them to get from A to B (around Europe) without delay. Markets can be broken up into `*benefit segments*' so that the communications can be tailored to develop the ideal positioning for a particular segment. In some cases, benefit segmentation demands different products for different segments, as in the case of the toothpaste market (page 68).

Attitudes

Attitudes affect buying behaviour. Attitudes are learned and they tend to stick; they *can* be changed, but not very quickly.

As Williams (1989) says: `If a marketer is able to identify the attitudes held by different market segments towards his product, and also to measure changes in those attitudes, he will be well placed to plan his marketing strategy. An attitude is a predisposition towards a person, a brand, a product, a company or a place.

An interesting question is `which came first, the attitude or the behaviour?' Are attitudes formed prior to purchase or post purchase? Can attitudes be formed without any experience?

The answer is 'yes' to both. Attitudes are sometimes formed without direct experience and, equally, products are often bought without any prior attitude. In the latter case, however, it is likely, that an attitude will form as a result of the good or bad experience which the buyer has with the product. Advertising, in this case, serves to reinforce attitudes rather than create awareness.

Attitudes can be broken down into three components, which are often explained as 'think, feel, do' or '*cognitive*', '*affective*' and '*conative*'. The cognitive element is the awareness or knowledge of, say, a brand. The affective element is the positive or negative feeling associated with the brand. The conative element is the intention to purchase. It can be important to measure all three components since an isolated element can be misleading. For example Rolls-Royce score highly on the cognitive and affective elements of the attitude, but few of those who express awareness of and liking towards a Rolls-Royce will actually buy one. Identifying the levels of each attitudinal element helps to set tighter communication objectives. For example, the creative strategy for increasing brand awareness would be different from the strategy required to change the target market's feelings (or reposition the brand). A different communications strategy (perhaps an emphasis on sales promotions) would be required if the objective was to convert high awareness and positive feelings into trial purchases.

Group influence

Much of human behaviour, and buyer behaviour in particular, is shaped by group influence. Whether cultural, religious, political, socio-economic, lifestyle, special interest groups or just family, social groups affect an individual's behaviour patterns.

The effects of group influence are often seen in a queue or waiting area where charity collectors are attempting to collect money. Success or failure is often determined by the reaction of the first encounter, ie if the first person acknowledges the collector and makes a contribution, the next person is more likely to do so also. I have often seen a whole platform generously giving money after a successful start. Equally, I have seen almost total rejection by a whole queue once the initial contact has refused to donate. This is a bizarre or perverse form of charity giving and seems to be about *peer group pressure*. In a sense a donation buys some relief from guilt or embarrassment.

Most individuals are members of some kind of group whether *formal (eg committees) or informal* (eg friends), primary (where face-to-face communications can occur, (eg family) or *secondary* (eg The Chartered Institute of Marketing). Groups develop their own *norms* or standards which become acceptable within a particular group. For example, normal dress among a group of yacht club members differs considerably from the norm or type of clothes worn by a group of punk rockers. Yet both groups adhere to the rules (mostly unwritten) of their own group. Both groups also go through some sort of purchasing process.

Roles are played by different members within a group. An individual may also have to play different roles at different stages of the same day, eg a loving mother, tough manager, loyal employee, client entertainer and, when returning home, a happy wife and, perhaps later, a sensuous lover.

Activities, interests and opinions can form useful segmentation criteria. Roles within groups help to target decision-makers and influencers in the *decision-making units*. Roles are also identifiable from the *family life cycle*, which shows how an individual moves from bachelor to newly wed to Full Nest 1 (youngest child under six) to Full Nest 2 (youngest child is six or over) to Full Nest 3 (dependent children) to Empty Nest 1 (children moved out) to Empty Nest 2 (retirement) or Solitary Survivor 1 (still working) to Solitary Survivor 2 (retired). The income levels, needs and spending patterns are often predictable as the income earner moves through various family life cycle roles. Spending patterns, influenced by changing roles, can be monitored and forecast before communicating any marketing messages. For example, direct mail companies often mail new mothers within a few days of the arrival of their baby.

SUMMARY AND CONCLUSION

The marketing professional must understand the target market's buying behaviour before, during and after the actual purchase. An examination of the apparently simple act of purchasing a hamburger can reveal a host of hidden motives. In-depth research reveals some deep and unconscious reasons which demonstrate some of the complexities of buying behaviour. The amount of time and effort spent in the buying process depends on the type of buying situation. Decision-making units affect the process. Buying models highlight some of the stages through which the buyer passes. This offers a kind of checklist for marketing communications to ensure that they carry the buyer through each stage successfully. The behaviourist school differs from the cognitive school of more complex buying models. Motivation, perception, learning, values, attitudes and lifestyles all interact and influence the buying process.

Equipped with a clearer understanding of both the motives for buying and the buying process itself, a marketing communications strategy can be developed to ensure that it covers as many avenues to the mind of the buyer as resources allow.

Reasons and motives range from the rational to the bizarre. But motives are, however, only one variable among many other intervening variables that integrate and influence buying behaviour. For example, beliefs and attitudes affect motives, which in turn, affect the way an individual sees or perceives things (images, ads, products, shops, etc). We learn these opinions attitudes and beliefs partly from groups (such as friends, colleagues) partly from commercial messages carefully aimed at us through advertising, sales promotion, etc and partly from real experiences of products or services.

All these psychological and sociological influences interact with commercial stimuli such as advertisements. The effects are ultimately reflected in our behaviour (or lack of behaviour in some circumstances).

In consumer markets, buying behaviour is affected by the complex web of mostly internal intervening variables (motivation, perception, attitudes, learning, memory,

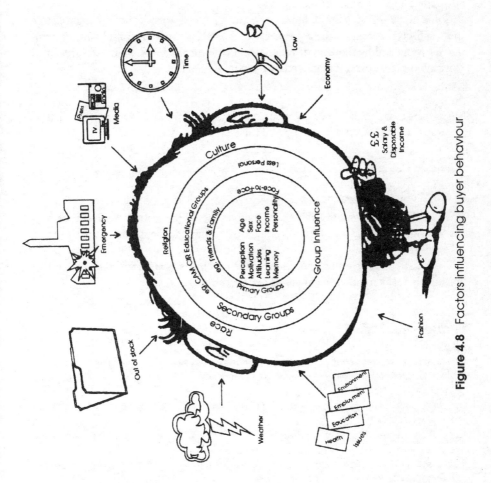

Figure 4.8 Factors influencing buyer behaviour

lifestyle, personality and groups). Sex, age, income and even an individual's face or body affect their behaviour. Other external variables such as laws and regulations, the weather, opening hours, an out-of-stock situation or an emergency can all change buying behaviour.

An industrial buyer is also influenced by internal and external variables, including the organisation's objectives, policies, procedures, structure and systems, and variables external to the organisation such as the state of the economy, level of demand and competition, the cost of money, etc.

Some argue that it is impossible, as Foxall (1992) says, to 'capture human nature in its entirety' because of the complexity of the decision-making process. This complexity is created by the web of rational and emotional factors which are generated from internal processes and guided by external influences.

Perhaps Oscar Wilde was too generous when he said that 'man is a rational animal except when asked to act within the dictates of reason'.

Key Points for Chapter 4:

1) A clear understanding of both the motives for buying and the buying process itself is vital if an effective marketing communications strategy is to be developed.
2) An effective communications strategy then covers as many avenues or channels to the mind of the buyer as resources allow.

Further reading

Chisnall, P (1984) *Marketing: A Behavioural Analysis*, McGraw Hill, Maidenhead

Dichter, E (1964) *Handbook of Consumer Motivations: the Psychology of the World of Objects*, McGraw Hill, New York

Engel JF, Blackwell, RD, and Kollatt, DT (1978) *Consumer Behaviour*, 3rd edition, Dryden Press, Hinsdale Ill

Engel JF, Kinnear TC and Warshaw MR (1991) *Promotional Strategy: Managing the Marketing Communications Process,* 7th edition, Irwin Shaw, Homewood, Illinois

Fishbein, M (1975) 'Attitude, attitude change and behaviour: A theoretical overview' in Levine, P (ed) *Attitude Research Bridges the Atlantic*, American Marketing Association, Chicago

Foxall, G (1992) *Consumer Psychology in Behavioural Perspective*, Routledge, London

Howard, JA and Sheth, JN (1969) *The Theory of Buyer Behaviour*, John Wiley and Sons Inc, New York

Kotler, P (1988) *Practice of Marketing*, Prentice Hall, Englewood Cliffs, New Jersey

Market Research Society Conference Papers (1986) 'Research is good for you — the contribution of research to Guinness advertising', MR, London

Packard, V (1957), *The Hidden Persuaders*, Penguin, Harmondsworth

Williams, KC (1989) *Behavioural Aspects of Marketing,* Heinemann, Oxford

Williams, TG (1982) *Consumer Behaviour*, West Publishing, St Paul, Minnesota

UNDERSTANDING MARKETS — MARKET RESEARCH

MARKET RESEARCH

The Card Trick

An Oxford Street card-trick man places four cards face down on a portable table. As the crowd gathers, he shouts '£10 to anyone who picks the ace'. Embarrassment, scepticism, even mistrust run through the crowd. No one responds to the offer of a simple £1 bet to win £10. As the card man leans forward to show the crowd a crisp £10 note, a grinning young man leans behind the card man and sneaks a look at the outside card. It's a jack of diamonds. Word quickly spreads through the crowd that the outside card is not the ace. Prompted by the fun (and the improving odds) someone shouts 'That's not a real tenner.' The card man responds by stepping into the crowd to allow a closer inspection of the £10 note. A second stranger boldly leans across and briefly turns the other outside card over. It's a two of hearts. The card man returns. 'Come on now. Who wants to win £10?' A well-spoken young lady replies 'If you show me one of the two middle cards, I will place a £2 bet against your £10.' The cardman accepts.

What has happened here?

Information reduces risk

As more and more relevant information became available the risk was eventually reduced to zero and a certainty emerged. The young lady could pick the ace as soon as she knew what the other three cards were. Market research (information) reduces risk also. So why not use research to reduce all risks? There are three reasons — it *costs men, money and minutes* — the three key resources (the three Ms). Firstly, knowing exactly what information you want and how to gather it (whether commissioning a research agency or handling the research in-house) is a relatively rare management skill. Secondly, research costs money. And thirdly, it takes time to define and write a brief, carry out the fieldwork, analyse the data, read a report, and ultimately, act upon the information. The *fieldwork* (asking the questions and collecting the answers) can also give competitors an early warning of intended activities. In a sense, it can give them time to respond.

Information is power

In both military and marketing strategies, information creates power. If an organisation knows what its customers really want and its competitors do not, then it has a powerful advantage. If the organisation knows what its competitor's next move is before they make it, then the organisation is in a stronger position to react or even pre-empt it. In negotiations, if one party knows more about the other party then the information-holder carries a hidden advantage. The classic salesman versus buyer situation emphasises how sales and profits can be increased as a direct result of information: the salesman desperately wants an order and is prepared to cut prices to get the business. The buyer desperately needs to buy the salesman's product because all their existing stocks were destroyed the night before in a fire in one of their factories and the salesman's company is the only company who can supply the goods immediately. If the buyer knows how desperate the salesman is then a low price will be negotiated by the buyer. On the other hand, the salesman seizes control over the negotiations (power) if he has been informed about the buyer's desperate situation. In addition, the salesman takes total control if the buyer does not know how desperate the salesman is for the order. In this situation the salesman will make the sale probably at a higher price. Information is power.

Notice how senior managers always seem to ask questions which are potentially embarrassing (because sometimes you don't know the answer). When they ask the

---

1992 World Chess Championship

To avoid giving his competitor too much information, Bobby Fischer wore a green visor to stop Spassky, the challenger, from looking into his eyes during an alternative world chess championship.

---

question you might think 'I wish I'd thought of that.' Questions are indicators of ability and seniority, or potential seniority. The ability to ask the right question is a precious skill that usually takes time and practice to develop. The ability to ask the right question is the precursor to providing the right answer.

Prioritise information

There is an unlimited amount of information available to all marketing managers.

There is more information available and obtainable than any manager can absorb, let alone pay for, in any one period. So the key is to *define what the problem is and outline the kind of information which might help*. An experienced market researcher (whether in-house or from an agency) can guide the marketing manager towards defining specifically what kind of information is needed. Since the research budget is usually limited, the manager may then have to *prioritise* which kinds of information are more important than the others. Ask for ambiguous information and a lot of ambiguous answers will be delivered.

A certain amount of discipline is needed to focus on relevant issues and not become side-tracked by indulging in 'interesting' bits of information. When briefing a market researcher as to the kind of information that is required, it is often tempting to add extra 'interesting' questions. Before adding extra information requests check that the following questions are answered satisfactorily:

- What will I do with this information?
- How will it affect my strategy or tactics?
- What action or withdrawal may result from this information?
- How much is the information worth?
- How much will it cost?
- Can I afford it?
- When do I need it?
- Have I checked all secondary sources (see 'Types of research' pages 91–3)?

Decision-making aid

Research is an *aid to decision-making* and not a decision in itself. As Torin Douglas (1984) says: 'In practice, most organisations have a continuous programme of research, often stretching back many years, which is designed not solely for advertising purposes, but also to help them run their businesses properly.'

TYPES OF RESEARCH

There are basically two types of research sources: primary and secondary. *Primary data* is gathered specifically for and commissioned by an organisation for a particular purpose (eg a research survey to find out about attitudes towards a company's brand). *Secondary data*, on the other hand, already exists and has been gathered by someone else for some other reason (eg government statistics, newspaper features, published reports, etc). *Desk research* can be carried out in a library or office since it requires researching secondary sources. It is worthwhile doing some desk research before embarking upon the more expensive primary research.

There are essentially two types of research: quantitative research and qualitative research. *Quantitative* research uses surveys based on a representative sample of the population or target group. *Qualitative* research involves an in-depth unstructured exploration with either small groups of individuals (group discussions or focus groups) or with individuals on a one-to-one basis (depth interviews).

Research can provide the marketing professional with *information on just about anything* from markets to distributors, to customers, to competition, to new products, new packs, new promotions, new advertisments, new prices and so on. Different types of research can reveal information about customers, where they are located, what they buy, read, watch on TV, how they spend their holiday time, which competitors they prefer and so on.

Ideas on new or modified products, packs, brand names or advertisements can be discussed initially in *focus groups* (six to eight people) which generate information explaining how people feel about a concept. This kind of '*concept testing*' can be used to reduce a number of ideas down to one or two for further testing, or can be used to give feedback to the creative people so that they can refine a particular concept. These qualitative interviews open up and identify areas that may need further investigation on a larger scale (quantitative survey) to find out how important certain aspects are among a statistically valid sample (minimum 400 in the sample). In the case of a new advertising concept, or a new pack or brand name concept, the refined concept can then be shown in a '*hall test*' (where respondents are invited into a hall to make comments). The packs and brand name concepts can be shown as mock-up artwork and the advertisements might be shown either as a storyboard or an animatic. A new product (concept) can be tested by using *in-home trials* or hall tests. Some data sources such as the *TGI Index* (see pages 95–7) are often used in the early research stages of consumer campaigns to identify buying behaviour, socio-economic groups, lifestyles, locations and appropriate media channels.

After all this, a new pack or brand name (or product) can be *test marketed*. This reduces the risk by holding back from national or international roll-out until the advertising campaign (or pack or name or product) can be tested within a representative test area. Due to the high cost of test marketing, and the increasing difficulty in the UK of truly isolating the test market area (especially in terms of distribution, where the national retail chains do not want to limit stocks to certain parts of the country), companies often prefer to conduct a *simulated market test* instead of carrying out a test marketing exercise. The main research companies in the field are Burke (BASES test), Nielsen (QUARTZ model) and Research International (MICROTEST). These models use information from the concept test or product test, simulate an expected level of distribution penetration (percentage of stores that will stock the product), assume a certain level of advertising spend required to generate certain levels of awareness, and then assume competitive activity, prices and other factors to predict the likely sales of a new product with an accuracy of +/– 20 per cent.

Since television advertisements are so expensive many companies prefer to do all the careful checking and testing through focus groups and hall tests instead of testing the advertisement in a specific test region. They can, and do, however, test the weight of advertising in different regions and measure the incremental sales to help them to find the most cost effective levels (frequency and timing) of advertising expenditure.

If a product is launched nationally or regionally, its launch can be monitored in several ways. Its usage (user profiles, frequency of purchase, etc) can then be monitored through *consumer panels*. *Retail audits* provide information about distribution penetration and how the product is moving off which shop shelves. It is also likely that *tracking studies* will monitor the immediate reactions and effects of the launch advertising. *Pre-* and *post-* quantitative surveys can monitor the levels of branded awareness before and after a new campaign breaks, and then be used again to measure the effect of the advertising and the product's development in the market place.

Summary table

Table 5.1 summarises some of the many different types of research information which are readily available. The cost figures only give a very rough indication of the budget requirements. They have been included so that the reader can get some idea of the costs involved. Costs will increase over time but these figures can be used as a 1993 basis.

Table 5.1 Types of research/information available

Information on:	Type of research/information	Sources	Approximate costs
Markets	Market reports (analysing market size, structure, market shares and trends, prices, key players, etc)	Mintel Jordans Keynotes Syndicated FT & trade magazines	£300 to £1,000 £500 – £10,000 £1
Distributors	Retail audit (analysing a brand's penetration into various retailer store categories, average stocks bought, held and sold per period, retail prices)	Neilsen	£10,000 – £30,000*
Customers' attitudes and awareness	Surveys — recommended minimum of 200 interviews; preferably a minimum of 500 interviews	Quantitative market research agencies Omnibus surveys	£10–£15 per person interviewed £500 per question
Customers' motivations and perceptions	In-depth research, sometimes using projective techniques	Qualitative market research agencies	£300 per individual, £1,300 per group of eight
Customers' lifestyles	Consumer profiles on product usage, lifestyle statements, media usage	TGI Index, tailormade (ad hoc)	£1,000 – £30,000
Customers' future lifestyles	Social forecasting, futurology, etc	Henley Centre for Forecasting	£ £

(continued)

Information on:	Type of research/information	Sources	Approximate costs
Customers' buying behaviour and trends over time	Who's buying what, when and from where; how buyers respond over time to various marketing activities, eg special offers, new ads and competitor activities, etc	Consumer panels, eg AGB's Super	£10,000 – £30,000
Customers' penetration	Penetration of product into % of homes and frequency of usage	Omnibus survey	£500 per question
Competition	As for markets, distribution and customers, if the budgets are available. The salesforce and marketing departments' 'ear to the market' can also provide much competitive information	As before	As already indicated
Simulated test market	Total mix test of product, brand name, price, positioning	Burke Nielsen Research International RSGB	£20,000 – £80,000
Test market	Running a new product or variation of its mix in a test area	Sales analysis plus above options	—
Product	New product concepts can be researched ('concept research')	Focus groups	£1,300 per group of eight
Packs	New pack design concepts can be discussed	Focus groups Hall tests	£1,300 per group of eight £1,000+
Advertisements	New advertisement concepts can be researched before going to expensive production	Focus groups Hall tests	£1,300 per group of eight £1,000+
	Pre- and post-advertising research measures levels of awareness before and after a campaign (tracking studies)	Quantitative survey	£10 – £15 per person

(continued)

Information on:	Type of research/information	Sources	Approximate costs
Exhibitions	Stand design, memorability, number of passers-by, number that stopped and looked, number that visited, % of total exhibition visitors	Exhibition surveys	

* Prices can vary enormously, eg a single brand retail price check might be carried out for as little as £500, while a full blown retail audit for multiple products can run into hundreds of thousands of pounds.

Anything can be researched and tested, including sales promotion ideas (concepts), mail shots and even press releases and journalists' attitudes to particular companies and brands (see pages 279–81, Chapter 14). Media research and planning is discussed in Chapter 7 'Understanding the Media'.

Qualitative research

An in-depth interview with an individual provides a lot of information. There are usually a series of individuals interviewed on a one-to-one basis. This type of research attempts to reveal what customers sometimes don't even know about themselves by delving deep into their unconscious motivations. As Wendy Gordon (1991) says: 'Consumers are often unaware as to why they do or don't use/buy/choose a particular brand. Asking for this kind of information in a direct way is like shouting at a foreigner in the belief that he will then understand English more easily.' In-depth researchers employ a range of techniques (including psycho drawings, word associations, metaphors, collages, picture completion, clay modelling and role playing) which throw the ego off guard and allow the subconscious feelings to be expressed. Chapter 4 considers the underlying motivations and complex information processes through which buyers pass on their journey towards a purchase.

Mommy's never coming back

In-depth research for an American manufacturer of security doors revealed deeply ingrained unconscious fears of being trapped inside, or abandoned, when doors are closed. The report suggested that a young child's first experience of a door is when its mother puts it to bed and closes the door behind her as she leaves. The child fears that it may never see its mother again. Many years later, the adult's unconscious mind can react to the sight of a closed door with an 'underlying feeling of discomfort and anxiety'. The Simpson Timber Company was reported as having gained a significant increase in its market share when they changed their advertisements to show partly-open security doors rather than their traditional images of securely closed doors.

(Source: Marketing Breakthroughs, December 1991).

Qualitative research: focus groups

Group discussions can be a more cost effective way of collecting information which is perhaps less in-depth but never the less useful in understanding why and how people (in the target market) feel about certain brands, advertisements or just new ideas (concepts).

Concept research

Concept testing helps every element of the communications mix. Whether it is an advertisement, new sales promotion, new piece of packaging, new direct mail leaflet or even a product or service, the concept should be researched and discussed at least among colleagues and customers, and, ideally, among unattached/unbiased focus groups who are representative of the target audience/customer.

Advertising *concept testing* measures responses to advertisements before they are fully produced (see the Hoffmeister example below). Storyboards, and key frames

Bear Concept 1	*Bear Concept 2*	*Bear Concept 3*
'Sartorial Elegance' was created to convey Hoffmeister as the best lager. Comments picked up through focus group discussions included: 'He looks like he's never been in a pub' and 'The advert's aimed at the higher class, but they drink wine — it's us yobs that drink lager — he's a snob!' *Result: Rejected*	'Sporting Bear' was perceived to be 'quite old'. Other comments from the discussion groups revealed: 'He's got a beer gut' and 'He looks grumpy, like a bear with a sore head — it should be a young bear to appeal to youngsters.' *Result: Rejected*	'George the Bear' pretested the best. Group feedback included comments like: 'It's the Fonz, a bit like flash Harry', 'a cool dude' and perhaps most importantly, he was perceived to be 'streetwise'. *Result: Developed*

The fully developed George the bear (concept 3) in one of the finished advertisements from Boase Massimi Pollitt (now BMP DDB Needham)

(see the milkman campaign concept, page 213, Chapter 11) or animatics (video cartoons) are made up and shown to focus groups. This kind of group discussion is used to identify the best idea from a range of different concepts, to iron out any glaring problems with a chosen concept or simply to help to refine the concept itself, as shown with the Hoffmeister bear concepts opposite.

Qualitative research is also used to define parameters or types of questions which should be asked in future quantitative research. For example, focus group/qualitative research into newspapers may have revealed that some readers feel mentally uncomfortable if they don't read all of their newspaper before throwing it out. This is obviously a problem if part of the paper's advertising proposition is 'the newspaper you can digest on the way to work'. So quantitative research will seek to substantiate the variables or issues revealed during the initial qualitative stage. The quantitative stage may be carried out by surveying several hundred or a thousand respondents. The interviewer's questionnaire might ask 'Which papers on this list do you find a quick and easy read/ long/difficult?' etc.

The TGI Index

The Target Group Index (TGI) collects and compiles information on consumer brands, and the profiles of heavy, medium and light users, and non-users, in a vast range of product categories and sub-categories. This is all cross-referenced to types of papers read, TV programmes viewed, and lifestyle/attitude statements. It can even

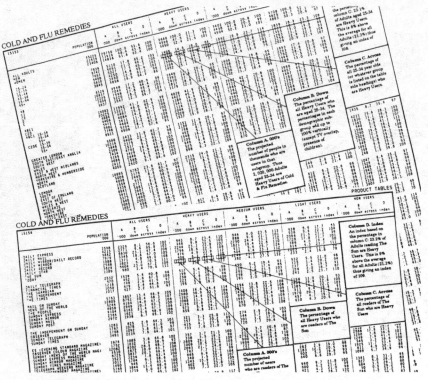

Figure 5.1 An example of the Target Group Index in use

classify 'light users' according to whether they buy a brand exclusively ('solus users'), whether they prefer it to another brand also used ('most often users') or whether they are more casual in their use ('minor users'), again cross-referenced to demographic data, lifestyles and media used. Advertisers use the TGI to find out who the users of a particular brand are and what they read, watch and listen to. The same information is available on competitors and their brands.

The excerpt shown in Figure 5.1 demonstrates how the index might be used by a company marketing cold and flu remedies. It identifies the heavy users, their age, the percentage of the total age group who are actually heavy users and finally, an index which compares the percentage of heavy users in this age group compared to the national average percentage of heavy users in all age groups. The excerpt (above) analyses which papers and magazines the heavy users use.

Elsewhere the index also gives lifestyle data, eg 'heavy drinkers of low alcohol lager'. This gives an insight into what motivates them. The excerpt in Figure 5.2 shows that they are keen pub-goers and have a propensity to try new drinks. They are highly image conscious, aiming to keep abreast of new fashions. They appear to be fairly 'flash with the cash' and admit to being no good at saving money. In spite of, or maybe because of this, they show a strong tendency to seek the advice of a financial consultant. They see their holidays as a way of achieving total relaxation, not wishing to do anything but eat, drink and lie in the sun.

Just about anything can be cross-referenced with any other variable. For example,

```
Base: MEN 18+
Pop: 20699
Private Eye Target: HEAVY DRINKERS OF LOW ALCOHOL BEER AND LAGER
Pop: 1155(000)    % of Base: 5.57

                                       -----  ------  --------  ------  ------
                                              UNWTD     PRJ     VERT    HORZ
                                       INDEX  RESP     (000)    (%)     (%)
                                       -----  ------  --------  ------  ------
 1  D8 DRINK LAGER RATHER THAN          176    183      366    31.68    9.83
    BEER THESE DAYS
 2  PA9 I LIKE TO KEEP UP WITH          165     53      121    10.47    9.20
    LATEST FASHION
 3  T7 HOLIDAY-ONLY WANT TO             165     75      158    13.67    9.18
    EAT,DRINK,SUNBATHE
 4  PA15 MEN'S FASHION MORE             161    105      238    20.60    8.96
    EXCITING NOWADAYS
 5  F7 I TEND TO SPEND MONEY            160     65      141    12.20    8.94
    WITHOUT THINKING
 6  SP3 CO'S/PRESTIGE SPONSOR           157     88      190    16.45    8.76
    ART/SPORT
 7  DH6 HEALTH FOODS ONLY BOUGHT        155     78      179    15.49    8.65
    BY FANATICS
 8  D9 I LIKE TO TRY NEW DRINKS         155     70      143    12.38    8.65
 9  D12 I REALLY ENJOY A NIGHT          146    164      345    29.87    8.12
    OUT AT THE PUB
10  P4 I WOULD LIKE TO BUY A            142     58      148    12.81    7.92
    HOME COMPUTER
11  F4 I AM NO GOOD AT SAVING           138     87      190    16.45    7.72
    MONEY
12  F15 USUALLY CONSULT                 138     62      114     9.87    7.68
    FINANCIAL ADVSR
13  PA2 IT'S IMPORTANT TO LOOK          137    104      247    21.38    7.65
    WELL DRESSED
14  T11 TRY TO TAKE ONE+ HOLIDAY        135     60      116    10.04    7.55
    ABROAD A YEAR
15  PA13 I REALLY ENJOY SHOPPING        134     70      130    11.25    7.50
    FOR CLOTHES
```

Figure 5.2 An example of lifestyle data from the TGI index

the index can identify Heinz beans users and what kind of cars they drive. The Haagen-Dazs ice cream short case (page 218, Chapter 11) shows how the TGI index was used to build up a picture of the typical kind of shopping basket of brands which their target market used. Another package, called 'trender', can be used to track product, brand, attitudinal, demographic or media trends. The index can also link into various on-line geodemographic packages.

Geodemographics

Geodemographics mix geographic population data together with basic demographic data. It uses neighbourhood types to predict the kind of people who live within them and thus their behaviour as consumers. If a brand is found to appeal to certain geodemographic groups their locations can be mapped and the subsequent communications can be targeted at the geographic areas which offer the greatest potential (see pages 250–3, Chapter 13, for examples of how precise geodemographic data is becoming).

ACORN (a clasification of residential neighbourhoods) uses post codes to identify 38 different types of house which generally give useful indications about buying behaviour (see Appendix 4, page 50, Chapter 2). Other UK on-line demographic analyses can be cross-referenced, eg PINPOINT which uses 60 different neighbourhood classifications. MOSAIC has 58 neighbourhood categories linked with financial information. SUPER PROFILES uses 150 neighbourhood types.

Test marketing

Test marketing refers to new packs, new brands and new products which are only marketed in a limited test region or geographic area, eg the Yorkshire TV area. A full marketing drive (distribution and advertising, etc) is released in the test area only. This gives the company a chance to spot any last minute problems which previous research has not identified. If the test market proves to be positive then the marketing campaign can be extended nationally.

Everything can be tested. A new advertising campaign, a new sales promotion or even a direct mail campaign can be tested among a few thousand names on a mailing list (in direct mail, some companies test right down to whether different colour signatures affect direct mail response levels). Some organisations do not, however, test market because of the associated problems of security, timing, costs and seasonality.

Some tests are considered to create *security* problems since they can alert competition with an early warning about, say, an intended new brand. Testing also costs *time* and *money*, which may not be available as launch deadlines loom closer. The limited time period of a test often restricts the accuracy of the measured results since additional time may be required to monitor whether repeat purchases continue beyond the 'trial period'. That is, do customers keep buying, or still remember a particular advertisement after the impact of the initial launch has died down? *Seasonal* products and services are further complicated since they may need to be tested 12 months in advance. Testing, of course, costs money, which needs to be budgeted for at the beginning of the planning period. Both freak results and results manipulated by competitors can also invalidate certain tests. If this kind of inaccurate information is used to decide whether to launch or not, or how much advertising spend is required nationally, etc, then the results could be disastrous.

Tracking studies

Advertising tracking involves *Pre-* and *Post-* advertising research which aims to measure levels of awareness and brand recognition before and after an advertising campaign. In fact, it can also be used to measure the series of mental stages through which a customer moves: unawareness, awareness, comprehension, conviction and action. These are the stages identified in *DAGMAR* (defining advertising goals for measured advertising results — see page 72, Chapter 4). It is worth remembering that some elements of the communications mix, like sales promotions, packaging and point-of-sale, can be more effective than advertising when pushing the customer through the final stage of 'action' or buying.

An analysis of the sales figures can identify an advertising campaign's effect on overall sales. Home audit panel data like SuperPanel can reveal information on what is happening within the total sales figures, like who is switching brands, who the heavy users are, etc. Quantitative techniques involving street surveys, in-home interviews or telephone surveys (obviously not used if prompting respondents with visual prompt material, eg storyboard, press or poster ad) can measure the other DAGMAR stages listed above.

The percentage of respondents with *spontaneous awareness* (which brands of beer can you remember seeing an advertisement for this week?) is always lower than those with *prompted awareness* (since the interviewer prompts the respondent by showing a list of brand names or a storyboard of the ad). See *Marketing Magazine*'s weekly brand awareness results for an example of who is leading the awareness tables. Incidentally, telephone surveys cannot currently be used for measuring prompted awareness of a TV campaign (they can be used to research a radio campaign) since prompt materials such as storyboards, press advertisements or lists of brands can only be shown to a misrepresentative sample (homes with video phones). Verbal prompts can

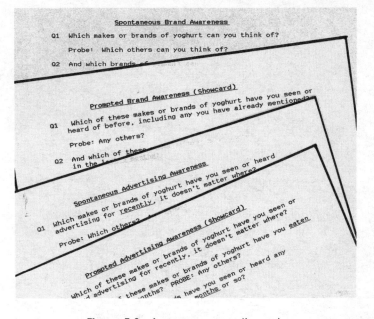

Figure 5.3 Awareness questionnaire

be made but this is obviously not the ideal situation. This situation may change as more homes begin to use video phones (ie, as penetration increases and 'the diffusion of innovations occurs').

Although awareness is of interest, '*salience*' is, as Wendy Gordon (1991) points out, 'a far more valuable tool for understanding what a brand means than brand awareness.'

Retail audits

Retail audits monitor share of shelf space, prices, and turnover of particular brands (including competitors') in a large and representative sample of retailers. It is worth noting that Boots, Sainsbury's and Marks and Spencer do not allow auditors to come in to their stores. This means that the audit results have to be weighted and adjusted. Where auditors are allowed access, they check shelves, facings, prices and stock levels. Most FMCG companies buy these audits since they provide a picture of what is happening at the retail level (average price of a product, stock levels in each outlet, and each product/brand's market share (See Figure 5.4 overleaf). *Bar codes* and laser scanning can provide much of this information on-line directly to the user. Sales out of shops do not necessarily reflect actual customer usage. Home audits (see below) can provide customer purchase information.

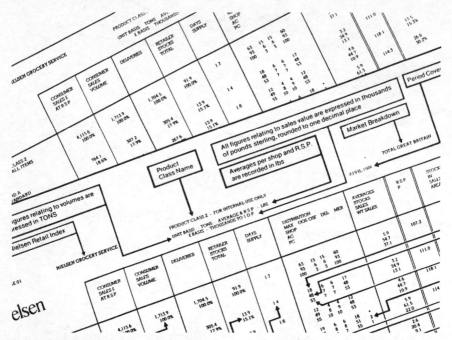

Figure 5.4 Sample extract from a Nielsen retail audit containing details of sales broken down by brand, regions, types of shops and national figures

Home audits

Instead of, or in addition to, researching the retail store, home audits research the customer directly. The retail audit data can be backed up with customer usage data. Representative families (sample size: 8,500) are recruited and asked to log all their purchases using a bar code recorder. The device asks for the name of the store and the price paid per brand, etc. All of this data is transferred to the central computer via a modem and telephone lines. Non-bar coded items are recorded on paper. Analysis of this wealth of data over time shows consumers' repertoire of brands, the effects of sales promotions on purchases, frequency of purchase, etc. This is automatically cross-referenced with the household's demographic data already held. Diaries and dedicated dustbins used to be used to collect this type of information. Today the automated on-line bar code system is preferred. The table excerpt in Figure 5.5 shows a small part of the monthly audit including the amount bought (by price and volume/weight); market share, and average price paid for any particular brand and its competitors.

Think 'secondary' first

All communication plans should be based on sound research. Expensive primary data should only be used when all possible secondary data sources have been checked. Why pay £20,000 for a market research report analysing your industry when it may

Figure 5.5 Sample extract from an AGB home audit containing details of amount bought by price and volume, market share, average prices, etc

be possible to subscribe for less to a *syndicated survey* carried out specifically for a group of companies in an industry sector (eg air travel or car manufacturers)? Alternatively, some markets are researched regularly by market report companies like Mintel and Jordans. These reports can be purchased by anyone for a few hundred pounds. Academic institutes often publish reports on various markets or aspects of the marketing process within a particular industry. Sometimes these are available at not much more than the cost of duplication and despatch. A newspaper like the *Financial Times* may have done its own analysis or survey which costs less than £1. Other research reports are available free of charge as the commissioning companies see published surveys as a useful marketing tool to generate free media coverage. It also gives them something to talk to clients and prospective clients about. On the other hand, some free survey results may be biased in favour of the organisation that commissioned the research in the first place, particularly if they have a vested interest in revealing certain positive results or trends.

THE MARKET RESEARCH PROCESS

The key to using information efficiently lies in the ability to *define exactly what information* is required. This is a valuable management skill. Defining the problem or defining the research objectives is the first step in the market research process shown overleaf.

1) **Problem definition**	Decide clearly what information is needed and why it is needed. Is it qualitative and/or quantitative? What will be done with it?
2) **Research plan**	Data sources: secondary/primary Research techniques: observation, survey, experiment, focus group Sample: size and type Degree of confidence Fieldwork: face-to-face, phone or post Questionnaire design Cost and timing
3) **Fieldwork**	Actual interviews/ data collection and supervision
4) **Data analysis**	Coding, editing, weighting, summing, consistency/check questions, extracting trends and correlations if any
5) **Report presentation**	The interpretation of the figures, summary and sometimes conclusions.
6) **Action taken/ not taken**	If the information is not used then perhaps it wasn't worth collecting in the first place

BRIEFS, PROPOSALS AND AGENCY SELECTION

Research brief

This can include a mini SOSTT + 3M formula (see page 34, Chapter 2):

*   Summary situation
*   Objectives of the research (problem definition — what information is required and what decisions should be made as a result of the research findings)
*   Strategy[*] (why the information is required/how the research findings may affect the communications strategies)
*   Tactics (how the research findings may affect the tactical communications activities)
*   Target market
    +
    Men (who will liaise with the agency)
    Money (how much is the research budget)
    Minutes (timing — when is the information needed?)

([*]Some clients prefer not to divulge too much strategic or tactical information for security reasons. On the other hand, the more the research agency knows the more useful their contribution to the success of the project will be.)

Research proposal

If an external research agency has been briefed, their research proposal should incorporate a research plan (point 2 above). You will also want to look at the agency's credentials.

Agency selection

If the organisation is not handling the research in-house, a market research agency will be chosen. The usual agency selection procedure will apply (see 'Advertising Agency Selection', page 121, Chapter 6).

A shortlist of agencies can be developed from personal recommendations from colleagues and advertising agencies, and from the organisation's own observation of research agencies and their advertisements or editorial coverage. Agency size, specialism/expertise, reputation, location and whether the agency works for any competitors can be used as shortlisting criteria. The agencies which 'pitch' or make a presentation will then be judged by the quality of their research proposal, security of data, cost, and spin-offs (like free training). Even small details can make an impression, like how many bound reports will be delivered when the research findings are eventually presented. The personal chemistry or relationship between the client and the agency presenter is often the key variable which swings the choice of agency one way or another. It is also important to find out who will be handling the project and, if it is a junior member of staff, the degree of supervision that will be offered. The *IQCS* (interviewer quality control scheme) follows rigid procedures to supervise and check the quality of the information.

Some agencies demonstrate great care about the security of the data they hold. Computer hackers pose a problem to any computer-stored data. Product test samples need to be controlled carefully and securely. All samples, mock-ups and concept boards need to be returned by the interviewers, and logged as returned once they are received by the research agency. Samples, mock-ups, concept boards can then be kept under lock and key.

My Girlfriend

About ten years ago my girlfriend used to work for a very well-known market research agency in London. On Fridays, I would come in and collect her before going to the pub. Whenever I was late I would dash in through the main front door, past the security guard and up the lift. Occasionally I jumped out at the wrong floor and found myself wandering through empty offices full of live, unattended, expensive (and competitor sensitive) research projects. Such a situation would not be allowed to happen today, and the particular agency has since changed its security procedures.

MARKETING INTELLIGENCE AND INFORMATION SYSTEM

Every organisation should have a marketing intelligence and information system (MIIS) which lists secondary data sources. The system can be a useful starting point. The basic checklist at the end can be refined as new and better sources are identified. Essentially an MIIS should be built and constantly refined as new sources become available and old ones become redundant.

Internal figures such as sales, percentage of sales expenditures (of say, advertising), response levels, cost per order/enquiry, etc can and should be compared with external industry averages or competitor activities. Not all the information is readily available immediately but competitors' sales figures (of grocery products and some other large markets) are available from companies such as *Neilsen Retail Audits*. Information on levels of advertising is available from MEAL (Media Expenditure Advertising Limited).

In an ideal marketing department, competitors' products, leaflets and advertisements should be filed, monitored and counted (so as to estimate the competitor's advertising spend) but busy marketing departments sometimes find this too time consuming. Certain monitoring companies offer to collect competitors' press clippings and published advertisements. They will also estimate a competitor's advertising spend, if this is not available from MEAL. Again, this costs money and therefore it may be deemed to be 'outside the budget', particularly if it was never included in the annual marketing budget in the first place. Estimating a competitor's advertising spend can also be done by collecting all the competitor's press ads and calculating the spend from rate card costs less bulk discounts.

A marketing log filing previous marketing activities advertisements, mail shots, editorial clippings, etc should be tagged with 'cost, objective and result'.

Comparing internal sales figures with external figures (eg total market size) gives you *market share* figures which can also be used to calculate your competitors' market share and, more importantly, whether it is growing. Figures in isolation are relatively useless. *Figures have to be pushed backwards and across*. Backwards gives you the trend over, say, the last five-year period, and across gives you a comparison across your market (including your competitors).

The *sales force* can, if trained, provide the most up-to-date and relevant information for the MIIS. They are closest to the market place and in touch with what is happening. They need to be encouraged to collect relevant information.

The Intelligent Rep

In the USA, one particular chain of stores which sold Christmas crackers held buying days when their buyers would see visiting sales representatives. Appointments were not accepted and once they had registered with the receptionist for the appropriate buyer 'reps' proceeded to queue in a waiting room on a first-come, first-served basis. The room had rows of desks with telephones where the reps sat down quietly filling in order forms, drafting letters, completing call sheets and making phone calls. Although it was only 7.30am a dozen registered reps were already busily working away. By 8.05am the room was packed. The large chap beside me was on the phone at 8.00am reporting some hot information which he had come across during another breakfast appointment earlier that day. He told his boss how the competition had offered the other buyer a new buyer-incentive scheme which would commence next month, followed by a new consumer-incentive programme scheduled four months down the road. They had now four months to react or pre-empt the competition!

Staff members throughout an organisation can be trained or briefed as to what type of information is considered important. Different members of the team can identify their choice of newspapers and/or trade journals. They can then scan for anything relevant. Alternatively, a *press clipping agency* (eg Romeike and Curtice) can be hired to do this work. An *on-line database* like Textline accepts key words, companies, products, people or issues. Once you have keyed in what period of time (three/six/twelve months, etc), what area (US, UK, Europe, etc) and types of journals or magazines, the screen will register how many references there are and ask the viewer if he would like to read/print the headlines, read/print all the abstracts, or refine the definition/choice of keyword if too many references are recorded.

Some of this information can then be used in a *SWOT analysis* (strengths, weaknesses, opportunities and threats). This is particularly useful in monitoring uncontrollable external 'OT' (Opportunities and Threats) variables such as political, economic, social and technical (PEST) factors. PEST developments can be difficult to forecast but the portents cannot be ignored (see Chapter 8). Many forecasting companies specialise in certain aspects (eg The Henley Centre for Forecasting). As well as social forecasting, they will also carry out *econometric forecasting*, which correlates the likely sales effect resulting from a change in pricing or advertising expenditures (price elasticity or advertising elasticity).

THE DIFFICULTY WITH RESEARCH

Researching new ideas

How can answers to questions about anything that is new, unseen or previously untried be valid? The first commercially-produced electric car, the Sinclair C5, had the benefit of some product research but how can research ask people about something they cannot experience? Driving a C5 in a hall is very different to driving one along a coast road or a busy, wet and windy dual carriageway with a 40-foot truck trying to over-take. Here lies one of the difficulties with researching a new idea: how can the reality of some markets and product usage be simulated? Another problem lies with the difficulty in taking the novelty factor out. When presented with something new, buyers may be prepared to give it a try but can the marketing people sustain the marketing effort after the excitement of the initial launch?

The same applies to advertising. Most advertisements try to be different, new and refreshing. So how can research help produce something which is radically different to people's existing levels of expectancy? One of the UK's most successful advertis-ing campaigns 'Heineken refreshes the parts other beers cannot...' had the normal focus groups/concept research carried out. It 'researched poorly', ie the results said 'This is rubbish. We don't understand this type of ad. Don't do it.' Frank Lowe (chairman of the advertising agency Lowe Howard Spinke) tells the story of how he had to tell the client (Heineken) about the negative concept research findings on their radically different advertising concept. 'He (the client) took a very brave decision and placed the research report document in the bin'. He said ''we had best leave that alone and get on with the ad!'' Expensive and carefully prepared market research findings are sometimes ignored.

Coke Flop

Philip Kotler (1988) suggests that even Coca Cola can get their research wrong. Although they researched the taste of the new Coke, their 1985 flop occurred because they failed to research how consumers felt about dropping the old Coke.

> Blind comparisons which took no account of the total product... name, history, packaging, cultural heritage, image — a rich mix of the tangible and the intangible. To many people Coke stands beside baseball, hotdogs and apple pie as an American institution. It represents the fabric of America. The company failed to measure these deep emotional ties, but Coke's symbolic meaning was more important to many consumers than its taste. More complete concept testing would have detected these strong emotions.

Dangers to guard against

Here are some of the areas where problems can occur:

1) Ambiguous definition of problem.
2) Ambiguous questions.
3) Misinterpretation (of the written question by the interviewer).
4) Misinterpretation (of the question by the interviewee).
5) Misinterpretation (of the answer by the interviewer).
6) Interviewer bias (street interviewers may select only attractive-looking respondents and exclude anyone else from the sample).
7) Interviewee inaccuracies (try to be rational, pleasant, offensive, disruptive, knowledgeable when ignorant, etc).
8) Interviewer fraud (falsely filling in questionnaires).
9) Non-response (a refusal to answer questions).
10) Wrong sample frame, type or size.
11) Incorrect analysis.
12) Freak clustering/result (an inherent danger of sampling).
13) Timing (researching seasonal products out of season).

The IQSC referred to on page 103 reduces these problems.

Dodgy data is worse than none. Having said that, good data can make the difference between winning and losing. Research is valuable but, as can be seen, it does require experienced advice and strict control if the data is to be usefully applied.

Defining exactly what you need to know makes life easy for the marketing professional. In fact, it can make life easier for everyone in general, as RD Laing's poem demonstrates.

There is something I don't know
    that I am supposed to know.
I don't know what it is I don't know,
    and yet am supposed to know,
and I feel I look stupid
    if I seem both not to know it
        and not know what it is I don't know.
Therefore I pretend to know it.
    This is nerve racking
    since I don't know what I must pretend to know.
Therefore I pretend to know everything.

I feel you know what I am supposed to know
but you can't tell me what it is
because you don't know that I don't know what it is.

You may know what I don't know, but not
    that I don't know it,
and I can't tell you. So you will have to tell me everything.

From RD Laing's *KNOTS*. Reproduced by kind permission of Tavistock Publications.

Key points from Chapter 5:

1) Budgets allowing, research can reveal anything required.
2) Consider carefully exactly what information is required because there is too much information out there.
3) Always check secondary sources before commissioning expensive primary research.
4) Set up a marketing intelligence and information system.

Further reading

Birn, R, Hague, P and Vangelder, P (1990) *A Handbook of Market Research Techniques*, Kogan Page, London

Crimp, M (1990) *The Marketing Research Process*, 3rd edition, *Prentice Hall*, Englewood Cliffs, New Jersey

Crouch, S (1984) *Marketing Research For Managers*, Heinemann, Oxford

Douglas, T (1984) *The Complete Guide To Advertising*, PaperMac, London

Gordon, W (1991) *Understanding Brands* (ed Cowley D), Kogan Page, London

Kotler, P (1988) *Marketing Management (Analysis, Planning, Implementation and Control)*, 6th edition, Prentice-Hall International, Englewood Cliffs, New Jersey

'Unlocking deep-seated reactions makes ads more sympathetic', *Marketing Breakthroughs* (ed Bruce Whitehall), December 1991, page 9

Marketing Guide 6: Market Research (13.4.89) *Marketing Magazine*, Haymarket Publishing Limited

Market Research Society Conference Papers (1986), 'Research is good for you — the contribution of research to Guinness advertising', MRS, London

Further contacts

Association of British Market Research Companies (ABMRC), Templeton Lodge, 114 High Street, Hampton Hill, Middlesex, TW12 1NT. Tel: 0181-977 6905

Association of Market Survey Organisations (AMSO), Millward Brown, Olympus Avenue, Tachbrook Park, Warwickshire CV34 6RJ. Tel: 01926 452233

The Market Research Society, The Old Trading House, 15 Northburgh Street, London EC1V OPR. Tel: 0171-490 4911

Media Expenditure Advertising Ltd (MEAL), 2 Fisher Street, London WC1R 4QA. Tel: 0171-833 1212

European Society for Opinion and Market Research (ESOMAR), Central Secretariat, JJ Viottastraat 29, 1071 JP Amsterdam, Holland. Tel: 31 20/664 21 41

UNDERSTANDING AGENCIES —
AGENCY RELATIONSHIPS

This chapter covers agencies, types of agencies, their structure, their fees and working relationships from shortlisting to briefing, selecting, hiring and firing. Although most of this material can be applied to all kinds of agencies and consultancies, the advertising agency is specifically drawn upon as it offers a broad base upon which other agencies and consultancies are often structured.

AGENCY STRUCTURE

Different types and sizes of agencies have different structures. The structure of a large advertising agency shown in Figure 6.1 illustrates the many different departments, people and skills which have to work together to create an advertisement. Companies which have their own in-house advertising departments, and smaller external agencies, will sub-contract in (or hire) any of the departments which they do not have. Many of the bigger agencies also hire or sub-contract directors, producers, camera men, photographers, film companies, print and production facilities. Any other agent, agency, consultant or consultancy — whether public relations, direct mail, sales promotion or corporate identity — also relies on many of the different skills/departments shown in Figure 6.1.

The account executive

Sometimes also called an account representative, the account executive is dedicated to a particular client. The account executive wears two hats — the client's when talking to the agency and the agency's when talking to the client. Responsibilities include: attendance at all client meetings, writing up 'contact reports' and general

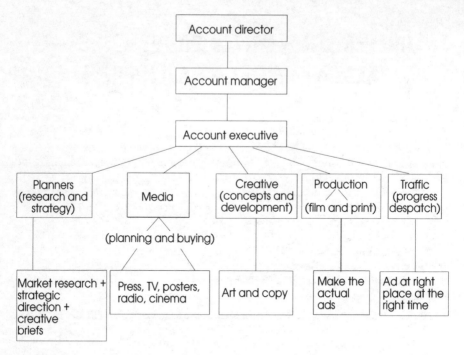

Figure 6.1 Structure of a large advertising agency

liaising between the many different members of the agency's team and the client. Many agencies write up *contact reports* (after each meeting) because they confirm and clarify all key points discussed, conclusions reached and any actions to be taken. This cuts out the opportunity for any misinterpretation as can happen further down the road when the client says 'I never said that' or 'I never asked for that'. When agreed by the client, vital documents such as a summary of the agency's interpretation of the client's brief, or concept proposals, are sometimes required to be signed by the client as 'approved'. This keeps communication clear, reduces ambiguities and, if a row does break out over a particular strategic direction or over the details of copy (the words in the advertisement), the agency can pull out a signed 'approved by'. This is particularly helpful when a manager leaves a client company because it confirms the stage-by-stage approval of the development of a campaign.

Planning department

Planners are more than glorified researchers. They have to know the right kind of questions to ask in the research, commission the research and interpret the results at two different levels. Firstly, they have to absorb, summarise and translate large market research reports into simple layman's terms for inclusion in the creative brief which they, in conjunction with the account manager, give to the creative team. Secondly, the information has to be interpreted at a strategic and tactical level for discussion with the account executive, account manager, account director and often the client.

Planners provide an objective voice, unhindered by both the account executive who sometimes wants to 'sell' an advertising concept to the client simply because the creative director wants to get on with it, and by clients who sometimes want to get on with it by quickly running some advertisements to satisfy the salesforce, who are anxiously waiting for news on the new campaign.

Creative department

It is unfair to stereotype creative people as unshaven, wearing faded jeans and silk shirts and who lie around dreaming up big ideas and concepts that drive all advertising campaigns. They usually work in pairs covering words and pictures, ie a copywriter (or wordsmith) and an art director.

Media department

The media department basically plans and buys the space where the advertisments are eventually placed (press, posters, TV, radio, cinema, etc). Media planners/schedulers are sometimes separate from media buyers, who negotiate and ultimately buy the space from the media owners. Both media planners and media buyers can be further separated into those that specialise in TV or press, etc. The emergence of cable and satellite TV and low-cost print technology increased the range of media available to media buyers. This media explosion presents new opportunites for schedulers and buyers. It also means that they need to analyse the appropriateness and cost effectiveness of much more media.

Production department

The production department actually makes the advertisement. Many agencies subcontract various parts of the production, eg hiring a studio, camera crew/photographer, director, editing suites, etc. This may involve flying around the world to take some photographs or simply working around the clock in an editing suite somewhere in Soho (London).

Traffic department

Despatch, or traffic, is responsible for getting the right artwork or film to the right magazine or TV network at the right time. This becomes complicated where posters, cinema, radio and magazine inserts are included in the media strategy. Mutliply this by several different campaigns for a range of different clients and the need for a traffic manager becomes self-evident.

The account management team

In a large agency this can involve an account director, account manager, account executive, planner, creative director, copy- writer, art director, TV producer, media director, TV media scheduler, TV airtime buyer, press planner and press buyer.

The three key components

The three key components of the agency are:

1) Planning/strategy
2) Creative
3) Media.

AGENCY TYPES

The larger agencies offer a *full service* including creative, research and planning, media planning and buying, and production. Some full-service agencies also have departments specialising in forecasting, market intelligence business planning and together with support services for the advertising campaign including point-of-sale design, sales literature, sales conferences and other below the line activities such as sales promotion, PR or direct mail. The agency, like any other business, has also got other departments which are of little interest to the client, such as accounting and finance, personnel, administration, etc.

Advertisers can choose to use only their own in-house staff to run a campaign. Do-it-yourself or *in-house advertising* also varies as some advertisers prefer to contract out some of their requirements to specialist services such as a specialist media scheduling and buying agency known as a '*media independent*'. Similarly, the creative work can be put out to a '*Hot Shop*', or '*creative shop*'. Saatchi and Saatchi started as a creative shop. Alternatively, the advertiser can go *à la carte* by picking and choosing separate agencies with specialist services for different parts of the process, eg using four different agencies for the research, creative, production and media planning/buying stages. There are other types of specialist agencies who focus on a particular industry sector.

A recent discrete development in the *à la carte* option is the agreement of a large, well-known, full-service advertising agency to sub-contract the large agency's creative services to the small communications consultancy on an ad hoc basis. This may only last while the agency has spare capacity or is searching for extra revenue during a recession. Some clients demand that their full-service agencies work alongside the client's separate choice of media independents. Some full-service agencies only get a portion of the full job. A recession can force some clients to cut back their own in-house advertising department and operate a less costly and more flexible ad hoc project arrangement with various agencies.

Different working relationships

At the end of the day the co-ordination of campaign development, launch and measurement requires time and management skills. Powerful personalities in agencies need to be controlled. *The ability to ask the right question* is a valuable management skill. The fatigue factor in negotiations or discussions can also cause rash decisions to be made. Marketing people tend to be energetic, enthusiastic, action-oriented achievers. Sometimes steely patience needs to be exercised. Perhaps a decision has to be

Table 6.1 The pros and cons of different working relationships

Aspect	Full services (under one roof)	Specialist services	In-house
Management and control	Easier since it is all under one roof	More work (co-ordinating)	Total control but more work involved
Security	Limited risk — sensitive information is shared with agency	More risk — more people have access to information	Minimal risk — no outsiders
Speed/response	Reasonably good	Possible problems if à la carte = more co-ordination	Fast since all decision-makers are available
Cost	Expensive, big overheads, but lower media costs with agency buying power	Cheaper, fewer overheads	Cheaper but less media buying power
Fresh views	Yes	Yes	No
Expertise	Yes (Jack of all trades, master of none?)	Yes (fill in gaps in client's skills)	No (lack of specialised knowledge)
Stress	Less pressure/work load	Delegate some work load	More stress — more work

delayed until further research can answer some emerging questions. Painstaking attention to detail may sometimes seem irksome to the advertising agency but it is often the mark of a true professional. On the other hand, a key resource, time, may be running out. More research reduces the risk but costs time and money. Can deadlines be moved? Is there money left for more research? A decision made in haste is rarely the best one.

How to ensure good agency relationships

1) Agree a system of remuneration — fees, commissions, mark-ups, time, expenses and method of billing in writing. Remember, it is better to argue over a quote than an invoice.
2) Trust the agency team (share research and information with them, involve them).

3) Make them become part of the marketing team. Use their expertise. See how suppliers (eg agencies) become extensions of the client's team through 'partnership sourcing' in the McGregor Cory short case at the end of Chapter 20.
4) Ask relevant questions. Listen carefully to the answers. Do not be intimidated by strong agency characters. All propositions should be justifiable. The final decision is the client's.
5) Explain to the agency who makes what decisions, ie who has authority for which decisions.
6) Sign/approve in writing each stage from brief to concepts finished artwork running proofs and so on.
7) Keep briefs short and unambiguous.
8) Regular reviews help to plug any gaps in performance, whether creative, strategic or personal.
9) Write an occasional 'thank you' note to the team.
10) A stable relationship builds a real team since the agency gets to know the client, the team, the company and the market inside out. In addition, the client does not have to worry about unfriendly, discarded agencies who have previously had access to sensitive information.

AGENCY REMUNERATION

Agencies have three basic methods of calculating their remuneration: commission, fees and pay-by-results.

Commission

Traditionally, media owners have given recognised agencies a 15 per cent discount off the rate card price. Thus in the case of a £10 million TV advertising campaign, the agency gets invoiced by the TV station at rate card £10 million less 15 per cent, ie £8.5m. The client then gets invoiced by the agency at the full rate card price, ie £10 million (this can be checked with British Rate and Data (BRAD) or the media owner's published rate card). The 15 per cent commission really represents 17.65 per cent mark-up, ie the £1.5 million commission is the mark-up which the agency adds on to their media cost of £8.5 million.

(£10 million ad campaign)

Agency invoiced by TV station less 15%	= £8.5 million
Agency invoices client at full rate card	= £10.0 million
Agency mark-up	£1.5 million
Agency mark-up £1.5m – £8.5m (cost)	= 17.65%

The agency will also apply its agreed mark-up to other services which it sub-contracts, such as market research and so on. Thus a piece of research which costs the agency £10,000 would be charged to the client (+17.65 per cent) at £11,765. One of the problems with the commission system is that it can tempt agencies to get clients to spend, spend, spend. Incidentally, the commission system does not necessarily cover all production costs, so production costs are often separately invoiced directly to the client by the agency.

Commission rebating

Specialist media-buying companies — with much lower overheads — can work with commissions as low as 2 or 3 per cent. Some clients insist that the full-service agency only takes a smaller commission, say 10 per cent, with the balancing 5 per cent going back to the client. Commission rebating occurs when an agency passes on some of its commission to the client. There is no actual refund or rebate. The agencies simply invoice the client at rate card costs less the level of rebate, in this case, 5 per cent. Commission rebating opens the door to agencies competing on price instead of, as they have done traditionally, on quality of service. Most industries dislike price wars and advertising is no exception. In 1984 Allen Brady and Marsh (ABM) once resigned their £3.5 million B & Q account after a request for rebates. They also took a large advertisement in the advertising trade press explaining that the 15 per cent commission left most agencies with 2 per cent profits after tax and any reduction would affect quality of advertising. They refused to become involved in commission rebating. ABM were a fantastic agency generating some classic advertising campaigns but sadly, they no longer exist. Many clients today are moving towards fees instead of solely commission-based remuneration.

Fees

Smaller clients with smaller media spends do not generate sufficient commission so a fee will generally be agreed. Larger clients are also moving towards fees — an annual, quarterly or monthly retainer or, alternatively, a project fee. No commission means *no media bias* since the agency is then free to recommend, say, direct mail, without losing any of its income (which would have been generated through commissions).

Many agencies receive a fee along with some level of commission. The agency's remuneration essentially depends on how much work is involved and how much the client is likely to spend (on media). The trend, particularly with larger clients, appears to be moving towards a fee basis or a mixture of fees, commissions and results.

. . Frowned upon by some agencies, pay-by-results can be mutually beneficial. It is sometimes disliked because of the lack of control which the agency has over its own destiny.

Pay-by-results

Some agencies, often young and new agencies, are prepared to put their heads on the block and offer their services on a pay-by-results basis. The problem is that some results are beyond the agency's influence, eg poor product quality control, late delivery or inadequate distribution, a price change, a strike at the factory or competitor activities such as doubling their advertising and cutting their prices. So if sales form the main criterion for payment then the agencies are vulnerable by the very nature of their dependency on so many uncontrollable variables.

If, on the other hand, the payment is linked to results directly influenced by advertising, say level of awareness or a shift in image or positioning, then the agency has more control over its own destiny. These, of course, have to be measured through market research. One area where results are easily measured and are directly related to the agency's input is media buying. If an agency achieves media buying at a price which is better than average then the saving is shared between client and agency. For example if the average advertising cost per thousand to reach say, housewives with children is £3.50, and if the agency gets this for 10 per cent less then the saving might be split 8 per cent to the client and 2 per cent to the agency. (Note: quality of the media is also taken into account.)

Pay-by-results extends beyond advertising into other disciplines as far away as design. This can apply to new product design (as a royalty) or even packaging design, where the packaging design consultancy bases its fee (or a portion of its fees) on the client's increase in sales occurring after the launch of the newly designed pack. Although payment-by-results appears attractive to the client, it can generate extra administrative work as exact results have to be measured, royalties/contributions calculated, invoices requested and cheques raised for each agreed accounting period.

The method of agency reimbursement is fundamental to the client/agency relationship (both working and contractual). An agency's range of reimbursement packages can influence the client's selection process.

AGENCY SELECTION PROCESS

Defining exactly what is required is the first stage of agency selection. This is because an appropriate choice is partly determined by a specific requirement. Some furniture retail chains may consider the strength of the media department the key criterion when choosing an agency, particularly if the store primarily wants maximum media coverage for its relatively straightforward black and white product information advertisements. Another client may be looking for a radically fresh approach and have a bias towards agencies with abundant creative talent. Either way a clear brief should be prepared to identify exactly what — in marketing and advertising terms — the new advertising campaign is trying to achieve (see 'The brief' on page 118).

The agency selection procedure can be as follows:

1) Define requirements
2) Develop a pool list of attractive agencies
3) Credentials pitch (by the agencies)
4) Issue brief to shortlisted agencies
5) Full agency presentation or pitch
6) Analysis of pitch
7) Select winner
8) Agree contract details
9) Announce winner

Some clients will prefer to get on with it by issuing a full brief to the shortlist of, say, six agencies without going through the agency credentials presentation. Other clients prefer to restrict the valuable research findings and strategic thinking to as few agencies as possible because the unsuccessful agencies are free to work for the competition at any time in the future.

Chapter 12, 'Sales Promotion', has a mock agency selection game which is somewhat biased towards the agency who made the advertisement (see page 232).

Pool list

Most advertising managers and marketing managers *observe* various campaigns by watching advertising and noting any particularly attractive campaigns. Agencies working for the competition need to be excluded or treated with extreme caution. Some desk research can reveal the agencies behind the brands by reference to Media Expenditure Analysis Limited (MEAL). Many marketing managers have a fair idea of who is doing what advertising in their sector by constantly reading the *trade press*. Other managers simply increase their advertising dosage by spending a few weeks watching more advertising than normal. Some clients sift through the agency *portfolio videos* which can be bought from Campaign Portfolio, Marketing Week Portfolio for a few hundred pounds (the agencies pay a lot more to acquire this advertising space in the first place). In these videos, agency after agency present themselves in a sometimes surprisingly tedious fashion. Some clients prefer to do their own screening and they request an *agency reel* (video) or an agency information pack directly from a particular agency so that they can view the agency's best work.

Another way of building a pool list is through the *professional associations*. Upon receipt of information about a potential client's basic requirements, professional bodies or trade associations such as the IPA (Insitute of Practitioners in Advertising), the ISBA (Incorporated Society of British Advertisers) and the AA (Advertising Association) all offer to provide lists of agencies which they feel are suitable to handle a specific type and size of business. Similar services are offered by the relevant professional institutes of other service sectors such as public relations, sales promotion, design, direct mail, etc (see 'Further contacts' at the end of each chapter). This service is normally free and the associations are extremely helpful to the uninitiated.

There are also *agency assessors* like the Agency Advertising Register and the Agency Assessements Limited, whose business is agency selection. They can handle the development of the pool list, pitch list, pitch analysis, agency selection and even performance assessment of the agency when it starts working for the client. The assessor services are popular with international clients who need help in all aspects of their quest for the right agency. The London-based Public Relations Register offers a similar service covering PR consultancies.

Credentials

Some clients, before issuing a full brief, prefer to ask the pool of agencies to present their *credentials*. This includes examples of current and previous work, team members' profiles, and company history, structure and facilities. It is worth visiting the agency, and sometimes at short notice, as this gives the client a 'feel' for the potential agency, and its atmosphere, organisation, professionalism, etc. From this a final *shortlist* is selected and issued with a detailed brief.

> *Long Shortlist*
> In 1992 Westminster Council invited ten agencies to pitch for their communications work.

Briefing, pitching and selecting take time and skills. Apart from creating a lot of work, a large pitch list leaves sometimes sensitive marketing information with many different people. Some cynics see it as an opportunity to get free strategic and tactical ideas from the best brains in each agency.

The brief

Briefs vary in size, structure and level of detail. Some clients may summarise on to a single A4 sheet of paper, others issue a much more detailed briefing document (Guinness's last brief was 100 pages). Essentially, the brief should incorporate as many of the key items listed in the SOSST + 4Ms approach as possible. (This approach is also used in the marketing communications plan — except in much more detail.)

The contents of the brief

1) Situation — where you are now — including competition, market share, position, current or previous campaigns, strengths and weaknesses (including features and benefits of brand and organisation).
2) Objectives — where you want to go — marketing objectives and communication/advertising objectives (see page 37, Chapter 2 for examples).
3) Strategy — how you are going to get there (including all the elements of the marketing mix).
4) Tactics — the details of strategy. Some of this can only be decided in conjunction with the advertising agency. It is unlikely that there will be very much detail here.
5) Target market — profiles, motivations, aspirations, habits, buying patterns of buyers and non-buyers within the defined target market.
   + *4Ms*
6) Money — budget available, commission arrangments, penalties for overspending, etc.
7) Minutes — timescale and deadlines.
8) Men — who makes the final decisions, members of the team, who to report to, contacts for additional questions, etc.
9) Measurement — some briefs explain how performance will be evaluated.

SOSTT is a checklist, not a sequence, eg target markets are often defined early on in the brief.

A smaller client may prefer to replace the advertising and/or marketing objectives with a statement of the problem and subsequently ask the agency to present a complete promotional plan. It is likely that the agency's first question will be: 'How much do you have to spend?' There are obvious dangers of releasing strategic information to several agencies, the majority of whom will never work for you (since there is usually only one winner or single agency selected). The corollary is that too little information reduces the quality (and possibly strategic direction) of the proposals.

Pre-pitch agency efforts

The shortlisted agencies are invited to make a full presentation or sales pitch. This usually involves several members of the agency staff and is viewed by several members of the client company. The cost of a major pitch varies from £2,000 to £20,000. Preparation for a pitch is usually an intensive affair and it can include researching the client's market, media, company structure and individual personalities (prior knowledge of who will attend the pitch and hopefully some background information on their personalities and interests), strategic planning, brainstorming, concept development (advertising ideas), slide shows, videos, rehearsals and even meditation. Without doubt, new business pitches increase the adrenalin flow inside agencies.

US-owned McCann-Erickson are reported to draft in a professional teacher of meditation and relaxation techniques before every pitch. JWT practise their pressure presentation techniques with bizarre scenarios like asking their teams to imagine that they discover one of their art directors pushing cocaine and that, as they prepare to fire him, they discover his wife is dying of cancer and in need of private medical treatment.

Real empathy, sound strategy, exciting creative work and reasonable costs are often considered to be the key factors during a pitch, but some agencies take initiatives before the actual pitch as Table 6.2 shows.

Table 6.2 Pre-pitch agency initiatives

Client	Agency	Stunt
Kiss FM Radio	BBDO	Delivered a framed poster to the Kiss MD bearing the legend 'we'll put your name on everyone's lips' *
Kiss FM Radio	Saatchi	Covered Kiss HQ with pink balloons on Valentine's Day.
Guardian	Publicis	Booked a 96-sheet (40' x 10') poster site opposite the newspaper's offices during the week of the pitch and ran flattering ads which changed each day *
Financial Services Company	Publicis	Sent a safe containing the agency's credentials

* won the account

Pre-pitch feelings — a client's view?

Will they love me?

'Our research has shown that generally speaking, clients are not happy about changing agencies. Such events are usually a signal that they are unable to sustain a productive relationship with other people, which is something that none of us is pleased to accept, however difficult the other people might be...the prospect (potential client) is under pressure from his boss to get it right quickly...so when he steps from the bustle and stress of his own trade into the palm-fringed oasis of Berkeley Square or Charlotte Street or Covent Garden it is possible that he has two questions in his mind: "will they love me?" and "Can they save my neck?"' (Source: Brian Johnson, new business director, JWT).

Other potential or prospective clients would deny any such self-imposed pressure. They may see the pitch as an exciting and stimulating process full of exciting new ideas and strategic thinking presented by clever, articulate (and sometimes entertaining) people. Client egos are massaged and generally the prospect is treated as a revered guest. Other prospective clients see pitches as a more tedious affair since they have to repeat their brief in detail several times over and then sit through the inevitable credentials bit before they get to the heart of the matter — the agency proposals.

Most selling situations, including pitches, are about the removal of uncertainty. So understanding the problem, and identifying clear solutions with enthusiasm and conviction, is a winning formula.

The pitch

After weeks of intensive preparation of exciting creative ideas, ingenious media plans and pitch rehearsals, copies of the proposal or pitch document are laser printed, bound and made ready for client distribution after the main presentation. The pitch itself is where an advertising agency has the opportunity to advertise or sell itself. Given that most campaigns try to be different, to grab attention and make an impression, it is understandable that some agencies should regard a pitch as a creative opportunity also. There are many stories of daring pitch techniques, some of which work and some of which do not. Here are a few.

ABM's classic British Rail pitch purposely created client tension when the top executives from British Rail were kept waiting in a smoke-filled reception area while the receptionist ignored them throughout her gossip-filled telephone conversation. Eventually a space was cleared among the empty cans and orange peels, and the executives were invited to wait as the agency people were 'busy'. After some minutes the British Rail executives had had enough. As they got up to leave, the agency chairman, Peter Marsh, clad in full BR uniform (complete with cap, whistle and flag), burst in and said 'You don't like it, why should your passengers?' He then invited them to listen to how he and his colleagues were going to solve their problems.

Don White of Benton and Bowles is reported to have once dressed up as a Butlins redcoat for a Butlins pitch. The client took one look, said 'Anyone dressed like that isn't suitable for my business' and left. David Abbott of Abbott Mead Vickers is reported to have greeted Metropolitan Police commissioner Sir Robert Mark with a high-pitched nasal 'Hello, hello, hello' as he arrived to hear the agency pitch. Not amused, Sir Robert left the building and was never heard of again.

Agencies pitching for the Weetabix breakfast cereal account were invited to make their pitches in a hotel. As ABM were the last agency to pitch on the final morning, they decided to redecorate the function room in the ABM colours. This required an overnight painting and carpeting exercise. A stage was built and a special chair was delivered to the function room for Mr Robinson, the arthritic and ageing Weetabix chairman. As the Weetabix panel seated themselves the next morning, the lights dimmed until they were all immersed in an enthralling darkness. A spotlight burst a stream of light on to the stage, where Peter Marsh kneeled as he opened his pitch with: 'As one of Britain's few remaining wholly owned independent advertising agencies, it gives me great pleasure to present to you, Mr Robinson, as chairman of one of Britain's few wholly owned cereal manufacturers...' ABM won the account.

One final ABM classic pitch was for Honda. ABM hired the 60-piece Scots Guard bagpipe band to play the Honda jingle 'Believe in freedom, believe in Honda', while marching up and down London's Norwich Street (where ABM were making their pitch). Again, ABM picked up the account.

Strict adherence to the time and type of presentation (specified by the client) is essential. When Burkitt Weinreich Bryant were pitching for Littlewoods they were asked to make a 'short and sweet' final pitch since the then 92 year-old chairman, Sir John Moores, would be in attendance. The trade press reported that 'after over 30 minutes managing director Hugh Burkitt was asked to finish as it became obvious that Sir John's interest and attention was waning.' A row broke out as Hugh Burkitt persisted and a senior Littlewoods executive tried to stop the pitch.

Analysing the agency

As Nigel Bogle, joint managing director of Bartle Bogle Hegarty, says: 'The key questions today are less about an agency's ability to execute brilliantly and more about visionary strategic thinking, razor sharp positioning, pinpoint targeting and ingenious media solutions.'

The order of importance of the following questions can vary depending on what the prospective client really wants. Some clients may consider the agency's location and car parking facilities as relevant, whereas other clients would discount this as trivial and irrelevant to good advertising. Here are some of the questions which help in the choice of the right agency.

1) Does the agency really have a feel for my product and market? Do they really understand my brand's situation and potential?
2) Have they got strong research and planning capability?
3) Do they know the best media to use? Will their media-buying skills make my budget go a long way?

AGENCY	Understand our product and company?	Research, planning & strategic thinking	Media planning and buying	Creative	Size In-house resources, full service	International	Location	Fee/cost	Will we get on?
1									
2									
3									
4									
5									

Figure 6.2 Choosing an agency — an assessment form

4) Have they got creative flair? Do they win awards? Do they suggest new ideas?
5) Are they full-service or does everything get sub-contracted out? Can they handle a pack redesign, public relations, sales promotion and direct mail if called upon?
6) Are they international? Can their headquarters force them to resign the account should they decide to seek business in the same industry overseas? Alternatively, can they take on a lot of our co-ordination work through their own international management network?
7) What will they charge? And on what basis?
8) Do they display cost consciousness?
9) How will they measure their effectiveness?
10) Are we a small fish in a big pond? Are they too small or too big for us? Do we have contact with the principal partners? Will they fire us if a competitor offers them a bigger account (should we insist on a five-year contract)?
11) Who will work on the account? Are we likely to get on together (chemistry)? Will the pitch team be involved? How stable will our account team be? Are the people who worked on the case histories still with the agency?
12) Do they have a good track record? Do clients stick with them and place repeat business with the agency? If not, why not?
13) Check their references. References of past clients can also be requested.

Choosing an agency — an assessment form

The assessment form shown in Figure 6.2 can be weighted and scored as appropriate for each client's needs. A rating scale of 1–6 can be used. Agencies should be assessed using the *same criteria*. Few agencies perform so outstandingly that they remove all doubt in the client's mind as to whom he or she should choose. The criteria should be agreed in advance by the team involved in the selection process. The sample agency selection score sheet in Figure 6.2 shows one approach which attempts to formalise the selection by using consistent criteria. Each company obviously tailors its own approach.

After the pitch — The agency awaits the decision

Post-pitch tension is agonising. Awaiting the outcome of a pitch is a tense and worrying time. When the phone eventually rings and it turns out to be the prospect everyone holds their breath. Rejection means total failure. All the brilliant ideas, the careful research, the buzz of excitement, the long hours — all down the drain. Selection means total success. The post-pitch wait makes the mind wander. Were there any clues as to what the client thought of the pitch? Len Weinreich of Burkitt Weinreich Bryant Clients and Company tells a story called 'Scratching an indecent living' (see page 124).

Agency rejection

A rejected agency's managing director has the difficult job of picking the shattered team up and building up the agency morale again. The rejected agencies usually ask the prospect for some feedback for future reference. Here are some answers which rejected agencies have recorded upon asking why they had failed:

- I just didn't like you.
- I'm afraid you are not European.
- You're too small.
- They (the other agency) have more experience of this sector.
- You have too much experience in this sector. We're looking for a fresh approach.
- If it wasn't for the other agency you would have come first.
- The final decision was evenly split and you lost 8 — 7.
- Although we preferred your creative work, the other agency does have a place to park in London on Saturdays — and it's terribly handy for the shops.

Scratching an indecent living

My ferrety acquaintance, Crispin Neat, intrepid slogan detective, telephoned recently. "Hello, Lenny," he burbled. "I thought you might like to know that I'm branching out. Diversifying."

"Excellent news, Crispin," I replied, feigning enthusiasm. "What other services will you offer the hard-pressed advertiser?"

"Scratch pad deciphering."

"What's that?"

"Simple, Lenny, old chum. You gather and despatch the scratch pads after a crucial meeting and we'll decipher the scribbles and the doodles. We'll interpret the curious, dubious squiggles that clients leave behind."

"Crispin, that is the most ridiculous scam I've ever encountered."

He paused to draw breath on the other end of the 'phone. "Lenny, Lenny," he admonished. "If cynicism is your only reaction to my new sca . . . I mean, venture, then I have to tell you that you've been ignoring one of the most invaluable sources of high-grade intelligence in the business."

"Talk me through it." I was compelled to listen.

"Well, look at it this way. You've got this captive audience. You're either presenting for the account, or pleading to retain the business. Either way, it's hypertension ad biz max stressworld for all participants and the anxious clients need to combust mega-kilojoules of excess nervous energy."

"Hence the doodling?"

"Correct. But (and here's the brilliance of the idea) it's their sub-

Len Weinreich

conscious that's doing the doodling. So, whatever materialises on the pad is an action diagram of the client's thought processes. See?"

"I see. But how do you decipher their darkest thoughts if they're only scribbly doodles? And anyway," I added, "some clients actually tear their encrypted messages off the pad and tuck them into pockets. What's your action then?"

"The rub, Lenny. The old brass rubbing lark. We massage the undersheet delicately with a 9B pencil and a palimpsest of the jotting appears, by magic. From then on, interpretation is everything."

"OK. I How do you interpret?"

"You mean you've missed my new book: *Corporate Doodling: The Direct Line To Your Clients' Intentions.* It reveals all."

"I missed the book. Supply the topline, please."

"Well, many symbols are clear. Sketches of knives, revolvers, bludgeons, barbed wire and strategic nukes mean that he or she

might be firing the agency."

"Crispin, what about clients who can't draw? Can you explain *their* scratch pads?"

"All in my book, old chap, £9.50 at leading booksellers. Since you ask, anything resembling a maze represents confusion on their part. Blurred shading or scratchy hatching means they think you're a shifty bunch of crooks."

"Crispin, in my experience, they generally scribble down a few low key phrases from the presentation or make a few critical comments for subsequent reference."

"Of course, Lenny, of course. But each one can be a telling pointer. In order to cope with that eventuality, we've cobbled together a computer program called SNOOP which correlates their scratch notes with the agency slides and overheads in order to present you with an Attention Rating Admiration Factor and Purchase Property Index on a scale of one to ten."

"What happens if they've only scribbled a 'phone number or an enigmatic address in SW10?"

Crispin was wounded. "Haven't you read *any* of my books?"

"Er . . . which of your *oeuvre* have I missed now, Crispin?"

"*Corporate Blackmail for Profit and Pleasure* one of my all-time chart-toppers and money spinners. A right little cash cow."

"Thanks, Crispin. Don't call us . . ." *Clickbrrrrrr*

Len Weinreich is a vice-chairman of Burkitt Weinreich Bryant Clients and Company

After the pitch — The agency still awaits

INSIDE VIEW

When no news is bad news

"Why don't they ring? It's been four, no, three, days since they were in for the presentation. Didn't they say they'd make their minds up the next day? God. No news is bad news. Or is it good news? I can never quite remember.

"Anyway, I don't think we won it. I mean, we would have heard, wouldn't we? That guy, the one down the end of the table with the woolly khaki tie, he never liked us. He asked the worst questions. Like that one about putting all their press money in TV. That was a stinker, maliciously inserted to distract me. Quite arrested my flow, log-jammed my drift. No sense of un-folding drama, silly sod.

"The woman liked us though. I had a feeling she'd marked us down because we had too few women in the presentation team. But I could tell she warmed to me. Smiled a lot when I projected in her direction. God! Why haven't they rung yet? It's not as if we really need their lousy business, after all it's only an account. Ad agencies are like re-volving doors: one account leaves and another one follows, I mean, enters. Have you seen this year's free-fall figures? The income from their billing would make good the loss of those bastards from . . .

"We won't get it. They hated the

Len Weinreich

creative work. Detested it. They sneered at the ads. You would've thought they'd never seen a real commercial before. On the other hand, they'd asked us to be radical. Their brief advised ignoring all re-straints. Still, I think it might have been wiser to check the script with the ITVA before the presentation. The naked couple and the golden retriever might be a little rich for today's audience.

"We spent a month assembling this presentation and now, a week, okay, maybe three days later, not a dicky bird. Not a peep. Not even a whimper. Not even one of those mysterious calls to the media de-partment dishing them undercover dirt. Nothing.

"Perhaps we should have bribed them. Maybe we should have taped a few large denomination notes to the inside covers of their docu-ments. Perhaps I really should have nobbled the top man when he dashed out for a pee.

"Quite frankly, I think they loathed the work. And my suit. And our media director. It didn't help that our creative (ho, ho) di-rector completely cocked up the or-der of the storyboards. Or that our dizzy planner addressed their com-pany by the wrong name, twice. This instant they obviously are ap-pointing someone else because they have no wit, taste, imagination, discernment or balls.

"I'm not so sure we'd be happy handling their business. They'd be terrible clients. Endless trips to their remote offices to niggle over a charity ad mechanical.

"Stuff their lousy business. Prob-ably seriously unprofitable. In fact, I shouldn't be surprised if they went belly up. I've heard some interest-ing City whispers concerning the bizarre hotel bedroom habits of their chairman. Apparently . . . ***, is that the phone?"

Len Weinreich is a vice chairman of Burkitt Weinreich Bryant Clients and Company

Occasionally the prospect client actually helps the agency by giving an answer which identifies where they saw a real weakness. The agency can then eradicate the weak-ness before the next pitch. Similarly, a successful agency will be interested to find out why they were chosen so that they can capitalise on their strengths.

Firing the agency

Agencies get fired for a number of different reasons. *Campaign* magazine ran a piece entitled '13 Ways to be a Loser'.

1 Control of brand's advertising switches to rival of client: Gold Greenlees Trott lost Fosters when Elders IXL and its Courage division took over control of marketing Fosters from Watneys, a GGT client.

2 Agency produces irrelevant or inappropriate advertising: Lowe Howard-Spink lost some of its prized Mobil account after its "breakthrough" Dan Dare campaign failed. Insufficient planning was cited as a reason behind the fiasco.

3 Client is unsettled over too many changes at agency: Foote Cone and Belding lost £22 million worth of business — including Heinz and Cadbury — because of management upheaval.

4 Client unhappy over excess negative publicity surrounding its agency: IBM is uncomfortable over the widely reported lawsuits involving its agency and breakaway Lord Einstein O'Neill and Partners. Could result in IBM choosing neither and picking a new shop.

5 Takeover of agency infuriates client: Goodyear, Philips, Pilsbury said goodbye to JWT after it was taken over by WPP. Most cite "disruption" as a reason for leaving.

6 Client rationalises its agency roster: Toyota chose its dealer agency Brunnings over its main agency Lintas London after a creative shoot-out. British Telecom reviewed its entire account and picked three main agencies — BBH, Abbott Mead and JWT.

7 Total breakdown in agency-client relationship: GGT resigns the *Daily Express* after repeated clashes an inability to work with title's marketing staff.

8 Agency fails to come to terms with account: BMP got the sack by Comet, its first major retail client. Former vice-chairman Paul Leeves said BMP won the business "one year too soon".

9 Lack of solution creatively: Abbot Mead couldn't crack the *Daily Telegraph*. Later the agency admitted to producing tasteless series of press ads which aroused the ire of women, among others.

10 New client arrives: Allen Brady and Marsh's long-standing Milk account was reviewed after new NDC chief Richard Pears joined.

11 Agency can't master the client's politics: JWT lost British Rail. Agency was allied to the central advertising body while the chairman, Bob Reid, was committed to devolution. Network SouthEast chief Chris Green was not keen on JWT after it produced two poor ads, one in which it was in legal hot water with the *Monty Python* people.

12 Agency merges with another, producing conflict and massive disruption: Difficulties surrounding the merger of Reeves Robertshaw Needham and Doyle Dane Bernbach resulted in massive client fall-out.

13 Client is subject of a merger or takeover: Fast becoming a major reason for account moves. Expect major international agency fall-out after the conclusion of the Nestlé/Rowntree/Suchard negotiations.

Reproduced by kind permission of Haymarket Marketing Publications Limited and Laurie Ludwick (Source: *Campaign* 1988).

A more recent *Campaign* survey identified the following reasons in order of clients' importance:

1) Receiving no fresh input
2) Account conflict at the agency
3) New marketing director arrives
4) Change of client's policy
5) Other accounts leaving the agency

Firing the client

Agencies sometimes resign accounts, particularly if a larger competing account is offered to them. Occasionally, they are obliged to resign if an agency takeover or merger brings in some competing accounts and thereby creates a conflict of interest. New demands by a client sometimes become so difficult that the account becomes unprofitable or, as in the case of ABM, a reduced commission was considered unsatisfactory.

Key Points from Chapter 6:

1) Clear communications between client and agency are important if the right messages are going to be successfully communicated to target audiences.
2) Agencies, consultancies and consultants can become more than just suppliers of marketing services; they can become strategic partners of the client.
3) Careful selection is crucial to ensure the development of a mutually beneficial long-term relationship.

Further reading

ADMAP (monthly) NTC Publications, Henley-on-Thames
Cowley, D (ed) (1987) *How to Plan Advertising*, Cassell, London
Douglas, T (1984) *The Complete Guide To Advertising*, Papermac, London
Campaign Magazine (weekly) Haymarket Marketing Publications Ltd, London
Marketing (weekly) Haymarket Marketing Publications Ltd, London
Marketing Business (monthly) Chartered Institute of Marketing and Maxwell Publications, London
Marketing Week (weekly) Centaur Communications, London
Media Week (weekly) EMAP Business Publications, London
Rijkens, R (1992) *European Advertising Strategies*, Cassell, London

Further contacts

Advertising Agency Registrar Services, 26 Market Place, London W1N 7AL. Tel: 0171-437 3357
The Advertising Association, Abford House, 15 Wilton Road, London SW1V 1NJ. Tel: 0171-828 2771
Agency Assessments, 7th Floor, Brettenham House, Lancaster Place, London WC2 7EN. Tel: 0171-836 4416
British Rate and Data (BRAD), 1A Chalk Lane, Cockfosters Road, Barnet, Herts EN4 OBU
The Incorporated Society of British Advertisers (ISBA), 44 Hertford Street, London W1Y 8AE. Tel: 0171-499 7502
The Institute of Practitioners in Advertising (IPA), 44 Belgrave Square, London SW1X 8QS. Tel: 0171-235 7020
PR Consultancy Registrar Services, 26 Market Place, London W1N 7AL. Tel: 0171-437 3357
The addresses of other professional institutes are listed at the end of the appropriate chapters

UNDERSTANDING THE MEDIA

INTRODUCTION — THE CHALLENGE OF THE MEDIA MIX

Whether it is an advertising or editorial campaign (see Chapter 14), careful analysis and selection of appropriate media is fundamental to the success or failure of any communications campaign. Deciding to include advertising or editorial campaigns in the communications mix is a relatively easy decision compared to deciding which media and which specific media vehicles (eg specific magazine title) to use. Should press, TV, radio, cinema or posters be used? If so, how much of each? Should they mixed together (the media mix)? If press advertising is chosen, which publications should be used — national dailies, Sunday newspapers, evening newspapers, daily or weekly regional papers, or magazines? How many times should the audience see or hear the ad (*optimum frequency*)? When should it happen? Even a great advertisement will not work if (a) it is in the wrong place (b) it is placed at the wrong time or (c) it is in the right place at the right time but not enough times (insufficient frequency).

Most of the advertising budget gets spent on the media (and not the creative side or production side). This is why careful attention to detailed media planning, knowledge and negotiating skills are so important. Expert media planners and buyers get the best out of advertising by finding the right spaces or places for an ad campaign at the lowest cost.

Media planning is both a science and an art. Traditionally, it has been based on 'number crunching' media analysis and the application of complex computer models. Today, media planners are also interested in the qualitative side, which tells them how audiences actually use (and feel about) different media. Before looking at media research and analysis, or media planning, scheduling and buying, it is useful to be familiar with the media vocabulary or jargon that is commonly used.

MEDIA JARGON/VOCABULARY

Cover, reach, coverage or penetration
Indicates what percentage of the target market comes into contact with, or has the *'opportunity to see'* (OTS) the ad at least once. If, for example the *News At Ten* reaches

10 million viewers, 70 per cent of whom are ABC1 male then an ad placed during the break will reach 7 million ABC1 men. If ABC1 men are the primary target group and there are, in fact, 9 million ABC1 men in the UK then the advertisement can reach seven out of nine of the total UK target market (77 per cent reach).

Frequency
Is the number of times an ad is shown/placed in a particular period of time. How many times should an ad be shown and seen? The *optimum frequency* is often really unknown. Should it be concentrated over a short period ('*burst strategy*') or spread steadily over a longer period ('*drip strategy*')? For example, an advertising frequency of 60 can be built up by either (a) having the same advertisement shown before, during and after the *News At Ten* every weekday for four weeks, or (b) having one advertisement every six days throughout the year.

Opportunity to see (OTS), impacts and impressions
The number of exposures or opportunities which a particular audience has to see a specific ad. The number of 'impacts' essentially means the same thing. The total number of impacts, impressions or OTSs which the previous example could deliver would be (7 million × frequency of 60) = 420 million impacts, impressions or OTS's over a four-week period.

Cost per thousand (CPT)
Calculates the average cost of reaching 1,000 of the population. If it costs, say, £100,000 to place a 30-second spot (advertisement) on national TV with a peak time time audience of, say, 10 million, then the cost per thousand or the cost of reaching each or any group of 1,000 people within the audience is £100,000 divided by 10,000 (10 million = 10,000 groups of 1,000 people). The CPT here is £10. CPT allows cross-comparisons across different media types and media vehicles. For example, a full-page advertisement in the *Sun* reaches, say, 4 million and costs, say, £40,000, then the CPT is £40,000 divided by 4,000 (4 million = 4,000 lots of 1,000 people), which again gives a cost of £10 per thousand. In fact, the real CPT would be lower because each copy of the *Sun* is read by, say, three people. This enlarges the audience and therefore reduces the CPT figure by two-thirds, down to £3.33. Pages 134–5 show a wide range of media vehicles and their CPT examples. The term 'CPM' (cost per mille/thousand) is the same as CPT and is commonly used in the US.

Ideally, cost per enquiry/order generated gives a truer picture but this can only be measured after the advertisement has run (and if the advertisement was designed to achieve these kind of responses rather than, say, increase awareness or change attitudes). Experience and knowledge provide useful insights into media scheduling and buying.

TV rating points (TVRs)
One TV rating point is one per cent of the target audience. The percentage of the target audience viewing a spot ('reach') multiplied by the average number of opportunities to see gives the TVR. Television companies will sell packages of guaranteed TVRs. For example, a target of 240 TVRs means that 60 per cent of the target audience will have, on average, 4 OTSs. It could also mean that 40 per cent have seen it six times. Reference to the media schedule quickly identifies the frequency. Four hundred TVRs

is considered to be a reasonably large campaign (80 per cent seeing the message five times). It has been suggested that some confectionery companies and record companies run a lightweight campaign and buy 100 TVRs so that they can tell the retail trade that they are running a television advertising campaign (the 'pull' helps the 'push' — see page 20, Chapter 1).

Impacts or impressions

The total number of people who saw the ad multiplied by the number of times they saw it. For example, if 30,000 see an ad three times during its campaign then it creates 90,000 impressions.

Position

Position refers to the place where the ad is shown. Back pages, inside cover pages, right-hand pages, TV pages and so on have greater readership and more impact than other pages (eg the third right-hand page has a bigger impact than the first left-hand page). Similarly, some positions on a page are more effective than others. Media buyers are aware of this and so are the media owners since their rate cards (prices) reflect the value of certain positions. Boddington's beer media strategy was built around position, ie they concentrated their advertisements on the back page of glossy magazines to the extent that they 'owned' the back pages for a period of time.

Environment

The environment or context in which an ad is exposed affects the message itself. The type of feature or editorial, and other advertisements, which run alongside an advertisement affect the likely effectiveness of that advertisement. For example, although the prime spot (first spot in the first break) was booked during the comedy TV film *Airport '77*, the TWA advertisement that followed lost its serious credibility. The same M & S dress advertised in *Vogue* and *Woman's Own* had a perceived value of £58 and £28 respectively.

WHICH MEDIUM?

Should press and/or radio be used? How should a client or an agency choose which media to use? Which TV stations and/or publications should be used? Which vehicles within a particular medium (eg *Guardian* or *Times*)? Press includes national dailies, Sunday newspapers, evening newspapers, daily and weekly regional papers, and magazines. Television, radio, cinema and posters are considered. Table 7.1 on page 134–5 summarises the key points which help to decide which media and vehicle is the most suitable. The key points are as follows:

1) Audience size (reach or penetration). Some media cannot carry national brands because they cannot offer national coverage. Media such as radio and regional press are generally considered to be local media since they talk to the community. Television can get to large audiences quickly.
2) Audience type (eg 15 – 24-year-olds don't watch much TV but do go to the cinema on the other hand, not many over 35+ year-olds watch the cable music station MTV).
3) Budget (production cost, media cost and CPT).

4) Message objective
   a) Creative scope: colour, sound and movement needed (eg TV's movement can show impulsive purchases)?
   b) Demonstration (product usage often best shown on TV, but all media can show product benefits).
   c) Technical detail — TV no good, press is better.
   d) Urgency (TV, radio and national papers can be topical and announce urgent commercial news).
   e) Compatibility, 'rub-off' or image effect of media and vehicle on product itself. For example, would Harrods advertise in the *Sun*? TV puts a product or company alongside the big boys and therefore enhances the image since many viewers think 'they can't be cowboys if they're on national TV'.
   f) TV adds credibility — 'as seen on TV'.
5) Ease of booking
   a) Lead times for space (magazines, TV and cinema have long lead times or notice of booking).
   b) Lead times for production (some press can be knocked out overnight whereas a cinema production takes months).
6) Restrictions. Some products are excluded from certain media, eg cigarettes on TV and alcohol in children's magazines.
7) Competitive activity. Advertisers watch, copy and sometimes avoid the places where their competitors advertise.

MEDIA SELECTION

Audience size

TV allows commercial messages to 'reach' large numbers of people on a national or regional level. TV used to be known as a mass medium but as the number of stations increase, more niche channels are emerging on cable, satellite and mainstream terrestrial TV which means that TV is becoming less of a mass medium. Radio attracts smaller regional audiences. Radio generally does not offer national coverage (although the *Network Chart Show* and *Newslink* are exceptions). Cinema attracts small audiences and can offer slow national coverage (among younger audiences). National and regional press deliver what they say — national and regional audiences respectively. Because posters can prove difficult to co-ordinate on a national scale, there are poster-buying specialists. Direct mail can address large national and international audiences but because of its high cost per thousand the target audiences are likely to be tightly defined and targeted. Finally, TV's audience size is seasonally influenced, with the audience increasing in winter and reducing in the summer.

Audience type

Generally, 15–24-year-olds, busy doing other things, don't have time to watch TV, whereas cinema tends to attract this target group. Radio is popular with housewives and commuters. The national daily newspapers tend to target specific socio-economic groups and political sympathisers, while magazines reach targeted groups defined by their lifestyles, income levels, ages and sex. Posters can target commuters who travel by car, bus and train.

Audience state of mind

Audience state of mind or receptivity to messages varies across the media spectrum. TV audiences can be relaxed and passive, sometimes viewing in a trance-like manner (the 'couch-potato syndrome'). TV and its ads become a form of visual wallpaper, sometimes used as company and sometimes used to 'warm up' a room. Radio can also be used in the background, but listeners do tend to work with the radio as they create visual images from verbal messages. The cinema delivers a captive audience who are happy to be involved in the suspension of disbelief, and they will not leave the room to make a cup of tea. In fact, many viewers thoroughly enjoy the special cinema ads. The national press is deliberately read as information is sought. Some research reveals unconscious feelings of guilt (waste and/or inadequacy of knowledge) if a newspaper is left unfinished. Magazines are absorbed in a more relaxed mood.

Cost of production

The cost of producing a TV ad can range from £1,000 to £1,000,000 depending on the length, complexity and actors involved, whereas radio has a lower cost of production ranging from £100 to £20,000. Stationary pictures with a voice-over promoting the local Indian restaurant can cost just a few hundred pounds, while a more lavish 90-second full production cinema advertisment could cost up to £1,000,000. Radio and press sometimes provide free help with basic productions. Posters can be produced for as little as £100 for a 4-sheet (5ft × 3ft 4in) poster or £5,000 for a 96-sheet (40ft × 10ft) poster campaign. Direct mail can be as cheap as the cost of a letter but if a four-colour brochure is specially designed and produced, then the costs can be anywhere from several hundred to several thousand pounds for design and artwork alone.

Minimum cost of space

Advertising space is rarely bought in single units. A single ad is unlikely to achieve as much as a campaign or a series of ads would. Ads are generally scheduled and bought over a period of time rather than as one-offs. The cost of space is relatively high on TV compared to radio where a single off-peak 30-second spot on a regional station could be as litle as £50 and £200 for radio and TV respectively. A national 30-second spot in the middle of *Coronation Street* could cost £100,000. A one-off full-page four-colour ad in the *Sun* or the *Financial Times* can cost nearly £40,000. Smaller space can be bought, right down to the single column centimetre (approximately £100 and £50 for the *Sun* and *Financial Times* respectively).

Cost per thousand

The CPT can vary widely, as indicated by Table 7.1 on page 134–5, Table 7.2 on page 139 and Table 7.3 on page 140.

Message

TV has sight, sound, colour and movement, which makes it an ideal medium for product demonstrations and impulse purchases, but the time constraint and viewing mode make detailed messages almost impossible. It is time constrained (whereas a press ad is not). Ads are viewed serially whereas press ads compete with other ads and editorial, often on the same page. Remote control zapping has made TV more vulnerable as an advertising medium. TV, radio and cinema are highly transitory in that the viewer cannot refer back to an ad once it is shown (unless taped). On the other hand, the audience can refer back to press, posters and direct mail. TV's fleeting messages leave no room for detail but can grab attention, create awareness and arouse interest. More and more ads across the media spectrum, including TV, are tying in with direct response mechanisms (0800 numbers or coupons to fill in) so that more detailed information can subsequently be delivered to the audience).

Ease of media buying

Some popular TV programmes (and magazines) require long lead times for booking space. Advertisements are still pre-emptable (they can be outbid and kicked off a particular spot on the day they were booked to be broadcast). Different rates or prices can be bid; the top rate guarantees the spot but agencies and clients want to avoid paying these extremely high rates so they make bids at prices lower down the scales (giving various amounts of notice about pre-emption). Both script and final film require approval/clearance from the Independent Television Association (ITVA). This takes time. Cinema has long lead booking times but shorter clearance time from the Cinema Advertising Association. Radio is the most flexible of all, with same-day clearance and short lead booking times. The national dailies tend to have flexible and short lead times, while magazines have longer lead times. The quality of audience research for some media, including cinema, is known to have been questioned. TV and radio can obviously offer a higher frequency since, in theory, an advertisement could go out every half hour all day. The lack of national network coverage makes radio, cinema and regional press a tough task for media planners and buyers involved in national campaigns.

Table 7.1 Summary of media characteristics

		TV	Radio	Cinema	PRESS Daily, evening and Sunday	PRESS Regional	PRESS Magazines	Posters	Direct mail
AUDIENCE	**Audience size**	Some wastage large and national (some international)	No national coverage	Small, no national coverage	Large and mostly national	Small, no national networks	Mostly national (and international)	National coverage is difficult	Large national and international
	Audience type	Few 15-24-year-olds	Many housewives, commuters	Many 15-24-year-olds	Socio-economic	Geographic segments	Lifestyle segments	Commuters, car drivers etc	Any target available
	Audience state of mind	Relaxed and passive TV couch potato = visual wall paper	Background/ audio wallpaper?	Captive audience — willing suspension of disbelief	Deliberately read		Relaxed and involved with magazine		
COSTS	**Cost of production**	High	Low	High	Low-med	Low	Low-med	Med	Low
	Minimum cost of space	High	Low	Low	Med	Low	Low-med	Low-med	High but can experiment in small quantities
	Average cost per thousand	Low less than £2	Very low less than £1		Low-med £8	Med £30	Med £12-£70		High £500
	Extra advantages	Adds credibility to product or company	Transportable medium	High impact and captive audience					

		TV	Radio	Cinema	Daily, evening and Sunday	Regional	Magazines	Posters	Direct mail
MESSAGE	Variable/ senses	Sight, sound, colour, movement time constraint	Sound and time constraint	Big impact enhanced sight and sound	Mostly black and white some colour	Black and white	4-colour	4-colour big impact	4-colour and 3-D possibility
	Serial ad sequence	Viewed serially — no competition from other ads or editorial but zap	Serially, less zapping	Serially and no zapping	Must compete with the other ads and editorial on same page			Ad clutter	
	Transitory	Highly transitory since you cannot refer back to ad once shown (unless taped)	Highly transitory since you cannot refer back to ad		Can keep clippings or refer back if desired			Can refer back, walk back or drive past	Can refer back and keep coupon
	Demonstration	Ideal for usage and impulse purchases	Difficult	Yes	Benefits or results can be shown but not product usage demonstration			Only short image benefit	Yes
	Detail/ technical	Viewer cannot absorb detail	No urgency and topicality	No	Yes	Yes	Yes	No	Yes
	Urgency/ topicality rub-off	No	Unique immediacy, urgency and topicality	No	Yes	No	Magazine image spills onto ad	Cult image?	
EASE OF MEDIA BUYING	Flexible	Inflexible and pre-emptible	Flexibility		Flexible			Inflexible	Flexible
	Lead times	Long	Short	Long	Short			Long	Short
	Clearance	Script (1-week) finished film (1-week) ITVA	Same day clearance ITVA	One week clearance cinema ad assoc.	Code of advertising practice (clearance is not compulsory)				
	Audience research*	BARB and TGI	RAJAR	CAVIAR	NRS	JICREG	NRS and ABC	OSCAR	
	High frequency facility	Hourly and daily	Hourly and daily	No	Yes	Weekly	Weekly/monthly		
	National coverage	Experts job but network exists and international cable/ satellite	No national network		Yes	No national network		Difficult	

* Audience research - see Further Cotacts on page 143.

HOW MUCH MEDIA SPACE?

Does the impact of a double-page-spread (DPS) justify the cost? Would the reach be increased by placing two single-page advertisements in two different magazines instead? Should TV be supplemented by radio, by posters, or by both (like the Guinness Genius campaign)? Is a *personal media network* worth creating so that the target audience is hit with a brand's message first thing in the morning on the radio, on posters in the neighbourhood area, in the appropriate paper on the way to work, on TV that evening, in the cinema that night and finally on the radio in the car coming home from the cinema?

Media buyers' computers churn out cost ranking analyses which list the publications in order of their cost per thousand — with the lowest at the top. CPT offers a quantitative criterion, but does it reveal *heavy-user* information? Perhaps a high CPT conceals within it a large chunk of the heavy users, which may make the advertisement more effective? Qualitative criteria (audience size and how they use the media, targetability, message type, ease of booking, restrictions and competitive activity) all affect the choice. In the end, experience, judgement, and a little bit of creative flair influence the decision to buy space.

WHEN TO GET THE SPACE?

Having selected the media type and specific vehicles within each media type, the next question is how much space and/or airtime should be booked. What season, month, week, day or hour should the advertisement appear? How many times should the ad be seen? How many times are too many times? Can the audience become irritated? Or is it just wasted advertising after so many impressions? What is the optimum frequency? This last question becomes more difficult when a campaign uses several different advertisements, particularly when each new ad builds on the last one. The creative side of the campaign can sell itself to the client but the media schedule often requires much more detailed justification. Once the media schedule has been agreed it can be passed on to the media buyer to start booking the space.

Media schedule

The media strategy is then refined into the tactical details specifying exactly what space should be booked where. Figure 7.1 shows the proposed media schedule for the Haagen-Dazs ice cream campaign which is featured in the short case at the end of Chapter 11.

MEDIA BUYING

A skilled media buyer can save enormous sums by playing one media owner off against another. After all, there are many different routes (or media vehicles) to the minds of the target audience.

There are series discounts (ten inserts or ads for the price of nine), and volume discounts if you spend over a certain amount. Many agencies pool their media buying

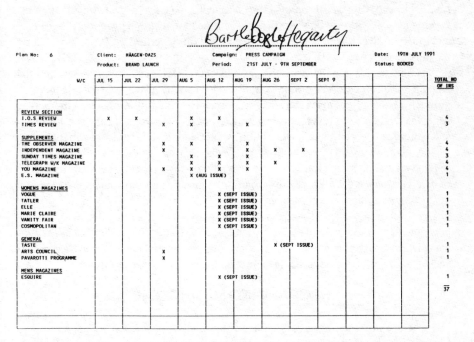

	W/C	JUL 15	JUL 22	JUL 29	AUG 5	AUG 12	AUG 19	AUG 26	SEPT 2	SEPT 9				TOTAL NO OF INS
REVIEW SECTION														
I.O.S REVIEW		X	X		X	X								4
TIMES REVIEW				X	X		X							3
SUPPLEMENTS														
THE OBSERVER MAGAZINE				X	X	X	X							4
INDEPENDENT MAGAZINE				X			X	X	X					4
SUNDAY TIMES MAGAZINE					X	X	X							3
TELEGRAPH W/K MAGAZINE					X	X	X	X						4
YOU MAGAZINE				X	X	X	X							4
E.S. MAGAZINE					X (AUG ISSUE)									1
WOMENS MAGAZINES														
VOGUE						X (SEPT ISSUE)								1
TATLER						X (SEPT ISSUE)								1
ELLE						X (SEPT ISSUE)								1
MARIE CLAIRE						X (SEPT ISSUE)								1
VANITY FAIR						X (SEPT ISSUE)								1
COSMOPOLITAN						X (SEPT ISSUE)								1
GENERAL														
TASTE									X (SEPT ISSUE)					1
ARTS COUNCIL				X										1
PAVAROTTI PROGRAMME				X										1
MENS MAGAZINES														
ESQUIRE						X (SEPT ISSUE)								1
														37

Plan No: 6   Client: HAAGEN-DAZS   Product: BRAND LAUNCH   Campaign: PRESS CAMPAIGN   Period: 21ST JULY - 9TH SEPTEMBER   Date: 19TH JULY 1991   Status: BOOKED

Figure 7.1 Proposed media schedule for the Haagen-Dazs ice cream campaign

together to gain the maximum discounts. Negotiating and discounting varies from country to country. Countries like Austria and Denmark allow very little negotiation with media owners. Media buyers and media planners/schedulers need to work closely together. Sometimes they are one and the same person. As Torin Douglas (1984) says: 'Some agencies prefer to have both the planning and the buying of a campaign done by the same person in that a good deal of negotiation can be done at the planning stage, where it will influence the way the schedule has been drafted.'

MEDIA RESEARCH

Media research basically tells the media buyer and scheduler which publications are read by what type of people, how many and what type of people are likely to watch a particular television programme, who listens to what on the radio, which kind of films attract what kind of audience, which poster sites are passed by most people, etc. The media buyer can then decide if the particular media vehicle's audience profile matches his target market, and if the audience size proves to be cost effective in terms of cost per thousand, coverage, frequency, OTSs, TVRs (see page 128) etc.

How many people watch *Neighbours* or the *Ten O'Clock News*? How many listen to Capital Radio's breakfast radio show? How many people read the *Sun*? Advertisers are even more interested in what type of people are in the audience and whether they are heavy, medium or light users of the product type or even the specific brand.

Although the *Sun* is considered to be a working man's paper, 30 per cent of its readership are ABC1s. So some strange anomalies do exist, and media buyers must tread cautiously. Information concerning socio-economic groups, product usage types and lifestyle data all help to build a *profile* which the advertiser can then use to target the most relevant audience.

An initial search into the British Rate and Data (BRAD) directory reveals a limited amount of information regarding circulation and audience type (socio-economic groups). This can be cross-referenced (or cross-tabulated) with the TGI index (see page 95, Chapter 5) to reveal, for example, types of audience according to lifestyles and typical product purchases in addition to the usual demographic information.

The qualitative data explains how the media are used by target audiences — the role the media play in people's lives. Some advertising agencies use focus groups to research the obscure media used by a particular group of opinion leaders or to investigate how an audience uses the media.

The short case at the end of Chapter 11 shows how careful quantitative and qualitative media research helped top advertising agency Bartle Bogle Hegarty to develop a media strategy which combined uniquely with the overall creative strategy to produce a highly effective advertising campaign for Haagen-Dazs ice cream.

THE CHANGING MEDIA SCENE

The control and regulation covering each type of media is discussed in Chapter 8, 'The Changing Communications Environment'. Here are some other changes that are occurring in the media world.

Print

Technology today allows low cost entry into the world of publishing. This has reduced the publishing industry's traditional high-investment barrier to entry. In effect, this means that we are seeing new magazines, journals and newsletters appearing alongside multi-edition, tailor-made magazines such as the *US Farmers' Journal* (which produces over 1,000 different editions of each month's publication targeted at over 1,000 different types of farmer). The result? More accurately targeted media which allow advertisers and PR people to target their messages more effectively.

Broadcasting

Cable and satellite TV have arrived. The new, wider choice means fragmented audiences tuned into discrete stations but with more zapping. More homes will have more channels. Thirty-five channels in the UK will not be uncommon.

Different stations attract different audience profiles or different psychographic and demographic segments. For example, religious channels, sports channels, children's channels, MTV music channel and now Chicago's Channel One (ten-minute high school news channel networked into 10,000 US high schools paid for by two minutes of advertising) all provide advertisers with more distinct target audiences.

Aerial advertising

Overlaps with point-of-sale, sales promotions and publicity. It includes aircraft-towed banners for a few hundred pounds per hour and hot air balloons for a £1,000 per day (see below).

Other advertising media

Parking meters for a few hundred pounds per 100 displays. *Advertee* golf displays (on the tee and now also inside the cup/hole). *Domestic videotapes, videos in the Post Office* (over £10,000 for a 30-second spot played every 15 minutes for five weeks). *Taxi cabs* carry exterior panels for over £20 per month. *Toilets* offer a captive audience. A network of toilets is currently being tested in the USA. A solus *leaflet drop* or house-to-house distribution costs approximately £25 per 1,000.

Direct mail has a 'ball-park' cost of £500 per thousand but its selectivity and cost per response can make it a very cost effective medium. Direct mail and sponsorship are dealt with in Chapters 13 and 15 respectively.

COST PER THOUSAND

Calculates the cost of reaching 1,000 of the population audience. Table 7.2 demonstrates the wide range of media vehicles available for pig farmers or builders' merchants, music lovers or bankers, etc. Please note that the figures below are calculated on rate card costs — substantial discounts are available, particularly during a recession, when it is a buyer's market.

Table 7.2 Cost per thousand of selected media vehicles

Vehicle	(Approximate 1992 Prices)		
	Cost £	Audience size	CPT £
The *Sun* (full page)	30,000	3,700,000	8.11
The *FT* (full page)	25,000	288,000	86.81

	(Approximate 1992 Prices)		
Vehicle	**Cost £**	**Audience size**	**CPT £**
The Word (full page)	61,000	5,250,000	11.62
The European (full page)	6,000	223,000	26.91
Basildon Evening Echo	1,900	62,000	30.65
Equine Welfare Magazine	610	20,000 (uncert)	30.50
Melody Maker	1,980	68,000	29.19
Love Story	960	19,000	50.78
Machine Knitting News	690	50,000	13.90
Saga Magazine	6,500	501,000	12.98
National Pig News	460	6,000	77.33
Baker's Review	560	8,000	70.63
Banking Technology	2,140	11,000	194.54
Builders Merchants News	1,330	7,600	175.00
New Civil Engineer	1,580	62,000	25.48
RADIO London Regional — Capital Radio	*30 sec spot* 650	*Weekly reach* 431,000	1.50
ILR Network National Chart Show	3,250	1,334,000	2.44
TV LWT area (*News at Ten* — London area	18,000	1,073,000	16.77
ITV National	60,000	5,255,000	11.41

MEDIA RESEARCH BUREAUX

TV audiences are measured by *BARB* (British Audience Research Bureau), who monitor a sample of 4,500 homes through their *people meter*. The meter records what stations are turned on and the hand-held remote control unit inputs data about who is watching the TV.

Radio audiences are measured by *RAJAR* (Radio Joint Audience Research). In 1992 RAJAR replaced JICRAR (Joint Industry Council for Radio Audience Research).

Cinema uses *CAVIAR* (Cinema and Video Industry Audience Research) to measure cinema and video audience size and profiles.

Newspaper and magazine readership is measured by National Readership Surveys. It carries out 28,000 in-home interviews each year. *ABC* (Audit Bureau of Circulation) audits the sales or circulation of over 2,000 different publications, including the nationals.

Freesheets or local newspapers use *VFD* (Verified Free Distribution system).

Posters use *OSCAR* (Outside Site Classification and Audience Research) and PAB (Poster Audit Bureau).

BRAD (British Rate and Data) is the media buyer's reference book because it lists all the above circulation/audience figures as well as the costs (rate card costs). It also gives detailed information on deadlines, mechanical data and commissions on over 2,000 newspapers, 2,400 consumer publications, 4,600 business publications, radio and TV networks, posters and much more. The monthly 600-page book costs over £130.00 and is available on disc.

APPENDIX 1

Cost per thousand in Europe

Peak Time CPT (adults & housewives)

Country	Channel	Adult CPT $	Housewives CPT $
Austria	ORF	10.19	20.90
Belgium	VTM	14.23	22.34
	TVB	16.37	25.59
Denmark	TV2	15.95	31.11
Finland	MTV	13.35	26.46
	Channel 3	11.60	24.98
France	TF1	5.64	13.52
	Antenne 2	6.29	15.12
	FR3	6.20	15.60
	Canal Plus	8.93	22.20
	M6	4.89	11.84
Germany	ARD	16.55	33.65
	ZDF	9.59	15.56
	Sat 1	10.82	18.57
	RTL Plus	9.19	16.24
Greece	ET-1	10.74	16.64
	ET-2	14.92	23.43
	ET-3	15.82	19.59
	Mega	7.18	10.84
	Antenna	7.97	12.20
	New Channel	14.81	32.59
Ireland	RTE TV1	6.22	13.23
	Network 2	7.30	16.19
Italy	RAI 1	8.67	18.77
	RAI 2	7.35	16.20
	RAI 3	5.56	11.69
	Canale 5	7.29	16.27
	Italia 1	5.84	14.43
	Rete 4	4.49	8.50

Country	Channel	Adult CPT $	Housewives CPT $
Netherlands	Nederland 1	6.67	n/a
	Nederland 2	9.27	n/a
	Nederland 3	7.98	n/a
	RTL-4	9.13	n/a
Portugal	RTP 1	6.01	10.87
	RTP 2	5.12	8.48
Spain	TVE 1	13.40	33.09
	TVE 2	14.20	36.29
	TV3	16.72	42.93
	Canal 33	24.71	75.18
	ETB 1	21.06	72.18
	ETB 2	15.20	41.25
	TVG	16.14	45.38
	Canal Sur	8.23	20.97
	TM3	24.64	67.34
	Canal 9	23.28	40.47
	Canal +	4.71	18.42
	Tele Cinco	16.04	41.60
	Antena 3	9.06	25.02
Sweden	TV4	22.65	52.58
Switzerland	DRS (German)	10.88	19.53
	TSR (French)	9.34	15.20
	TSI (Italian)	11.16	18.62
	SRG (National)	10.53	18.34
UK	ITV	9.73	16.83
	Channel 4	9.73	16.83
	TV-am	9.04	14.57

Note: In some cases, CPTs are the cost of reaching the total population however these channels are not necessarily available to everyone

(Source: Saatchi & Saatchi; Worldwide Advertising, 1992)

Key Points from Chapter 7:

1) The proliferation of new media vehicles (TV stations and magazines) creates more 'noise' but also offers discrete communication channels to better defined audiences.
2) More money is spent on buying space than producing the ads themselves.
3) Media planning and buying is a highly skilled area.

Further reading

Advertising Association (1993) *The Marketing Pocket Book*, NTC, London
Davies, M (1992) *The Effective Use of Advertising Media,* 4th edition, Business Books, London
Douglas, T (1984) *The Complete Guide To Advertising*, Papermac, London

Engel, J, Warshaw, M and Kinnear, T (1991) *Promotional Strategy: Managing the Marketing Communications Process*, Irwin, Homewood, Illinois
The Account Planning Group (1987) *How To Plan Advertising* (ed. Cowley D), Cassell, London
Campaign Magazine, Haymarket Marketing Publications Ltd, London
Media Week, EMAP Business Publications 33-39 Bowling Green Lane, London EC1R ODA
Media International, (monthly), Reed Publishing Services 27 Wilfred Street, London SW1E 6PR

Further contacts

For trade associations and professional bodies, see Chapter 6, page 127.

Audit Bureau of Circulation (ABC), Black Prince Yard, 207-9 High Street, Berkhamsted, Herts HP4 1AD. Tel: 01442 870800

British Audience Research Bureau (BARB), Glenthorne House, Hammersmith Road, London W6 0ND. Tel: 0181-741 9110

British Rate and Data (BRAD) see page 127.

Cinema and Video Industry Audience Research (CAVIAR), 127 Wardour Street, London W1V 4AD. Tel: 0171-439 9531

Joint Industry Committee for Regional Press Research (JICREG), Bloomsbury House, 74–77 Great Russell Street, London WC1B 3DA. Tel: 0171-636 7014

National Readership Surveys Ltd, 11-15 Betterton Street, Covent Garden, London WC2H 9BP. Tel: 0171-379 0344

Outside Site Classification and Audience Research (OSCAR), NOP Posters, Tower House, Southampton Street, London WC2E 7HN. Tel: 0171-612 0100

Radio Joint Audience Research (RAJAR), Collier House, 163-169 Brompton Road, London SW3 1PY. Tel: 0171-584 3003

Verified Free Distribution (VFD), Black Prince Yard, 207 High Street, Berkhamsted, Herts HP4 1AD. Tel: 01442 863344

8

THE CHANGING COMMUNICATIONS ENVIRONMENT

INTRODUCTION

This chapter looks at how marketing communications are affected by the business environment and its many apparently uncontrollable factors.

Markets are pulled and pushed in different directions by forces which are outside an organisation's immediate control. New laws; changing regulations; fluctuating economic cycles; demographic shifts; new social values, attitudes and cultural norms; fast-changing technology and agile competitors are some of the key factors which constantly move markets away from the existing status quo. Today's marketing mix and marketing communications mix can soon become obsolete.

This means that the *MIIS* (marketing information and intelligence system) discussed on page 104 of Chapter 5 should constantly feed back information on patterns, trends or sudden changes in any of these uncontrollable forces. This requires, in turn, a constant alertness and preparedness to change products, services, advertisements, images, communications and even an organisation's attitudes or culture.

Part of a *SWOT* analysis (strengths, weaknesses, opportunities and threats) monitors the external opportunities and threats which emerge in the business environment. The *PEST* acronym provides a useful starting point to scan the business environment for any of these change factors which directly or indirectly affect a business and how it communicates:

- **P**olitical (including legal and regulatory)
- **E**conomic (cycles of recession and boom)
- **S**ocial (new values, attitudes lifestyles, ethics and demographics)
- **T**echnological

Competition could also be added as a key factor operating in an organisation's environment. For the purposes of this chapter, the focus will be on the PEST factors. Any of these change factors could ultimately push a business into extinction if the changes are constantly ignored. There is a tendency to resist change, perhaps because of the insecurities which it heaps upon an individual. Some organisations wait until the last moment before changing. Others see an advantage in being pro-active rather than reactive. We will now consider how these PEST factors affect the organisation's marketing activities and its communications in particular.

POLITICS

Legislation and regulation

Pan Am's Downfall

It was claimed that *Pan Am* failed because `it never got a handle on how dereg-ulation of the 1970s would affect a powerful world airline.'

(Source: *Fortune*, 13 January 1992)

National and international laws and regulations change. This can affect the basic product or service and methods of communication.

UK legislation provides laws which essentially support the principles of being honest and truthful. The laws are bolstered by a host of self-regulatory professional codes which draw on the same set of basic business principles eg marketing profes-sionals should conduct their business in a *legal, decent, honest and truthful* manner.

Before looking at the laws, it is worth mentioning that short-term, dishonest deals (`rip-offs') which slip through the system generate short-term gains but they tend not to generate long-term sales since repeat business does not come back. The `*everlasting customer'* or the `*lifetime customer'* concept is a long-term winning strategy since the marketing perspective is broadened towards selling ten cars, ten fridges, or thousands of cans of food or beer, or 50 years of office cleaning to one customer over a long period of time instead of grabbing a one-off, short-term sale. It *costs five times as much* to sell to a new customer as it does to an existing customer. Fooling a customer is myopic. You can *only cheat a customer once*. Flouting the law or regulations restricts a business to a short-term vision. Incidentally, Japanese management guru *Kenichi Ohmae* claims that the most fundamental difference between eastern and western business strategies is the *time horizon*. Japanese companies build long-term strategies while western companies plan short-term profits.

There are many laws that affect business, and marketing communications in partic-ular. UK television advertising alone has at least 56 statutes and regulations which affect it. These include the 1987 Consumer Protection Act, the Sex Discrimination Acts 1975 and 1986, the Race Relations Act 1976, the Telecommunications Act 1984, the Copyright Designs and Patents Act 1988 and many more. Here is a brief descrip-tion of some of the laws which directly affect marketing communications.

The *1968 Trade Descriptions Act* legally obliges companies and individuals to avoid making false or misleading statements about the goods or services being mar-keted.

The *1979 Sale of Goods Act* demands that goods sold match the description.

The *Control of Misleading Advertisements Regulations 1988* provides the safety net of the *Office of Fair Trading*, where complaints about marketing communications (advertising, shop-windows displays etc) can be referred for scrutiny.

The Data Protection Act 1984 requires any organisation or individual to register if they hold names, addresses or data on individuals *on computer*.

There are, as we have mentioned, many other laws and regulations, both national and international, that affect a business and its marketing communications. Some of the legislation may not appear to affect the marketing communications directly, eg product liability laws, but caution, coupled with expert advice, is required, particularly in the international arena. *Product Liability* puts an increasing onus of responsibility on both manufacturers, distributors and retailers to make sure that the products they market are safe and sound. It also affects marketing communications (in the case below, packaging communications). The '*borderless world*' knows few barriers when it comes to liability.

Sparkling Wine Shooting

The 15-year-old case of a US consumer suing a UK paint company (for alleged injurious effects of a lead-based paint) strikes fear into the heart of many potential exporters. According to Mickey Pohl, a growing awareness that a manufacturer carries a heavy and detailed obligation to warn potential users about any dangers which might lurk in the use of its products has prompted some sparkling wine manufacturers to print disclaimers on the packaging warning against possible risks involved in uncorking their products.

(Source: Pohl M (1991))

EC legislative process

On a local scale, centralised *EC* legislation is beginning to affect every European company in some way. Many organisations are only now reluctantly accepting the new European environment. Many will react with some urgency but how many have really seized the opportunity of selling in the world's most competitive market? And how many will get wiped out within 10, 20 or 50 years? More and more legislation may come from a centralised European state. The process of European legislation is shown in Figure 8.1. It is vital to make an organisation's voice heard so the advice from the DTI (Department of Trade and Industry) is to find out how proposed legislation could affect a particular organisation, then get in early and have a say in the emerging EC regulations. Chapter 9 on International Marketing Communications considers the effects of the EC on the communications mix and on client/agency relationships in more detail.

This legislative process is particularly relevant to regulations which affect *marketing communications*. Here some EC countries prefer central legislation over self-regulation and its voluntary codes of practice. For example, draft EC legislation aims to outlaw cigarette advertising across all promotional media (sponsorship is also in the

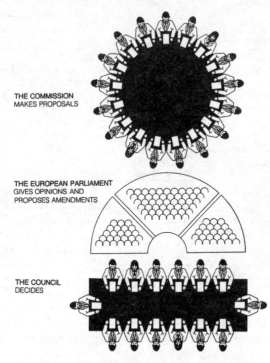

THE COMMISSION
MAKES PROPOSALS

THE EUROPEAN PARLIAMENT
GIVES OPINIONS AND
PROPOSES AMENDMENTS

THE COUNCIL
DECIDES

Figure 8.1 The EC legislative process

European definition of promotion). Currently, in the UK, voluntary agreements specify the amount of space and precise wording of warnings on packs or on advertisements for cigarettes. These agreements also specify that no positive claims can be made about tobacco and that no tobacco advertising is permitted on television. It is this self- regulation which has moved the market, and its communications, in new directions as voluntary codes change. Once there was a time when cigarettes were promoted as being good for you. Today they are advertised as being bad for you (the mandatory health warnings).

The EC directive on cross frontier broadcasting was adopted in 1989 and implemented on 3 October 1991. It basically covers television and can be summarised as follows:

- Allows television channels to cross frontiers of member states.
- Limits the total amount of advertising airtime to 15 per cent of daily transmission.
- Sets guidelines for broadcast sponsorship (see Chapter 15 page 291 for examples of programme sponsorship).
- Bans tobacco advertising and prescription medicine advertising.
- Sets guidelines for children's advertising.

European countries have no central set of detailed controls over marketing communications. Table 12.2 on page 238, Chapter 12 demonstrates the extreme differences that exist in Euopean countries over what is accepted as a form of sales promotion. Table 8.1 shows the lack of European agreement across many products and services. Some

Table 8.1 Television Advertising Restrictions

	ALCOHOL	Children & Adv.	Cleaning products	Cosmetics/ personal hygiene	Food	Non-prescription /medical products	Political advertising	Religious advertising	Tobacco
Austria	B/RV	RV	P	R	R	RV	R	B	BV
Belgium	R	RV	R	RV	R/RV	B	B	B	B
Denmark	R	R	P	P	R	B	B	B	BV
Finland	R/B	RV	R	R	R	R	B	R	B
France	B	R	R	R	R	R/RV	R/RV	R	B
Germany	RV	RV	P	P	R	RV	P	P	B
Greece	R	R	RV	RV	P	B	P	R	B
Ireland	B/R	R	P	R	R	R	B	B	B
Italy	B/RV	R	RV	RV	R	R	B/R	B/R	B
Netherlands	RV	RV	RV	RV	R/RV	RV	B	B	B
Norway	B/R	P	P	P	R	B	P	P	B
Portugal	R/B	RV	P	P	P	R	R	R	B
Spain	RV/B	RV	R	R	R	R	P	P	B
Sweden	B/R	B	P	P	RV	B	P	P	B
Switzerland	B	P	R	R	R	R	B	B	B
UK	BV/R	R	R	R	R	R	R/RV	R	B/R

B = Banned by law   BV = Banned voluntarily
R = Restricted by law   RV = Restricted voluntarily

types of advertising are either permitted, restricted or banned by either legislation or voluntary codes (regulations).

Self-Regulation — Codes Of Practice

Various professional bodies draw up their own codes of practice to which their members must adhere. Failure to do so may result in expulsion and sometimes negative publicity, along with a form of blacklisting. A breach of a code can also result in the withdrawal of an advertisement or sales promotion, etc. This can be expensive as the development of any campaign costs money. The risks are arguably higher in television where a 30-second advertisement could cost anywhere up to a million pounds. Most advertisers want to stand out from the crowd. To do this they sometimes have to be daring, bold and controversial. The advertiser's dilemma here is whether to (a) be so controversial that the advertisement teeters on the brink of being pulled off the air or (b) play safe with a less controversial creative treatment.

Although marketing communications must adhere to the laws of the land, ie one cannot misrepresent or blatantly mislead, the voluntary codes are both *cheaper and quicker* to apply should any complaints or claims be made. The codes also offer useful guidance to the advertiser so that most problems are ironed out before an advertisement goes out on air or is published in the press. Essentially, the advertisements should:

• be *legal, decent, honest and truthful*;

- show *responsibility to the customer and society*;
- follow the *basic business principles of fair competition*.

Professional bodies need to be vigilant in order to maintain the credibility of their profession. This is particularly true in advertising where the consumer's scepticism and resistance to advertising is heightened or lowered according to the advertising's credibility. This credibility is founded upon the industry's reputation and determination to maintain standards of legality, decency, honesty and truthfulness.

Press and Print Advertisements and the ASA

Press and print means all non-broadcast media ie press, posters, leaflets, direct mail, video cassette commercials, teletext and cinema advertising. In the UK, the Committee of Advertising Practice *(CAP)* is the custodian of the British code of advertising practice. They provide a rulebook for all advertising except radio, TV and cable (which is covered by the ITC — see below). The code offers guidelines as to what is acceptable and what is not.

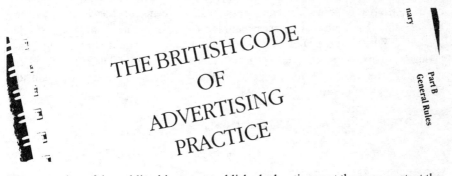

If any member of the public objects to a published advertisement they can contact the Advertising Standards Association *(ASA)* and complain in writing. The ASA is the customer side of the CAP; the CAP deals with the trade or the advertisers directly. Complaints are analysed to determine whether they are worth further investigation. If the complaint is deemed to be reasonable, and the association consequently uphold the complaint, then the advertiser is asked to *withdraw* it immediately. The ASA is not a legal body and therefore has non-statutory powers. Some advertisers may choose to ignore a request to withdraw an advertisement. The ASA will then issue a *media warning* to all CAP member organisations (including media owners). This effectively blacklists the advertisement. The result is that the advertiser will find very few media owners prepared to sell them any advertising space. The media may implement their terms and conditions of business, which require adherence to the codes. Agencies who persistently breach the codes *jeopardise their membership* of professional and trade organisations. This means trading privileges and financial incentives may be forfeited, and potential new clients may exclude agencies who are not members of recognised professional bodies. If all else fails, the association can invoke the final legal backstop of the *Control of Misleading Advertisements Regulations 1988*. Although rarely needed, these empower the Director General of Fair Trading to obtain an injunction against the advertiser.

It is worth checking with CAP before printing a mail shot or publishing an advertisement. Having said that, many campaigns are published without prior CAP approval and run the relevant risk.

It has been suggested that some of the more controversial short campaigns seek to gain free editorial coverage by being banned. There are, of course, risks associated with this kind of exposure (see 'Lack of Control', page 279, Chapter 14).

Television Advertisements and the ITC

TV advertisements, on the other hand, must gain approval before broadcasting. The *ITC* (Independent Television Commission) and the Radio Authority publish free guidelines (the ITC Code of Advertising Standards and Practice – see below). The ITC and the Radio Authority replaced the IBA (Independent Broadcasting Authority) in 1991.

Initial scripts are approved by the *ITVA* (Independent Television Association) and a *clearance certificate* is issued. However, this does not guarantee that the finished production will also be acceptable as the film's treatment is sometimes difficult to envisage from a script or storyboard, and so it also screened for final approval before broadcasting. Even after an advertisement is cleared for broadcasting, it can still be 'pulled' off the air if the ITC requests it. Their attention would be aroused by complaints from the public. If, after they have examined the material and considered the complaint, they feel that the complaint should be upheld, they can then pull the advertisement off the air.

The ITC code of advertising Standards and practice

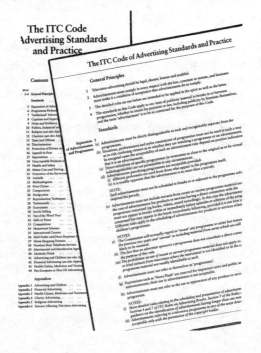

The ITC code of advertising Standards and practice colour leaflet

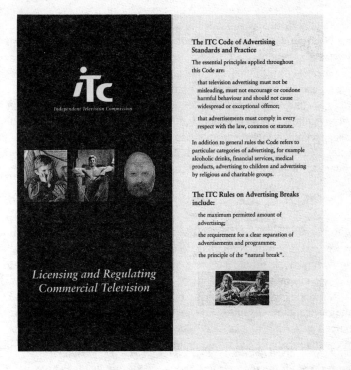

In addition to advertising, other marketing services have their own regulations and codes. For example the *Code of Sales Promotion Practice* is also published by the CAP and basically provides guidelines for sales promotion activities. The *IPA* (Institute of Practitioners in Advertising, *IPR* (Institute of Public Relations), *PRCA* (Public Relations Consultants Association), *ISP* (Institute of Sales Promotion) and other professional bodies all have their codes of practice to which their members must adhere. Any breach of the code can result in a member being warned or ultimately struck off the institute or association 's member list. This may have some short-term negative publicity plus, in the medium to longer term, exclusion member from some pitch lists. Some clients refer to the appropriate institution/association when choosing a new agent/consultant.

Direct marketing

From January 1992, the ASA/CAP acquired the responsibility for regulating the direct marketing industry. Essentially this is to ensure that consumers receive as much or as little direct mail as they want. The CAP's new rules require direct marketing campaigns to:

1) Give consumers a choice before transferring their names to other companies.
2) Remove names from lists on request.
3) Correct personal details immediately upon notification.

The direct marketing industry is currently under scrutiny from the EC. The *European Advertising Standards Alliance* (EASA) consists of the organisations in Europe that already operate self-regulatory codes of advertising practice. It hopes to co-ordinate the disparate activities and act as focal point for pan- European consultation. Whether voluntary codes of practice will be preferred to centralised legislation remains to be seen.

This will affect *all direct marketing* activities including *telemarketing*. At present there is little EC harmony in either regulations or legislation, eg cold calling is banned in Germany. Equally, sales promotions, incentives, premiums and free gifts are generally unacceptable in Germany and also cause problems in France (see page 238, Chapter 12). The EASA may provide a platform for promoting self-regulation and harmony across Europe.

Macro-political effects on business and communications

We now move from national and international regulations and legislation, which affect marketing communications, to international political negotiations, which affect the world economy. It should be remembered that the larger international trading companies need to monitor the results of worldwide political agreements. Plans are prepared to meet a range of scenarios built around possible results from, say, the current major economic disputes. *Fortune* magazine describes two scenarios used by an oil company.

Scenario 1: Sustainable world and global mercantilism
This assumes that all the major international economic disputes are solved. There is European unity. US and Japan agree trading terms (and avoid a trade war).

Free trade prevails across the globe and stable growth is maintained. As a consequence, environmental issues receive more attention. The implications for Shell: new emission restrictions and a reconfiguration of the energy industry in which less oil and more natural gas is used.

Scenario 2: Global mercantilism
This assumes a gloomier world where regional conflicts basically destabilise the world.

Trade wars and recessions rage. Trading blocs form and consensus on environmental issues is never achieved. This scenario implies less regulation, a piecemeal approach to environmental issues and much more oil consumption.

Worldwide political agreements not only affect product portfolios (the range and types of products or services), they also affect the social agenda which determines what are considered to be the most important social issues in the minds of customers. This, in turn, affects the organisation's social responsibility policies and subsequent communications programmes (see 'Marketing and public relations', page 273, and 'The PR Mix', page 274, Chapter 14). The social factors examined on page 155 also consider how the agenda can change over relatively short periods of time. First, we will consider how the national economy affects organisations and their marketing communications.

ECONOMICS

Effects on markets and communications

Industrial and consumer markets are directly and indirectly affected by the state of the economy. Exchange rates, interest rates, unemployment, levels of disposable income, etc, all affect how much money is around, how much will be spent and, in a sense, the size of many markets or industries.

During a recession almost everyone cuts back on spending. Consumers spend less. Companies spend less. Many organisations cut back on all types of spending, including marketing (although there are exceptions like Procter and Gamble, who according to Bill MacNamara, ex-ASDA divisional marketing director 'automatically raise their marketing expenditure in a recession.' A classic fall in derived-demand emerges: as primary consumer demand falls, the secondary demand (for the commercial products and services required to make and market the consumer products) also falls. This reduces growth in the marketing service industries like advertising and design. It becomes a buyer's market as prices tumble and better deals are demanded by clients. Several agencies and clients go into liquidation. There is therefore an increased need to check the financial stability of any agency/partner/supplier/customer.

Meanwhile, advertisers have to address the difficulty of encouraging people to buy amidst a serious recession. Appendix 1 explains how some American advertisers fight the enemy of recession by using its own images. During a recession many buyers search for better deals, which include price cuts, extended terms, value-for-money sales promotions, etc. These promotions may not enhance the brand loyalty (see Figure 12.4 on page 236, Chapter 12). The scars of an economic recession may be permanently expressed in terms of buying patterns, attitudes, values and, ultimately the advertising imagery which reflects the changing norms, roles and values of a culture.

Recession-induced psychological change

Even a phenomenally strong economic recovery may not bring back the consumer spending patterns of the 1980s. Values, attitudes and lifestyles may combine to create lower levels of consumption, new buying processes and an overall pattern of trading down (away from premium price brands). The worldwide recession brought job cuts and quality of life worries out of the headlines and into millions of homes. Some feel that consumer markets have changed because of a recession-induced psychological change which moved people away from the self-indulgence and excess of the 'me, mine, more' mentality of the 1980s to the 'learning to live with limitations' of the 1990s.

This could affect buying behaviour and the supporting advertising messages. For example a move away from images of personal achievement to images about personal relationships, or even a move away from advertising that is built around the user imagery (where 'the user is the hero') to where 'the product is hero'. This suggests that advertising will have to provide more hard information as consumers buy more carefully, seeking out the best deal, and display a price consciousness which rejects premium price brands for better-value products that provide relevant benefits and excellent performance.

A 1992 survey by the Grey International Advertising agency appears to support this theory, at least in America, where many of the trends are often transfered across the Atlantic within a few years. Ninety-one per cent said that they themselves, or a relative, or a friend had been affected by the recession (this is further supported by a *Time*/CNN poll which found that 23 per cent of Americans were out of work because of the recession at some point during 1991). Other key findings in Grey's survey showed:

- Eighty-five per cent have cut back on spending
- Eighty-two per cent say they are learning to make do with less
- Ninety per cent say the simple joys in life are what matter most
- Eighty-seven per cent are more aware of the importance of the family
- Eighty-one per cent are yearning for more lasting values

This compares with a 1987 survey by Grey which found that Americans in every social and economic stratum were involved in an all-out quest for ego-gratification demonstrated by the top four goals (1) Making life the best it can be (2) Enjoying what I do (3) Being able to afford the things I enjoy (4) Staying physically fit.

SOCIAL CHANGE

Norms, roles and values change. Fathers change nappies and cook dinners. Many women earn more than their male partners. Roles are becoming less clearly defined. It is no longer abnormal to have two working parents. Attitudes towards issues change. Once environmentalists were considered to be hippies, communists, anarchists or outcasts because of their lack of conformity with other people's beliefs, values and attitudes. Today, most political parties and major corporations recognise the importance of environmental groups.

A new interest in ethics

Social consciousness among buyers is increasing. Consumers want to know more about products and their producers. Do they damage the environment? What do they do in the community? Do they donate political funds? Do the organisations disclose information, and so on?

A relatively new UK publication called *Shopping for a Better World* (Adams et al, 1991) ranks household brands according to nine different ethical criteria (see Figure 8.2). Many buyers are becoming aware that the supermarket is the economic ballot box of the future.

And investors also are becoming increasingly interested in the corporate citizenship of organisations which they might consider funding.

Banks are becoming weary of lending funds to higher-risk, unenvironmental companies. Insurance premiums will also reflect the higher risk of non-green companies. The corporate responsibility record is now a criterion in joint ventures. For example, who wants to invest time and money in an organisation which has a poor environmen-

SOFT DRINKS AND MIXERS											Alert!
7 UP	PEP	x	?	?	xx	✔	x	x	y	n	
Apeel	PHM	x	?	?	xx	?	xx	x	y	n	AT
Aqua Libra	GRM	✔✔	✔	x	✔	✔	✔✔	x	Y	n	Atg
Britvic 55 *	BAS	x	?	x	xx	✔	✔✔	x	y	n	AtG
Britvic Fruit Juices *	BAS	x	?	x	xx	✔	✔✔	x	y	n	AtG
Britvic Quencher *	BAS	x	?	x	xx	✔	✔✔	x	y	n	AtG
C-Drinks	NES	✔	?	x	✔✔	?	x	x	Y	n	a
C-Vit	SKB	x	?	?	✔	?	✔	?	Y	C	
Canada Dry *	BAS	x	?	x	xx	✔	✔✔	x	y	n	AtG
Capri-Sun	RHM	x	?	?	x	?	?	x	n	C	
Cherry 7 UP	PEP	x	?	?	xx	✔	x	x	y	n	
Cherry Coca-Cola	COC	✔	x	✔	✔✔	✔	x	x	y	n	
Cherry Pepsi	PEP	x	?	?	xx	✔	x	x	y	n	
Citrus Spring *	BAS	x	?	x	xx	✔	✔✔	x	y	n	AtG
Coca-Cola	COC	✔	x	✔	✔✔	✔	x	x	y	n	
Corona *	BAS	x	?	x	xx	✔	✔✔	x	y	n	AtG
Cottee's	CAD	✔✔	✔	✔	x	✔	✔✔	x	Y	n	
Crush	CAD	✔✔	✔	✔	x	✔	✔✔	x	Y	n	
De L'Ora	RHM	x	?	?	x	?	?	x	n	C	
Dexters	GRM	✔✔	✔	x	✔	✔	✔✔	x	Y	n	Atg
Diet 7 UP	PEP	x	?	?	xx	✔	x	x	y	n	
Diet Coca-Cola	COC	✔	x	✔	✔✔	✔	x	x	y	n	
Diet Fanta	COC	✔	x	✔	✔✔	✔	x	x	y	n	
Diet Lilt	COC	✔	x	✔	✔✔	✔	x	x	y	n	
Diet Pepsi	PEP	x	?	?	xx	✔	x	x	y	n	
Diet Sprite	COC	✔	x	✔	✔✔	✔	x	x	y	n	
ED Smith	CAD	✔✔	✔	✔	x	✔	✔✔	x	Y	n	

											Alert!
Fanta	COC	✔	x	✔	✔✔	✔	x	x	y	n	
Ferguzade	SKB	x	?	?	✔	?	✔	?	Y	C	
Five Alive	COC	✔	x	✔	✔✔	✔	x	x	y	n	
Five Alive Citrus	COC	✔	x	✔	✔✔	✔	x	x	y	n	
Five Alive Lite	COC	✔	x	✔	✔✔	✔	x	x	y	n	
Five Alive Tropical	COC	✔	x	✔	✔✔	✔	x	x	y	n	
Five Alive Tropical	COC	✔	x	✔	✔✔	✔	x	x	y	n	
Gini	CAD	✔✔	✔	✔	x	✔	✔✔	x	Y	n	
Groosome Joosome	RHM	x	?	?	x	?	?	x	n	C	
Hires	CAD	✔✔	✔	✔	x	✔	✔✔	x	Y	n	
Holland House	CAD	✔✔	✔	✔	x	✔	✔✔	x	Y	n	
Hycal	SKB	x	?	?	✔	?	✔	?	Y	C	
Idris *	BAS	x	?	x	xx	✔	✔✔	x	y	n	AtG
Just Juice	RHM	x	?	?	x	?	?	x	n	C	
Kia-Ora	CAD	✔✔	✔	✔	x	✔	✔✔	x	Y	n	
Libby	NES	✔	?	x	✔✔	?	x	x	Y	n	a
Lilt	COC	✔	x	✔	✔✔	✔	x	x	y	n	
Lucozade	SKB	x	?	?	✔	?	✔	?	Y	C	
Moonshine	NES	✔	?	x	✔✔	?	x	x	Y	n	a
Mott's	CAD	✔✔	✔	✔	x	✔	✔✔	x	Y	n	
Mr & Mrs 'T'	CAD	✔✔	✔	✔	x	✔	✔✔	x	Y	n	
Napolina	CPC	x	?	?	xx	?	✔✔	x	n	n	
Oasis	CAD	✔✔	✔	✔	x	✔	✔✔	x	Y	n	
Old Colony	CAD	✔✔	✔	✔	x	✔	✔✔	x	Y	n	
One-Cal	RHM	x	?	?	x	?	?	x	n	C	
PLJ	SKB	x	?	?	✔	?	✔	?	Y	C	
Pepsi Cola	PEP	x	?	?	xx	✔	x	x	y	n	
Quosh *	BAS	x	?	x	xx	✔	✔✔	x	y	n	AtG

Figure 8.2 An example of brands coming under increasing ethical scrutiny

tal record? To put it another way, who wants to inherit a *green time bomb*? Similarly, eastern European companies look towards the community record of potential western partners.

There is a fascinating publication for investors and chairmen called *Changing Corporate Values*. Basically it gives a 'three or four-page profile of major organisations' corporate ethical record, as shown in Figure 8.3.

Some estimates suggest that a 'green screen', or false green claims by corporations, will only last approximately six months since probing pressure groups, investigative journalists, scrutinising financial analysts and information-hungry customers will eventually reveal a much bigger problem than that which was originally hidden. This implies that the marketing people have a vested interest in ensuring that an organisation operates in a socially responsible manner. Corporate attitudes towards altruism and ethics are changing, as are personal religious beliefs. For example one advertising agency forecasts that by the end of this century Britain will have more practising Muslims than Christians.

Finally, one extraneous factor which affects the business environment is the environment itself. If the world continues to heat up, northern European attitudes, emotions and feelings about different stimuli (particularly colour) may change. This would affect almost all forms of marketing communications, and possibly even radio.

As mentioned previously, the state of the economy can influence the social agenda.

GUINNESS PLC

* ✓ ✗ * Y Y ? A

...ess name is synonymous with the company's brewing oper-r dominate the group's affairs. incipal activities are the distill-ting of Scotch whisky, gin and followed by the brewing and beer. Spirits now account for Guinness turnover.

...thur Guinness used £100 left to rchbishop of Castel to buy a small St James's Gate in Dublin, on the ne River Liffey, negotiating a nine-year lease at £45 a year. His extra ..er was the beer that swept Ireland ...ne known as Guinness stout. ...oubled' £2.7bn takeover in 1986 the y acquired the Distillers Company; it ns Arthur Bell Distillers. In 1988 Guin-bstantially reinforced its commercial vith LVMH (Louis Vuitton Moet Hen-a French luxury goods company whose famous brands include Christian Dior ...ivenchy perfumes, Dom Pérignon, Moët handon and Veuve Clicquot champag-; LVMH now owns 24% of Guinness, and rness has a 24% beneficial interest in MH. Other interests include the Glenea-...s Hotel, the French gourmet chain Hediard, e best selling *Guinness Book of Records* and hampneys health resorts. Following the investigation in the United ...tates of convicted stock manipulator Ivan ...—v funder Ernest Saunders, Guinness had ...m of which has

of Distillers (now incorporated in Guinness as United Distillers). They found that during the Argyll-Guinness duel for Distillers, top people in Guinness (with the help of friends in New York, Zürich, Luxembourg and London) had manipulated the stock market to drive up the price of Guinness shares. It was an illegal ma-noeuvre that worked because the Guinness offer for Distillers was partly in stock, and the higher price made its bid more valuable than Argyll's. On 14 January 1987 the Guinness board of directors fired Saunders and asked for the resignation of his associates on the board. On 7 May Saunders was indicted on charges of trying to pervert the course of jus-tice.' The Guinness/Distillers takeover scan-dal was the subject of a major criminal trial, the chief defendant being the former Guinness chairman and chief executive Ernest Saunders.'At the heart of the case were indem-nities to cover losses sustained by those who bought Guinness shares to support the share price and success fees paid to supporters who included Anthony Parnes (a city stockbroker), the financier Sir Jack Lyons, Gerald Ronson (the Chairman of Heron International, one of Britain's biggest private companies), and Tho-mas Ward (ex-legal director of Guinness). The payments totalled £23m.' The total cost of Guinness's £2.7bn takeover of Distillers was over £182m.' In August 1990 Ernest Saunders, Gerald Ronson, Anthony Parnes and Sir Jack Lyons were convicted for their part in the illegal deal.

In 1989 Guinness was ordered by the Take-over Panel to pay out '£85m in compensation over former Distillers' shareholders as a result of ...ormer Distillers' tactics used to clinch the

information, they say, they would need to refer also to the well-documented evidence relating to the reduced incidence of coronary heart disease and lowered blood pressure.' The *1989 Annual Report* contains the following statement on moderate drinking: 'The encour-agement of moderate drinking follows logi-cally from our focus on value. We have worked to promote moderation which, of course, is entirely compatible with a healthy lifestyle.' The company offers counselling for employees with problems with alcohol abuse. 'Guinness has been instrumental in the found-ing of The Portman Group, a pan-industry organisation devoted to an objective explora-tion of alcohol issues.'

Guinness owns three subsidiaries in South Africa, but these are 'brand-own-

While the c...... Africa, none of its beer there (though they are sold widely ... African countries).

Guinness's partial disclosure in... cated a variable set of policies on so... issues, and a company culture un... going some considerable change in light of its involvement in a n... criminal trial. Modest as the pany's initiatives on alcohol abu... they are progressive for the br... industry as a whole.

HANSON PLC

SECRET ♀ ~ * 🌳 🐦 ? C/F

✗ * * ✓ ✗✗ ✓ Y Y

Hanson is an industrial management com-pany whose subsidiaries are involved principally in consumer, industrial, and build-ing products operations in the UK and USA. The company was formed in 1950 under the name of Wiles Group Limited. The present chairman, Lord Hanson, joined the board in 1964 following the company's acquisition of Tillotson. In the company's *1987/88 Annual Report* he wrote: 'Over the last 25 years our principal objective has remained unchanged since I stated in my first report: "to expand profitability while achieving careful expan-sion through acquisitions". Improving shareholder value has always been our first consideration.'

In recent years the Hanson story has indeed

been one of expansion thr... tions. In the 1980s major ... included Ever Ready, Ur... the London Brick Comp... Group. It made history ... Consolidated Gold Fiel... – the largest takeover ... UK. Hanson's consum... comprise Imperial Tol... bacco – major bran... Embassy, Lambert ... British Ever Ready ((natural health pro... sumer companies ... houseware and re... has substantial i... (electronic typew...

Figure 8.3 An example of corporations being subjected to ethical scrutiny

The changing public agenda illustrated in Figure 8.4 shows the environmental issue losing its position of importance in the space of just three years.

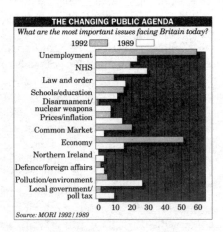

(This chart first appeared in *PR Week*, 15 October 1992.)

Figure 8.4 The changing public agenda

Demographics

The statistical analysis (or division) of a population/audience by age, sex and social status helps marketers to segment and target markets (see the socio-economic data on pages 48–50, Chapter 2). This can be combined with location/geography and hence the term *geodemographics*. In addition, there are demographic cycles, trends and movements which can help an organisation to learn about its market many years in advance. According to Matthew Gwyer (1992), we know that by *2030 the UK population will start to shrink* and deaths will exceed births. The period total fertility rate (PTFR) is now at 1.8 children per family, which is below the replacement level of 2.1. By 2030 the 80-year-old plus market will expand to 3.4 million (three and a half times more than in 1961).

The demographic shift during the 1980s *pulled the market away from Guinness* as a disproportionately large number of younger drinkers (20-year-olds) emerged after the 1960s baby boom. Guinness was positioned as an older, unfashionable drink. To chase the moving market, Guinness and the now extinct but then brilliant advertising agency, Allen Brady and Marsh, repositioned the product as a younger and more fashionable drink. The early 1990s saw the demographic bulge move on to create a disproportionately large number of 30-year-olds. Guinness are chasing this swell by using a maturing blond-haired man to help to position the drink appropriately. During the early 2010s Guinness may reposition itself as a 50-year-olds' drink. The *beer market will shrink* since volume customers are the younger session-drinkers who pour as many as a dozen pints down their necks on Friday and Saturday nights. Or perhaps the *ozone* layer will crumble and the weather will warm up, followed by increased liquid consumption, including beers. Or will there be *another baby boom* of the 1990s (as less women use the pill because of cancer scares) creating a vast 18–25-year-old market by the early 2010s? Or then again, perhaps an even bigger *health trend* will curtail all regular drinking behaviour. Or will the *EC ban* all alcohol advertising? Maybe real estate companies will force *pubs to increase their prices* and thereby push drinkers back into their homes to consume canned draught beers? Or perhaps the *decline of western civilisation* will follow the decline of the Roman and Greek empires with over-indulgence and decadent lifestyles, including heavy drinking, and thereby create a short- or medium- term boost in the beer market?

1995 will see more UK consumers over the age of 45 than under the age of 30. What are the implications of an *ageing UK population*? Bigger typefaces and print to help older eyes read commercial messages? Many products and services repositioned as the more mature person's choice'? There will still be youth markets but they may not be as attractive since they will shrink in size and competition may become quite ferocious. Then again, *AIDS* may wipe out a whole middle generation leaving behind a polarised society of very old and very young.

The falling marriage rate, the increasing divorce and the increasing number of births outside marriage contribute towards the sad term, '*disintegrating family*'. In addition, the single-person household is expected to increase by more than one million between 1990 and 2000. The traditional happy-family advertising formula is becoming obsolete. A few years ago Oxo showed the husband cooking the family lunch while the wife was out at play. More recently, Persil have cast comedian Robbie

Coltrane as a friendly adult grandchild who helps his grandmother to wash up by using a top brand of liquid. The traditional housewife/woman shopper is no longer the sole key decision-maker. Just take a look around a local supermarket on a Saturday morning, where you will see male shoppers buying Fairy liquid, Ariel and Palmolive soap.

Decision-making units (DMUs) are changing (see 'Target Markets' page 40, Chapter 2). Over 60 per cent of mothers in the UK work either part-time or full-time, compared with 10 per cent in the 1930s and 20 per cent in the 1950s. Incidentally, it has been suggested that *guilt-ridden working mothers* may ease their discomfort by buying the 'best' brands for their families instead of buying the less expensive store's own-brand. A recent Gallup poll suggested that 90 per cent of working mothers suffer some psychological discomfort in combining the roles of mother and worker.

The effects of the changing structure of DMUs apply to a broad sweep of products and services and not just *FMCGs*. Insurance, health care and double glazing target both partners instead of just the head of the household or the main income earner. Most telesale phonecalls only fix an appointment to visit when *both* partners/spouses are available for a sales presentation.

Futurologist Alvin Toffler forecast many years ago that technology could facilitate vast demographic shifts as populations migrated from the cities to work in their own electronic cottages (complete with phone, fax and computer). Although there has been some movement, the vast demographic shift has not yet occurred. Technology, meanwhile, has relentlessly marched on into new realms of marketing.

TECHNOLOGY

Technology keeps changing the face of marketing communications. You only have to think of taped customer care announcements, automatic bank dispensing tills, robot-manned compact disc stores, and outbound and inbound telesale voice machines to see how this is true. *Home computer shopping* in the US allows customers to move their home computer's mouse to scan aisles, pick up products, examine them in three dimensions and put them into an electronic basket. Payment is by credit card and delivery comes the next day. Bar codes and information-collecting technology have increased in diversity and accuracy. Interactive TV programmes and *interactive TV advertisements* are on the way. *Satellites* provide new programmes and new conference facilites for *sales meetings*, *press conferences*, *training programmes* and much more. Here is what the director-general of the European Association of Advertising Agencies has said about satellites.

> What satellite broadcasting is going to mean for us, apart from reach, is greater emphasis on non-verbal communication: the big visual idea, and the use of visual symbols. Where the message transcends national frontiers, it will often transcend national languages. Remember, we have nine different national languages in the EC. This is going to put a premium on the visual and musical content of commercials, with less emphasis on verbal communication...
>
> (Source: Rijkens (1992))

Computers can even do a lot of a manager's *reading* by scanning journals, newspapers and trade magazines for relevant material and printing out headlines, summary abstracts or complete articles (see on-line research databases in the Marketing Intelligence and Information System section, Chapter 5, page 104). Database marketing is where a real technological opportunity lies for all types of organisation both large and small (see Chapter 13).

Print technology allows magazines to run liquid-filled ads, heat sensitive ads, double-image ads (which create the effect of movement), 3-D ads, scratch 'n' sniff ads (in fact 3M used scratch 'n' sniff in their 1992 annual report), perfumed ads and, of course, singing and speaking press ads. According to *Marketing Breakthroughs* in October 1992, a Canadian publisher was reported to have been worried about the declining presence of its daily newspaper on the breakfast table. 'So it had its logo printed on millions of fresh eggs'.

Novelty marketing gadgets have been employed for many years now, ranging from robots to *light-sensitive supermarket displays* which react when triggered by a passing customer. Shopping carts can carry video screens promoting 'today's special offer' as the customer passes various sensors discretely placed around the store.

Packaging technology has provided self-heating tins and special Coca Cola cans for use in American spaceships. In fact technology permeates every aspect of marketing and marketing communications, even selling. This is only the start.

10,000% Increase in Technology

All the technological knowledge we work with today (1992) will represent only 1 per cent of the knowledge that will be available in 2050.

(Source: Marvin J Cetron and Owen Davies (1992))

Perhaps we might yet see Philips projecting their logo, through a laser beam, on to the moon?

APPENDIX 1

Fighting the enemy of recession with its own images

Moods, aspirations and tones of communications also vary according to the state of the economy. This is how some US advertisers are reported to advertise during a recession.

During a recession everything out there repeatedly tells the consumer 'don't spend, don't spend'. People are irritated if tempted to buy things they think they cannot (or should not) afford. So some US recession-related campaigns use the recession as part of the 'reason to buy'. The advertisements give the consumer 'permission' to buy. This breaks down into three basic arguments:

1) *You need this* — advertisements like those for Armani go back to basics with copy

which reads: 'Clothing. Basics. Period.' Professor Ralph Whitehead of the University of Massachusetts says that they are 'back to basics in content but very slick and stylish in form; in substance they recall the older practice of citing product features rather than lifestyles, but they achieve this with contemporary cinematic style.' The Gap clothing store has attempted the 'basic but best' with the 'no frills dressing, essentials not whims' approach.

2) *You deserve this* — arguably a more feminine and soothing approach to help to soothe the bruising from the recession. Advertisements and images articulate how many of the recession-bruised consumers really feel inside. They conjure up feelings of sympathy and understanding followed by a suggestion that consumers should treat themselves. The permission can be reinforced by rationalising with suggestions like 'if you don't give yourself a break or a treat then you are likely to under-perform anyway.'

3) *It is your responsibility to buy this* — the outgoing US president, George Bush promoted spending during his last Christmas in office. Ellen Goodman of the Boston Globe reported: 'There is the implication that anyone who truly loves their country and wants it to recover from this recession will contribute this season to the hundreds of needy malls. We're all supposed to be buying not just for Aunt Evelyn but for Uncle Sam.'

APPENDIX 2

Sample of complaints against advertisements upheld by the ASA

ASSET WINDOWS LTD
Unit 16
Clifton Industrial Estate
Cherry Hinton Road
Cambridge CB1 4WT

Complaint: Objection to a drop leaflet for windows, featuring the written testimonial "My wife and I have never seen such dedicated craftsmanship. I am pleased that we chose Asset Windows." The complainants, whose names were printed below the testimonial, maintained that although their windows were installed by Asset, they did not make the statement, nor did they give their permission for the use of any such testimonial. (B.10.2/3/7; B.17.1.1)

Conclusion: Complaint upheld. The advertisers submitted a copy of the completion document relating to this particular job. It included a questionnaire and carried, in handwriting, the comments reproduced in the advertisement. On being sent a copy of this document by the Authority, the complainants said they had not seen it before, denied making the comments it contained and disowned the handwriting. The Authority was concerned that the advertisers had presented what appeared to be fictitious testimonial, and noted that this would have been apparent if the complainants had been asked to sign the statement and give express prior permission for its use in advertisements (both requirements of the Code). The advertisers were requested to comply with the Code in future testimonial claims.

Complaint from: March,
Cambridgeshire

Barclays Bank Plc
PO Box 120
Longwood Close
Westwood Business Park
Coventry CV4 8JN

Agency:
Dean Street Marketing

Leaflet

Complaint from:
West Midlands

Complaint: Objection to a leaflet to enter Barclays Bank Christmas Competition which included, under "Competition Rules", the condition that "The Bank may amend these rules or withdraw the competition altogether at any time without notice". The complainant objected that this condition was in breach of the Code. (BCSPP 4.2; 6.2.2)

Conclusion: Complaint upheld.
The advertisers stated that the clause had been introduced in order to allow withdrawal in the event of unforeseen circumstances that might be detrimental to either the advertisers or the customer – eg. new legislation deeming the competition illegal, or where a promotion was considered politically insensitive. While the Authority concluded that such a clause would be acceptable if it were made clear that it related to circumstances outside the control of the advertisers, they were requested to amend future advertising material accordingly.

British Airways
Heathrow Airport
Hounslow
Middlesex TW6 2JA
(Previous complaints upheld
during last 12 months: 1)

Agency:
Saatchi & Saatchi Advertising Ltd

Press
Complaints from:
Middlesex, Warwickshire

Complaint: Objections to a national press advertisement headed "British Airways would like to offer you a flying start to 1992. An extra 500 Air Miles." The complainants objected that the advertisement, which gave details of when the offer applied, did not make clear that the offer was limited to one application per person. (BCSPP 4.5; 5.8)

Adjudication: Complaints upheld.
The advertisers acknowledged that there had been an oversight and apologised. The Authority noted that the advertisement would not appear again, but advised the advertisers to take greater care when devising advertising for future promotions and reminded them that sales promotions should be designed and conducted so as not to cause avoidable disappointment.

Benetton Spa
Villa Minelli
31050 Ponzano
Veneto Treviso
Italy
(Previous complaints upheld
during last 12 months: 2)

Press

Complaints from:
London, Leicestershire

Complaint: Objections to an advertisement in The Face magazine captioned "United Colors of Benetton" featuring a man with wasted features apparently suffering from AIDS, prostrate on a bed, being comforted by two other men one of whom had his cheek pressed against the sufferer. The advertisement also featured a distressed woman at the bedside comforting a child. The complainants considered the advertisement extremely offensive and distressing. (B 3.1; B 15.2)

Conclusion: Complaints upheld.
The Authority considered the advertisement to be in breach of the Code. It was noted that, before publication, the Committee of Advertising Practice had advised both the advertisers and media that the advertisement was likely to cause offence and occasion distress. The Face magazine stated that, while they considered that the advertisement may cause offence to some readers, they had published it so that readers would be aware of Benetton's disregard for the sensitivities of the public. The Authority was concerned that the advice of the Committee of Advertising Practice had not been heeded. It deplored the advertisers' apparent willingness to provoke distress with their advertising approach and requested them to withdraw the advertisement.

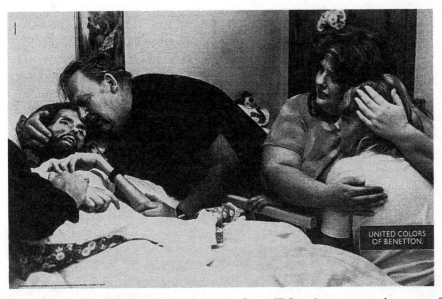

Benetton's controversial tragic death scene of an AIDS patient generated a wave of complaints which the ASA upheld.

APPENDIX 3

Major European satellite channels

PAN EUROPEAN MEDIA

MAJOR SATELLITE CHANNELS

Channel	Main Language	Countries Reached*	Homes Reached (millions)
Superchannel	English	14	23.0
MTV	English	13	20.1
TV5	French	13	20.3
RTL Plus	German	7	14.3
Screensport	Multi	14	23.0
Sat 1	German	3	11.6
Pro 7	German	6	11.8
3 Sat	German	3	11.6
CNN	English	12	9.1
Tele 5	German	2	9.3
Eins Plus	German	1	11.0
BR3	German	1	7.1
WDR3	German	1	6.6
BBC WSTV	English	3	11.6
RTL 4	Dutch	1	5.4
RAI	Italian	4	4.0
Children's	English	7	2.2
Lifestyle	English	9	6.8
TV3	Scandinavian	3	3.4
Kindernet	Dutch	1	3.9

* Maximum of 14 countries (i.e. the countries featured in this book less Italy, Portugal and Turkey).

(Source: Saatchi & Saatchi. Worldwide Advertising, 1992)

Key Points from Chapter 8:

1) Markets constantly move away from products.
2) Monitoring and exploiting the changing PEST factors can create competitive advantage.

Further reading

Adams, R, Carruthers, J and Hamil, S (1991) *Changing Corporate Values*, Kogan Page, London
Adams, R, Carruthers, J and Hamil, S (1991) *Shopping for a Better World*, Kogan Page, London
The Central Statistical Office, *Social Trends* (annual) gives demographic breakdowns and forecasts.

Cetron, M and Davies, O (1992) *The Futurist* (World Future Society), summarised in *Crystal Globe: The Haves and Have Nots of the New World Order*, St Martin's Press, New York

Doyle, P (1992) 'What are excellent companies?' *Journal of Marketing Management* 8, pp 101–116

Grey International Advertising Inc (1992) *The Post-Recession Marketplace: Life in the Slow Lane*

Gwyer, M 'Britain bracing for the age bomb', *Independent on Sunday*, 29 March 1992

Knowlton, C 'Shell gets rich by beating risk', *Fortune*, 26 August 1991, pp 51–53

MacNamara, W 'A New Discipline', *Marketing Week*, 6 December 1991, pp 34–37

Ohmae, K (1983) *The Mind of the Strategist*, Penguin Business Library, London

Ohmae, K (1985) *Triad Power: The Coming Shape of Global Competition*, Free Press, New York

Ohmae, K (1990) *The Borderless World*, Collins, London

Pohl, M 'UK unaware of legal pitfalls in US', *Marketing Week*, 13 September 1991

Rijkens, R (1992) *European Advertising Strategies*, Cassell, London

Further contacts

The Advertising Standards Authority (ASA), 2 Torrington Place, London WC1E 7HW Tel: 0171-580 5555

The Committee of Advertising Practice (as above)

The Department of Trade and Industry (DTI), European Community Information, Ashdown House, 123 Victoria Street, London SW1E 6RB. Tel: 0171-200 1992

The Independent Television Commission (ITC), 33 Foley Street, London W1P 7LB Tel: 0171-255 3000

Independent Television Association (ITVA), 200 Grays Inn Road, London WC1X 8HF. Tel: 0171-843 8000

Institute of Practitioners in Advertising (IPA), 44 Belgrave Square, London SW1X 8QS Tel: 0171-235 7020

Institute of Public Relations (IPR), The Old Trading House, 15 Northburgh Street, London EC1V OPR. Tel: 0171-253 5151

Institute of Sales Promotion (ISP), Arena House, 66-68 Pentonville Road, London N1 9HS. Tel: 0171-837 5340

Public Relations Consultants Association (PRCA), Willow House, Willow Place London SW1P 1JH. Tel: 0171-233 6026

9

International Marketing Communications

GLOBALISATION AND EUROPEANISATION OF MARKETS

Is it really happening?

Today, in Britain, yoghurt, pizza, spaghetti, rice, kebabs, Indian and Chinese foods, American burgers and bangers 'n' mash are popular with the majority of the population. Meanwhile, in China, there are more people learning English than speak it in the USA. Back in 1985 approximately one billion people from different time zones across the world watched the Live Aid concert live. Perhaps the global village is still emerging? Or are cliches like 'the world is getting smaller' nothing more than oversimplified generalisations cast upon a culturally complex world?

Some say human beings have more things that bind them together than separate them. Others say that *market differences* are greater than market similarities. There are, in fact, what Young and Rubican advertising agency call *cross cultural consumer characteristics*. These identify the common ground. The man or woman living in a smart apartment block in London's Knightsbridge has probably got more in common with his or her counterpart living in a smart apartment block off New York's Central Park than he or she has with someone living in some drab south London suburb.

There are indeed some common denominators — some common sets of needs and aspirations — which can be identified, particularly in similarities of lifestyle. The manufacturers of the few true world brands can therefore position their products in a similar manner in the minds of many different cultures. This is the result of careful analysis and planning by expert marketing professionals rather than a trial and error approach to market extension. The significant benefits derived from a world brand and a world communications strategy are reserved currently for a relatively small number of players who recognise the right conditions and apply thorough research and planning to exploit the strengths of the appropriate brands on a worldwide scale. Although Rein Rijkens (1992) has identified a *'trend towards greater inter-nationalisation and centralisation'* it should be remembered that a single communications strategy rarely works for all the players operating in international markets.

Failed International Advertisements

'Yet despite the experience, money, time and attention of large intenational advertisers more attempts to internationalise advertising fail than succeed.'

(Source: Dudley, J (1989))

This chapter examines various strategies, restrictions, options and problems facing organisations operating in the international marketing communications arena. The desire to harness the global opportunity is natural because international markets offer huge rewards. They also present intricate problems. Careful cultural homework needs to be included in the detailed research and planning.

Similar buying behaviour and buying patterns do not necessarily mean a uniform market with uniform needs, uniform communication channels, uniform decision-making processes, uniform decision- making units, or even uniform reasons for buying. The example below demonstrates *'unreal similarities'*. Although the buyers behave similarly by purchasing expensive water, they are in fact from totally dissimilar groups with different aspirations, motivations, lifestyles and attitudes, not to mention disposable income.

Consumers Pay Premium Prices for Prestige Water?

'In a Khartoum slum an impoverished and homeless family are buying water from a street vendor at nearly 20 times the price paid by households in the city with mains connections. Half a world away, a middle class family are loading up their supermarket trolley with bottles of mineral water at maybe a thousand times the price. The irony is that what is regarded as a very tangible measure of deprivation in one country is seen as a mark of status in another.'

(Source: Gill, L (1990))

On the surface there is a market for private water in both countries, but the distribution channels, communication channels, advertising messages and levels of disposable income are poles apart. Other, less extreme cases, like the soup buyers discussed on page 66 of Chapter 4 suggest a common market. An analysis that goes below the surface (or below the sales results) will reveal a range of different motives, aspirations, lifestyles and attitudes to the same product.

Surface information can create a false sense of simplicity. International markets can also suggest surface solutions that ignore the cultural complexities and intricacies of a new market. As Sir John Harvey-Jones points out: 'Operating in this milieu requires much greater sensitivity to national differences than we are accustomed to having. The mere fact that one stays in the same sort of hotel almost anywhere in the world, that one arrives in the same sort of car, that it is now possible to call by telephone or telex directly from almost anywhere in the world, all gives a *superficial feeling of sameness* which is desperately misleading and must never be taken for granted.'

Globalisation, intertwined with cultural idiosyncracies, appears to be emerging in many markets around the world. The marketing maxim *'think global act local'* remains valid. The challenge goes beyond communicating with new international customers and into working with international partners whose idiosyncracies and languages pose many problems. Take nomenclature for a moment. The French normally refer to advertising as 'publicité'' which can cause some confusion, while the Yugoslavian word for advertising is 'propaganda'. Other cultures have difficulty translating 'marketing', 'marketing communications' or 'advertising' as they have not yet created such words. We look at cultural idiosyncracies later.

Before considering how organisations deal strategically with the international opportunity, we will look briefly at the underlying forces driving the globalisation process.

Globalisation — the driving forces

Cheap *travel* combined with higher disposable *incomes* allows travellers to leap across borders, visit other cultures and return home with a little bit of that culture's soul in their own. *Television* itself has brought into the sitting rooms of British homes pictures and images of America's *Miami Vice*, Australia's *Neighbours*, Africa's famines and Tiananmen Square's students. It has also brought stunning scenes from the depths of the oceans, to the balmy beaches of the Caribbean, to the rugged beauty of the bush and on to the once rich and fertile Amazon forest. This global awareness is exploited by the *corporate push* for growth, which has forced many suppliers from saturated local markets to venture into overseas markets. *Improved production, distribution and marketing* techniques have accelerated the movement of products and services from all around the world into local markets. *Political barriers* are falling in China and the eastern bloc and, of course, Europe's own internal political barriers are being dismantled also. The doors of the world's markets are opening.

The key, it seems, is to identify *core benefits* which are common to different cultures along with the major *differences* that also exist.

The strategic impact of globalisation

More and more businesses have to compete in the global arena. For many companies there is *nowhere left to hide*. Those that do not move into the international arena will probably find that the international arena will come to them as new competitors target the once safe local market. There is a need to be pro-active rather than reactive. In 1989 there were an estimated *500,000 European companies* circling the UK, ie analysing the UK market and preparing to enter it (Business Consultants 92, Single Market News, Spring 1989). Those that ignore this small part of the globalisation process may not be around in 50 years' time.

A *defensive strategy* (eg consolidate existing customer base, stay native, and block competition from entering with, for example, a series of flexible distributor promotions) may safeguard the company, at least in the short term. *Offensive strategies* are required if a company is seeking entry into new markets, eg increasing promotional spend in key national markets, supported by a flexible operations system. *Strategic alliances* and joint ventures offer a lower-cost, lower-risk (and possibly lower-margin) method of entry into these new, large and increasingly competitive markets. Global competition has even prompted global co-operation in the marketing communications industries. Advertising and PR independent networks are popping up alongside the multinational agencies who have expanded to meet their clients' global requirements. The issue of centralised advertising and single source agencies are discussed later in the chapter. First we will consider Keegan's product/communication strategies.

Strategies for multinational marketing

Warren Keegan (1984) identified five product/communication strategies for multinational marketing. These were determined by the state of the various international markets. The state of the market was analysed by (a) whether the need (or product function) was the same as other markets; (b) whether the conditions of product use were the same as other markets and (c) whether the customer had the ability to buy the product.

The five strategies are:

1) Same product/same communications

   This applies to markets where the need and use is similar to the home market, eg Coca-Cola with its centrally produced advertisements which incorporate local differences in language.

2) Same product/different communications

   This applies to markets where the need or function is different but the conditions of product use the same, eg bicycles in Europe and bicycles in Africa (recreation and transport respectively).

3) Different product/same communications

   This applies to markets with the same product function or need but with different conditions of product use, eg different petrol formulae but same advertising image — Esso's tiger.

4) Different product/different communications

   This applies to markets with different needs and different product use, eg greeting cards and clothes are held to be 'culture bound' but it should be noted that some clothing companies like Levi's use the same, centrally produced, wordless advertisments internationally.

5) New product(invention)/new communications

This applies, for example, in the case of a hand-powered washing machine.

The question of whether the advertising can be standardised (same communication) is a source of great discussion. Kahler and Kramer (1977) suggest that successful standardisation

> is dependent on the similarity of the motivations for purchase and the similarity of use conditions. For *culture-free products* such as industrial goods and some consumer durables the purchase motivations are similar enough to permit high degrees of standardisation. *Culture-bound products*, in contrast, require adaptation. Customs, habits and tastes vary for these products and customer reaction depends on receiving information consonant with these factors.

James Killough (1978) felt that '*buying proposals*' (the benefits proposed in the advertisement) had a good chance of being accepted across large geographic areas, whereas the 'creative presentation' (creative treatment) did not. Essentially, if the international market had a similar set of needs and interests (to the established market), then a successful adaptation of the advertising message was more likely.

Simon Majaro (*1982*), observed that

> ...the gap between the time a product reaches its decline stage in the most advanced market and the introduction stage in the slowest market is narrowing. If this trend continues the point will be reached where the pattern of the *life cycle* in a domestic market will become identical with the pattern in the foreign markets. This will of course have tremendous impact on the communications strategy of firms operating internationally. It would mean that in time it would become possible for the commmunications objectives of such firms to become more and more homogeneous, thus allowing for a larger measure of standardisation. In other words if the trend continues it should become possible for the same campaign, subject to the manipulation necessitated by linguistic and cultural variations, to be undertaken in all markets. This is indeed the kind of standardisation that Coca-Cola has achieved in world markets. This strategy stems in the main from the fact that the product life cycle profile of Coca-Cola is pretty homogeneous throughout the world.

Rein Rijkens (1992) confirmed the trend towards 'greater internationalisation and centralisation' where basic creative ideas are centrally produced for international use. Kahler and Kramer felt that *transferability of advertising* was dependent on the possibility of a more homogeneous consumer who might, for example, evolve out of the ever-integrating European Community.

> If the European consumer showed a willingness to accept the products of countries within the community and if that consumer was motivated similarly to those in other countries, a common promotional approach would be practical;

but if national identities prevailed, separate campaigns would be more likely to succeed.

Communication strategies

The four basic strategies available for international marketing communications are:

1) Standardised/centralised: advertisements are controlled and produced by the head office (or its agency). This includes message modification, like translations and tailor-made editions for various markets.
2) Decentralised/autocratic: advertisments are controlled and produced by the local subsidiary and its agency specifically for the local market.
3) Central strategy and local production (pattern advertisements): the pattern provides uniformity in direction but not in detail, which allows the advertisements to be locally produced but within the central strategic guidelines (see page 170 for some examples).
4) Central strategy with central *and* local production: centrally produced non-verbal commercials are used to to build a unified identity, while local productions supplement this platform. This is demonstrated by the Levi's example on the next page.

Although 'standardised' generally refers to production it can also include centrally controlled media strategies, planning and buying. The centralised/standardised global campaign problems are discussed later in this chapter. First, the advantages and disadvantages of standardised/centrally controlled advertising are discussed.

Examples of standardised centrally produced advertisements

Coca-Cola's emotion-packed 'General Assembly' advertisement showing the world's children singing happily and harmoniously together was similar to their 1971 'I'd like to teach the world to sing' (McCann's) in that it was packed with emotion and carried a universal theme. The 21 language editions of this advertisement opened with 'I am the future of the world, the future of my nation' and ended with the tag line 'a message of hope from the people who make Coca-Cola'. Each country then edited in their own end shot of the appropriate child's face. Incidentally, the German edition was dubbed slightly out of synchronisation since they associate quality films with dubbed (slightly out of sync) American and British films.

Scottie's nappies save production costs by omitting any dialogue and just using a different voice-over for each country.

Levi's do not bother with voice-overs, dubbings or translations as there is no dialogue — just music by Steve Miller. Their unified logo and brand image does away with the need for different pack shots (close-ups of the pack/label) for each country, so their commercials produced by the London agency BBH, are used throughout Europe.

Standardised central and local productions supported by local productions

As Rein Rijkens (1992) says:

> As far as advertising is concerned, the company will continue its policy of central production of *non-verbal* commercials and cinema films, to be shown throughout Europe and intended to establish a uniform identity for Levi Strauss as a business and for its products. Advertising produced locally by the Levi Strauss subsidiaries will respond to local circumstances and to the local competitive scene. This formula, also applied by other companies marketing a uniform product and using one advertising strategy on an international scale, has proved successful and may well be further developed once the single market comes about.

Examples of pattern advertisements

This is where head office guides the strategic direction of the advertisements but allows local production. These advertisements work to a formula.

In the *Blueband Margarine* advertisements whether in Scandinavia or Africa, the appropriate happy mother can be seen spreading margarine on bread with her happy family sitting around eating it.

Impulse fragrance use a 'boy chases girl' formula across Europe but still allow for cultural idiosyncracies like eye contact, sex appeal and law abiding citizens to be tailored into each country's different production.

Renault's pan-European strategy was to 'endow the car with its own personality'. In France the car was shown with eyes. In Germany the car talked back. In the UK the end line was 'What's yours called?'

Advantages of standardisation

The advantages of centrally controlled advertising, whether centrally produced or pattern advertisements, are as follows:

1) *Consistent image* — a consistent image (and positioning) is presented around the world, allowing consumer awareness and familiarity to prosper.
2) *Consolidated global position* — leaves the brand in a stronger position to protect itself from any attack.
3) *Exploits transnational opportunities* — reduces message confusion arising when (a) advertising in one country spills over to another (eg boundary-bouncing satellite TV), or (b) when migrants and tourists are also in the target customer group.
4) *Saves costs* — economies are enjoyed by not having several different creative teams (and production teams if central production) working on the brand around the world (saves re-inventing the wheel). Possibility of centrally produced (or at least centrally designed) point-of-sale material also.
5) *Releases management time* — and/or reduces the size of the marketing department, which might otherwise be tied up briefing creative teams, approving creative concepts, supervising productions, etc. It may even save time invested with pack-

aging designers, sales promotion agencies, etc if pack designs and promotions are run from central office.

6) *Facilitates transfer of skills* within the company and around the world since, in theory, it is the same job anywhere around the world. It also stimulates cross-fertilisation of company ideas if staff are moving around internationally.

7) *Easier to manage centrally* since there are, in total, a smaller number of decisions and projects to manage:

   a) One creative decision facilitates harmonisation of creative treatments, particularly in areas of media overlap.

   b) Media policies — manage the media overlap between countries to maximise effectiveness and recommend preferred media choice in specific territories.

   c) Budgets — determine local budgets for each product in each market so that the method of allocating resources is consistent worldwide (and therefore easier to control).

   d) Agree activity programme and a specific reporting system to facilitate a simple management system.

Disadvantages of standardisation

The disadvantages of standardisation are as follows:

1) *Stifles creativity* and stops local creative contributions from both company staff and local advertising agency (whether part of an international group or independent agency). The account may be considered by the local agency staff to be dull and boring with the top minds (in creative or media planning) avoiding being involved with it.

2) *Frustrated local management* — although the local office may be accountable for its performance, it does not have control over its own destiny since advertisements are centrally produced or directed. This may lead to a sense of frustration.

3) *Minimal effort from local agency* (if using an international agency with its network of overseas branches). The high global advertising spend may put the brand high on the agency's head office list, but the local agencies may find it is uneconomic to spend too much time and top brains on it.

4) *Lost opportunities* — The opportunity to react quickly to changes in the local market is lost.

5) *Different product life cycles* — different markets may be at different stages of their life cycles, which may make the standardised approach unsuitable. It may, however, still be possible to standardise each stage of the brand's development, eg Boot's launch of Eurofen in the UK and northern Europe.

6) *Wrong idea* — some central advertising concepts may simply not work as well as another locally created original idea. Sales therefore perform below their potential.

7) *Difficult translation* — other ideas just do not lend themselves to translation, eg Pepsi's 'Come Alive' was translated in some countries as 'come from the dead' or 'come out of the grave'.

8) *False savings* — local language adaptation/modification costs may negate the cost savings generated by the centrally controlled creative work.

9) *Market complexities* or the many other local market differences (eg variations in consumer protection regulations and media availability, etc) may make a standardised message extremely difficult if not impossible.

10) *Inexperienced staff* — a lack of suitably qualified expert staff who can manage the co-ordination of transnational standardised campaigns may make the whole centrally controlled advertising concept too risky.

Difficulties with global campaigns

> Kenya's third largest ethnic group, the Luo, have a creation myth which blames women for bringing the curse of work to men.
>
> (Source: Ferraro (1990))

International markets are riddled with hidden cultural differences that make global advertising an intriguing challenge even for the most capable international marketing expert. Here are some of the intricacies which contribute towards the difficulty of global marketing.

1) *Language* obviously requires translating, although there are exceptions to the rule (where the language reflects beneficial cultural aspects of the product, eg Audi's 'Voor Sprung der Technic' strap line). Some expressions simply do not translate. For example, the New York Tourist Board found 'I love New York' difficult to translate into Norwegian since there are only two Norwegian verbs that come close: one translation is 'I enjoy New York', which lacks something, and the other is 'I have a sexual relationship with New York'.

   Other expressions are sometimes imprecisely translated, eg US cigarettes with low asphalt (tar), computer underwear (softwear) and wet sheep (hydraulic rams).

   Humour is rarely globally appreciated, and even basic body gestures are not global. For example, in some parts of India shaking the head from left to right means 'yes'.

   See Majaro's translating tips in Appendix 2.

2) *Literacy*: in many developing countries literacy is low (Dudley, 1989). This limits the amount of explanation in advertising. Even with high literacy, the reading of translated western-style advertisements still causes problems, eg before and after toothpaste advertisements which are not adjusted for Arabs, who read from right to left.

3) *Culture* creates a quagmire of marketing problems: religion, sex, eating, greeting, habits, lifestyles, the role of women, the list is endless. Ferraro (1990) points out nine critical dimensions that contrast the US with the rest of the world's cultures. She says that US culture places a high value on (a) individualism, (b) a precise reckoning of time, (c) a future orientation, (d) work and achievement, (e) control

over the natural environment, (f) youthfulness, (g) informality, (h) competition and (i) relative equality of the sexes.

4) *Original national identity* can be an asset or a liability. For example Dudley (1989) reports that Marathon Oil make a point of stressing its US association in Italy, where American high technology is beneficial, but in Germany Marathon avoids the issue of its American parentage because of the German concern over US control in the German energy industry.

5) *Media availability*: television is sometimes unavailable since (a) developing countries do not have a high penetration of televisions in domestic households, (b) some countries do not have commercial TV stations and (c) others do but they restrict the amount of advertising time. Unilever and BAT make their own medium available in East Africa by running their own mobile cinemas.

6) *Media overlap*: television and radio from one market can spill over into other markets, eg half the Canadian population has access to American television. Kahler (1977) reports that 'Belgium, with no commercial TV can be reached through two Dutch, three French, three German, two English, and one Luxembourg channel.'

7) *Lack of media data*: Great Britain and Ireland have well-structured and categorised media analysis data (audited data). Without reliable media data, the optimum cost and effectiveness of the overall campaign is unlikely to be achieved. Properly structured media markets are easier to work in.

8) *Lack of media credibility*: in some countries unregulated or poorly regulated media in some countries may flaunt the principles of legality, decency, honesty and truth, which in turn may make these media untrustworthy or create audience scepticism about the particular source of information.

9) *Varying media characteristics*: coverage, cost and reproduction qualities can vary from country to country.

10) *Different media usage*: Kahler and Kramer (1977) suggest that the British tend to see TV as a visual medium while TV to the Americans is a visual accompaniment to words.

11) *Different media standards*: a lack of uniformity of standards means different types of both film and artwork may be required for different markets, eg different page sizes may require different artwork, which increases cost.

12) *Different cost structures*: different forms of negotiation and bartering.

13) *Legal restrictions*: whether voluntary codes or actual law, there is as yet no harmonised set of laws or regulations. This presents the advertiser with different problems in different countries. As Majaro (1982) says, 'In Germany, superlatives are forbidden by law. In Sweden, misdemeanours by advertisers may be charged under the criminal law with severe penalties'. See International Regulations and Codes in Chapter 10.

14) *Competition*: different markets have different key players using different strengths. For example, Ford's position of 'safety engineering' worked in many countries but not in Sweden, where, of course, Volvo occupied the position.

15) *Non-global names*: some brand names simply restrict themselves from seizing the global opportunity. Here are a few examples:
Sic (French soft drink)

Pschitt (French soft drink)
Lillet (French soft drink sold in wine bars)
Creap (Japanese coffee creamer)
Irish Mist (in Germany 'mist' means manure)
Bum (Spanish potato crisp)
Bonka (Spanish coffee)
Trim Pecker Trouser (Japanese germ bread)
Gorilla Balls (American protein supplement)
My Dung (restaurant)
Cul toothpaste (pronounced 'cue' in France, which means 'anus')
Scratch (German non-abrasive bath cleaner)
Super-Piss (Finish car lock anti-freeze)

These problems are not insurmountable. For example Curtis shampoo changed its name from 'Everynight' to 'Everyday' for the Swedish market since the Swedes wash their hair in the mornings. Mars changed their well-known 'Marathon Bar' to 'Snickers' to fit in with the worldwide brand name communications strategy. In the attempt to get the packaging, advertising and branding right, global marketers can sometimes forget the fundamental product and whether it is suitable for the market in the first place. Here are some examples of international product failures arising from the basic product itself.

International product failures

Many other campaigns fail because the product or package is not suitable for the market in the first place. Examples include Christmas puddings in Saudi Arabia or toothpaste to combat beatlenut stains — (stained teeth implies wealth in some cultures, as does being overweight in others). Other examples include Kellogg's 'Pop Tarts' in the UK since (unlike the US, too small a percentage of British homes have toasters). General Foods' packaged cake mixes found the Japanese market too small for them (3 per cent of homes had ovens). Coca-Cola had to withdraw their two-litre bottle from Spain because few Spaniards owned refrigerators with large enough compartments. Tennent's Caledonian successful Scottish lager flopped initially in the UK because it came in 24-packs rather than 6-packs. Phillips had to change the size of its coffee makers to fit into the smaller Japanese kitchens and its shavers to fit smaller Japanese hands.

AGENCIES

Types of agency

There are several different types of agency from which an international advertiser can choose:

1) International agencies (multinationals)
2) Independent networks/associations/confederations of agencies
3) Local independent agencies

4) House agencies.

In addition to deciding whether to centralise control over advertising (and effectively standardise it), another dilemma facing the international marketing manager is whether to put all international advertising in the hands of one international agency or hand it out to local independent agencies.

Many local independent agencies have grouped themelves into networks or associations, which means that they have a ready network of contacts with the other network member agencies in the various international regions. A fourth and less common option is for the client to set up its own house agency specifically to handle its own worldwide advertising. The two extreme options will now be considered, ie whether to choose a single international agency or choose several independent local agencies.

Choosing an international agency or independent local agency

This question is linked to whether the communications should be controlled centrally or left to run autonomously. Should the marketing team at headquarters work with just one large multinational advertising agency or should they allow a range of independent agencies to use their unique skills on a local basis? A co-ordinated message can be developed in either situation. For example, centrally produced advertisements (with local modifications/ translations, etc) and pattern advertisements (formula advertising) can work under either system.

Although a centrally produced advertisement is more likely to be handled by a large international agency, there are exceptions where local independent agencies with local media buying and production skills (if pattern advertisements are required) may be preferred. It is possible to choose to work with a range of independent local agencies while adhering to centralised policies. These policies can help the client to manage the whole advertising process by giving specific guidance on creative directions, media strategies, budgets and activity programmes.

As Majaro (1982) says: 'Obviously where the product profile justifies communications standardisation, it may be advisable to use the services of an international agency with offices in all markets'. Majaro continues: 'Hoping to attain the same results by using a host of local agencies with no international expertise is a formula for waste in worldwide marketing.'

Advantages of using an international agency

Compared to local agencies, the international advertising agency claims the following advantages:

1) *Full service* — because of the international agency's size, it can offer a full range of services, including research, planning and translation under one roof (see Chapter 6).
2) *Quality* — some clients feel reassured by the quality feeling of a large international

agency (as opposed to taking a chance with a smaller local agency). Quality and standards should, in theory, be universal.

3) *Broad base of experience* — training and transferring personnel is common among the international agencies.

4) *Presence* — in major adverising centres, the agency branches are located at the centre of most major cities/ marketing territories.

5) *Cost saving* — less duplication in areas of communication, creative and production departments.

6) *Easier to manage* — a single central contact point combined with the points listed in 'Advantages of Standardisation', page 170.

Disadvantages of using an international agency

It is arguably easier for a single international agency to standardise the message. The disadvantages of standardisation (see page 171) therefore apply where central control moves in. In addition, the overseas agency subsidiary may *lack enthusiasm* if the account was won elsewhere. It is as if, by necessity, various branches of the international agency are brought in. The lack of excitement may be compounded, particularly where all the creative work has been handled by head office. In a sense, the branch's job is relegated to media scheduling and planning.

EUROPE

Europe's single market

The single market has the potential to expand beyond the initial European Community and into northern, central and eastern Europe. The EC's single market means freedom of goods, services, people and capital. The new single market is just what it says — one big new market with many *more customers, more competitors, more suppliers, more choice* and *lower costs*. This brings with it a *web of cultural idiosyncracies, language barriers* and a reported sense of *xenophobia* that sometimes translates into a pattern of what the Henley Centre for Forecasting call, '*patriotic purchasing impulses*' (though this does not stand in the way of getting good value for money, which proves that behaviour does not always follow attitudes and aspirations). Net result? Opportunities (and threats) galore.

Is it really single?

In practice, the single market is splintered by different levels of economic development (north and south), culture, attitudes and lifestyles, languages, retail trends, direct mail trends, sources of information, time taken to make a decision and so on. John Mole (1990) says that 'southern Europeans work to live and northern Europeans live to work.' The agency Ogilvy and Mather say that 'The national cultural, social and psychological differences will remain for so many years to come that the reality of a truly *common market may never exist*.' Some of the EC idiosyncracies reported by Philip Kotler (1988) are that the average Frenchman uses twice as much cosmetics

Table 9.1 Main trends in retail and mail order

Main trends in retail and mail order   *Source: O&MD Survey, April 1989*

	Belgium	Denmark	France	Germany	Greece	Ireland	Italy	Netherlands	Portugal	Spain	UK
Retail											
Concentration to large stores	★	★	★	★			★	★			★
Shopping moving out of town			★	★	★				★	★	★
Proliferation of credit cards	★		★	★		★		★			★
Retailers offering financial services			★	★							★
Shopping becomes leisure activity											★
Development of specialist shops											★
Customer revolution underway					★	★			★	★	
Mail Order											
More working women: consumers need convenience	★	★									★
Becoming fashionable/more acceptable			★	★		★	★	★		★	★
Rapid growth			★	★			★			★	★
Mail order companies offering financial services				★							limited
Retailers entering market				★							★
Developing specialogues for niche needs				★				★			test ★
Electronic media in use/experiments			★	test ★				test ★		test ★	test ★

and beauty aids as does his wife. The Germans and the French eat more packaged branded spaghetti than the Italians while Italian children like to eat a bar of chocolate between two slices of bread as a snack.

Some of the differences in lifestyles across Europe are reflected by the different trends in retailing and direct mail shown in Table 9.1.

Different mixes for different EC countries

Different marketing mixes and communication mixes are required for different European countries. *Oral B toothbrushes* found different distribution and promotional routes in different countries. In Holland, dentists derive 40 per cent of their turnover from the sale of products like toothbrushes. In Germany, supermarkets are expected to sell only cheap, utilitarian brushes, while the pharmacies handle the premium brands. In Italy, a premium brush has to carry a fashionable, exclusive label. This makes *any above the line* campaigns difficult. The communications mix was built around direct mail to dentists supported by point-of-sale and product literature, packaging design and sales presenters.

In the *business to business* sector *different communication mixes* are used in different countries. Table 9.2, again from Ogilvy and Mather Direct, shows how buyers from just three countries (France, Germany and the UK) have wide variations in their

Table 9.2 Preferred information sources

Rank	France		Germany		UK	
1	Magazines/ Journals	44%	Magazines/ Journals	65%	Magazines/ Journals	43%
2	Trade fairs/ exhibitions	35%	Trade fairs/ exhibitions	32%	Word-of-mouth	39%
3	Sales visit	25%	Direct mail	29%	Catalogues	17%
4	Catalogues	17%	Sales visit	26%	Direct mail	16%

choice of information sources (communications mixes) when buying Rank Xerox machines. In Germany, magazines dominate while word of mouth or networking (meaning buyers talking to other buyers) is not common. In the UK trade fairs are not important whereas France and Germany rate then highly.

Different purchasing decision processes

Table 9.3 shows the *varying amount of time taken* to make a final decision, again for the purchase of a Rank Xerox machine

Table 9.3 How long does it take to make a final decision to purchase

	France % Co's	Germany % Co's	UK % Co's
One week or less	61	12	36
Up to one month	29	19	9
1-3 months	19	20	19
3+ months	4	10	9
Average no. of weeks	**4.9**	**5.1**	**6.8**

EC effect on client – agency relationships

Advertising agencies may see a *concentration of clients* with bigger (and fewer) marketing communications budgets. It will be interesting to see if client head offices and advertising agency head offices will concentrate geographically. Arguably, this will lead to the *big agencies getting bigger*. Perhaps there will still be room for the small local agency, while the medium-sized agencies may be caught in *no man's land* and become extinct?

This may lead to many more *mergers and acquisitions*, even stock market listings to raise more funds. Whether this will improve the quality of *client service* is debatable. Agency management may have to devote resources to their stockholders and focus on half-yearly profit figures rather than client service. In the short term these priorities can be mutually exclusive, with one being chosen at the expense of the other. Clients obviously do not like being treated as second class citizens. The larger, *less personal*, listed corporation may lose the charm of having direct and immediate access to the agency's chairman. The *inevitable staff changes* may cause key teams to leave. Sometimes the clients go with them. At other times the client fires the new agency because it is now part of a group that holds competing accounts, or the agency *resigns* the account because the new corporation has acquired some competing accounts which create *a conflict of interest*.

CULTURE

The complexities of working within EC cultures

To some overcoming local customers' idiosyncracies may seem relatively easy compared to overcoming local partners' working practices. Whether they are suppliers, distributors, sales agents, advertising agents, strategic partners or just prospect contacts, understanding and overcoming each other's approach to business is essential. Here are some excerpts from John Mole's excellent book on other cultures, *Mind Your Manners* (1990). The first set of extracts consider how various Europeans see each other and the second set consider how other Europeans view the British.

The Europeans

Somewhere in the world there are people who think the Germans are messy and unpunctual. (The chances are they are in Switzerland). There are countries where Greece is regarded as a model of efficiency. There are countries in which French bosses would seem absurdly egalitarian and others where Italian company life would seem oppressively regulated.

They are so inefficient. It is hard to get them to do things. At home I ask for something to be done, politely of course, and it gets done on time without any fuss. Here there are always reasons why it can't be done the way I want it. If it gets done at all. Sometimes they just ignore me. You have to follow up much more here. Set deadlines. They always want me to discuss things instead of doing them. Punctuality? Meetings never start on time. And they always drag on. You invite a customer to lunch at one o'clock and he arrives three quarters of an hour late and thinks nothing of it. It is very frustrating. I get very irritated and I don't know how to handle it.

Was this said by a Danish manager about working with British employees or by a British manager working with Italians? The answer is yes to both parts of the question.

(Mole, J (1990))

Those weird Brits

When asked about planning most British managers immediately think of financial forecasting and budgeting. The annual budget is the backbone of the organisation and the major exception to the otherwise inconsistent approach to systems.

...the British aversion to working within a rational and systematic framework. They take pride in 'muddling through', in 'getting there in the end'. This should not necessarily be construed by outsiders as intellectual idleness. British thinking is interpretive rather than speculative. It prefers tradition and precedent and 'common sense', in other words the interpretation of experience untrammelled by theory or speculation. This usually involves finding the expedient rather than the innovative solution. There is a deep scepticism about great schemes and constructs on a macro or a micro economic level.

(Mole, J (1990))

Western weirdos

Nose blowing

Where most North Americans are repulsed by an Indonesian who blows his nose onto the street, the Indonesian is repulsed by the North American who blows his nose in a handkerchief and then carries it around for the rest of the day in his pocket.

(Ferraro, G (1990))

Ballroom dancing

It is common in such dancing for the front of the bodies to be in constant contract — and they do this in public. In spite of the close physical touching involved in this type of dancing (a form of bodily contact not unlike that assumed in sexual intercourse), our society has defined it as almost totally asexual. Although ballroom dancing can involve high levels of intimacy, it is equally possible that there is no sexual content whatsoever. Many adult men in the United States have danced in this fashion with their mothers, their sisters, the wives of the ministers at church socials without anyone raising an eyebrow. Yet many non-American cultures view this type of dancing as the height of promiscuity and bad taste. It is interesting to note that many of those non-Americans for whom our dancing is a source of embarrassment are the very people we consider to be promiscuous, sex-crazed savages because their women do not cover their breasts.

(Ferraro, G (1990))

Kissing

What's so strange about a kiss? Surely kissing is one of the most natural things in the world, so natural indeed that we might almost ask what are lips for if not for kissing? But this is what we think, and a whole lot of people think differently. To them kissing is not at all natural. It is not something that everybody does, or would like to do. On the contrary, it is a deplorable habit, unnatural, unhygienic, bordering on the nasty and even definitely repulsive.

When we come to look into the matter, we shall find that there is a geographical distribution of kissing; and if some enteprising ethnologist were to prepare a 'map of kissing' it would show a surprisingly large amount of blank space. Most of the so-called primitive races of mankind such as the New Zealanders (Maoris), the Australian Aborigines, the Papuans, Tahitians , and other South Sea islanders, and the Esquimaux of the frozen north, were ignorant of kissing until they were taught the technique by the white men...The Chinese have been wont to consider kissing as vulgar and all too suggestive of cannibalism...the Japanese have no word for it in their vocabulary....

(Pike, R (1967))

Drinking tea

In England, tea breaks can take a half hour per man, as each worker brews his own leaves to his particular taste and sips out of a large, pint-sized vessel with the indulgence of a wine taster...Management suggested to the union that perhaps it could use its good offices to speed up the 'sipping time': to ten minutes a break...The union agreed but failed...Then one Monday morning, the workers rioted. Windows were broken, epithets greeted the executives as they entered the plant and police had to be called to restore order. It seems the company went ahead and installed a tea vending machine — just put a paper cup under the spigot and out pours the standard brew. The pint-sized container was replaced by a five-ounce cup imprinted — as they are in America — with morale building messages imploring greater dedication to the job and loyalty to the company...The plant never did get back into production. Even after the tea brewing machine was hauled out, workers boycotted the company and it finally closed down.

(Stressin, L (1979))

The complexities of working with other cultures

The total global concept suggests that the big global marketing players can accelerate the globalisation process by transcending cultural boundaries and bringing their messages, goods, services and traditions to the markets they choose. Here are some seemingly bizarre cultural norms which suggest that the total global concept will not happen, at least not in the next few generations.

Lailan Young (1985) reports that the Barusho bride in the Himalayas has a tough time on her wedding night as she has to share the bridal bed with her mother-in-law until the marriage is consummated. The Kagába women of North Colombia not only practise free love but free rape — few men are safe. On the other side of the world in the Southern Indian state of Kerala, Puyala women return to the fields to tend the crops after the birth of their babies, while the husband goes to bed. The rest of the family ministers to his needs until he recovers. In the Andaman islands specially anxious husbands will stay in bed for anything up to six months. The lost kingdom of the Minaros was 'discovered' in a mountain hideaway 16,000 feet up the Himalayas by a French explorer in 1984. The Amazon-like women totally dominate their men, marrying several at a time and keeping them in line by brute force.

According to Browne (1963), the former Kwakiutl of Vancouver Island demonstrate what is almost a parody of industrial civilisation: the chief motive of this tribe is rivalry, which is not concerned with the usual concerns of providing for a family or owning goods, but rather the aim of outdoing and shaming neighbours and rivals by means of conspicuous consumption. At their potlatch ceremonies these people compete with each other in burning and destroying their valuable possessions and money. This is in contrast to the Dobu of north-west Melanesia. This culture is reported (Browne (1963)) to encourage malignant hatred and animosity. Treacherous conduct unmitigated by any concept of mercy or kindness and directed against neighbours and friends is expected. The Zuni (a branch of the Pueblos of New Mexico) are a people whose life is centred on religious ceremonial, being prosperous but without interest in economic advancement. They admire most those men who are friendly, make no trouble and have no aspirations, detesting on the other hand those who wish to become leaders. Hence, tribal leaders have to be compelled by threats to accept their position and are regarded with contempt and resentment once they have achieved it.

Even cultures that are relatively better known have their own intricacies over something as simple as a handshake, eye contact and the use of colours. For example, brown/grey is disapproved of in Nicaragua; blue in Iran is immoral white, purple and black are the colours of death for Japan, Latin America and Britain respectively.

The pious and the superstitious

...the world...does not divide into the pious and the superstitious...there are sculptures in jungles and paintings in deserts...political order is possible without centralised power and principled justice without codified rules the norms of reason were not fixed in Greece, the evolution of morality not consummated in England...We have, with no little success, sought to keep the world off balance pulling out rugs, upsetting tea tables, setting off fire crackers. It has been the office of others to reassure; ours to unsettle.

(Geertz, C (1983))

APPENDIX 1

An international business dialogue gone wrong

Bob: *How long are you here for, Renee?*
Renee: Since last night.
Bob: No, I mean when do you have to leave for the airport?
Renee: Oh. Twelve o'clock at the latest.
Bob: Well in that case, we'd better press on.
Renee: Sorry?
Bob: Let's resume, shall we, or would you like some more coffee?
Renee: *No, let's resume.* Would you like to?
Bob: What?
Renee: Resume.
Bob: Yes, suits me. Over to you then.
Renee: Oh. Well, perhaps we could turn to the new quality control system. You say you're not very happy about the effect on throughput.
Bob: That's right. It's slowing things down very badly. This week, for example, we're already two days late for one of our regular customers.
Renee: Uh-huh. What sort of an order is it?
Bob: XB-90's. Three thousand.
Renee: *Ah, not so important, then.*
Bob: Well, I think it is.
Renee: *Oh. What's your usual delivery delay?*
Bob: We don't usually have any delay at all, if I can help it.
Renee: But how much time do you need to turn an order round?
Bob: We quote fourteen days.
Renee: *And how long does it actually take?*
Bob: Well, fourteen days, of course! What sort of an operation do you think I'm running?
Renee: I don't see the problem then.
Bob: The problem is that the new system is causing delays.
Renee: *Look, I'm sure I mustn't tell you this,* but the board are very keen to see it in operation in all subsidiaries before the end of the year.
Bob: *That's hardly news.*
Renee: Oh, sorry, I thought they told you already.
Bob: Of course they have. I mean, we can all see benefits coming from a really effective control system, but ...
Renee: *I think it's too early to talk about benefits.*
Bob: Oh I don't know. Look, do you think there's any chance the board will change their minds?

Renee:	*Eventually, but ...*
Bob:	... but it'll take a few more meetings?
Renee:	No, I was going to say it's not very probable.
Bob:	I see. Oh well. What's next?
Renee:	Sorry?
Bob:	*Have you got your agenda?*
Renee:	Why? Do you want to fix our next meeting?
Bob:	No, I just mean what other points ...

Explanations

Renee is a composite European. Her 'language' refers sometimes to the Latin based languages like French, Italian, Spanish, sometimes to Germanic ones.

The italics show where Renee and Bob are talking at cross-purposes. Here's why they misunderstand each other:

How long are you here for, Renee?
Renee responds to this question as if it meant 'How long have you been here?' because, translated word for word, that's what it means in her language.

Let's resume.
Renee mistakes this for a similar word in her language meaning 'summarise'. She therefore thinks she's inviting Bob to sum up the meeting so far and is surprised when Bob doesn't do so.

Not so important.
In her language, 'important' refers to size as well as status and priority. Renee is not necessarily dismissing Bob's order as 'unimportant', just noting that it's not very big.

What's your delivery delay?
To Renee, 'delay' simply means a period of time, and doesn't necessarily carry any suggestion of lateness.

And how long does it actually take?
To Europeans, 'actually' means currently or at the moment. Also, many non-native speakers confuse 'I do it' with 'I'm doing it'. So Renee thinks she's saying 'How long is it taking you at the moment?' It's therefore no wonder that she doesn't see the problem!

I'm sure I must not tell you this.
Non-native speakers often confuse 'mustn't' with 'don't have to'. Renee in fact thinks that Bob already knows the board's opinion. Bob's reply:

That's hardly news.
compounds the misunderstanding, as Renee takes 'hardly' to mean 'hard' or 'tough'. So she not only misses the irony, but also thinks Bob is disappointed.

I think it's too early to talk about benefits.
Renee thinks that 'benefits' carries the same meaning as in her language — 'profits'. This is clearly inappropriate here.

Eventually ...
... in Renee's language, means 'conceivably' or 'possibly' and carries no idea of 'finally'. Hence the misunderstanding.

Have you got your agenda?
'Agenda' to Renee means diary.

(Reproduced by kind permission of Canning International Management Development from *The New International Manager*, 1993.)

APPENDIX 2

Translation tips

Simon Majaro (1982) suggests the following tips for advertising copy that is going to be used in a foreign language.

1) Avoid idioms, jargon and buzz-words.
2) Leave space to expand foreign language text (Latin languages take 20 per cent more space and Arabic may need up to 50 per cent more space).
3) Check local legal requirements and codes of conduct.
4) Ensure that the translators speak the every day language of the country in question. UK English and American English differ, as does the Spanish spoken in Spain and Argentina.
5) Brief the translator thoroughly so that they get a feel for the product, its benefits, the customers and competition. Do not just hand over the copy and expect it to be translated.
6) Check the translation with distributors and customers in the particular market. This also gives local users the opportunity of being involved and raising any criticisms of the promotional materials before they are published for use. Having it translated back into English can be an additional safeguard.

Key Point from Chapter 9:
   1) Think global. Act local.

Further reading

Browne, J A C (1963) *Techniques of Persuasion: From Propaganda to Brainwashing*, Penguin, Harmondsworth

Dudley J. (1989) *1992 Strategies for the Single Market*, Kogan Page, London

Ferraro, G P (1990) *The Cultural Dimension Of International Business*, Prentice Hall, Englewood Cliffs, New Jersey

Geertz, C (1983) *Local Knowledge: Further Essays in Interpretive Anthropology*, Basic Books Inc, New York

Gill, L 'Water everywhere but is it fit to drink?' the *Sunday Correspondent*, 27 May 1990

Guy, V and Mattock, J (1993) *The New International Manager*, Kogan Page, London

Harvey-Jones, J (1988) *Making It Happen*, Collins, London

Kahler, R and Kramer, R (1977) *International Marketing*, South Western Publishing Company

Keegan, W (1984) *Multinational Marketing Management*, 3rd edition, Prentice Hall International, Englewood Cliffs, New Jersey

Killough, J 'Improved Pay-offs from Transnational Advertising', *Harvard Business Review* July/August 1978, pp 102-10

Kotler, P (1988) *Marketing Management: Analysis, Planning, Implementation and Control*, 6th edition, Prentice-Hall International, Englewood Cliffs, New Jersey

Lodge, C 'Developing a taste for the new Europe', *Marketing Week*, 7 July 1989

Majaro, S (1982) *International Marketing*, Allen and Unwin, London

Mole, J (1990) *Mind Your Manners*, The Industrial Society, London

Paliwoda, S J (1986) *International Marketing*, Heinmann, Oxford

Pike, R (1967) *The Strange Ways of Man*, Hart Publishing,

Rijkens, R (1992) *European Advertising Strategies*, Cassell, London

Stressin, L (1979) 'Culture shock and the American businessman overseas' in *Toward Internationalism: Readings in Cross Cultural Communication*, eds Smith, E C and Luce, L F Newbury House Rowley, Mass.

van der Vliet, A 'Marriages of convenience (strategic alliances)', *Marketing*, 26 January 1989

Winick, C 'Anthropology's contribution to marketing', *Journal of Marketing*, 25, 1961

Young, L (1985) *Love Around The World*, Hodder and Stoughton Ltd, Sevenoaks

PART TWO

THE MARKETING COMMUNICATION TOOLS

10

SELLING AND SALES MANAGEMENT

INTRODUCTION

> I used to have a territory where I was a free agent...today the computer recommends which calls I should make...my sales aids remind me what to ask and say...my manager knows where I am and I spend half my time on training courses...but I do sell 30 per cent more per annum.
>
> A domestic appliance executive.

In an increasingly impersonal world of faceless faxes and voicemail, *face-to-face* communications or personal selling can provide a reassuring, personal touch. In addition, the salesperson can respond immediately to a buyer's changing needs and moods. The salesperson can also provide instant feedback from the customer or marketplace (see 'The Intelligent Rep', page 104, Chapter 5). On the other hand, a salesforce can be expensive in terms of cost per thousand contacts and sometimes it can prove to be uneconomical on a cost per order basis. This largely depends on the size and profitability of the order, the distance travelled to get it, the number of meetings required, etc.

Size and importance of the salesforce

The word 'sales' is conspicuous by its absence on business cards. 'New business development', 'account manager' or 'marketing executive' are often preferred, yet its impact on most markets at some stage is vital. The 'selling' stigma is surprising given the size and importance of selling. A recent study called 'Balancing the Salesforce

Equation' (Abberton Associates, 1991) indicates that there are approximately 300,000 professional sales people in the UK alone. The London Business School's Associate Professor of Marketing, P J S Law, cites selling as a vital ingredient: 'I cannot think of a product or service which has not, at some stage on its journey from producer to customer, been the subject of face-to-face negotiations between buyer and seller'. The salesforce budget allocation varies according to industry type (see below) but average percentage of turnover spent on selling is estimated to be between 3 and 4 per cent. To put it another way approximately £12 billion is spent on selling compared to some £9 billion spent on advertising or £1 billion spent on PR (see pages 25–6, Chapter 1).

Industrial markets

Some markets, particularly industrial markets depend on personal selling more than others — winning an order for, say, a heavy industrial machine cannot be done by advertising, direct mail or telesales (telephone selling). This kind of selling requires a top level sales professional. Consumer goods, on the other hand, rarely use personal selling to the end user or consumer because of the high cost per visit, (ranging from £22 to £400 depending on the seniority of the salesperson, the frequency and length of the visit etc). Having said that, there are always exceptions to the rule. Avon are reported to be training 3,000 new Avon Ladies to sell their cosmetics in China. Two other forms of salesforce, *field marketing* and *multi-level marketing* are both growing in popularity. These are discussed later in this chapter.

Integrating with the communications mix

An organisation's own salesforce, or a distributor's or agent's salesforce all have to be kept abreast of any new advertising or sales promotion campaigns. Their product knowledge has to be kept up to scratch. Some advertisements are wasted when they succeed in pulling customers into stores only for the customers to find out that the sales staff behind the counter are not familiar with either the advertisement or the particular offer being made. Equally, salespeople may spend considerable time ensuring that wholesaler and retailer point-of-sale materials are professionally co-ordinated with a national advertising campaign (see Thomson's Holidays short case Chapter 9). The amount and type of personal selling required changes as a product or service moves through its life cycle (see 'Types of Salespeople', page 191).

Figure 1.3 on page 28 of Chapter 1 showed how more of the marketing budget was spent on personal selling in industrial markets than in consumer markets. Figure 1.2 on page 27 indicated that as a customer moves through the mental stages towards buying (AIDA), selling became more effective in the final stages. This suggests that *selling needs to be integrated with other communication activities* such as advertising, direct mail, telesales etc.

SALESFORCES

Types of salespeople

Some sales reps (sales representatives) are excellent at winning new business (*'order getters'*) and find the servicing of regular accounts to be dreadfully tedious compared to the exciting buzz of new business. Other reps are meticuluous professionals who service an account (*'order takers'*) with such professionalism, pride and affection that they create barriers for competition by building a *'wall of warmth'* around their customers. In reality, most reps have to do a bit of both jobs. Shiv Mathur (1981) wrote an intriguing article about 'transactional shifts' which suggested that different types of marketing managers (and salespeople) were required as a product passes through its life cycle since the product requires different levels of service support as it passes through the various stages of its life cycle.

Types of salesforce

The three key resources, the three Ms (men and women, money and minutes) are limited. Selling soaks up all three resources. There are various combinations of types of salesforce. An organisation's field salesforce can be supported by an in-house telesales (telephone selling) team who do the prospecting and appointment setting, thereby freeing the field salespeople to do what they are best at — selling. Resources can also be invested in agents, distributors, wholesalers, retailers and their reps so that they become an extension of the salesforce. Alternatively, a temporary sales team can be contracted in to screen and make appointments (telesales) or to go out and sell (see 'field marketing' page 194). There is no single correct *salesforce mix*.

> ...within the commercial tyre market one company achieves 200 calls per executive per annum while its largest competitor achieves over 1600. The former company has focussed on large accounts and uses agents to service the independent trade. The latter sells direct to customers of all sizes. Both companies are highly profitable and both have highly efficient sales organisations.
>
> (Source: Abberton Associates (1991))

The correct approach is, of course, to monitor constantly the effectiveness of the each salesforce mix (sales, market share and profitablity) and the efficiency (number of calls, cost per call, conversion rates of enquirers to customers, etc.) There is always room for improvement.

Functions of selling

A ridiculous heading? The purpose of selling is to sell. However, research suggests that as little as 5 per cent of a salesman's time is in fact spent actually 'selling' (see

'Time the Scarce Resource' page 198). In addition to prospecting, appointment setting, letter writing, travelling, training and administration, many salespeople are also responsible for some customer care, post-sales service, entertaining, intelligence gathering, forecasting, understanding customers, developing customised solutions, team selling, etc. As Law (1991) says: 'Customers seek longer-term relationships with fewer suppliers than formerly, and in return for security of business ask their suppliers to do more for them.' (See the McGregor Cory short case in Chapter 20 for an example of how longer-term relationships are built. Forecasts suggest that there will be a concentration of key accounts (large customers) and they will need suppliers who work with them as *strategic partners* instead of adversaries (see 'Consultative Selling', below). *Team selling* may become more popular as R and D, production, distribution, sales marketing and even legal and financial people may be called into discussions with the customer. Everyone sells in some way or other. Constable and McCormack's (1987) management survey highlighted the need for leaner, flatter and more flexible, multiskilled managers in the future. Team selling endorses this forecast.

Collecting feedback

Since the salesforce is in the frontline of the market, it provides a fast and accurate *feedback* mechanism. Competitor activity, customer needs, and new opportunities and threats can and should be picked up by the salesforce and fed back, without delay, to the sales manager or marketing manager. Reasons why an old customer is lost or a new customer is won should be fed back without delay.

Consultative selling

Looking at customers as partners with whom a company wishes to develop a long-term, repeat-business relationship requires a shift in the business paradigm from 'selling *to* them' to 'working *with* them'.

Offering expert advice and consultancy demands an attitude shift where the customer is seen as a partner rather than just a sales target. The short-term 'win-lose' scenario (the seller gains at the customer's expense) is replaced by the longer-term *strategic partnership* 'win-win' scenario. This builds customer retention through enhanced customer satisfaction, which in turn creates a sustainable marketing advantage. These new parterships may involve joint development programmes which might not bear fruit for five or more years. This may seem inefficient in the short term but highly effective in the medium to long term. If this approach is to work, longer time horizons have to be shared by the salesforce, sales manager, marketing manager and even the board of directors. In the case of new product developments, this approach may clash with *time-based competition* as *competitor catch-up periods* shorten. In the case of a low technology product a well trained contract field salesforce might accelerate the initial distribution penetration level by selling into the independent stores (thereby blocking some of the gaps inviting entry from a competitor).

EXTENDING THE SALESFORCE

Mindshare

In business-to-business or industrial markets, many manufacturers and importers sell into distributors who, in turn, sell into wholesalers and/or end users. Winning the battle for the distributor's *'mindshare'* (or share of mind) can be an important part of salesforce management. Mindshare means the amount of attention and effort which a distributor's salesforce gives to a particular manufacturer's product. A distributor often carries many different product lines supplied by several competing suppliers. The mindshare concept aims to develop the distributor's salesforce into a part-time extension of the supplier's salesforce.

All suppliers would obviously like to have the distributor's salesforce recommend, select, or push their particular brand to the end user (ultimate customer). Mindshare can be won by creating and maintaining a *partnership approach* which develops a mutually beneficial business relationship. This means the manufacturer must supply:

1) A reasonable quality of product (and price and delivery).
2) Creative and frequent sales promotions* (eg a distributor sales rep club where the top distributor's reps are presented with awards, in front of the distributor's own management, once they attain a certain level of sales. There might be a silver, gold and platinum club for 50, 100 and 200 unit salespeople respectively).
3) Product training.
4) Joint visits (manufacturer and distributor visit end user together).
5) Co-operative advertising (where the manufacturer shares the cost of the distributor's advertising when it promotes both the parties).
6) Merchandising and display services.

Mindshare requires a longer-term approach to selling since the sales reps' efforts do not necessarily result in an immediate order. But mindshare will contribute to longer-term sales. It is therefore management's responsibility to develop a suitable time horizon and a mindshare strategy that works.

Mindshare benefits

An American marketing consultancy, the Richmark group, claims that a mindshare strategy has been found to be more powerful than strategies based on product differentiation and other more traditional market strategies. Manufacturers who successfully implement this strategy have built a market position that is almost impossible for competitors to duplicate (Richmark, 1990). The three examples below show how mindshare can make a competitor's marketing communications totally ineffective. Imagine the manufacturer makes electrical cable Z100, the distributor is an electrical

---

* Many effective salesforce sales promotions are based around psychic income (see 'Motivating', pages 196–7) since recognition often packs more punch than money.

wholesaler and the end user is the electrical contractor who will buy and install the cable under the floorboards of the new house.

An end user (electrical contractor) customer asks a distributor rep (electrical wholesaler's rep) for a competing brand, say brand A1000. The distributor rep recommends and offers the Z100 cable instead.

The end user seeks advice in selecting a specific brand. The distributor rep recommends the manufacturer's brand, Z100.

The distributor rep actively solicits orders for the Z100 brand.

Field marketing

It is possible to hire flexible salesforces for ad hoc tactical activities or regular repeat activities. Reduced cost, flexibility and direct measurability make a contract salesforce or field marketing team attractive compared to a full-time in-house field sales team. Cost can be further reduced by using a syndicated or shared team as opposed to a dedicated team devoted to one particular product only. There are, of course, inherent dangers associated with letting someone else represent your organisation, particularly if they have a tendency for hard selling, misrepresentation or even rudeness. Careful scrutiny and supervision can usually identify these potential problems before they develop into a full-blown crisis. Field marketing tends to be used by FMCG or impulse goods manufacturers but can be used by a wider range of organisations (see below).

Typical field marketing activities include:

1) Selling into independent retail outlets, eg field sales teams sold Christmas charity cards to almost 18,000 outlets during January, February and March.
2) Merchandising and display — arranging stocks and literature in retail stores and other outlets, eg 25,000 newsagents and doctor's surgeries had the Department of Social Security's Family Credit information point-of-sale material placed in them within 14 days.
3) Sampling/promotions — providing teams (eg the Pepsi Challenge in shopping precincts, superstores and national events and exhibitions).
4) Market research into shelf facings, stocking levels and positions in store (including number of shelf facings or number of units that can be seen).
5) Monitoring customer care/service — with mystery shoppers who are employed to observe service and report back details of the specific levels of in-store service and customer care.

The Thomson's Holidays short case at the end of Chapter 19 has an example of how a field marketing team can operate flexibly and efficiently.

Multi-level marketing

Multi-level marketing is a system of selling goods directly to customers through a network of self-employed salespeople. The manufacturer recruits distributors, who in turn recruit (or sponsor) more distributors, who in turn recruit more distributors and so on. Each distributor is on a particular level of discounts (depending on the size of stock purchased). The distributor effectively earns income on his own direct sales to the distributors he has recruited. The distributor also earns a percentage of all of the other distributors connected through his chain or line of distributors.

Multi-level marketing is sometimes called network selling, retail networking and pyramid selling. Several companies have proved that network selling can be a legal and successful method of marketing. Pyramid selling has a bad image because it was exploited unscrupuously, with new distributors being promised fortunes in return for large investments in stock which never sold. In addition, these selling systems tend to exploit personal contacts and networks, which can cause an individual to view all his friends and family (or anyone who comes into contact with them) as sales prospects. This mercenary perspective is sometimes enveloped in a kind of corporate evangelism which gives this sales and distribution method a poor image, despite the several legitimate and successful systems that thrive in the USA.

The Pyramid Selling Schemes Regulations 1989 allow a maximum initial fee of £75 (within the first seven days) to be charged for enrolment as a distributor. Goods are then purchased at a discounted wholesale price which allows the newly enrolled distributor to add its own margin of profit when selling the goods to an end user. Goods are returnable (and 90 per cent of the cost recoupable). Any training fees must be clearly stated in the written contract and training must not be compulsory.

MANAGING THE SALES FORCE

The primary responsibilties of the salesforce manager include *recruitment, training, motivating*, controlling and *collecting feedback*.

Recruiting

Determining the right size and structure of the salesforce is vital. What is the *optimum call frequency*? Who should service the account? As an organisation changes or grows, so too the salesforce and its responsibilities must change. *Salesforce attrition* is a fact of life. Some salespeople move to new companies, some are promoted, others retire or are fired. This means that recruitment is a continual process which demands skills, cash and time. Recruiting the right salesperson is a resources-consuming management activity. Recruit the wrong people and sales can actually be reduced instead of increased. Keeping the right sales team together is largely determined by levels of training, motivation, control and feedback.

Training

Training is an ongoing affair, not a one-off activity. It is a continuous process. Like thinking, it requires practice (Tony Buzan's books (1988 and 1989) emphasise that thinking is a skill which needs development and exercise). Basically the salesforce has to acquire and maintain three pieces of knowledge and one set of skills — selling skills. The three pieces of knowledge which the professional salesperson must have are:

1) Product (4Ps, features/benefits and USPs).
2) Market (customers and competitors).
3) Company (history, structure, etc).

Appendix 1 shows a list of questions which salespeople can use to assess their levels of knowledge. The art of selling, salesmanship, sales techniques or selling skills require separate training.

The 7-P approach to selling skills

There are several different stages involved in selling. The 7-P sequential approach identifies areas for skill improvement. The seven stages are:

- Prospecting (looking for potential customers).
- Preparation (objective setting, customer research etc).
- Presentation (demonstration, discussion).
- Possible problems (handling objections).
- 'Please give me the order' (closing the sale or getting the order).
- Pen to paper (record accurately all relevant details).
- Post-sales service (building a wall of warmth).

Each stage requires a certain amount of training and practice. Training should also include non-selling activities (information gathering time management skills, personal expense control, etc).

Motivating

Maintaining the salesforce's motivation is a vital part of sales management.

It can be as easy as publishing the monthly sales figures against targets for each sales rep and circulating the figures among the sales team. This can lead to competition among members, which may inhibit them from sharing ideas, contacts, leads and even closing techniques. On the other hand, it can keep everyone focused on targets, with peer pressure as a source of motivation. It is the sales-manager's job to build a team feeling and get everyone working together, sharing ideas rather than hiding them from each other.

'Psychic income' is often a stronger motivator than financial income, yet it does not need to cost the company any more money than the old traditional financial incentive. Psychic income offers rewards aimed at the higher levels of need, such as being valued, recognised, rewarded and challenged (see Maslow's hierarchy of needs on page 82).

This is how it works: A bonus cheque for £1,000 tends to get spent on dull and boring things like reducing the overdraft or paying the mortgage. On the other hand, the same £1,000 spent on a holiday for two or a spectacular piece of Waterford glass acts as a constant reminder of the job well done. Even a clap on the back, a thank-you note, a presentation ceremony, a photograph in the newsletter (or in the annual report) can arouse feelings which satisfy the higher levels of Maslow's hierarchy of needs. This contrasts with the £1,000, which is probably used to satisfy the dull, boring and soon forgotten lower levels of need. The reward is soon forgotten here, whereas the psychic income reward tends to linger longer and therefore offer better motivational potential.

Two holes of golf with Jack Nicklaus

The Maritz corporation specialise in psychic income packages. They even give out pyramid-shaped paperweights which list Maslow's needs. They tailor their awards so that individuals are offered an appropriate range of stimulating options. Some of their choices have offered trips to the moon, ballooning across the wine fields of Burgundy or two holes of golf with Jack Nicklaus. As you approach the eighteenth green there is an 80 piece orchestra perched on a scaffolding playing the tune of your choice.

The *annual sales conference* should be a motivator and act as a forum for sharing ideas ('How I made a sale' contest), identifying and solving problems improving techniques, and recognising and rewarding achievements. The conference should also provide a pleasant environment which reinforces feelings of being glad to work with the company.

Controlling

Controlling the salesforce involves analysing sales:

1) By product
2) By market/region
3) By salesperson.

Sales can also be analysed by profitablity or the 'contribution' which each order makes towards the overall profitability of the organisation. This encourages the saleperson to sell higher margin products/services rather than succumbing to the temptation of (a) giving discounts and (b) pushing easier low margin items.

The bottom line tends to be turnover or sales, number of new accounts (customers) won and old accounts lost, and the quality of those accounts (size and creditworthiness). Further analysis reveals number of orders (and average order size), calls to orders ratios etc. Even miles driven gives some indication as to whether a rep is chasing his tail or leaving room for improvement. Good planning helps control.

Good sales forecasting provides targets and yardsticks for measurement. Sales forecasts can be drawn up by sales reps for each customer for each month and eventually put together to form an overall sales rep forecast. This can be modified to allow for low forecasts which reduce target sales figures thereby reducing pressure on the rep and making it easier for them to attain their daily, weekly, monthly, quarterly and annual targets. There are, of course, more sophisticated forecasting models which take into account a host of factors including prices, competitors, state of the economy, etc.

Typical quantitative standards are as follows:

1) Sales volume as a percentage of sales potential.
2) Selling expense as a percentage of sales generated.
3) Number of customers as a percentage of the total number of potential customers in the territory.
4) Call frequency ratio, or total calls made divided by total number of customers and prospects who are called upon (or visited) by the salesperson.

Time — The scarce resource

The average salesman spends *less than 20 per cent* of his or her time actually engaged in face-to-face selling (Institute of Sales and Marketing Management, 1992). The rest of the time is spent filling in report forms, travelling, setting up appointments, attending internal meetings, etc. Is this the optimum use of a key resource? Definitely not, so some companies use other communication tools (eg direct response advertisement, or a mail shot) to generate enquiries, then categorise or qualify the quality of the enquiry or lead into 'hot, medium or cold' prospects. A telesales team can then further qualify the lead by determining how urgent, immediate or serious the enquiry is (see the hybrid marketing system on pages 252–3, Chapter 13, for further examples). They can even set up appointments in a way that minimises the travel between appointments. 'The Extinguisher' on page 199 is an extreme example where the salesman seizes the relatively rare face-to-face opportunity and makes a sale every time (although he may also soon be locked up!)

Reducing the call frequency

Servicing customers with a mixture of telephone calls and personal visits, instead of visits only, allows sales reps to become more efficient by reducing the frequency of their visits but maintaining the frequency of contact/service by phone. There is obviously a fine line between the less personal telephone call and the more personal visit. Some buyers may prefer to avoid the interruption of a sales visit and appreciate a courtesy call ('just checking to see if everything is all right or if there is anything you need') This minimises time wastage (for both parties) while maintaining the customer service facility. Getting the balance between calls and visits is vital since competition is also out there, every day, knocking on the same doors. Optimum call frequencies need to be carefully planned.

CREATIVE SELLING

There is always room for creativity in marketing, and particularly in selling. Whether it is a new form of presentation, a new way of prospecting or a new way of showing determination to win the business, the list is endless. The extinguisher's creative approach (on page 199) is not to be recommended. The short case, 'Selling Life Assurance' at the end of this chapter shows how a small budget and a smart salesman can create an effective and integrated marketing activity.

The extinguisher

I recall a story of an interesting sales pitch that was written about in a marketing magazine many years ago.

Having recognised the weary tread of a door-to-door salesman coming up the stairs, the giggling office staff scrambled behind doors and under desks to avoid the approaching salesman's eye contact. I only realised that a salesman was looming when I noticed the sniggering bodies scattered behind the furniture. Too late. I turned around to see a shabby little man in a greasy raincoat and coffee stained briefcase move towards me. Before I knew it he had opened his briefcase and poured a jar of petrol over himself. Out of his inside pocket he drew a lighter and set fire to himself. Then, while standing in the classic sales-man pose (right arm holding out a spray can and left arm pointing to the label), he said 'and this ladies and gentlemen, is the FlameZapper miniature fire extin-guisher...' As he proceeded to spray himself he continued '...you can carry it anywhere...' He left several cans lighter and several pounds heavier.

Short case

Selling life assurance

This short case demonstrates how innovative sales people can be when motivated to create new methods of prospecting and selling.

Situation

The traditional marketing methods of advertising, exhibitions, seminars, mail shots and cold calling are commonly used by many organisations in the fiercely competitive life assurance market.

Objective

To find a new, competition-free, low-cost way of getting in front of groups of prospective clients in a friendly (non-hard selling) atmosphere.

Strategy

To develop good relations with independent NHS and private hospitals whereby the hospitals can benefit from some fundraising while the sales team gain access to new prospects in an informal non-hard selling environment.

Tactics

Life assurance and hospitals work in much the same way — both offer a service which nobody really wants to use. The NHS and private hospitals in south Hertfordshire, Middlesex and north London were approached to establish which hospitals were having summer fetes. Those having fetes were then offered assistance and support in return for permission to do some soft selling. A children's bouncy castle was provided and all the profits (castle admission fee) would go to the hospital. As the children bounced around, their parents were approached by asking if they would like to enter a free prize draw and simultaneously identify whether any of the financial services would be of interest to them. The sales team's dress was strictly casual (no suits).

In addition to the fete's visitors, the hospital administrators/ managers were approached with a view to extending the services on an ongoing basis to the hospital staff. This presented further opportunities to give seminars to junior doctors and to sponsor various activities including a squash competition. One hospital agreed to distribute details of the company's AVC (additional voluntary contribution/pension scheme) with the staff's pay slips. Other hospitals, after careful consideration, allowed the assurance salespeople access to the internal phone directory.

Men

One manager
Three associate salespeople
One castle supervisor

Money

One bouncy castle supervisor	£15.00
One bouncy castle	£30.00
Eighteen prizes	£63.00
Total	£108.00

The cost of the castle was paid out of the bouncy castle takings on the day and the balance or surplus was donated to the hospital. Life assurance branded mugs, T-shirts, golf balls and torches were used as prizes. Eighteen prizes ensured that each associate salesperson had another opportunity to get back in front of six prize-winning prospects to present them with their prize. This was in addition to the other prospects who actually requested an appointment. The cost to each salesperson was £26 (cost of the prizes + supervisor divided by three).

Minutes

It takes several months of visits and discussions to build up a certain level of trust in the relationship between hospital administrators and the assurance company. Once permission has been given to participate in the fete, it only takes a matter of days to book a castle and brief the associates. The real time-consuming activity is the follow-up. Unless all leads are meticulously followed up, the whole effort is wasted. Several hospitals have since invited the assurance company to participate in their Christmas fairs, etc.

Measurement

The results to date have been positive in terms of sales of new policies, associated services and recruitment of new sales people.

APPENDIX 1

Salesman's self-assessment questions

The product

1) How does it work (what does it do?) Can you demonstrate it with ease and professionalism?
2) Features v benefits.
3) What are its advantages to the consumer (benefits)?
4) What are the advantages and disadvantages over the competition?
5) How old is the design?
6) Where is it made?
7) What safety, health or environmental standards or regulartions are relevant?
8) Does it meet those standards? (What do those standards mean in layman's terms?)
9) What materials are used?
10) What back-up service do you offer?
11) How is it packed, from where is it delivered, order lag/lead time, minimum order quantities?
12) Are there any back-up promotions (point-of-sale, literature, promotions, co-operative advertising, samples, etc)?
13) What is the price (FOB, CIF, Ex-works, Ex-VAT, £ sterling, cash discounts, trade discounts, bulk discounts, credit terms, validity)?

Your customers

Don't
Know Know

1) How many different customer types can you identify?
2) Who are the major customer/prospects in your area?
3) Who do they buy from you (benefits)?
4) Why have they all not placed orders?
5) Do they buy at particular times only?
6) Who are the decision-makers?
7) Do different customers/prospects look for different benefits?
8) What is the exact number of your customers?
9) What is the exact number of your prospects?
10) How much time do you need to cover them all?

Major customers

11) What is their total buying power (how much do they buy)?
12) What other suppliers do they use?
13) What is the major customer's turnover/sales for the last three years?
14) Who will be your most important customers this year?
15) What are the key trade journals in your market?
16) Do you know when each of your top six customers orders?

How many knows?

15–16 excellent
12–15 very good but room for improvement
10–12 room for improvement
Below 10 clean up your act!

Questions for experienced salespeople

Yes   No

1) Do you regularly check your records/files?
2) Do you have all customers ranked in order of importance (usually business volume)?
3) Do you allocate your selling efforts to customers in direct proportion to the customer's importance (ie spend a long time with major accounts and less time with minor accounts)?
4) Do you control your sales appointments (ie have you mastered the art of keeping customer contacts to a practical time minimum without appearing brusque)?
5) Do you avoid personal visits where a telephone call might suffice?
6) Are you at all times contactable (answer machine, bleeper, ring in every morning/afternoon)?
7) Do you send customers Christmas cards (and sometimes even holiday cards)?
8) Have you got a system which picks up customers who have passed their normal ordering cycle without placing an order?
9) After every sale, do you check to see if delivery was OK, etc?
10) Do key accounts (major) have your home telephone number?
11) After losing an account (customer) do you always find out the *real* reason why?
12) Do you keep a file on lost accounts (reasons why)?

How many YES's?

11–12 excellent
10–12 very good but room for improvement
8–10 room for improvement
Below 8 clean up your act!

Some general questions on competition

1) Have you examined their product?
2) What are the advantages and disadvantages of their product?
3) How do they compare with your product?
4) Why do your customers buy your product and not competition's?
5) What about competition's actual company (structure, history, staff, etc)?
6) Price, delivery, promotion, etc.
7)
8)
9)
10)
11)
12)
13)
14)
Add your own questions to test your sales team's knowledge.

Your company

1) Do you know the full (registered name) of your company?
2) Do you know who founded the company?

3) Do you know why it was founded?
4) Do you know who currently owns your company?
5) Do you know who sits on the board?
6) Do you know whether you have any environmental policies?
7) Do you know if you have any ethical policies?
8) Do you know what are the last three years'
   a) turnover
   b) market share
   c) number of employees?
9) Do you know your company's
   a) strengths
   b) weaknesses?

Key point from Chapter 10:

1) Consider and evaluate different types of salesforces.

Further reading

Abberton Associates (1991) *Balancing the Salesforce Equation (the Changing Role of the Sales Organisation in the 1990s* (Foreword by PJS Law), CPM Field Marketing Ltd
Buzan, T (1989) *Use your Head,* revised edition, Pan Books
Buzan, T (1988) *Make The Most of your Mind,* Pan Books
Constable, J and McCormack, R (1987) *The Making of British Managers,* CBI/BIM
Mathur, S (1981) `Strategic industrial marketing: transaction shifts and competitive response', City University Working Paper Number 33

Further contacts

The Institute of Sales and Marketing Management, National Westminster House, 31 Upper George Street, Luton, Bedfordshire LU1 2RD. Tel: 01582 411130

11

ADVERTISING

MANAGING AN ADVERTISING CAMPAIGN

This chapter focuses on how an advertising campaign is planned and managed. The first three elements of the SOSTT + 4M approach to planning (previously discussed in Chapter 2) are used here to give structure to the development of an advertising campaign.

• Where are you now? (Situation)	S
• Where do you want to go? (Objectives)	O
• How will you get there? (Strategy)	S

The advertising campaign planning process incorporates an analysis of the current situation (research) and a clear definition of the goals or objectives. Only then can the advertising strategy be devised. The strategy summarises broadly what to say (message), how to say it (execution, tone or creative strategy), who to say it to (target audience), where to say it (media choice or media strategy), when to say it (timing) and sometimes, how much it will cost (budget).

THE SITUATION

There is a lot of research to be done before any exciting creative work can be started. *What* are the current sales trend, market share trend and overall market trend? Are there any regions or segments that buy more than others? *How* big are the competition's sales (per region and per distribution channel)? What is the profile of the customer and of the non-customers who potentially might be converted? *Who* is the target market now and in the future? Who are the heavy users? *When* do they buy? *Where* do they buy?

How is the brand positioned in the minds of various target markets? *Why* do people use/not use the brand? This can be the most difficult question to answer because real reasons are often deeply hidden beneath apparently rational buying behaviour. What are the current features and benefits of your product or service? A feature is translated into a benefit by using three words: '..which means that..' For example, 'this car has a crush loading of over five tons which means that it can roll over without the roof caving in'. Many advertising campaigns can demonstrate benefits without having to use words (in fact wordless advertisements like Levis may become more popular as satellite television grows — see Chapter 9), but it is the application of this three-word formula that helps to identify real benefits which can then be demonstrated. Spending time 'interrogating the product' is a good investment.

Product interrogation

In addition to the previous questions, further questions, or product interrogation, can sometimes reveal hidden benefits which advertising can subsequently highlight. Is there anything unique about the product (USP — unique selling proposition)? How does it compare against the competition's features and benefits in both people's imagination and in reality?

The cunning K Shoe lady

Some years ago shoe manufacturer K Shoes and their agency BBH discovered a hidden USP. This was that the quality of the leather in their shoes was such that their shoes did not creak or squeak. This subsequently opened up the opportunity of dramatising the benefits of squeak-free shoes. One of the TV advertisements showed a lady wearing K Shoes quietly entering an apartment in which her lover was dining with another woman. The K Shoes lady proceeded to dump a bowlful of slimey noodles on the head of the two-timing man. The K Shoe lady turned silently and walked confidently out of the apartment.

How does the product or service compare with competitors' products in the minds of the customer (how is it positioned)? Or have they even heard of it (what percentage are *spontaneously aware* of your product or service? Is it *top of the mind* or *front of mind*, ie do customers include it in the first three brands they think of when considering your product type?) What is important to the target customers? Or perhaps there is a high level of awareness but low level of preference, possibly because of poor product or poor image? What do customers consider to be the most important factors (key buying criteria) when making a choice? What is their *ideal product*?

Trend identification

What new values, trends, attitudes or lifestyles/business styles are emerging which may affect the organisation's product or service? Guinness identified two trends which helped them to modify their advertising: individuality and advertising literacy. Their advertisements now reflect these trends.

Review of past advertisements

An analysis of competitor advertising campaigns can trigger ideas and, more importantly, provide some insights into competitor strategies, thereby helping the strategic thoughts of the advertising for the brand in question. Even the brand's past campaigns can give some guidance as to how the campaigns reflect the state of the market what that objectives are, and what works and what does not. The following summary review of Guinness campaigns from the recent past, mixed with advertising results and market research (identifying consumer trends), provides guidance for Guinness's future advertising strategy.

Consumer research and trend identification

Another major exercise was embarked upon to understand the consumer environment that the new advertising executions would have to operate in.

The central thesis was quite simply that in the early and mid 1980s, consumers felt most comfortable following the crowd and feeling a collective sense of involvement. In this context advertising that showed session-drinking in the pub (men making wisecracks) was quite appropriate. Brands in the main lager arena prospered. The role these brands occupied was to lubricate the session-drinking of the male dominated pub. In the late 1980s this climate appears to have changed and the process of change continues. Now the consumer wishes to stand *out* from the crowd and express his *individuality* much more. He does this by demonstrating his discernment in the clothes he wears and the brands he chooses. The premium lager boom coincides with this, where the brand acts as a kind of badge of individual choice.

If this was so then the implications for the advertising were fundamental. It suggested a more sophisticated audience, a change in the pub environment, less session-drinking orientation and a different attitude to premium brands. Indeed a significant opportunity if Draught Guinness, already moving in the more fashionable image arena, could catch the crest of this wave and exploit it fully. In order to do so, this social change needed to be confirmed and understood in some detail.

Source: Ogilvy & Mather

Review of past Guinness ads, their effects and future directions

In the early 1980s the 'Guinnless' campaign was created as a means of confronting lapsed Guinness drinkers with a message which made the Guinness brand relevant to their pub drinking lifestyle. High increases in consumption among young session- drinkers resulted but were not sustained and consumption among the old guard declined.

By 1985, a need was perceived to establish a stronger, more long- term consumer franchise — one that was positive and made greater use of essential product values to maintain a growing brand loyalty.

Consumer attitudes were changing fundamentally and it was no longer enough

to show two lads in a pub drinking Guinness to make the brand sociably acceptable. While significant improvements had been achieved in the fashionableness
of the brand, the mood of the consumer environment had evolved and left the
old advertising executions behind.

The advertising had not only to convert the 'Guinnless' trialists to a more
permanent relationship with the brand but had also to satisfy the brand's generally older loyal drinkers.

Source: Ogilvy & Mather

Answers to all of the questions raised in the situation analysis/review are required
before setting advertising/communications objectives. In a sense, researching the current situation reveals the objectives for the campaign. *Good research makes objective
setting easier.*

Research, however, costs time and money (and people) so it needs to budgeted for
or, ideally, built in to a *continual system of information gathering* (see 'Marketing
Intelligence and Information Systems,' page 104. Chapter 5) to help both objective
setting and subsequent measurement of the campaign's effectiveness.

OBJECTIVES

After analysing the situation through secondary and primary research sources (see
Chapter 5) a clear picture of where you are emerges. The next step is to define exactly
where you want to be. 'If you don't know where you're going, any road will take you
there.' Ideally, *objectives should be quantified* in terms of success/failure and time-
scale. This makes control easier since actual results can be measured against quantified objectives. The previous year's objectives, and corresponding results, help to
make the planning job a little easier, as previous experience provides a better idea of
what are realistic objectives for the future.

Objectives should be *SMART:*

* **S**pecific
* **M**easurable
* **A**ctionable
* **R**ealistic
* **T**ime Specific

A clear strategy (how to get there) is not possible without clearly defined objectives
(where you want to go). Without a clear strategy, a loose set of tactics, lacking
cohesion (and sometimes pulling in different directions), is likely to emerge.

Establishing clear objectives is necessary to give a focus to the organisation. Clear
objectives also give direction to the subsequent creative efforts. Some marketing
managers and agencies break objectives into many different types. We focus on just
two types here:

1) Marketing objectives

2) Communication objectives.

Marketing objectives

Typical marketing objectives refer to sales, market share, distribution penetration, launching a number of new products and so on. See the objectives on page 37 (Chapter 2).

Communications Objectives

You will find examples of communications objectives on page 38, Chapter 2. As mentioned in that chapter, communication objectives typically refer to how the communication should affect the mind of the target audience, eg generate awareness, attitudes, interest or trial. The DAGMAR (defining advertising goals for measuring advertising results) and AIDA (awareness, interest, desire and action) hierarchical models reveal some of the mental stages which many buyers have to move through before buying. Again, these objectives (eg 'to increase awareness') are more useful when quantified ('to increase awareness from 35 per cent to 45 per cent within a six week period').

Another way of looking at communications objectives in a competitive market for, say, the purchase of a car would be as follows:

Total Set	Awareness Set	Consideration Set	Choice Set	Decision
Vauxhall	Vauxhall	Vauxhall	Vauxhall	Nissan
Ford	Ford	Ford	Ford	
Nissan	Nissan	Nissan	Nissan	
Volvo	Volvo	Volvo		
Toyota	Toyota	Toyota		
Volkswagen	Volkswagen			
Renault	Renault			
Fiat	Fiat			
Skoda	Skoda			
Lada				
Canto				

A particular campaign's objective may be to move a significant number of prospects from one set to the next. Some advertisements go further by seeking to reinforce/reassure existing buyers.

STRATEGY

With the situation fully researched and clear objectives identified, the campaign or advertising strategy can now be developed. It will include positioning, objectives, target audience, key benefits, secondary benefits and often a statement on what kind of media will be used. The strategy will not get bogged down in detailed tactics or any specific creative messages. It should offer strategic direction to the client and agency

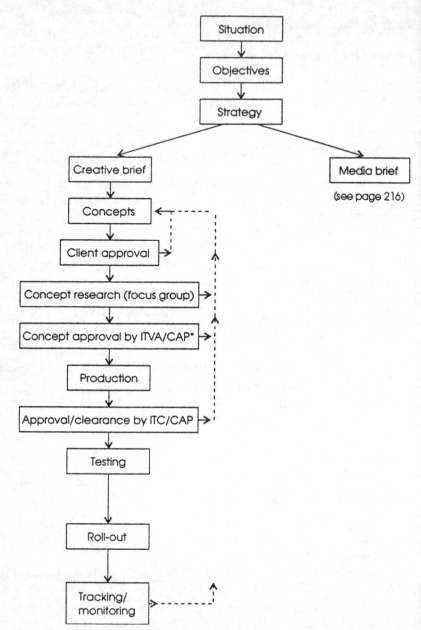

Figure 11.1 The remaining stages of the campaign planning and execution
*Contact with the ITVA/CAP (see Chapter 8) may occur earlier.

team. Some clients will work with the agencies to develop this key statement. Other agencies do all the work and present the campaign strategy to the client for approval.

The campaign strategy forms the foundation for the more detailed planning and development of the actual message (or the advertisement itself), and the selection of

SUMMARY CREATIVE BRIEF

Why are we advertising at all?
Every pint of milk which is sold through a supermarket rather than a milkman loses the dairies 10p in profit. More and more people are moving some or all of their order to the supermarket. What is more, the tendency is to consume less milk when it is bought from the shops — because it is less "on tap". The fundamental benefits of having milk delivered have not been presented in advertising for a very long time and there is evidence that these benefits have become back of mind among the people who are drifting away. Rather like a big brand which has been unadvertised and allowed to drift, what we need is a big, impactful relaunch of the delivery service.

What is the advertising trying to do?
1. Re-present the strongest rational and emotional arguments for having a milkman.
2. Add to the self esteem of the milkmen.

Who are we talking to?
1. Busy mums, who have moved some or all of their order from the milkman to the supermarket.
2. Milkmen.

What do we know about them that will help us?
Busy mums are the people most in need of the convenience a milkman offers. They get through about ten pints a week and on top of carrying it all home, it is yet another thing that they constantly have to bear in mind. Their needs for milk may vary wildly, eg. at the weekend, people dropping in. If, as is common, they have whole milk for some of the family and low fat for others, they have even more to keep track of.

Lapsing users are the people who have most forgotten what benefits the milkman offers. Everyone agrees that the main advantages are "don't have to go out" and "don't have to carry home". On a more emotional level the milkman brings a personal, human-scale service, making your house seem more of a home. These fundamental advantages have become progressively back of mind among those who are lapsing.
(We should also bear in mind that some of the people we are talking to still have a milkman at the moment).

What is the main thought we need to put across?

The milkman delivers help to your doorstep.

What's the best way of achieving this?

1) The milkman delivers the benefit, personifies the service and is the secondary audience and should therefore be central to the advertising idea.
2) We need to make this benefit concrete.

   - he carries a full range of milks, including semi-skimmed milk.
   - he is flexible; he can juggle the most complicated orders and can deliver a bumper supply for the weekend.
   - he carries all that heavy milk for you.
3) If it is useful, we could also support the argument with the recycling of bottles (Green).

Why do we think we are saying the right thing in the right way?
(Summarise the evidence)
The need for a comprehensive re-launch comes from NDC research which shows that, in particular, those who are lapsing have a lower awareness of the advantages of a milkman order.

The central thought of help from a milkman is universally recognised as the main reason for having a milkman — whereas the secondary points appeal to different sub-groups and support this main benefit by giving concrete examples rather than an empty promise.

Essential practical Considerations?
- logo
- tel no.
- address etc.
- budget discipline

Any other Client expectations we must consider?

Tone of Voice
The style of the commercial should be charming, friendly and witty because this is how people see and want to see the milkman.

End Line
The end line for milk must be incorporated — (see separate brief).

ID No. 615

Source: BMP DDB Needham

Figure 11.2 National Dairy Council creative brief

the media. Figure 11.1 illustrates how the initial SOS forms the basis for the subsequent development of the message and media plan.

Strategy first and tactics later?

Quite apart from the fact that a good deal of post rationalisation goes on to justify in marketing terms what seems like a good idea, the advertising objectives and strategy can often be devised simultaneously.

(Source: Douglas, T (1983))

THE REMAINING STAGES

Creative briefs

With the review complete, objectives set and strategy agreed, the creative team can finally be called in and briefed. The creative brief is a key document. Each agency has its own style (see top advertising agency BMP DDB Needham's style on page 211). It is here where all the volumes of research findings and weeks of discussions have to be concentrated into a single page creative brief which translates the details and research jargon into relatively simple layman's terms which explain exactly what the advertisement should do.

This is the brief which the planner or account manager gives to the creative team. It succinctly covers all the key information such as the target audience and its perceptions, motivations and buying criteria; advertising objectives, proposition, tone and how the audience should feel after the advertisement; and constraints and choice of media. It is an important document and should be signed (or approved) by an account director before being passed to the creative team. Sometimes the clients want to approve it also.

Both the agency and client need to have a clear focus on exactly what the advertising should say or what it should achieve. Many creative people don't want too much detail ('just tell me exactly what you want!'). They will then set about delivering a creative idea or concept. Page 211 shows the summary creative brief which BMP DDB Needham used for the National Dairy Council. Note: at the suggestion of the client, one extra task was added — targeting milkmen themselves (as a secondary audience) to improve morale.

CONCEPTS

Ideas or concepts are roughly designed into 'roughs' or 'scamps' which can be developed into a storyboard (like a comic version — see Figure 11.3). The idea can be further developed into better quality visuals known as key frames (see page 214). These, in turn, can be shot on to video to create an animatic (moving cartoon of the advertisement complete with music, voice-over and sound effects). Any of these

Figure 11.3 National Dairy Council storyboard

visual presentations of the advertising concept (concept board, storyboard, key frames animatics) are discussed and/or *researched* before the idea is allowed to go on the expensive production stages and eventually to the even more expensive media stage (buying space and actually advertising). If the concept 'researches well', ie gets good feedback from the focus groups, it can be taken forward for further refinement and eventual production (see the Hoffmeister Bear concept research, page 94, Chapter 5). Despite poor research findings (ie the focus groups do not like the concept), some clients and agencies sometimes pursue an idea regardless of the negative research. For example, Heineken's long-running 'refreshes the parts other beers cannot reach' campaign did not research well but was, nevertheless, produced. It eventually went on to become a successful campaign.

Figure 11.4 National Dairy Board key frames

Advertising agency BMP DDB Needham's rough concept idea for the National Dairy Council (Figure 11.3) was developed from the initial creative brief (shown on page 211). This is the birth of an award-winning advertising campaign that generated over 250 per cent return on investment (see advertising budgets on page 25, Chapter 1).

Client approval

Concepts have to be justified or explained to clients. Agencies support their concepts with a 'message rationale' which basically explains why the concept is brilliant and guaranteed to achieve outstanding results! (See Appendix 1 at the end of this chapter for an example of message rationalisation for the unusual and sometimes bizarre Guinness Genius campaign).

Meanwhile the previous milkman concept was developed into key frames. This was

"2 semi-skimmed, 1 silver
top, number 18 - mmm,
rice pudding tonight"

"Lads, lads, what are you
playing at, you know
they're away for a fort-
night. But next door want
2 extra. Go on then..."

VO. Whatever your order,
your milkman can
deliver all the fresh
milk you'll ever need.

"Empties..."

Figure 11.5 Finished National Dairy Board advertisement

then presented along with the message rationale to the client. The key frames can also be shown during focus group research. Figure 11.4 shows a selection of the National Dairy Council's key frames.

Production

The production of an advertisement requires time and careful attention to detail. It may involve overseas locations, casting, contracts, rehearsals, special effects, weeks or months of sophisticated computer graphics, studio shoots, editing and more.

The finished milkman campaign took over 14 weeks from brief to completion. Figure 11.5 shows what the finished television advertisement looked like.

Clearance

The finished advertisements should be checked before publication or broadcasting by the regulatory bodies (the CAP for non- broadcast advertisements and the ITVA for broadcast advertisements — see Chapter 8 for full explanantion of how these bodies work). ITVA clearance is compulsory while CAP is voluntary.

Testing

With the production stage completed, some clients or agencies *test* the finished advertisement in a hall test (see page 90, Chapter 5). Others will test the advertisements in a geographical region (eg Anglia TV or Ulster TV Region) before rolling out nationally or internationally. Other clients put their advertisements out without testing because of time constraints. The `first to market' with a new product or idea can often steal the initiative.

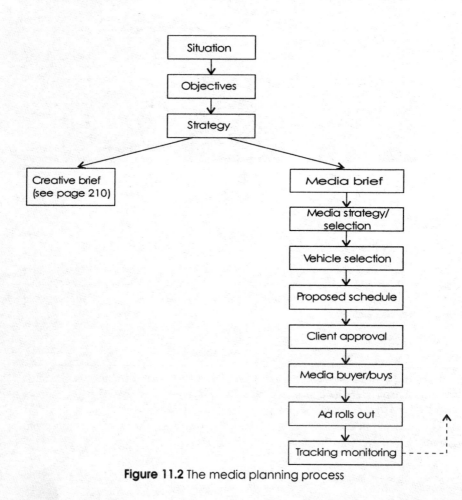

Figure 11.2 The media planning process

Roll-out

If an advertisement has been produced and subsequently tested (successfully), then it can be released, or rolled out, across its whole market.

Tracking

The advertising campaign can and should be monitored, or tracked, to see how it is working, eg what level of awareness it is generating or whether it is affecting attitudes or even sales. This allows any problems to be corrected sooner rather than later.

While the advertising messages are being developed the media planners are busy devising media strategies and plans to ensure the advertisements get the optimum exposure.

MEDIA PLANNING

More money is spent on media than on the production of the advertisement itself. It is here that large savings can be made. Media planning is becoming increasingly scientific as press and TV proliferate. Although, media buying, some argue, is an art in itself. Some media planners understand the qualitative side of the media as well as the quantitative side and can therefore use media in a creative manner. The media awards in *Media Week* give an insight into the creative use of media.

Subliminal Advertising?

PURE GENIUS.

Expert media planning and buying can also save vast sums of money, which can either be redeployed to buy more advertising space or saved and used elsewhere in the communications mix. There is, of course, the temptation to keep the saving and add it on to the bottom line profits (by taking it away from the bottom line expenses). Figure 11.2 on page 216 showed the process of media planning.

Media strategy

Chapter 7, 'Understanding the Media', also looks at media research, planning and scheduling. Here are some additional examples of how media strategy can work creatively and effectively.

Haagen-Dazs ice cream used the weekend press to allow the advertisements to be savoured and enjoyed at leisure, while, according to *Media Week* awards (1992), 'the intimacy of the experience could be hinted at better through the personal communication of the press.'

Part of Guinness's media strategy was to use black and white 'fractionals' (small space) advertisements in newspapers, which as *Media Week* awards put it meant that they 'effectively dominated the mono newspaper world with fresh and extensive copy rotations, so that no reader would see any one execution more than once over a period of seven months.' (See the sample fractional on page 217.)

Media Schedules

In addition to the creative use of the media, careful analysis can identify the optimum media schedules. A media plan is then developed and presented to the client. This plan shows the types of places where the advertisement could be used.

The space is then negotiated and bought. (See 'Media Planning, Scheduling and Buying', Chapter 7.)

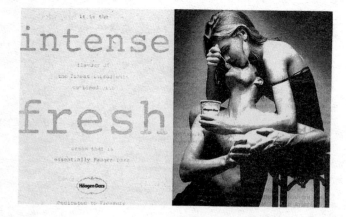

SHORT CASE

Haagen-Dazs Ice Cream Advertising Campaign

Here is a case where the media department and the creative department worked closely together to develop a campaign that first created consumer excitement, then newsworthy PR, then trade excitement and consequently more and more consumer interest to the point where the whole launch gained an unstoppable momentum.

Situation
Haagen-Dazs luxury ice cream previously had very little above the line activity. The limited amount of local advertising used radio, posters, local press, cinema and sandwich boards to launch the openings of Haagen-Dazs shops. There had been no previous brand launch activity.

Objectives
1) To launch Haagen-Dazs brand nationally.
2) To build brand awareness.
3) To position it as the finest ice cream in the world.

The campaign also had to generate strong consumer response since the campaign took place when many of the major multiples were testing the brand.

Strategy
Build brand leadership by creating a new language for ice cream.

Other ice creams focus on ingredients or images of happy families. The new advertising, instead, talked about end benefits that are sometimes hidden deep below the surface of traditional and conscious feelings expressed about ice cream.

Customer research
After being briefed, agency Bartle Bogle Hegarty (BBH) immediately started researching. Focus groups were set up among premium ice cream consumers to try and identify the main differences and reasons for purchasing a super premium ice cream over other ice creams. After a lifelong diet of other ice creams, individuals found it difficult to describe the experience of tasting Haagen-Dazs. They kept lapsing into the language of sensual satisfaction. Some elements of this were more tangible than others. The lavishness of the ingredients (fresh cream, egg yolks, skimmed milk and no E numbers at all) invited comparisons with indulgence. The special flavour of the ice cream elevated it to an experience more sensual than just eating. People also seemed to want to enjoy the ice cream quietly and intimately — to savour it without interruptions. They wanted to concentrate on the experience without the distraction.

The *target market* was not easy to define. Although the ice cream was expensive its market was not casually defined as 'upmarket, frivolous and young'. Instead the target market was defined by attitude — they enjoy the best, believe that quality is worth paying for and that they themselves are worth treating (see below how this was translated into media selection).

Media research

Rather than conducting independent research into the Haagen-Dazs audience, answers were sourced from the extensive qualitative research which was used to guide the creative development of the advertising message itself. Despite the attraction of television advertising for a new brand and the popularity of television with other ice cream suppliers (87.5 per cent of the total ice cream spend went on television), press was preferred since it created a 'feel' with the advertising that could itself be savoured and enjoyed at leisure. In addition, the intimacy of the experience could be better hinted at through the personal one-to-one communication of the press. Television is often a family or social medium which might, in itself, devalue the communication by exposing it to the comment and reaction of third parties. Strategically, a series of press advertisements allowed a relationship to be built with the target audience rather than just a one-off advertisement.

Although weekend colour supplements and weekend reviews are considered to be highly optional reading and lack the immediacy of their parent newspapers, the weekend's 'leisurely read' aspect (being read for leisure rather than for information) lent itself to the creation of the values which the brand advertising was trying to develop. The qualitative research highlighted those lazy Saturday or Sunday afternoon moments, languishing in the garden. This is just the moment to whisper 'Haagen-Dazs', instead of having to shout the message on television.

Research showed that women were particularly expressive of these special moments when they are left alone with their favourite magazine. They often save up the magazine for the sheer joy of being alone with a cup of coffee, disconnected from the rest of the world for a few moments of self-indulgence (ideal for Haagen-Dazs).

Media schedule

Original research and TGI data was used to blend the shopping and reading habits of the target customer (see TGI data, page 97, Chapter 5). To ensure that the target market would be exposed to more than one of the four advertisements, the media schedule was compiled with meticulous attention to duplication (see page 137, Chapter 7). The media planners researched and analysed the extent to which readers of each magazine also read the weekend reviews or the weekend magazines. The titles eventually chosen also had to share a commitment to the quality lifestyle which was appropriate to the brand itself.

Campaign measurement

Although this advertising campaign only had a 6 per cent share of voice (share of all the advertising money spent by UK ice cream manufacturers), it helped to make Haagen-Dazs the most talked about ice cream brand of the year — in fact, the 'New Product of the Year' according to the Marketing Society. It had become brand leader of the take-home premium ice cream sector. The results below confirm the power of good advertising.

1) The 'propensity to purchase' (or try it) increased by over 500 per cent.
2) Sales through Haagen-Dazs' own outlets broke all records.
3) Distribution penetration increased through the retail multiples with Waitrose

increasing distribution from their test stores dramatically and Safeway going to national distribution immediately.

4) Prompted awareness almost quadrupled.

5) Haagen-Dazs had a unique positioning as they were 'Dedicated to Pleasure' — effectively redefining what 'premium' meant to the consumer.

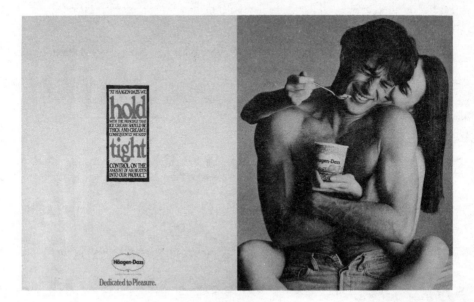

APPENDIX

Guinness genius message rationale

In the case of the 'Man With The Guinness' campaign initially discussed on page 57, the style and type of advertisements created were explained by the agency Ogilvy and Mather as follows:

> The 'Man With The Guinness' campaign is designed to allow consumers to access their individualism via the commentary provided by a man who is an embodiment of Guinness itself.
>
> The man is black, blond, enigmatic, mysterious, powerful, redolent of inner depth — all the classic attributes of draught Guinness.
>
> He walks through conventional life communicating modern-day parables.
>
> Not philosophies or theories. But using wit and wisdom to draw our attention to our real values — life's experiences, life's ups and downs, life's lessons.
>
> It's not only modern in look and style, it's modern in the way it talks to the viewer, rather than at him. It is designed to create a visual and verbal dialogue with each individual who views it.
>
> The advertising is able to provide this complex symbolism because of the brand which it carries. The character of Guinness — original, authentic, an acquired taste, different,

difficult, `a logo within a glass' — make it entirely eligible as a shorthand statement of user independence.

The man is independent, able to make choices. His dialogue privately encourages and provides consumers with access to their own individualism.

The campaign is recruiting new drinkers to Guinness and, most importantly, retaining them as regular Guinness drinkers. 1992 figures show sales of draught Guinness to be booming.

Key Points from Chapter 11:

1) Media planning can be creative.
2) Research can be used at all stages of the development of a campaign.

Further reading

Aaker, D and Myers, J (1987) *Advertising Management*, third edition, Prentice Hall International, Englewood Cliffs, New Jersey

Cowley, D (ed) (1987) *How to Plan Advertising*, Cassell in association with The Account Planning Group

Douglas, T (1983) *The Complete Guide to Advertising*, PaperMac, London

Hart, A and O'Connor, J (1985) *The Practice of Advertising*, second edition, Heinemann, London

Further contacts

Advertising Standards Authority (ASA), 2 Torrington Place, London WC1E 7HW. Tel: 0171 580 5555

The Committee of Advertising Practice (CAP) (as above)

The Institute of Practitioners in Advertising (IPA), 44 Belgrave Square, London SW1X 8QS. Tel: 0171 235 7020

The Incorporated Society of British Advertisers (ISBA), 44 Hertford Street, London W1Y 8AE. Tel: 0171 499 7502

The Independent Television Commission (ITC), 33 Foley Street, London W1P 7LB. Tel: 0171 255 3000

Independent Television Association (ITVA), 200 Grays Inn Road, London WC1X 8HF. Tel: 0171 843 8000

12

SALES PROMOTION

INTRODUCTION

Sales promotion is big business in fact. It is bigger than advertising in the UK (see page 26, Chapter 1). The UK sales promotion industry has enjoyed an average 10 per cent growth pa during the period 1981 – 1991. In 1991, this £9 billion industry pipped advertising's £8.8 billion spend. Isolating and calculating the exact industry figures is difficult since forfeited revenue from price reductions is included in this figure. Some companies pay for the publishing of free information booklets out of their sales promotion budget and others see it as part of public relations. Whichever way it is looked at, sales promotion is a *below the line* activity which can be used externally with end user (customers), and intermediaries (trade distributors), and also internally with an organisation's own salesforce. Sales promotions, premiums, incentives and motivation schemes are used for both products and services in consumer, business-to-business and industrial markets. There are three main categories:

1) *Customer* (premiums, gifts, prizes and competitions, eg on the back of breakfast cereal boxes).
2) *Trade* promotions (special terms, point-of-sale materials and free pens, diaries, competition prizes, etc).
3) Salesforce (incentive and motivation schemes — see page 196, Chapter 10, for an explanation of how these become a form of psychic income).

Whether they take the form of competitions, price reductions, free gifts, coupons, samples, special demonstrations, displays or point-of-sale, consumer sales promotions tend to *affect the latter stages of the communications/buying process* (ie triggering action) such as a purchase or increased usage of a particular brand, whereas advertising tends to affect the earlier stages such as awareness, interest and desire (there are exceptions, particularly where direct response advertising is concerned).

Promotions are action-oriented particularly, as they often tempt the buyer to buy or at least to try a product or service. These kinds of promotions often provide the final shove which moves a customer towards buying a particular product or service.

In terms of *learning* about brands and learning to use them frequently, many sales promotions and the involvement they create (by filling in forms, collecting coupons, posting application forms, trying a free sample etc) are considered by some to be a form of *operant conditioning* as demonstrated by Skinner's rats (see pages 78–9, Chapter 4). Advertising, on the other hand, is thought by some to help buyers to learn and remember brands and their benefits by repeating the message and building associations between brands, logos, images and benefits — a form of classical conditioning as demonstrated by Pavlov's dog (see page 78, Chapter 4). There are, of course, many exceptions to this today, as more advertising tries to involve the audience rather than just beat it over the head with a repeated message.

FACTORS DRIVING THE USE OF SALES PROMOTIONS

1) The *recession* has fuelled the emergence of *price consciousness* and the customer search for value-for-money offers or promotions.
2) As FMCG distribution concentrates into the hands of a few big retail chains, the battle for shelf space (often competing against the retailer's own brands) has intensified. Sales promotions provide another tool with which the manufacturer can negotiate with this *retail power*.
3) *Spiralling TV advertising costs* combined with the *constant search for cost effectiveness* force marketing managers to look for more cost effective below the line tools such as sales promotions.

Integrated promotions

Sales promotions integrate with other marketing communication tools, particularly packaging ('on-pack' promotions), point-of-sale, merchandising, sponsorship, PR, advertising and selling. Media-supported promotions do better than ones which are not supported. There are, however, many occasions when media support cannot be afforded or where point of sale materials flagging the offer are considered to be more cost effective than above the line support. The Miss Pear's Soap competition at the end of this chapter demonstrates how a unique promotion combines with PR to maintain the brand's market share without any above the line or point-of-sale support. Even a great sales promotion fails if no one knows about it. Some support, whether advertising, point-of-sale or PR is therefore generally required.

Promotions warfare

Competitors compete with each other using different elements of the marketing mix, marketing communications mix, and the sales promotion mix. In the 1960s petrol retailers competed against each other by using advertising to differentiate the products with claims such as more power (tiger in your tank), more mileage, more secure ('you can be sure with Shell'). Towards the end of the 1960s the competitive edge shifted away from product claims and into an increasingly popular sales promotion called

Green Shield Stamps. Securing an exclusive Green Shield Stamp franchise was the key competitive tool as the stamps came to dominate the battle for market share right up to the first oil crisis in 1973. Then competition became focused on basic supply and distribution of a scarce commodity. Spurred on by higher and higher prices, a price war eventually broke out in 1974 and marginal sales (brand switchers) shopped around for the best deal. This carried on until the second oil crisis in 1979. Price cutting meant lower margins, which required higher sales volumes, so developing new distribution networks of bigger and better-designed service stations became the key competitive tool at the beginning of the 1980s. Larger forecourts, free of queues, attracted drivers and distracted their attention from prices. Buying time (created with faster service) became more important than penny pinching. Bigger canopies, double-sided multiple pumps, space for passing lanes and self-service all quickened the speed of service while the forecourt shops offered more than just spark plugs and fan belts.

The mid-1980s saw the battle move back on to the sales promotion plain with a variety of games offering a variety of prizes to lucky winners. These were soon replaced by guaranteed winners as collecting gifts or tokens delivered better rewards for both petrol company and consumer. The late 1980s followed with a sales promotion war where different, better and more extensive ranges of guaranteed gifts became the key competitive weapon in the forecourt battleground. Large advertising budgets were used to support and promote various sales promotion campaigns.

Then one oil company spotted a chink in the armour of a competitor's sales promotions when research suggested that consumers were beginning to tire of the endless stream of cheap free wine glasses. The battle moved on to another plain. A new advertising campaign was launched not to promote a 'better' range of free gifts but to attack the competition's 'inferior' range of free gifts. No inferior competitor product claims were made, only inferior competitor sales promotion claims. One advertisement showed a driver opening his glove compartment only to find a wave of free glasses pouring out on to the floor of his car.

In addition to using advertising to promote a product or a sales promotion, or to criticise a competitor's sales promotion, in 1991 advertising was used to promote a sales promotion which promoted a sales promotion (see below).

Esso launched the UK's biggest ever T-shirt promotion featuring a single design. It was designed to promote not only the Esso brand, but also Esso's main promotional medium — the Esso Collection (gifts for tokens promotional scheme). In less than two month's over 800,000 T-shirts were given away through some 2,100 UK service stations. The subsequent 800,000 walking advertisements (people wearing the T-shirt with the striking design) helped to achieve the promotion's objective of stimulating additional consumer interest in the Esso Collection.

Television advertising gave the promotion a high profile and stimulated high levels of redemption (number of responders claiming their gift). The T-shirt supplier immediately had to increase their daily T-shirt shipment from 10,000 to 40,000 units.

Since promotions can be expensive, the 1990s' battle for petrol market share may be fought with other tools such as service facilities (on-site shops, phones, food, tapes, etc), location and corporate identity, as well as advertising and sales promotions.

As Drayton Bird (1990) says, 'In the 1930s the national newspapers got into an incentive war that proved so crippling that finally all agreed to stop it.' In 1984 the newspaper market suffered its own bingo war with million-pound prizes squeezing bottom line profits. What started as an exciting promotion for one paper was quickly copied by another. Success attracts imitators, copiers or me-toos' (similar products and similar ideas). If all the players offer similar incentives then the competitive advantage is nullified. Some customers simply expect a sales promotion. Trading stamps swept the UK in the 1950s and 1960s, 'the problem being that almost everyone started offering them and the whole exercise became virtually pointless'. In this situation the promotion can become a '*dis-satisfier*' ie the sales promotion does not motivate the customer towards a particular store or brand but without the sales promotion, the buyer will avoid the promotionless brand or the promotionless retailer.

Creativity

There is always room for creative innovation. If it is stunningly successful it is likely that the competition will follow unless the innovation relates uniquely to the brand in a creative way. This is demonstrated by the *Sunday Sport* newspaper.

> *Is your mother-in-law an alien?*
>
> The *Sunday Sport* tabloid newspaper offered a free test kit which helped the readers to determine whether their mother-in-laws were in fact aliens.

This 'alien mother-in-law' type of promotion is arguably just a stunt designed to generate publicity which may, at least temporarily, increase levels of awareness, boost circulation and also reinforce reader loyalty by rewarding them with a gift which appeals to their mentality. Because the gift is relevant to both their target reader's sense of humour as well as the newspaper's image, it adds to the paper's branding. In a way it adds to the brand franchise or builds consumer franchise (see page 277).

Creativity and originality can work well together, as in the case where Nat West bank's sales promotions and direct marketing were combined as a '*direct promotion*' (most mail shots use an incentive of some description). Nat West moved away from the traditional clock/radio/calculator/travel bag type of incentive which is used by banks from time to time. Instead they offered a choice of one of ten limited edition prints which were specially commissioned from five artists. They mailed 65,000 names (who they thought had £25,000+ to invest) and received a 12.3 per cent response (instead of the targeted 5 per cent response level).

Free Ladas boost sales by 36 per cent

After several seasons of declining gates, Russian football club Zenit have used a simple sales promotion to boost attendances up to 26,000. Entry costs 1.5 roubles and tickets for the Ladas lottery cost 1 rouble. Ladas cost 8,000 roubles (equivalent to three years' salary for the average industrial worker). The biggest roar of the evening comes not as the two teams run out on to the pitch but when the three cream-coloured Ladas are driven on to the running track. The opportunity of winning a Lada just pulls in the crowd.

(Source: The *Observer*, 23 October 1988)

Consumer franchise building (CFB)

Some promotions can enhance or add value to the image of the product or service. These types of promotions build '*consumer franchise*'. This means that the gift is in some way related to the brand, its image or its properties. As Torin Douglas puts it, a brand property encapsulates 'the image of the product and ensures that extra mileage can be obtained out of the advertising over a period of several years' (eg Esso's tiger and Johnny Walker's gentleman with the top hat and tails). Franchise building promotions contrast with price/discount offers which dilute brand values and do not enhance brand loyalty, despite boosting short-term sales. The Miss Pear's competition (at the end of this chapter) reinforces the brand image of gentle-natural soap. Esso's tiger T-shirt was also franchise building. CFB promotions tend to have longer-term implications and are therefore more strategically driven, while non-CFB promotions can be driven by shorter-term tactical goals.

SALES PROMOTION OBJECTIVES

As the name suggests, a promotion is a limited period offer. It is therefore not surprising to find that sales promotions tend to have shorter-term tactical objectives (although, as previously explained, this need not be the case).

Some typical sales promotion goals might be:

1) Increase sales (although it may only be a temporary increase because customers can either simply stock up with the goods or temporarily switch brands while the promotion is running).

   a) reward loyal customers;

    b) lock customers into loyalty programmes (where they have to keep buying the product or service over a period of time in order to collect the number of coupons, vouchers or items in a collection);

    c) increase repurchase rates of occassional users;

    d) generate 'trial' among new customers (by triggering an impulse purchase);

    e) demonstrate new features/modifications or introduce a new product/service;

    f) develop new uses;

    g) image development (awareness or repositioning);

    h) deseasonalise seasonal sales (eg skiing holidays in the summer).

2) Develop new sales leads.

3) Satisfy retailers with a complete package — gain trade acceptance.

4) Move excess stock.

5) Block a competitor (by offering incentives to customers to stock up).

6) Match a competitor (petrol tokens).

7) Build a database (some promotions also act as database builders (see how Rothman's offer of a free pack collected 750,000 customer names in the section on direct mail in Chapter 13).

Matching types of promotions with specific objectives

As shown below, some sales promotion techniques are more appropriate than others in achieving certain objectives.

Objective:	Promotion tool
	Consumer
Trial	Sampling; couponing; free draw; price-off; self-liquidator (send in some money which pays the costs of the promotion); premiums; in-pack; on-pack; near-pack; Re-usable container; Personality promotion
Retrial	Coupon for next purchase; price-off
Increase usage	Collections; games; competitions; extra quantity/ bonus packs price-off multiple purchase
Develop new uses	Companion brand promotions; publications; workshops
Image development	Publications; sponsorship; charity
	Trade
Increase distribution/ shelf facings/displays	Discount; extended credit; POS materials; tie-in with advertising
In-store promo	Above + consumer offer + promotion allowance
Increase sales	Sales competitions & rebates (mostly independent stores/wholesalers)
Cement good relations	Gifts, holidays and awards

Sales and distribution

Salesforce
Psychic income and financial income

Some efforts have been made to rank the effectiveness of specific tools ('mechanics') against various objectives. Julian Cummins (1990) identified how certain sales promotion techniques match up with various objectives (Table 12.1).

Table 12.1 Linking the objective to the mechanics: how they match up

Objectives \ Mechanics	Immediate free offers	Delayed free offers	Immediate price offers	Delayed price offers	Finance offers	Competitions	Games and draws	Charitable offers	Self-liquidators	Profit-making promotions
Increasing volume	9	7	9	7	5	1	3	5	2	1
Increasing trial	9	7	9	2	9	2	7	7	2	1
Increasing repeat purchase	2	9	2	9	5	3	2	7	3	3
Increasing loyalty	1	9	0	7	3	3	1	7	3	3
Widening usage	9	5	5	2	3	1	5	5	1	1
Creating interest	3	3	3	2	2	5	9	8	8	8
Creating awareness	3	3	3	1	1	5	9	8	8	8
Deflecting attention from price	9	7	0	7	7	3	5	5	2	2
Gaining intermediary support	9	5	9	5	9	3	7	5	1	1
Gaining display	9	5	9	5	9	3	7	5	1	1

Each square is filled with a rating from 0 (not well matched) to 10 (very well matched). Use it as a ready reckoner for linking your objective to the mechanics available.

(Source: Cummins, J 1990)

STRATEGY OR TACTICS?

The short-term tactical approach

The general short-term, 'immediate action', tactical nature of sales promotion contrasts with the longer-term image and brand building capability of advertising. This need not be the case because sales promotions *can* be planned on a strategic level. But first, why is there a tendency towards short termism?

Perhaps the short-term focus is a result of:

1) Management *pressure to boost quarterly sales*. This therefore encourages the use of quick response sales promotions.
2) This may be exacerbated by the *shortening product life cycles* which demand quick sales results.
3) *Increased competition* and increased *new product introductions* increase the need for tactical defensive sales promotions.
4) Sales promotions often lend themselves to the *speedy response required to handle business problems when they arise.*
5) *Full-service agencies* may try to sell the client additional services such as sales promotion on an ad hoc 'add-on' tactical basis.

The strategic approach

All promotions should be part of a bigger and longer-term strategy. Longer-term strategies are about building and reinforcing brand image, strengthening user loyalty, and even inviting new users to join the club, as opposed to short-term tactical sales boosts. Whether planned on a one-off tactical basis or on a more structured strategic approach, the sales promotion can have an impact on the brand or organisation's overall image (nb Hoover). Corporate image is central to the longer-term strategic communications of the organisation. Tracking studies (or continual market research) can monitor changes in specific aspects or dimensions of an organisation's corporate image. These changes can be caused by many different communications tools including sales promotions.

Sales promotion's strategic impact

Years ago, Heinz used to say that they saw more far reaching effects on image dimensions of their tracking studies from their sales promotion schemes than they ever saw resulting from advertising campaigns.

(Source: Jim Castling, 1989)

Some organisations only see promotions as a short-term tactical tool to support what they call the more strategic communication tools such as advertising. Realistically, however, *it is not always possible to achieve strategic goals if the client does not want them in the first place.* Roger Hyslop (1989), managing director of the Marketing Triangle, gives an example of a retailer who says: 'I don't need this promotion to add to my brand image, otherwise I wouldn't be spending millions on television. What I need is to bring 50,000 people in to see my store opening.' The difficulty is compounded by the fact that strategic promotions may sometimes not generate maximum customer response in the immediate short term. Should the longer-term image building capability of a sales promotion be forfeited for the shorter-term tactical 'trial sales' objective?

Julian Cummins (1990) explains why a strategic approach is preferred:

1) It enables one offer to build on the previous one, and to establish a continuity of communication.
2) It makes it possible to communicate image and functional values, so promotions work harder.
3) It can produce considerable savings in time and money.
4) It enables offers to be fully integrated into the other activities in the marketing programme (eg linking with advertising and PR).
5) It facilitates a better approach to joint promotions (see below).

A strategic approach does not exclude the use of tactical promotions since it can provide a framework within which shorter-term tactics can be determined. In this way a sales promotion strategy makes the tactical planning easier and more productive.

How to develop a strategic approach

1) Identify the long-term strategic marketing and communications objectives (see Chapter 2 for examples of separate types of objectives).
2) Create guidelines for each product or service showing the style of sales promotion that is most appropriate to the brand's long-term health. Ensure that this style contributes towards the strategic marketing goals (as opposed to sometimes going in opposite directions).
3) Determine exactly how much of the total marketing communications budget is available for sales promotions.
4) Ensure that there is support and commitment from senior management (eg marketing director) so that sufficient management expertise and funds are available to ensure the promotions are professionally carried out.
5) Develop a method of evaluation so that longer-term performance can be measured against longer-term objectives. Ideally, this might then be compared to other types of marketing expenditure. Agencies and consultancies can review the effectiveness of their activities at the end of the year. Some agencies/consultancies are then asked 'which communication tool is more effective and why?'
6) Develop a 'promotions file' which compiles ideas and costs throughout the year. These can then be reviewed closer to the time of planning.
7) Plan and forecast the sales promotions' results. This is obviously difficult to do, particularly for the first time. Usually a best/worst/medium range of forecasts helps to build some kind of management control and criteria for success or failure.

Joint promotions

Joint promotions and cross-promotions offer economical routes to target the same customers with relevant offers. Cathy Bond (1991) gives this example: Coca-Cola led its army of soft drinks brands into a joint promotion with Cadbury in spring 1991. It was only a matter of time before arch-rival Pepsi popped up with another mega-brand deal — in this case with Kellogg. Caution must be exercised when choosing a partner. Equal standing brands, budgets and branding details need to be clarified, with nothing left to chance. Stuart Hardy, managing director of WLK (who married Mothercare and Lever's Persil in a joint promotion) says: 'In any true relationship each side is going to have 50 per cent of the say. A lot of marketing people want 100 per cent of the say and only 50 per cent of the costs.' Although there are lots of opportunities, relatively few joint promotions seem to get off the ground. 'For every one joint promotion that gets off the ground, ten never make it', says Roger Hyslop (1989).

MANAGING A SALES PROMOTION

Choosing an agency

As with advertising campaigns, a sales promotion can be handled in-house or given

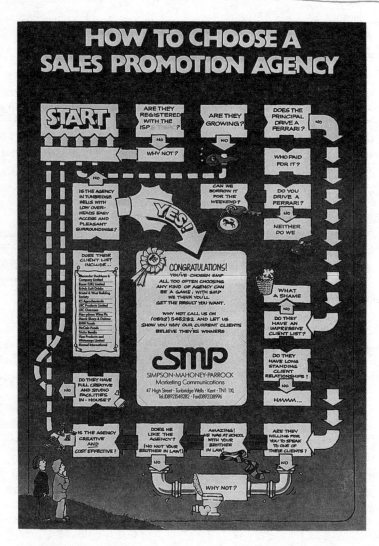

Figure 12.1 How to choose a sales promotion agency

to an external agency. If the work goes outside to an agency the usual selection procedure applies (see Chapter 6) ie develop a pool, list possible agencies; invite them to present credentials; check references; select a shortlist; brief them; pitch; evaluation; selection; written contract. Figure 12.1 shows an advertisement placed in the trade magazine *Sales Promotion* by a marketing communications consultancy. It shows their interpretation of how to select an agency (while simultaneously doing all the selection work for the potential client).

Planning the campaign

The SOSTT + 4Ms checklist can be used to build a sales promotion plan (see Chapters 2 and 11 or the Miss Pear's Competition at the end of this chapter for applications of the SOSTT + 4Ms planning checklist). The situation analysis requires research into past, present and possible future campaigns combined with a clear analysis of the target market.

Research

Research is required at most stages of the development of the sales promotion. An initial review of previous promotions (including competitors') can be followed by further research into the target market. In addition to the usual demographic and psychographic information (see 'Target Markets', page 40 Chapter 2), further analysis may reveal what Philip Kotler identifies as three types of people who respond to sales promotion offers: (a) users of a competing brand in the same category, (b) users in other categories and (c) frequent brand switchers. This 'deal prone customer', the brand switcher, tends not to be loyal and is likely to switch away to the next low price or free gift offer that comes his or her way. In the UK, Peter Holloway, managing director of MS Surveys, calls this last group 'promiscuous nomads' who can be easily bought and lost the next day — but at what cost? The group at the other end of the

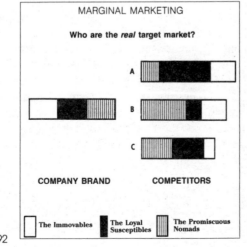

Source: MS Surveys, 1992

Figure 12.2 Who is the *real* target for a sales promotion?

target market loyalty spectrum are called 'the immovables' who are locked into brand loyalty. 'No amount of promotional effort will move them, so there is no point wasting money on them', says Holloway. The real target group within the target market is called the 'loyal susceptibles' (see Figure 12.2). Holloway says that 'they are there to be won (or lost if they are your brand customers) and once their loyalty is broken, their new found loyalties can well be worth having.'

Knowing exactly who these people are and why they are more susceptible is the key to the sales promotions tapping into their susceptibilities, which in turn will increase market share beyond a short term temporary boost.

Crossing the bridge

Crossing the bridge from your own island of subjective presumptions to the land of the real-life target consumer can be as revealing, remove as many uncertainties and avoid as many clangers as having a full medical check up, or consulting a map before you go somewhere new. The first step towards making promotions, etc work better for you is knowing who you really ought to be talking to.

(Source: Peter Holloway, MS Surveys)

After analysing the real target market, the sales promotion concept should be researched in focus groups or at least with customers, suppliers, friends and colleagues. When the idea or promotional tool is agreed it is still worth testing it in a limited area or customer group to reveal any hidden problems or even opportunities before launching nationally or internationally.

Attention to detail

The choice of promotional tool can be directly affected by the availability of resources. The three key resources, men and women, money and minutes (the 3Ms) are tied up with a promotion. Careful contingency planning should cater for an unexpectedly large response. Insurance can help here because things do go wrong and costs can rapidly escalate (see 'Sales Promotions Problems page 237'). Although creating a promotion is exciting, finishing it is dull and boring, yet this is the mark of a true professional. Cut-off dates, logistical arrangements (returning unused stocks), and even announcing the end of the promotion, cost time and money. Shell wanted to avoid the flush of irritation that would undoubtedly rise up if their customers failed to cash in their carefully collected gift tokens before they expired and became worthless.

So they advertised the end of the promotion.

Checklist

Here is a checklist covering some key sales promotions details:

1) Does the promotion *exploit key strengths & USPs* (unique selling propositions)?

2) Is it a *franchise building* promotion? Does the gift, incentive or premium relate to or enhance your product/ service or organisation's image? Does it carry a *selling message* or at least a subtle reminder of some selling message? Unrelated premiums, contests, refunds price discounts do not reinforce brand or enhance corporate values.

3) *What can go wrong?* Contingency planning, crisis management and insurance are worth considering (see 'Sales Promotion Problems' on page 237).

4) Has the promotion got *legal clearance?* Should it be checked with the Code of Advertising Practice (CAP) Sales Promotions department?

5) Will the promotion only generate a *temporary gain* while customers stock up and do not repurchase for twice the normal period? (see Figure 12.3.) Will existing/old stocks (not carrying the promotion) waste?

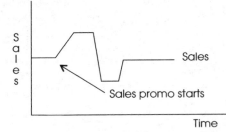

Figure 12.3 Temporary gain, illusions and sales promotions

6) Does the promotion need *advertising and PR support?* Is it newsworthy (ie can the PR people get some media coverage anyway)? With a consumer product, will the retail trade demand some *above the line* support? A great promotion will die on its feet if no one knows about it.

7) What other *communication tools* are required — new packaging, POS (point-of-sale) materials, new literature, contract field sales teams? Are these in the budget (time and money restrictions)?

8) Is there an *administrative* burden created by new order forms, coupons, judging, choosing winners, despatching gifts, etc? Or will this all be handled by an external agency?

9) *Time* a) cut-off date (clearly state when offer closes); b) sell-off time (estimate how long it would take to use up the stock of incentives/gifts); c) lead time (period required to set up the whole sales promotion through to launch date).

10) Is the sales promotion going to be *costly?* Does it fit the budget available? Is it cost effective? Can it be measured?

Measurement

The fourth M, measurement and monitoring, forms the loop in the management system. How can the success or otherwise of the promotion be measured? The number of respondents, redemptions and increased sales are all relatively easy to calculate. But these are only the surface figures. They may be hiding the fact that many of the responders are the wrong people (promiscuous nomads), or existing customers who simply buy twice as much this week (stocking up) but do not buy next week. In fact, it may be that less than a quarter of the respondents actually represent new business. Figure 12.4, considers this.

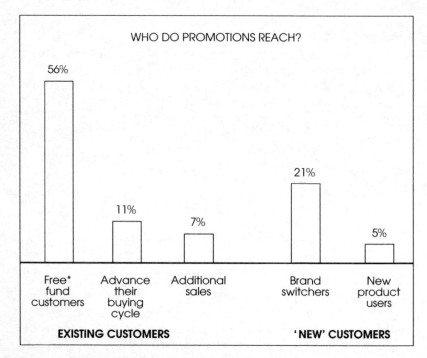

*'Free fund' customers are those who are going to buy the brand anyway–just giving them a discount, ie funding them for no reason.
(Source: MS Surveys, 1992)

Figure 12.4 A breakdown of who responds to sales promotions

The promotion may have worked well in one respect but failed in another. The purpose of measurement and monitoring is twofold:

1) To control current campaigns
2) To improve future campaigns by learning about what did and did not work with the current campaign.

Each promotion has to work successfully across a number of communication stepping stones for it to succeed. As Holloway puts it:

'It has to be: seen, interesting, understood, believed, relevant and compatible, persuasive, and produce the desired response among the right people... "Being seen" questions the suitability of the vehicle of communication (in-pack, on-pack, off-pack, POS, etc) and the design characteristics of the visual elements, eg many on-pack flashed offers are simply never seen by the target market. The middle criteria of communication effectiveness relate to the nature of the offer, the platform involved and the visual/copy elements of the promotion. Persuasion and response are dependent on the combination of the lot. There are few promotions we've come across in our pre- or post-testing which don't leave considerable room for improvement somewhere in the mix of essential ingredients.'

Figure 12.5 indicates how the total sales promotion package (including advertising support, if any) has worked.

PROMOTIONAL PENETRATION

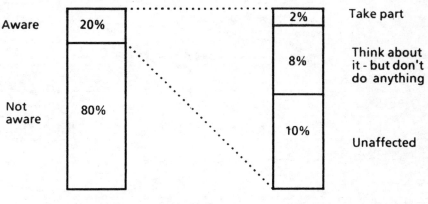

(Source: MS Surveys 1992)

Figure 12.5 Promotional presentation

SALES PROMOTION PROBLEMS

As with most marketing communication tools, Sod's law runs rampant across sales promotions and destroys many excellent ideas that have apparently been meticulously planned. Whether the sample packs burst and destroy other goods, premiums are pilfered, misredemption (non-buyers acquire other buyer's coupons), malredemption (large scale fraudulent coupon redemption), over redemption (with millions claiming their prizes), or door-drop samples that the dog or child gets to before the adult, the possibilities of a mini-marketing disaster seem endless. In addition, the *Competitor's Companion*, a monthly subscription magazine, publishes news and views on which competitions are running, what prizes they offer, exactly where to get entry forms, which qualifiers are required (eg a label etc) and the closing date. According to the magazine 'you receive advice on the answers to their questions plus a regular list of winning slogans and tie breakers...that way, you can read what's catching the judge's eye today and make them work for you tomorrow.' Here are a few cases of promotions that went wrong.

In 1984 syndicates cracked *Typhoo Tea's Cash Pot* promotion. Cadbury Typhoo were reported to have had to make cash payouts of more than one million pounds. According to *Marketing Week*, their insurers were reported to have issued a High Court writ against Cadbury Typhoo seeking a 'declaration that some claims made by

Table 12.2 Summary table showing which different sales, marketing and advertising methods are legally permitted in which European countries

One Law? – No!

As with every aspect of its day-to-day life, each European nation has its own laws in relation to Sales, Marketing and Advertising. It is this complex legal diversity that makes the appointment of a genuine European agency network even more vitally important to the International Marketer.

	UK	Irish Republic	Spain	West Germany	France	Denmark	Belgium	Netherlands	Portugal	Italy	Greece	Luxembourg	Austria	Finland	Norway	Sweden	Switzerland
On-pack price reductions	●	●	●	●	●	●	●	●	●	●	●	○	●	●	●	●	●
Banded offers	●	●	●	◄	●	◄	◄	●	●	●	●	○	◄	●	◄	●	○
In-pack premiums	●	●	●	◄	●	◄	◄	●	●	●	●	○	◄	◄	◄	●	○
Multiple-purchase offers	●	●	●	◄	●	●	◄	◄	●	●	●	◄	●	●	●	●	◄
Extra product	●	●	●	◄	●	◄	◄	●	●	●	●	○	●	●	●	◄	●
Free product	◄	●	●	◄	●	◄	◄	●	●	●	●	●	●	●	●	●	●
Reusable/alternative use pack	●	●	●	●	●	●	●	●	●	●	●	●	●	●	●	●	●
Free mail-ins	●	●	●	○	●	●	○	◄	●	●	●	◄	○	●	◄	●	○
With-purchase premiums	●	●	●	◄	●	●	●	●	●	●	●	●	◄	●	●	●	○
Cross-product offers	●	◄	●	○	●	◄	◄	◄	●	●	●	○	●	●	◄	◄	○
Collector devices	●	●	●	○	●	◄	●	◄	●	◄	●	◄	○	●	○	○	○
Competitions	●	●	●	●	●	◄	●	●	●	●	●	●	◄	●	●	◄	○
Self-liquidating premiums	●	●	●	●	●	◄	○	●	●	●	●	○	●	●	○	●	○
Free draws	●	●	●	○	◄	○	○	○	●	●	●	◄	○	◄	○	◄	○
Share-outs	●	●	●	◄	◄	○	◄	●	●	◄	●	○	●	●	◄	◄	○
Sweepstake/lottery	◄	◄	●	○	●	○	●	●	●	◄	●	◄	○	●	○	◄	○
Money-off vouchers	◄	●	●	○	◄	◄	○	●	●	◄	●	○	◄	◄	○	◄	○
Money-off next purchase	●	●	●	◄	●	○	●	●	●	○	●	◄	◄	◄	◄	●	○
Cash backs	●	●	●	●	◄	○	●	●	●	●	●	○	●	◄	○	●	○
In-store demos	●	●	●	●	●	●	●	●	●	●	●	●	●	●	●	●	●

● Permitted
○ Not permitted
◄ May be permitted

Extract from IMP Europe legislation document – 1/03/92.

© IMP Europe
197 Knightsbridge, London SW7 /RP, England

Cash Pot competitors are outside the rules of the competition'. Nevertheless, the expensive promotion apparently increased its market share to its 'highest level since its relaunch in 1982', but at what cost?

In 1990 *Coca-Cola's MagiCan* US promotion was supported by a massive $100 million push. The MagiCan looked and felt (even when shaken) like a regular can but when the tab was pulled a mechanism inside the can pushed real rolled-up dollar notes through the hole in the top of the can. Prizes ranged from $5 to $200. Inevitably there were a few duds. Most of them just didn't work but in a few cases the seal that held the 'liquid that gives the can the feel of the real thing' had broken. Although it was not harmful, one small boy (who was not aware of the promotion) drank the liquid and public health officials were called in. Massive media attention followed. 750,000 cans were held back while each one was shaken to determine whether the seal was broken or not. An immediate TV and press campaign was put into action to explain the promotion and to warn customers not to drink the liquid if the seal was broken. (*Marketing* 31 May 1990).

Kraft Foods 'Win a free camper van' promotion had a computer error which generated hundreds of winners. As the prize-winners' claims kept coming in, Kraft realised there was a problem. Some disappointed customers vowed never to buy the firm's food products again. Others sought legal action.

According to *Marketing Breakthroughs*, half a million special free sample minipacks of *Vidal Sassoon* shampoo were distributed in 1991 throughout Poland. When news of the promotion spread, around 2,000 mail-boxes (mostly at apartment blocks) were pillaged. The sample packs then started appearing in street markets and they soon sold out. The extra costs incurred by the damage added a new dimension to the sales promotion review process.

There is, arguably, a worse scenario. No one responds to the sales promotion. Large stocks of premiums are left in the warehouse, and teams of order fulfilment staff (who despatch the prizes) sit around with nothing to do.

As Table 12.2 shows, the international arena further complicates the life of the sales promotion professional. Regulations vary enormously.

To a Haggis

Sales promotions come in all shapes and sizes. Here is a leaflet that was in a 'please take one' point-of-sale dispenser sitting on top of the counter in a butcher's shop in Edinburgh. Some would call this simply a free leaflet, others point-of-sale, others packaging, others sales promotion, others PR. Regardless of what budget it comes out of, it promotes the brand while reinforcing the brand properties in a simple, low-risk, cost effective and friendly manner.

A TRUE TASTE OF SCOTLAND

SHORT CASE

The Miss Pears Competition

This short case demonstrates how sales promotion and PR work together.

Situation

Pears, the original transparent soap, was invented over 200 years ago by a Cornish barber, Andrew Pears. It was an instant success and has remained market leader for over two centuries. Despite the premium price, Pears Transparent Soap enjoys 3 per cent of the highly competitive soap market. The key qualities of Pears soap are those of purity and gentleness. Nostalgic childhood ideals have been upheld throughout the brand's history and the soap has always been completely natural.

Objective

The original marketing objective behind the Miss Pears competition was to 'sell full capacity from the Port Sunlight plant (built in 1890) at minimum marketing cost to maximise profit'.

Strategy

To create a competition suitable for anyone in the country and which is capable of repetition, and which, most importantly, enhances Pears caring family image. In 1958 the 'Preparing to be a beautiful lady' advertising campaign was brought to life and consultancy Welbeck Golin/Harris created an annual nationwide search for a natural and attractive little girl to star in the campaign.

Tactics

This classic competition, which harnesses public relations, sales promotions and advertising, still runs today, but without the advertising. The winning child is featured on the Pears soap cartons — which carry entry forms for the following year's competition. Proof of purchase is a prerequisite for entry and the chosen winner is used to promote the soap in the following year.

The competition is promoted editorially and on-pack with an annual closing date of 1 July. Around 20,000 entries are received each year. Each entry photograph is considered by a panel of independent judges before a shortlist of children is prepared in each regional judging area.

In 1992 the judging areas were increased from six to ten to bring the number of shortlisted children to 50. At no point do the judges meet these 50 children they work exclusively from photographs until the winner is chosen. Shortlisted children are photographed again and the judges choose ten regional winners. It is from this final ten that Miss Pears is chosen at the finals in August. The ten families travel to London and are photographed under identical studio conditions. It is from these pictures that the judges pick the eventual Miss Pears.

A national photocall is held at the crowning ceremony. This is then supplemented

by additional regional publicity/editorial generated by the nine other finalists and 40 national runners up — who all receive prize cheques.

Targets
Premium price soap aimed at all ABC1C2 mothers. There tends to be an AB buyer bias.

Men
Welbeck Golin/Haris Communications (the consultancy who created the competition in 1958 and still runs it today) allocate a team to work closely with the Pears brand manager for soaps throughout the year. The 20,000 entries are judged by a panel of independent journalists and photographers who are recruited each year.

Money
The 1992 campaign was run on a budget of £150,000 including publicity, cost of the final event, prize money, and handling of the entries. The special Miss Pears soap cartons are updated by simply substituting the new Miss Pears photograph on the existing artwork.

Minutes
The competition is open for entry in February/March every year, when the promotional packs appear on the shelf. The publicity campaign is launched at the same time and entries are generated until the closing date, 1 July. The shortlisting and judging process takes place throughout July and the ten finalists are announced at the begin-

ning of August. The crowning ceremony takes place at the end of the month and the 40 national runners up are informed during September.

Measurement
Each year 20,000 families enter their little girl, which means there are probably at least 80,000 people involved with the entries alone. In editorial terms (or free publicity) the

competition generates over 100 million OTS's (opportunities to see) through national and regional publications, consumer magazines, television and radio. Market share is maintained despite the intensity of the big ad-spending competitors.

Key Points from Chapter 12:

1) Sales promotions can be used strategically rather than simply as short-term tactical tools.
2) Sales promotions must integrate with other elements of the marketing mix.

Further reading

Bird, D 'No mileage in frequency marketing', *Marketing*, 10 October 1990, p.12

Bond, C 'Marriages of some convenience', *Marketing*, 10 October 1991, pp. 23–26

Britt, B, 'Coke's magic spells trouble', *Marketing*, 31 May 1990

Castling, J 'Buying strategic sales promotion', *Sales Promotion*, July 1989, p.11

Chapman, N, 'Cadburys pays up in Typhoo game', *Marketing Week*, 17 May 1985

Cummins, J (1990) *Sales Promotion: How to Create and Implement Campaigns that Really Work*, Kogan Page, London

Douglas, T (1984) *The Complete Guide to Advertising*, PaperMac, London

Ehrenberg, A, Hammond, K and Goodhaedt, G (1991) *The After Effects of Large Consumer Promotions*, London Business School

Farrell, J 'Which countries allow which promotions?', *Marketing Week*, 16 June 1989, pp.75 — 77.

Hyslop, R 'Round table discussion', *Sales Promotion*, July 1989, p14

Holloway, P 'Can research really help?', *Sales Promotion* July 1989 pp 12 and 13

Holloway, P 'Getting it right in the 90s', *Sales Promotion* February 1989 pp. 23 and 24

Kotler, P (1988) *Marketing Management: Analysis, Planning, Implementation and Control*, sixth edition, Prentice-Hall, Englewood Cliffs, New Jersey

Marketing Breakthroughs (1991) 'Polish giveaways struggle to reach target', *Marketing Breakthroughs*, December

Further contacts

British Promotional Merchandise Association (BPMA), Suite 12, 4th Floor, Parkway House, Sheen Lane, East Sheen, London SW14 8LS. Tel: 0181 878 0738

Institute of Sales Promotion (ISP), Arena House, 66–68 Pentonville Road, London N1 9HS. Tel: 0171 837 5340

Sales Promotion Consultants Association (SPCA), Arena House, 66-68 Pentonville Road, London N1 9HS. Tel: 0171 702 8567

DIRECT MARKETING

WHAT IS DIRECT MARKETING?

Direct marketing brings the market directly into the home or office of an individual buyer instead of the buyer having to go to the market. This is why it is sometimes called *armchair shopping*. There are, however, occasions when an immediate sale is not appropriate so direct marketing techniques can be used here to move buyers through various stages of the buying process, eg to get buyers to visit an exhibition, call into a showroom for a test drive, establish contact, etc. The Direct Marketing Association in the US defines direct marketing as:

> An interactive system of marketing which uses one or more advertising media to effect a measurable response *at any location*.

Direct marketing should not be used solely as a tactic, eg a one-off mail shot designed to win an initial sale. It can and should be used on a more *strategic* basis by integrating it with other marketing communication tools and in the longer term by developing a database (see page 254).

Direct marketing includes:

1) Direct mail;
2) Telemarketing;
3) Door-to-door selling (pyramid, multi-level, network retailing and field sales forces (see Chapter 10);
4) Direct response advertising (TV and press advertisements which solicit an immediate response, eg 'phone now' or 'fill in the coupon');
5) Computerised home shopping (link home computer with a store so that one can browse around the aisles, pickup merchandise, inspect it by turning it around on screen, etc);
6) Home shopping networks (have turned millions of living rooms into shopping

malls, eg Sky's Lifestyle channel; in the US in 1989, Home Shopping Network was carried on cable into 60 million US homes);

7) Miscellaneous (stuffers, inserts, leaflet drops/house-to-house distribution).

This chapter examines the growth of direct marketing and the development of database marketing and planning while focusing on two popular types of direct marketing techniques:

1) Direct mail;
2) Telemarketing.

As with all the marketing communication tools, the opportunity to integrate direct marketing is endless.

The marketing communications strategy should seek to link and *integrate* direct marketing techniques with other communication tools such as mainstream above the line TV advertising. For example, according to Ogilvy and Mather, some research shows that awareness for a TV ad campaign can be increased by including a picture from the ad in a mail shot. This integration can work both ways, ie advertisements linked to direct marketing (direct response advertisements). According to D P & A Associates, estimates suggest that as much as 75 per cent of US advertising now carries a direct response mechanism (eg coupon or toll free number).

Unintegrated communications activities can result in different messages being sent out through different media. This, in turn dilutes the message impact, splinters the image and sometimes generates plain confusion in the buyer's mind.

A strategic decision to integrate the communication tools increases the communications' effectiveness. Similarly, a longer-term strategic decision to build a database for direct marketing purposes can also create competitive advantage.

WHAT IS DATABASE MARKETING?

A database is more than a list of names. A database is distinguished by the amount and quality of relevant marketing data held on each customer/prospect file. There are two types of information kept on a database which a simple mailing list does not provide: *historical data* and *predictive data*. Historical ('transactional data' or 'back data') includes name, address, recency and frequency of purchases, responses to offers and value of purchases. Predictive data identifies which groups or subgroups are more likely to respond to a specific offer. This is done through statistical scoring: customer attributes (eg lifestyle, house type, past behaviour, etc) are given scores which help to indicate their future behaviour.

Database marketing is a not a short-term, tactical, one-off marketing activity. It is a medium to long-term commitment which facilitates the development of a *dialogue* and a *relationship* with each customer and prospect. It involves careful selection, collection and constant analysis of computerised customer records/data (and prospect customers' data also). Customers can then be telephoned or mailed with relevant offers at appropriate times in their buying cycles. The database can target, for example, 'customers who have bought three out of our four services and who are due this month, to buy a service similar to our fourth service'. A mutually useful relationship can then blossom through properly managed database marketing.

Never sell to a stranger

Think of the old corner shop. If the shopkeeper ordered a new type of pickle, he wouldn't expect strangers to flock in and buy it. He'd recommend it to his regular pickle buyers and to people buying cheese and pork.

You wouldn't call that hard sell. You'd call it personal service, based on the shopkeeper remembering the preferences of individual customers and using this knowledge to anticipate their needs. No matter what the size and character of your market place, direct marketing now lets you offer that personal service to every customer.

(Source: Miles Young, Ogilvy & Mather Direct)

A database gives an organisation access to its own private market place. Databases are discussed further on page 254. Suffice it to say, at this stage, that organisations with properly managed databases enjoy a *competitive advantage* over competitors without databases. This is compounded by the fact that no one has an exclusive right on their customers. The customers are probably listed on several databases, which means that a competitor will probably talk to these same customers through their own database marketing activities sooner or later.

The diner

The diner whose ego is bolstered by the head waiter recalling his name is more likely to to remain loyal than the diner whose repeat custom is incentivised by a voucher redeemable for a glass of house wine. Recognition of past custom is a powerful inducement to award future custom.

(Source: Graeme McCorkell, chairman, the Direct Marketing Centre)

ADVANTAGES OF DIRECT MARKETING

In addition to exploiting the power (and reduced costs) of computer technology, direct marketing can also open up a new distribution channel offering delivery from the supplier to the customer directly. This can save money by saving margins previously given to distributors or retailers but it can also damage relations with distributors if they feel the direct marketing competes unfairly with them. It can, of course, work with them by referring enquiries to or generating leads for them, or simply expanding the market. Other advantages include:

1) *Targeting* — to isolate and talk to tight, well-defined, appropriate target markets, eg 'slimming pill buyers who read the Sun' and to exclude waste associated with promoting to a mass audience (see 'List Explosion', page 249).

2) *Cost effective* — although initially a higher cost per thousand contacted, the cost per enquiry/order can be substantially lower, particularly with repeat sales.

3) *Control and accountability* — easy to measure results as the responses are directly attributable to the direct marketing activity. This facilitates continuous improvement and clearer direction for future activities. It also helps subsequent forecasting and budgeting.

4) *Immediate and flexible* — this applies to telemarketing in particular as responses can be logged as soon as contact is made. Scripts can be rewritten overnight or discussion varied according to contact's reactions.

5) *Opportunity to test* — and retest — any variable, eg prices, promotions, timing, lists and even the colour of a signature and/or the colour of the envelope (split mailings — 50 per cent blue and 50 per cent black).

6) *International* — can offer an alternative route for new market entry. Direct contact by mail or telephone may be cheaper and faster than a personal visit at the early stages of the buying cycle.

7) *Opportunity to build a database* — and win repeat sales by developing a personalised or individual dialogue and ultimately a continuous relationship with the customer base. A database also facilitates testing and researching the impact of, say, TV advertisements on different segments (see 'Building a Database', page 254).

8) *Tailored messages* — customers with different needs or even different levels of loyalty can receive separate offers, eg brand-loyal customers can receive different offers from brand switchers.

9) *Long-term customers* — the opportunity of developing long-term active relationships with customers through the database.

10) *Multi-functional* — applies particularly to telemarketing since it can be used to 'profile' or segment existing customers into clusters, generate leads, qualify leads, sell, give customer service and collect information about reactions to advertisements, promotions, mail shots and even reasons for buying or not buying as the case may be.

Buying a loan?

A building society's telemarketing campaign included the revealing question: 'What factors did you consider/are you considering with regard to taking out a mortgage at another bank or building society apart from the name of the bank?' In order of priority the top four criteria were: 1) price or interest rate, 2) special deal/discount, 3) recommendation and 4) convenience. This kind of feedback helps to determine the best sales and marketing strategy. The criteria, however, may change over time or as a recession lifts, etc.

DISADVANTAGES OF DIRECT MARKETING

In addition to sometimes upsetting the middleman (as mentioned previously), direct marketing has a problem with its image. Direct mail has connotations of 'junk mail' and is therefore vulnerable to criticism from environmental pressure groups. Although research shows that a large majority prefer to receive direct mail, there is a percentage who consider it to be an *intrusion* or *invasion of their privacy*. This is particularly true if they are telephoned in the evening or if a door-to-door salesperson knocks on their door after they have had a long day at the office. Telemarketing can be uniquely intrusive if a consumer has just come in from a hard day's work and wants to be left alone to relax. Whether someone is watching a football match, listening to Beethoven or simply sleeping, a telephone call, even from a friend, can sometimes be considered a downright nuisance.

The initial *customer acquisition costs* are high (subsequent transactions are much cheaper). Direct marketing has high cost per thousand (people contacted) compared to above the line advertising. The very rough industry average response of 2 per cent response* suggests, by definition, that *98 per cent of mailings get chucked in the bin* (albeit mostly after being read). There can also be a *heavy investment cost in developing a database*. Direct marketing can prove to be expensive for a one-off sale. Used inefficiently, ie simply to make a single sale, direct marketing can be extremely costly. Used effectively, ie to develop repeat sales and 'lifetime value' (see page 254) it can prove extremely profitable.

Finally, there is, of course, the *risk* involved with any marketing communications activity. A bad mailing, for example, can not only lose money but reduce sales and damage the company's corporate image.

---

* Many direct mail shots achieve much higher responses. The issue is largely to do with targeting and relevance. In addition, where the objective is to generate enquiries rather than make an immediate sale, a higher response is likely. A further percentage of the enquirers are then converted into sales, eg 15 per cent respond as enquirers and 30 per cent of those are converted into customers, giving a net response of 4.5 per cent.

THE GROWTH OF DIRECT MARKETING

Many years ago advertising guru David Ogilvy forecasted that one day all advertising agencies would be direct marketing agencies. The growth of direct marketing has been fuelled by:

1) Market fragmentation
2) Tailor-made technology
3) The list explosion
4) Sophisticated software
5) Hybrid marketing systems
6) The constant search for cost effective communications.

Market fragmentation

In the 1960s we had mass marketing. The 1970s developed *segmentation*, while the 1980s moved into *target marketing* and *niching*. The 1990s and beyond are now in a new era — that of *one-to-one-marketing* or direct marketing. Today, *mass markets*, by and large, are *dead*. They have fragmented into more discrete sectors or niches. This is clearly demonstrated by the plethora of product development and modification shown below.

Once there was one cola; today there is ordinary cola, sugar-free cola, caffeine free cola, and so on. Once there were a dozen or so breakfast cereals; now the consumer can choose from over one hundred different types. Once there was just a running shoe; now there are tennis, squash, basketball, indoor soccer, walking, running, jogging and aerobics shoes for both men and women. Once there was just coffee; then came instant coffee, powder, granules, freeze-dried granules, filter and percolator coffees, and *caffeine-free coffee*. Now we have 'politically correct' coffees from certain developing countries. Oxfam shops sell other 'ethical coffees' (coffees supplied by working co-operatives in developing countries) and there is even a brand of coffee sold in Amsterdam called 'Fair Wages For Coffee Pickers'.

The shampoo market has gone full circle. Initially it fragmented into dry, greasy and normal shampoos. Split ends, dandruff, sensitive scalp and blow dry shampoos followed. Then TV audiences were informed that the shampoos didn't work very well and conditioners were needed. There is today a new shampoo targeted at the busy person, which has shampoo and, wait for it, conditioner all in one. These new, emerging, discrete needs, niches or mini-markets have a growing range of specialist magazines and new minority radio and television programmes which offer tightly targeted communication channels. The trend towards individualism, the increase in personalised products and the resulting bespoke solutions to buyers' needs are evidence of the continuing fragment of markets.

Tailor-made technology

Personalised products, eg inscribed silverware and handwritten letters have been around for a long time. Technology today allows thousands or millions of personalised items (eg personalised letters or maybe even personally labelled shampoo) to be produced economically in the course of a few days. This matches our increasing desire to be treated as individuals (see the Guinness Genius research findings, page 207, Chapter 11). Many years ago futurologist *Alvin Toffler* forecasted that there would be a proliferation of personalised, tailor-made products. One of his many challenging books, *The Third Wave*, considered tailor-made remote *satellite* manufacturing systems which design individualised products on a computer screen in one country, and are electronically linked to an automated factory in some less developed country where a laser could cut out the design as directed by the designer, on a screen, many thousands of miles away. A single product would then be produced to suit an individual's need.

Underwater and space manufacturing have not fully caught up with Toffler's predictions but it seems as if America's *Farmer's Journal* is getting close. Its 825,000 circulation now receives a tailor-made magazine with a minimum of 2,000 and a maximum of 8,896 different editions per issue. Essentially, the pig farmer's edition will not carry features or advertisements about cereal farming, etc. The farmer prefers his magazine to carry relevant materials. The advertisers like it because it offers better targeting. The magazine saves money on paper and post. The environmentalists might prefer it too. It has been suggested that one day everyone will have their own *personalised magazine*. *Personalised interactive TV programmes* are already running in Spain and France.

The list explosion

The third factor fuelling the growth of direct marketing is the proliferation of lists or databases available. The *only restriction is imagination*, or one's ability to define a target market or customer profile in a range of different ways. For example, home decorators could be redefined as 'home movers'. The million or so UK home movers could then be reduced to those moving into certain geographic locations or even neighbourhood areas which might indicate their propensity to undertake the decorating themselves (as opposed to hiring someone else to do it for them). A list, or a section of the list, can be hired or bought, and tested and/or refined (by using certain software packages (see 'Sophisticated Software', page 251). It is important to select and check lists carefully since the quality of many of the UK's 'cold' lists has long been a problem for UK direct marketers.

The diversity of the lists available is intriguing and sometimes bewildering. The lists range from 'cynical humorous intellectuals' (23,000 *Punch* magazine subscribers) to 'slimming pill buyers who read the *Sun*' to 'young mothers' to 'fork lift truck-buyers'. Just about anything can be targeted. There was even a list of 'right-wing, money oriented gamblers who are influenced by advertising, react to new ideas and have disposable income' (the three million British Gas shareholders is available from the British Investor Database). The Companies Act requires firms to hand over their registers to anyone for a minimal fee.

It is worth phoning list brokers and list owners to request a catalogue of lists (consumer or business to business) and spending an hour browsing through the range and types of lists available from just one particular source. A *compiled list* is collected from public records, directories, trade show registrations, etc. According to *World List News*, a *mail-responsive list* can produce a 300 per cent increase in response over a compiled list. The best list is an organisation's own house list of customers, enquirers, visitors, employees, shareholders, etc.

Some examples of lists

Here is a small selection of lists which could be relevant for the three types of target customers shown below.

Prominent people: 25,000 Rolls-Royce, Lamborghini and Jaguar owners, 2,500 UK millionaires, 10,000 rich ladies, 7,000 tennis court owners, 13,000 private plane owners, race horse owners, greyhound owners and even cat owners.

Entertainment seekers: 190,000 theatre goers, 27,000 Shaftesbury Theatre goers, 186,000 club goers.

Improvers: 47,000 named clergy, 26,000 buyers of self-improvement books, 106,000 house improvers, 1,000,000 house movers, and even a list of owners of Black 'n' Decker drills.

The diverse range of lists is, to the uninitiated, extraordinary. Here are some other odd lists of odd target groups.

100,000 aerial home photograph owners (people who have aerial photos of their homes), 15,000 personalised car number plate owners, 62,000 buyers of military prints and memorabilia, 49,000 tall ladies, 5,000 car phone enquirers, 160 prisons, borstals and detention centres, 21,000 women executives, 295,000 hypochondriacs, 4,100 management consultants, 43,700 librarians, 246,000 educational children's book buyers and so on.

These are just a selection from a few list catalogues. They do not represent the whole universe of people who fall into each category. They only represent those who have been trapped on to a list. The lists can be bought or hired on disc, printed labels, envelopes and so on.

The best list is the house list or an organisation's own customer files/lists. In the USA it is estimated that 80 per cent of all direct mail is targeted at existing customer lists.

Sophisticated software

Basic technology today allows different mailing lists and databases to be added together and even superimposed on each other. Lists can be *merged* and any overlap or duplications can be '*deduped*' (deduplicated).

Geodemographics mix geographical location, type of neighbourhood and demographic data such as age, income and family life cycle. Everyone fits into a cluster. Key in an address and the database will identify the neighbourhood's cluster type or profile. This *geodemographic typecasting* uses shorthand names to identify cluster types. For example, in the US one database company classifies people with mature families living in affluent suburbs as '*pools and patios*' whereas poorer rural areas are called '*shotguns and pickups*'. People living there may have aspirations to move towards '*golf clubs and Volvos*'.

They know you better than you do

An investigative journalist decided that he wanted to find out about himself as he was soon moving to south east San Francisco. Having keyed in his new address, the database company told him that he was classified as a *'young influential'*. He was moving into a 'thirty something childbearing neighbourhood'. They also told him that 'he may still be in a town house or a row house and may not have graduated to the detached single home but they were definitely starting to have children, making the transition from a couple-oriented lifestyle to a family-oriented lifestyle.' (See 'UK Sagacity Family Life Cycles' on page 49, Chapter 2.) Furthermore, the 'young influentials' typically were aged 20 – 35, had a median income of $39,500, enjoyed jogging, travelling, new wave music and investing, they read magazines like *Rudder*, *Scientific*, *American* and *Town and Country*, and they also liked to eat yoghurt, wholemeal bread, Mexican food and drink low-fat milk.

This profile almost exactly matched the journalist's profile.

It is said that demographics say *'you are where you live'* (meaning your neighbourhood is a good indicator of your lifestyle and the kinds of products you are likely to buy) and psychographic databases say *'you are what you do'* (meaning your behaviour patterns and buying preferences can be estimated from collected data on your (or similar people's) lifestyle, eg whether you are likely to own a compact disc. In the UK, geodemographic packages such as *ACORN* (see page 51, Chapter 2), *PINPOINT*, *MOSAIC* and *SUPER PROFILES* are easily cross-refenced with media usage, product usage and lifestyle statements. Another system called MONICA classifies databases into age and social status by analysing the Christian or first name alone.

If you run up a bad debt...

...the computer will know about it, if you subscribe to a dubious magazine, forget to return library books or collect parking tickets, everyone with access to a computer will know about it!

This light hearted suggestion was made in an article in *Marketing Week* (3 December 1982) but try to hire a TV if you have a county court judgement against you — the retailer will find out through their on-line database, United Protection of Traders Association.

Hybrid marketing systems

The addition and integration of new communication channels (eg telemarketing) to existing communication channels (eg advertising or the salesforce) can create a hybrid marketing system. Harvard professors Moriarty and Moran (1990) recently said that 'a company that designs and manages its (hybrid) system strategically will achieve a powerful advantage over rivals that add channels and methods in an opportunistic and incremental manner'. A well managed hybrid system allows an organisation to achieve what Moriarty and Moran call '*a balance between its customers' buying behaviour and its own selling economics.*'

Direct marketing can, and should, integrate with other communication tools. It can link different direct marketing tools to create a more cost effective method of marketing communications. Depending on the quality of the lead, the lead can be followed up by mailing a brochure, or a hot prospect might be telephoned to set up an appointment or to invite the prospect to an event.

The *lead generation* might be created in the first place by a *direct response advertisement* which invites readers/viewers/listeners to send in for a free gift. Research suggests that approximately 45 per cent of business enquirers will buy within 12 months. The challenge then lies in identifying the hottest prospects and directing the salesforce to the one out of every 2.2 enquirers who will buy within the 12 months.

Identifying the hottest prospects or 'screening' can be carried out by following up with an *outbound telephone* interview to determine the prospect's status. Alternatively, the analysis can be carried out directly from the coupon if the coupon was designed to capture the required detailed information. The outbound phone call can screen and ultimately fix an appointment for the sales representative to visit and make a presentation, and consequently close the sale or progress to the next appropriate stage in the buying process. Alternatively, an *inbound* phone catering for an 0800 or free-phone number can accomodate enquiries generated from either a direct response advertisement or a mail shot.

This is only the start. After the initial sale, *database marketing* can then help to keep in touch with the customer as he moves towards a repeat purchase. Conservative estimates suggest that it is *five times easier to sell to an existing customer* than to a new one.

The constant search for cost effectiveness

Falling computer costs have opened up computer database facilities to organisations large and small.

Ideally, costs should be measured against results, not simply outputs. The cost of testing* a telesales campaign (1,000 names at £10 per call) might be, say, £10,000 but the result might be 2 per cent success or 20 new customers. The cost per order or cost per customer can then be calculated as £500. How does this compare with the current cost per new customer generated by other marketing techniques, such as exhibitions, advertising and field sales?†

---

* Since the set up costs of a test remain fixed, it follows that a larger test run will reduce the cost per order anywhere from £500 to £50.
† The real cost of a salesman on a basic salary of £19,000 plus bonus, car (including depreciation), expenses, national insurance and perks such as medical and life insurance is closer to £50,000. Five visits a day times four days a week (one day in the office per week) times

The results, and costs, may vary if, for example, the telesales team is only focused on appointment setting and the field sales team handles the rest. This may result in, say, 15 per cent appointments (150); the sales team then convert, say, 30 per cent of these into 45 new customers. The telesales cost of £10,000 is added to the field sales cost of £8,550 (see note 2 below). £18,550 divided by 45 gives a cost per new customer of £412. A recent Datapoint survey suggested that companies could increase their salesforce's productivity by at least one third by providing in-house telesales marketing support.

The *lifetime value* of the customer can then be calculated by multiplying the average value of expected orders p.a. by the number of years the customer will exist. The cost per order of subsequent orders will be significantly less than the cost of the initial order as estimates suggest that it is at least five times cheaper and easier to sell to an existing customer than a prospect.

One last international question — what are the *marketing costs of entering a new market*? Could any of the marketing costs be reduced by telemarketing or direct mail?

Telesales can be used to *support a sales force* by servicing accounts over the phone instead of having a sales rep visit every month. Telesales can also be used to generate or even screen leads. At a cost of anywhere between £5 and £60 per appointment set up, a telesales campaign can release the salesperson from prospecting and even administration into doing what most reps are best at, face-to-face selling. Some estimates show that sales people spend less than 20 per cent of their time actually selling; the rest is prospecting, travelling, form filling, etc. The average cost of a single sales visit of £150 (per call) can be reduced if sales people are released from other duties and therefore make more visits. Some telesales campaigns link in with computer models which select the optimum call plan to minimise travel time. All of these activities, including order fulfilment, can be handled by an outside agency if needed.

Not surprisingly TV ads and mail shots can link together both activity wise and image wise. Drayton Bird's excellent *Commonsense Direct Marketing* (1989) revealed that awareness for a particular airline's TV ad four months later was 50 per cent higher among those who had received a mail shot which featured a scene from the TV ad than among a similar panel who had not received the mail shot. The database can also be used to research the impact of, say, a TV advertisement or a sponsorship package among different types of audiences.

DATABASE MARKETING

Building a database

A customer database or a list carrying customer information can be an organisation's most valuable asset. Databases can be bought, borrowed or built. Guarantee slips, subscription lists and sales promotions all trap names and addresses. Often the best

---

50 weeks = 1,000 sales visits a year. Each visit costs £50.00. Some customers could be serviced by a telesales call (@ £10) while others need a sales representative to be there on the spot, face to face with the customer. The trick is to identify which ones need the extra attention. See Chapters 10 and 16 for further salesforce cost analysis.

source lies dormant, tucked in the bottom of a file somewhere in an organisation. Every customer and their purchasing pattern, every enquiry and every complaint comment or feedback can be logged into a database. The database then builds up a detailed picture of the customer's profile, which lets the company get to know its customers better. The database can identify which customers/prospects are in which stages of the buying cycle. This facilitates *sequence selling*, where attitudes are moulded and interest is aroused by a series of communications rather than going for an immediate straight sale. In a sense, prospects are moved up the 'ladder of loyalty' (see Figure 13.1) from suspects up to devoted loyal customers who advocate an organisation's product or service. Raphel and Considine's *The Great Brain Robbery* (1981) gives a full explanation.

Figure 13.1 The ladder of loyalty

Customer *acquisition* is the immediate goal. Customer *retention* is the long-term, financially-rewarding relationship which, ultimately, the database aims to achieve. Welcome cycles (welcome letters, new member offers), upselling (moving the customer on to higher quality levels), cross-selling (other products/services) and reactivation (of previous customers) all help to nurture the relationship. The system should develop a *dialogue* or a two-way flow of information between customer and the organisation. Every time a customer responds he or she can be encouraged to give information about their needs and situation (eg whether they want to stay on the database). Questionnaires are sometimes sent out to existing customers to gather even more specific data. The *art lies in the retrieval of the data* in an appropriate format, eg a list of 'all enquirers from the south west in the last six months', a list of a particular category of business customer (SIC code), a list of 'customers that have bought all our products except product X' and so on. Can the database identify the key characteristics of the customers on file? Careful thought and considerable advice is needed in setting up a database since the system has to be told specifically what is expected of it.

Information gathering is strategic, it has a long-term purpose and it costs time, money and expertise. *Information is an investment.*

In consumer markets, a database allows an individual to be targeted by *overlaying* lifestyle and geodemographic data which analyses our behaviour patterns. And this data is saleable. Why then are databases not included as assets on the balance sheet? Like fixed assets, databases can be realised or sold. They also deteriorate or depreciate (business lists deteriorate at 25 per cent or more p.a.). They need maintenance and (need to be cleaned or adjusted/updated). Equally, an uncleaned or decayed list should be considered a liability to the extent that the data is so inaccurate it generates much higher costs per order/response than orders generated from a properly maintained database or list. An inaccurate list can also damage the corporate image and even cause resentment, eg when mailing dead members of a family.

Some years ago Rothmans used a *sales promotion* to build a database by offering their cigarette smokers a free pack of cigarettes when they had collected ten coupons and returned them with a completed form. They generated 750,000 names within 18 months. 500,000 of the customer database were subsequently offered *FGF* promotion ('friend get a friend', similar to *MGM* 'member get member'). The database members received a free draw ticket after sending in their own name and address and a 'draw partner's' name and address. The draw partner had to be over 18 and a smoker of a competitive brand. 250,000 smokers of competitors' brands were named. Follow-up market research showed that 90 per cent were genuine. These names may provide an invaluable communication channel as fewer and fewer communication channels become available to cigarette companies. The lifetime value of a smoker may be around £29,000 (for an average 20-a-day smoker). This would represent over £7 billion (£7,250,000,000) worth of sales if all 250,000 converted permanently to this brand.

Dunhill have also advertised a free product trial and gave a direct response phone number which could be used to claim a free pack of cigarettes.

There are, of course, other methods of compilation, some of which may cause concern. For example, Manhattan psychotherapists Muriel Goldfarb and Daniel Ruinstein compile their own lists of *mild neurotics* so that they can market counselling by mail. Lists of those recently divorced and widowed, and previous patients, are added, together with bereavement notices. These prospects are then offered a ten-session programme with the first one free 'plus' a free tape recorder if they pay in advance.

In the UK it is now illegal to store any data about an individual on computer unless registered with the *Data Protection Registrar* (1992 cost was £75.00). The *Mailing Preference Service (MPS)* is a free service for people who do not want to receive unsolicited mail, or who only want to receive mail in certain categories. They can put their names on an MPS application form (which they can get from the post office) and their names are then entered on to a disc which is used by reputable list owners and mailers so that these names are cleaned from their lists. Reputable agencies subscribe to the MPS and therefore use *MPS clean lists*. Any response mechanism (coupon, guarantee slip, order form, etc) should give the respondent the opportunity to choose not to receive further mailings, or *opt out* by ticking an opt-out box (see the example opposite).

Address..

....

....Postcode.................

Signature................................... ....Date....................

Prices may be subject to alteration without notice

☐ As a service to our readers we occasionally make our customer lists available to companies whose products or services we feel may be of interest. If you do not wish to receive such mailings, please tick the box.

TR 0123456789 ABCDE TM

Database manipulation

Database manipulation creates further opportunities for tighter targeting. In the early 1980s, Grattan's ladies' fashion mail order company decided to experiment with a new product, a grandfather clock. They guessed the likely target profile would be something like middle-aged, well off ABs living in ACORN types J35 (villages with wealthy older commuters) and J36 (detached houses, exclusive suburbs — see page 52, Chapter 2.) They then asked their computer to print out names and addresses which fitted this profile. The subsequent mailing produced 60 orders at £1,000. They then analysed those 60 orders with a view to identifying any hidden characteristic which could be added to the profile and fed into the database again to produce a different, more accurate target list. When they mailed this list they sold every one of the 1,000 limited edition clocks.

In the absence of completely reliable data, a *less scientific analysis* is sometimes used to separate or take out names that do not fit the target profile. For example, Rediffusion cable services felt that older home dwellers did not fit their hot prospects' profile so they took out older- generation Christian names commonly used by elderly relatives, office tea ladies and popular Falkland Island names such as Albert, Alfred, Arthur, Bertram, Harold, Samuel, Victor, Winifred, Alice, Amelia, Constance, Grace, May, Mildred, Rose, Sabena and Violet.

Constant analysis not only seeks to identify the best prospects for various direct marketing activities, it also provides guidance for future communication strategy, creative strategy, product strategy, and pricing and offer strategy. The responses are then fed back into the database so that a *spiral of prosperity* develops (see Bird D, 1989). This is shown in Figure 13.2.

Accurate feedback of results by key code (identifies which lists, media and tests were used) is absolutely essential.

Database maintenance

Like any other asset the database has to be maintained or '*cleaned*'. It is estimated that business lists decay by 25 per cent p.a. because of constant career moves. During a recession redundancies can increase the '*gone aways*' (obsolete addresses, positions or job titles) to give a *decay rate* of over 30 per cent.

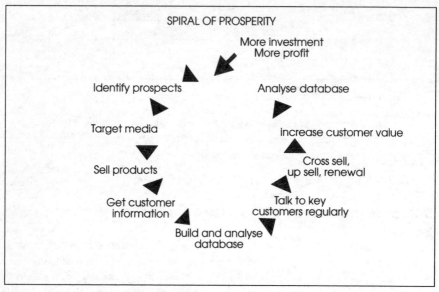

Figure 13.2 The spiral of prosperity

Marketing Business reported in June 1992 that one company maintains its core list of 900,000 names with 40,000 calls a month. Other companies send their database names a reply-paid card asking them whether they wish to be kept on the mailing list. Non-respondents get wiped. This may seem costly but it can increase the accuracy of the list and ultimately improve the cost effectiveness of the responses. This, in turn, reduces wasted brochures, envelopes, handling costs and postage. It simultaneously maintains this asset's value.

PLANNING A DIRECT MAIL CAMPAIGN

Whether an organisation is planning an advertising campaign or a direct mail campaign, a similarly disciplined approach should be taken, ie research, message development (creative mailing), media planning (list selection and timing), testing and monitoring, etc. In addition the SOSTT + 4Ms can be used as a checklist (see Chapter 2).

A direct marketing campaign can be planned in the same way as an advertising campaign, ie by using SOSTT + 4Ms. The following six factors will now be examined in more detail:

1) Timing
2) List selection
3) Creative mailings
4) Budgeting
5) Operational implications
6) Testing.

Timing

The mailing schedule illustrated in Figure 13.3 shows why a minimum of 12 weeks, preferably *six months*, is needed to set up a direct marketing campaign which feeds into a database system from scratch. As Drayton Bird (1989) says: 'The faster you need something done the more likely there will be mistakes. The answer is either give more time, or pay a great deal more money.' Deciding whether the campaign should be multi-stage (generate enquiries, screening, follow-up phone calls and sales visits, etc) or single stage (straight order), multi-media or single media, and so on, is arguably less important than determining strategically how each mailing forms part of an overall campaign which develops a cumulative effect. *One-off large mailings should gradually be replaced by smaller, more frequent mailings* as the database identifies what is needed by whom and when. Many direct mail agencies can develop a campaign in four to six weeks but, ideally, the campaign should be researched and planned strategically.

Timing also refers to identifying when a target market buys and how often. Markets are constantly moving. Buyers drift in and out at different stages. Other markets are seasonal and others again have peaks and troughs on different days of the week. Are target respondents more receptive to a mail shot which lands on a Friday morning or a Monday morning?

The development and scheduling of the campaign is shown in Figure 13.3. Essentially it follows the normal advertising campaign development sequence: brief, concept development, research artwork, production, and roll-out (note that research can be supplemented by continual testing).

As in advertising, a *creative brief* is followed by *concepts* which are subsequently approved, amended, *researched* and eventually developed into *final copy and design*. This is turned into *artwork* which is checked/*proofed* and eventually turned into *final approved artwork* which goes to the *printer*. Prior to this (or sometimes simultaneously) a *list brief* is agreed. This defines the target market. Lists are carefully researched and checked.

A list proposal is subsequently approved for ordering (purchase or hire). *The letter shop* puts the required letter into the system ready for *laser printing* on to personalised letters. Proof letters are checked and approved while the lists are prepared, merged and purged (duplicate names withdrawn). The printer despatches the brochure to the letter shop, who then press the button. The letters are lasered, *folded, collated and inserted* with the brochure or mailing piece into lasered (or window) envelopes (sometimes preprinted with teaser messages or images) and *posted*. Then a dreadful quietness descends as the bags of mail are driven off into the sunset and the long wait begins. Pre-mail-shot tension can run riot with nightmares about postal strikes, redundant lists, a printing error, a wrong expiry date or, worse still, a nil response level.

Good planning ensures that the best lists are used (perhaps based on test results), print, proofs, dates, etc are checked, and acceptable results projected. Even in a situation where a lot of variables are unknown, careful planning can reduce the chance of failure.

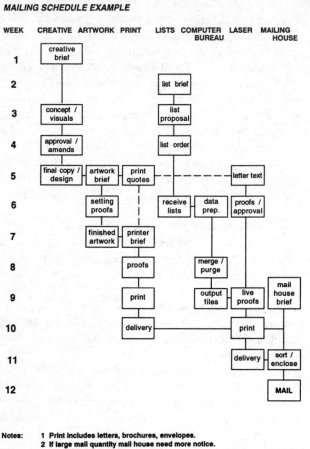

MAILING SCHEDULE EXAMPLE

Notes: 1 Print includes letters, brochures, envelopes.
         2 If large mail quantity mail house need more notice.
         3 If envelopes special their make-up requires longer lead time.

(Source: Direct Marketing Centre, 1992)

Figure 13.3 Example of a mailing schedule

List selection

Five key planning questions

These are patently obvious questions which can be applied to any communications campaign but as Bird (1989) says, surprisingly few people do ask these questions.

1) Who are you trying to influence?
2) What are you selling?
3) Why should your prospect buy it?
4) Where will you find your prospect?
5) When should you speak to them?

Tips for selecting a list

List selection is the most important stage in the whole direct marketing process. Sixty per cent of any project's time should be spent on list selection. 'There's no point fishing in the pool if the pool ain't got any fish.' Here are some questions which should be asked before using a list.

1) Where do the names come from (eg compiled, previous mail responsive, subscription lists, etc)?
2) When was the list built?
3) How often is it cleaned (updated)? Is it MPS cleaned?
4) When was the list last used (and by whom) and what was the percentage of gone aways (redundant names/addresses which the post office return to the sender)? Are there any known results or any references from past users?
5) What is the rebate per gone away which is returned to the list owner for future cleaning?
6) What proportion of the target's total universe does the list represent, eg does the one million list of home movers represent all the home movers or half or what?
7) What selections are available (eg geographic split, job title, etc? Are there any additional costs?
8) What 'net names' percentage is quoted (ie net useable names after deduping with other lists)?
9) Are there any rental restrictions (minimum quantities, competitive products subject to the list owner's approval, etc)?
10) Assuming the list has an appropriate profile (similar to your specified target market), clarify whether:
    a) it has named individuals as opposed to job titles or 'the occupier'
    b) the list is in an appropriate format, ie labels, disc, etc. If disc check that the disc format suits the lettershop's requirements
    c) the list is postcoded (for post office Mailsort discounts)
11) How much does it cost? What is the lead time from order to delivery?

If the list is hired, permission is usually given for one use only. *Sleeper names* are planted in the list to ensure that the list is not used more than once (the sleepers immediately notify the list owner if they receive two mailings). Hiring charges vary from £30 to £200 per thousand. Many lists are not available for purchase but those that are are often priced at least four times higher than the rental price. Prices in the US are cheaper. For example, every single residential phone number in the US is in 'Phone Disc USA', which is available on interactive compact disc (CDI) for $1,850 annual subscription.

Creative mailings

Creative mailing devices

Opportunities for creativity abound. Most mail competes with bills and statements. Many of the top creative people still feel television advertising is sexier, so perhaps most mailings are restrained either by the people that create them or the managers who commission them. Here are some odd exceptions:

A *plastic green cucumber* was mailed by the Direct Mail Sales Bureau to all UK media buyers to raise awareness of the direct mail option.

The Prince's Trust, when targeting company chairmen, mailed a box containing a *ceramic bowl* created by one of the very businesses the Trust had supported (the bowl provided a gift for the chairman's secretary, to encourage her to pass on the pack it also brought the achievements of the trust to life for the chairman).

A *briefcase* was mailed to car distributors. When opened the briefcase resembled a car dashboard complete with audio cassette and car phone. Insert the tape and lift the phone to hear a sales pitch about why the particular car phone was outstanding. The briefcase further doubled as a point-of-sale item for the distributor.

The mailing piece and the incentive can affect the budget significantly. Not all creative mailings need anything other than a few clever words. A recent mailing simply said '*Good Morning*'. This generated a lot of interest, anticipation and eagerness to get the next mailing in the sequence.

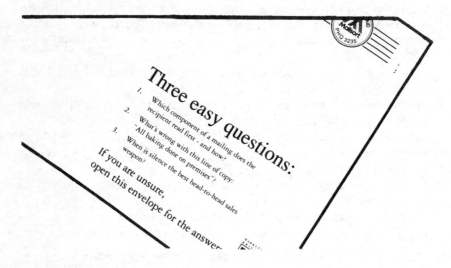

Budgeting

One way of budgeting is by asking: 'how much can the organisation afford to spend to recruit a new customer? How much is a new customer worth or what is the allowable cost per customer? What is their *lifetime value*?' Then multiply this by the number of customers required and bingo, a budget emerges. Another way to build a budget or at least a *ball park cost figure* is to calculate 50p per shot. Thus if an organisation is running a 20,000 mail shot then ball park costs to cover everything (design, artwork, print, list, letter shop, insertion or collation incentive, envelope and postage) would be £10,000; a 500,000 mail shot would obviously enjoy economies of scale and cost less than £250,000.

Cost per thousand
This translates into £500 per thousand contacts compared with:

Table 13.1 Direct mail budgeting worksheet

DIRECT MAIL BUDGETING WORKSHEET

CAMPAIGN TITLE: Est   Actual
BUDGET: PROMOTION DATE:
TARGET: MAIL QUANTITY:

		Estimated Costs	Actual Costs	Invoice Y/N	Comments
1 ORIGINATION	- Copywriting/Design - Artwork Production				
2 DATABASE LIST PREPARATION	- List Rental - Data Preparation - Merge/Purge - Mailsort				
3 LASER PRINTING	- Text Setting - Printing				
4 PRINT PRODUCTION	- Letterhead - Continuation sheet - Brochure - Flyer - Order Form - Other				
5 ENVELOPES	- Outer - Reply				
6 LETTERSHOP	- Folding - Collating - Enclosing				
7 POSTAGE	- Postage -(Discount)				
8 MISC.	-couriers etc				
9 TOTAL COSTS					
10 COST PER 1000 MAILED = (Total Cost/Qty. Mailed) x 1000					
11 COST PER RESPONSE = Total Cost / No. of Responses					
12 COST PER SALE = Total Cost / No. of Sales					
13 TOTAL REVENUE					
14 REVENUE TO COST = Revenue / Total Cost					

(Source: The Direct Marketing Centre, 1992)

Telesales (@£10)	£10,000
Door-to-door drop	£250
Inserts (inc. print)	£100
Magazine ads	£50
National press	£10
TV ads	£1

Cost per response and cost per order give the bottom line of success or failure. Percentage response levels vary from half of one per cent to 2 per cent. Enquiries, as opposed to orders, are easier to get and therefore *pull* higher response levels.

The direct mail budgeting worksheet shown in Table 13.1 helps to identify and control costs.

Operational implications

A strain on your office?

Even if the response is fairly modest it can still be a strain on your office resources. Could your telephone system handle thousands of calls in an hour? Could your staff still treat customers with enthusiasm at the end of a whole day of frantic answering? Do you have space for sackfuls of mail? Do you have time to answer every reply quickly? If not a specialist fulfilment company can help.

(Source: The *Royal Mail Guide to Successful Direct Mail*)

If carefully thought out, *the operational requirements* clarify how the campaign will actually work. For example, what happens to the information that is collected during a telephone conversation? How do the sales representatives' diaries get updated and who monitors their availability? 1990 research by RSCG Direct found '*an irresponsible use of response handling mechanisms*' with only a 70 per cent chance of respondents receiving information. The majority of this 70 per cent were never contacted again. Only 5 per cent ever received a follow-up telephone call. Is there a plan/system which ensures 'follow-up'? Who controls and delivers stocks of goods or stocks of brochures? How and when are invoices generated?

Marketing is the last bastion of under automation, whereas manufacturing and production have generally been automated to the point where labour costs account for only 8–12 per cent of production costs. Sales and marketing costs can account for between 15 per cent and 35 per cent of corporate costs. According to Moriarty and Swartz (1989) 'few companies have automated any part of their marketing and sales functions. Even fewer appear to understand the significant strategic benefits that can accrue from marketing and sales automation.' *Voice recognition* or robot-answering phones are also starting to come into action.

Testing

Test, test and test

One of the advantages of direct marketing is the ability to test, retest, change, monitor and learn what works best. Everything can be tested including the colour of the signature. Bird (1989) suggests that a white envelope will do better than a manilla envelope and a brightly coloured envelope will do better than a white one (but will it damage the long-term corporate image?). If 10 per cent of a direct marketing budget is allocated to continual testing then response levels will be continually higher.

Bird tested 12 different 'appropriate' lists, three different prices, two different ways to pay, different times for the mailings, alternative ways of responding and several creative approaches. He found that the best combination of all these factors produced a result *58 times better than the worst combination*. By identifying the best and worst responses for each variable, the maximimum response variation (difference between best and worst) was found. Table 13.2 shows the result:

Table 13.2 The impact of different direct mail variables on response levels

Variable	Different repsonse between worst and best
List	x 6.0
Offer	x 3.0
Timing	x 2.0
Creative	x 1.35
Response	x 1.2

Ideally, everything should be tested in isolation to give more realistic results. There are sometimes so many combinations that testing might appear endless. However, the big variables (those likely to have a *significant* impact on the bottom line) should be tested. Work down the list but stop when the cost of testing outweighs the benefits. As we have mentioned, direct mail lends itself to testing. It allows the marketing manager to become more scientific and more precise — basically a better manager. Testing the colour of signature may only yield one twentieth of one per cent difference in response, but even so it still generates increased revenues so it is worthwhile testing everything.

TELEMARKETING

As Michael Stevens (1991) says:

> The telephone is such a commonplace, every-day piece of business equipment that is often treated as something more akin to the office photocopier than a powerful means of communication. It requires planning and skill to get the best from a telephone call, yet the majority of business communication over the telephone lacks both. In some areas this can have a seriously damaging effect on the company's image, marketing efforts and resulting profitability.

What is telemarketing?

Telemarketing, or telephone marketing, is used for many different purposes including selling, lead generation, customer care or even shareholder communication. In contrast with advertising, telemarketing's two-way communication flow offers the opportunity of conversing with a customer. This interactive *dialogue* can constantly collect and give new information. In marketing, fast *feedback* is invaluable. It allows an early assessment of, say, a special offer, an advertisement, or even the telesales campaign itself. The *flexibility* of a telesales campaign is dependent on feedback. Depending on the previous day's results, a telesales campaign can change on a daily basis if required. A telesales script can be rewritten overnight and *tested* the following day. This kind of flexibility increases an organisation's ability to seize sudden opportunities. Ideally, telemarketing should be linked into a *database/hybrid marketing* system (see page 252). This is not exclusive to large companies. Relatively inexpensive software packages for databases are available for both large and small companies.

An *outbound* campaign requires telemarketing professionals to make the calls, as opposed to an *inbound* campaign which receives calls generated from 0800, freephone, local phone or standard phone numbers listed in either direct response advertisements or mail shots.

The growth of telemarketing

The following factors are contributing to the growth of telemarketing:

* Management's constant search for cost effectiveness;
* New ways of competing;
* Market fragmentation;
* The emergence of niches;
* Fading costs;
* The increasing capacity of computer technology.

Running a telemarketing campaign

In-house telemarketing departments are still relatively rare in the UK. The decision to set up a telemarketing department is a long-term strategic decision which often requires approval at board level. Over 40 weeks are required to set up and train the department. An in-house unit with six callers could cost £300,000 p.a. to run and £100,000 to set up. On the other hand, a variety of telemarketing agencies are available. They can run projects and even assist in the development of an in-house department. Either way, the campaign process is as follows:

* *Brief*;
* *Agree brief*;
* *Research target audience*;
* *Develop contact strategy*;
* *Detailed objectives*;
* *Campaign costing*;

- *Action plan*;
- *Script development*;
- *Clarifying operational requirements*;
- *Team briefing/training*;
- *Test calls*;
- *Campaign roll-out*;
- *Monitor and control*;
- *Campaign completion, analysis and reporting.*

The basic *brief* should cover the SOSTT + 4Ms checklist as outlined in 'Briefs' on page 118, Chapter 6. The objectives can include list building/cleaning, market research, appointment setting, selling, etc. The telesales agency or in-house manager needs to determine if the *objectives* are realistic and comprehensive (exploit all the opportunities available within the budget). Having agreed the objectives, there is usually some further *research* into the target audience to find out where the potential contacts can be found (lists or old records); how to contact (mail, phone, etc); when to contact; how they buy (several stage/sequential selling or simple straight sale?); profile — their potential life time value; existing levels of awareness and previous contact with the company; ideal marketing message; back-up information required; types of objections, etc.

Developing contact strategies involves establishing the sequence of stages required to achieve the objectives. For example, qualifying the prospect could be by telephone interviews. Stage two may involve entering all the data on to a bespoke marketing database. Prospects with less immediate needs might then be mailed a brochure, while telemarketing contacts the more immediate buyers with a view to setting up an appointment. Another stage will emerge when the not-so-urgent prospects who received the brochure start to mature into the buying mode. The database can prompt some telesales action and so on.

Detailed objectives for the campaign such as total number of calls, number of calls per person per hour, conversion rates, minimum amount of information to be collected, etc can be agreed.

Campaign costing and target setting can be refined once the research and contact strategy has been developed. The *action plan* co-ordinates who does what and when. For example, the telemarketing manager needs to know when the mailings go out or when the sales team are available for appointments. *Script development* draws on the features, benefits and unique selling propositions (USPs). It will also include open questions, presentation, objection handling and closing techniques.

Finally, the telemarketing team is ready to be *briefed and trained*. Telemarketing lends itself to *testing* and this is relatively simple to carry out. Lists, scripts, incentives, prices and timing can all be tested. The results will be carefully monitored and used to develop the optimum combination for the full roll-out of the campaign. These results should be analysed to continually build on previous success.

SHORT CASE

Woolworths Kids Club

Situation

Woolworths were brand leaders in confectionery and toys but not in kids' wear. They were losing share to other multiples. In fact Woolworths *were* considered to be a slumbering giant. Acquisition of the exclusive Ladybird range of children's wear sowed some of the seeds of a major high street success story. The Ladybird brand name had previously been owned by a high quality childrens' wear range sold through independents. Profitable potential lay in the expanded franchise of this brand.

Marketing objectives

- Short term: build one-to-one relationship with customers.
- Medium term: increase 'acceptability' of the range.
- Long term: drive incremental profit.

Communications objective

- Talk to parents of 0–7-year-olds via their children in a responsible, relevant and relationship-building fashion.

Strategy

- Develop a database to expand the Ladybird franchise.
- Launch a free-to-join children's club – the Kids Club at Woolworths.
- Create exclusive branded characters to reinforce the merchandise link.

Tactics

- Promote membership through in-store leaflets and the Ladybird catalogue, ie build Woolworths' own database from own customers and not from anyone else's lists. Print one million leaflets.
- Restrict membership to age range of Ladybird merchandise.
- Incentivise membership via offer of regular communication and free gifts.

- Mail to members *regularly* via parent/guardian including Comic, parents' newsletter, product offers, incentives (provided by suppliers free of charge) and birthday and Christmas cards.
- Comic featured, Ladybird characters, and supplier funded advertorials, and activity pages.

Targets
Parents of 0–7 year old children within the Woolworths store catchment areas (mosly within a seven mile radius).

Men
The Ingram Sales Promotion Company were appointed to be an important adjunct to the small and extremely busy marketing department. The agency quickly isolated the Ladybird brand as having potentially highly profitable growth and used an innovative combination of promotions and database marketing to maximise the benefit. The result was a strong team effort between client and agency.

Money
The agency was retained on a long-term remit and paid a monthly fee which represented about 10 per cent of the total project budget. A six-figure budget was allocated to the launch phase and subsequent mailings had an average cost of 75p per member.

Minutes
The club was launched in 1987 on a national basis. The development and planning was started almost a year prior to this. It was not felt that regional testing would be beneficial because the high production values required would have escalated costs on smaller print runs.

Measurement
The club initially recruited 200,000 children. Subsequent recruitment ran at approximately a minimum of 2,000 a month. In 1992 the database stood at 750,000 children, which represents about 500,000 households and about 10 per cent of the total UK population of 0–7-year-old children. `Dotty', the Ladybird team captain, gets thousands of fan letters a month.

Ninety-five per cent of parents thought the club was as good or better than other clubs.

Partnership with suppliers was founded early on in the club relationship and swiftly became approximately 30 per cent of the funding.

Kids Club members were found to spend significantly higher than average; they also visited the stores more often. Depending on the offer, coupon responses from subsequent mailings achieved 15–17 per cent redemption levels.

Kids' participation levels in all club activity was equally rewarding with up to 20 per cent response rates to competitions.

The database has mounted a successful series of relationship-
building promotions and subsequently has been used for a number of highly cost effective additional activities. These include:

1) Off-the-page selling of exclusive Kids Club merchandise.
2) Joint mailing with other Kingfisher companies.

3) Local level tactical activity, ie new store openings, competitive defence tactics and other short-term requirements.
4) `Calls to action', ie traffic builders via `Dotty', the Ladybird Club character, and in-store visits, birthday parties, etc.
5) Time-delay promotions such as bringing forward of seasonal shopping missions, ie Christmas shopping evenings for parents of club members with results of *six* times the seasonal average spend achieved.

Key Points from Chapter 13:
1) Databases can and should be developed for all types of organisations.
2) Organisations that ignore direct marketing and database techniques will suffer a competitive disadvantage.

Further reading

Bird, D (1989) *Commonsense Direct Marketing*, second edition, Kogan Page. London

Brann, C (1984) *Cost Effective Direct Marketing*, Collectors' Books

Considine, R and Murray, R (1981) *The Great Brain Robbery*, The Great Brain Robbery, 521 South Madison Avenue, Pasadena, California 91101

The Direct Marketing Centre (1992) *The Practitioner's Guide To Direct Marketing*

Howard, M (1989) *Telephone Marketing vs Direct Sales Force Costs*, commissioned by Datapoint (UK) Ltd, London

Moriarty, R and Moran, U `Managing hybrid systems', *Harvard Business Review*, November – December 1990

Moriarty, R and Shwartz, G `Automation to boost sales and marketing', *Harvard Business Review*, January – February 1989

Royal Mail (1991) *The Royal Mail Guide To Successful Direct Mail*

Toffler, A (1980) *The Third Wave*, Collins, London

Stevens, M (1991) *The Handbook of Telemarketing*, Kogan Page, London

Watson, J `The direct marketing guide', *Marketing Magazine*, 9 February 1989

Further contacts

The Direct Marketing Association (UK) Ltd, Haymarket House, 1 Oxendon Street, London SW1Y 4EE Tel: 071 321 2525 The Direct Mail Services Standards Board, 26 Eccleston Street, London SW1W 9PY Tel: 0171 824 8651
(confers `recognised status' on suppliers of direct mail services who meet the required ethical and professional standards.)

The Institute of Direct Marketing, 1 Park Road, Teddington, Middlesex TW11 0AR. Tel: 0181 977 5705
(organises the Direct Marketing Diploma and other educational and training initiatives.)

European Direct Marketing Association (EDMA), 36 rue du Gouvernement Provisoire, B-1000 Brussels. Tel: 0032 22176309

The Mailing Preference Service, Freepost 22, London W1E 7EZ. Tel: 0171 738 1625

The Office of the Data Protection Registrar, Wycliffe House, Water Lane, Wilmslow, Cheshire SK9 5AF. Tel: 01625 535777
(provides guidance on the laws governing the holding and use of personal data.)

PUBLICITY AND PUBLIC RELATIONS

INTRODUCTION

Positive publicity is dependent primarily on good relationships with the media (media relations). This is only one of the responsibilities of *public relations*. There is some overlap between public relations, public affairs, corporate affairs and community affairs, community relations, corporate relations, and corporate communications. Many organisations have different structures with separate departments serving specific requirements. Public relations integrates with most aspects of an organisation's activities. The first part of this chapter considers public relations in its entirety while the second half of the chapter focuses on one aspect of public relations — publicity.

PUBLIC RELATIONS

Public relations is regularly, and sometimes worryingly, referred to as 'PR' which is often confused with 'press releases' or 'press relations'. These are, in fact, only a part of real public relations. A simple definition of public relations is: 'the development of and maintenance of good relationships with different publics'. The publics are the range of different groups on which an organisation is dependent. These include, employees, investors, customers, legislators/regulators/ governments, the trade, the community, pressure groups and even competition. Most of these groups have different (sometimes conflicting) interests in any particular organisation.

While marketing traditionally focuses on markets or just three of the publics, ie customers, distributors (the 'trade') and competition, public relations is concerned with many more publics. The UK's Institute of Public Relations (IPR) use the following public relations definition: 'the planned and sustained effort to establish and maintain goodwill and mutual understanding between an organisation and its publics'. The 1978 world assembly of PR Associations in Mexico agreed what is now known as *the 'Mexican statement'*:

> PR practice is the art and science of analysing trends, predicting their consequences, counselling organisation leaders and implementing planned

programmes of action which will serve both the organisation's and the public interest.

Marketing and public relations

The previous definitions give an indication of the diverse nature and far reaching effects of public relations. It is *not a subset of marketing nor is marketing a subset of public relations*. They do, however, integrate with each other. Dr Jon White, in his excellent book *How to Manage and Understand Public Relations* (1991), says that

> public relations is *a complement and a corrective to the marketing approach*...it creates an environment in which it is easier to market...public relations can raise questions which the marketing approach, with its focus on the market, products, distribution channels and customers, and its orientation towards growth and consumption, cannot. Public relations concerns are with relations of one group to another, and with the interplay of conflicting and competing interests in social relationships.

Publicity objectives can vary from promoting a product (*product PR*) to promoting a company (*corporate PR*) among employees, customers, investors, the community, local government, etc. Marketing will tend to be sales/market share oriented while public relations can, but not always, be sales/market share oriented eg, a PR objective may be to win permission to build a new factory, recruit the best employees, etc. A manager responsible for product PR would ultimately report to the marketing manager, whereas a manager responsible for corporate PR would probably report to a board director or the board itself.

Norman Hart (1992) gave an interesting interpretation in an article he wrote entitled 'Is there a new role for PR in marketing?' Taking the IPR definition, which talks about relationships between an organisation and its publics, he made the point that the definition says nothing about products and nothing about the media. PR can be interpreted as more of a corporate activity, such as corporate communications, than a product activity, such as product publicity (product PR):

> The fact is that advertising is just one of a number of channels of communication available to promote a product (and thus a subset of marketing) or to promote an organisation (and thus a subset of public relations). Equally, editorial can contribute powerfully to product promotion (marketing) or corporate promotion (public relations). The simplest way of expressing the difference is to discriminate between brand or product image and corporate or company image.

The *influence of public relations stretches far beyond product marketing* and into corporate strategy, particularly where long-term decisions affecting choice of markets, products, factory locations, production processes, etc are concerned. External groups are becoming more demanding and organisations are beginning to have to demonstrate their social responsibility on a global basis. Ethics and social responsibility have traditionally been the bastion of public relations. Today, all managers need to develop their awareness and understanding of at least the PR implications of both board room and marketing department decisions, strategies, policies and actions (or the lack of these).

More than communications

The PR mix (see figure 14.1) gives an indication of the diverse nature and far reaching effects of public relations. It is more than just communications; it is part of the broader business disciplines such as corporate planning, finance, personnel, production and marketing. It cannot work effectively unless it is integrated into these areas and unless it also links with product quality, customer care and design management (corporate identity). These are the *credibility* elements which build a platform for subsequent publicity, which, as can be seen from Figure 14.1 is just one of the many *visibility* tools.

Marketing communications and publicity

Some organisations insist that the public relations people and sales promotion people sit in on various advertising/direct marketing meetings so that they cross-fertilise ideas and create synergy through integrating the marketing communications at an early stage. Chapter 1 mentioned the British Airways free flights promotion which PR exploited to the point where massive awareness was generated from carefully orchestrated and integrated below the line activities. Here is another example of how product PR and advertising can work together.

Nine million Jim Dunks

PR support created an additional nine million opportunities to see (OTS's) Molsen's branding device Jim Dunk. This followed research which showed that most consumers do not taste the finer points of beer: they buy the image created around it. Editorial profiles of Jim Dunk, the actor who featured in the commercials telling viewers 'not to drink Molson' appeared on the news pages of national newspapers like the *Daily Express* and the *Sun* while rationale on the negative aspects of the advertising appeared on the *Financial Times* marketing page. The publication of a booklet on 'What's in and what's out' in London linked Dunk as an arbiter of taste. Joint promotions with specialist magazines like *City Limits* were tied to selected bars and pubs throughout London. Additionally, editorial competitions with Molson prizes helped raise brand awareness in the regions linked to outlets via local papers. The integrated communications contributed to a 70 per cent increase in awareness, quadrupling of the distributor base and tripling of sales — all within 12 months.

The PR mix

Figure 14.1 also shows how the *visibility* activities such as news releases, news

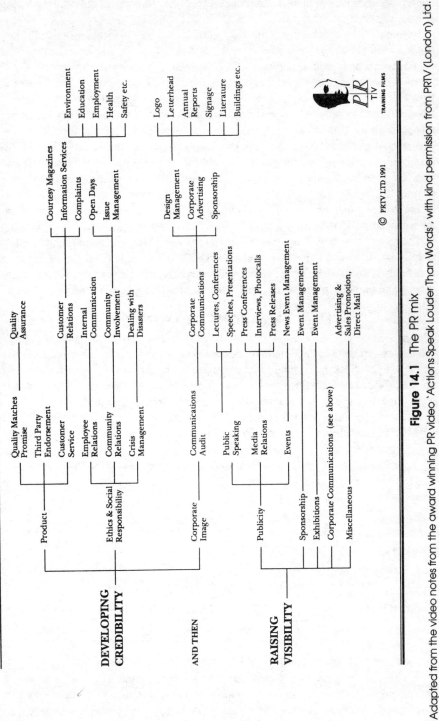

Figure 14.1 The PR mix

Adapted from the video notes from the award winning PR video 'Actions Speak Louder Than Words', with kind permission from PRTV (London) Ltd.

conferences, publicity stunts, conferences, events, exhibitions, sponsorship and sales promotions can integrate.

Before looking at publicity in more detail it is worth mentioning again that the key to long-term success is to *develop credibility before raising visibility*. Credibility is created by a proper product and/or quality of service. This means that the product must match the promise made by the marketing communications, ie do not sell a Rolls-Royce and deliver a Mini Cooper. False expectations only lead to disappointment, frustration and extremely high post-purchase dissonance. This kills off any long-term repeat business. Good customer service makes doing business a pleasurable experience for all parties. Having the right sort of people or institutions associated with, using and *endorsing* a product improves credibility. So too ethics, social responsibility (see Chapter 8) and corporate image (see Chapter 17) all contribute towards building a credible image.

There is no point waving a flag, shouting, leaping, roaring, advertising or raising an organisation's visibility if it has not got a solid platform of credibility supporting it. The days when the two aspects were held separately are gone. Spending thousands or millions on raising a profile is not just wasteful but actually damaging if a lack of credibility is exposed. So today, more than ever before, it is worthwhile investing men, money and minutes in getting the credibility right before raising visibility.

MEDIA RELATIONS AND PUBLICITY

Take a look in the local and national newspapers, trade journals, radio programmes and television. Spot the commercial news items or features that have made it into the press or TV. Like advertising, this kind of editorial publicity can achieve many similar communication goals such as increasing awareness or repositioning.

News and feature editors do not have time to scout around for all the items they cover. They depend on a constant feed of professionally presented news items and news releases from organisations. Despite this about 121 million press releases (out of 125 million sent out) get thrown into editors' bins every year in the UK alone. Many of them are badly written and inaccurately targeted (sometimes even addressed to people who have long left the newspaper).

Dead editors

I have even seen news releases addressed to people who have died.

(Source: Rosemary Unsworth, Business News Editor, The *Independent*)

Publicity can be generated through *press releases*, *news releases* (*video news releases* for a television programme and *syndicated radio tapes* for radio — see appendices 1 and 2), *press conferences*, *press receptions* and *media events* what the media less reverently call 'stunts'), and *public speaking* (at conferences, lectures, seminars, dinners, chat shows etc). The Hewlett-Packard short case at the end of this chapter shows how carefully planned conferences are a potent PR tool which also directly affect lead generation and sales. The other visibility tools such as sponsorship, exhibitions, corporate identity, advertising, sales promotions and direct mail are all dealt with as separate chapters elsewhere in this book.

Positive *editorial* is usually the result of carefully managed *media relations*. Organisations and/or individuals must take time to understand what the journalist or editor wants, the news angle, the relevance of the piece, the appropriate time to deliver it to a news organisation, the correct format or layout of the press release and so on.

There are three important points about editorial coverage:

1) There is no media cost.
2) The message has higher credibility.
3) There is no control over the message.

No media cost

There is *no media cost* since, unlike advertising, the space is not bought. There are, however, *some other costs* since news releases have to be written, carefully targeted and distributed to the right editor at the right time in the right format. This can be done by an in-house press officer or public relations department or it can be handled by an external public relations agent or consultancy. There are news release distribution companies who specialise in getting releases physically or electronically to news editors' desks at the right time.

The 'TSB sponsorship of Roy Of The Rovers' press release and montage of press clippings on page 278 shows the kind of free publicity that a well written, carefully targeted and properly timed news release can generate. (For a full explanation of how the sponsorship worked see the short case at the end of chapter 15.)

This kind of editorial coverage creates valuable positive publicity. The editorial coverage has higher credibility than advertising copy. No space was bought and therefore no media costs were incurred. However, whether it is in-house PR people or an external consultancy (in this case, QBO Consultancy), it does cost someone's time and expertise to:

1) Select the right target media (appropriate press and editors) at the right time.
2) Write the news releases.
3) Print, address, pack and post the news releases.
4) Handle any press enquiries. There are, of course, other minor costs, some of which are hidden: photographs, stationery, stamps, phone calls, wear and tear of the word processor, laser printer and so on.

Editorial coverage is used increasingly to stretch the above the line advertising campaigns. Good press officers push the knock-on PR potential of advertising. The controversial £300,000 Haagen-Dazs ice cream advertising campaign (featured in the short case on page 218, Chapter 11) enjoyed an estimated £750,000 worth of additional free editorial coverage (*Creative Review*, October 1992). The calculation is simple : add up the column inches of coverage and find the equivalent cost for the same amount of advertising space. There are more sophisticated methods of eval-

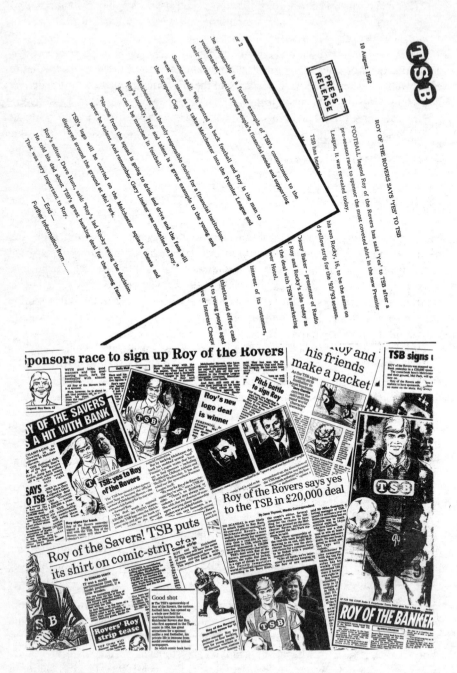

Media clippings (bottom) generated from the news release (top)

uation which include: positive/negative comments; the position on the page; whether a picture is shown; the number of times a brand name is used, etc. Forte Hotels' constant quantitative report on editorial coverage is outlined on page 282.

Higher credibility

Editorial coverage has *higher credibility* than advertising, probably because it is perceived to be written by an editor or journalist and not an advertiser trying to sell something. There is arguably less resistance to the message. Some estimates suggest that a message carried in a piece of editorial has three times more credibility than a similar message carried in an advertisement. Despite the attraction of the message credibility factor, editorial coverage is risky because there is *no control over the message*. An editor can take a news release and criticise the sender for sending it. Advertisers, on the other hand, can control the message since they buy the space and publish exactly what they want to say (within the law and advertising regulations).

The adage '*any publicity is good publicity*' is not always true. The negative editorial coverage shown on page 280 is, arguably, good publicity, but this is not always the case. Retail jewellery giant Ratners discovered this when they fell foul of the power of negative publicity. Their chairman, Gerald Ratner, told the press that his jewellery was 'crap'. It gained national coverage but it also kept customers away from his shops and lowered morale among his employees. He has since relinquished his joint position of chairman/ managing director.

Lack of control

The uncontrollable element of media relations is demonstrated by the montage of press clippings (editorial coverage) generated by PRTV's 'Nuclear Missile' news release (see page 280)). This shows how the same news release gets totally different editorial coverage by two different editors. On the one hand, the *Wall Street Journal* gives it brief but positive front-page exposure, while *Personnel Today* treats the same news release with a lot of cynicism and, arguably, negative editorial coverage, despite a lot more detail about the promotion.

Reducing the lack of control

Red faces can be avoided by checking to see if any events clash with a particular news release or event (like launching a new hamburger bar on national vegetarian day). There are directories available (like *Foresight*) which list events and categorise them by type, region, date, etc. There are other directories which list editors' names, addresses and numbers (again categorised by type of magazine or programme). This is, of course, available on disc also. The publication *Advance* helps to ensure better targeting of news releases by identifying editorial topics which will be covered by particular media in the future.

Editorial risk can be further reduced with the help of companies like CARMA International, who compile lists of journalists, who have written articles on a particular organisation or on its products, or any particular issue together with a favourable

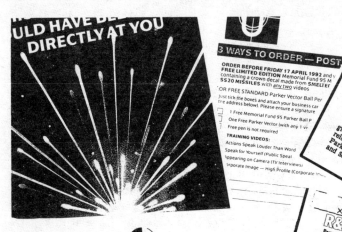

NEWS
RELEASE

P|R
T|V

10 March 1992

PRTV TRIGGER NUCLEAR MISSILE

Europe's first public relations training video called, 'Action
Speak Louder Than Words' is now at the centre of an internati
exchange of nuclear missiles. Decommissioned US Pershing a
USSR SS20 missile casings have been smelted and inserted in
crown decal of a limited edition series of Parker Pens. Th
world's first peaceful nuclear missile product comes boxe
numbered certificate of authenticity and is available fr
buyers of any two videos from a four video public relat
training package being launched (13/3/92) by PRTV.

Working with BBC and Central TV the new PRTV package
videos on 'Public Relations', 'Public Speaking',
Interviews' and 'Corporate Image'. Each collector'
contributes to the Worldwide Memorial Fund For Dis

The introductory-level public relations video, 'A
Louder Than Words' actually shows Presidents Bus
signing nuclear agreements with pens from the l
range. They subsequently shake hands and excha
the film's three years of research and develo
for the 'ultimate product endorsement'. Whe
this White House footage we felt, at last w
gem." PRTV Managing Director, Paul Smith.

-----End-----

Further Information: Contact Paul Smith,
(081) 567 4659 and Fax: (081) 567 6843
THE SPECIALISTS IN PUBLIC RELATIONS TRAINING FILMS
PRTV LIMITED THE STUDIO 2 BELSIZE AVENUE EALING LONDON W13 9TF
TELEPHONE: 071-792 8480 FAX: 071-792 1329

*The same news release and brochure can generate totally different types of
editorial coverage as indicated by the press clippings*

or unfavourable rating for each article. A further analysis compares the incidence of solicited and unsolicited press coverage, which can be cross-referenced with the ratings to identify any apparent bias in specific journalists' relationships with organisations. Sandra Macleod of CARMA said at the 1992 IPRA (International Public Relations Association) Hong Kong Conference that: 'Once a journalist calls, by punching in a few key words on his or her desk terminal, the PR manager is able to call up the profile of the caller on the screen even before the preliminary hellos'.

Controlled integration of publicity

Publicity should be *integrated with other elements of the marketing communications mix*. Chapter 1 explained how many major advertising campaigns are now supported by press launches and followed up with a press and publicity campaign to maintain the visibility generated by the public relations people. The example on page 280 shows how PR, sales promotion and direct mail work together in the case of a nuclear missile pen promotion. The TSB sponsorship was totally integrated with the media relations (editorial) campaign. The Miss Pears promotion (see Chapter 12) demonstrates how an integrated packaging, PR and sales promotion campaign maintains the brand's share without any above the line support. In other cases, blown-up press cuttings can look effective at trade fairs and exhibitions. Third-party endorsements can be used in advertising, news releases, sales literature, packaging design, sales promotion and so on. A single photographic shoot can produce a range of material suitable for advertising, packaging, exhibitions, direct mail, press packs, etc. Strategically, the marketing communication tools should all work together (eg consistent positioning) rather than pull in different directions.

Ideally, each activity should be planned for maximum integration. Unforeseen opportunities and threats invariably emerge which make it *difficult to plan* for everything. For example, editorial is difficult to forecast (even if an editor promises to use a news release it often gets 'spiked' or replaced by some other news item at the last moment, at other times the news release gets used later than expected). Successful positive publicity can trigger all sorts of ideas for mailings, promotions and further press coverage. *Crises* and negative publicity are equally difficult to forecast and plan, although many top companies today invest in *crisis management programmes* before crises occur. This allows them to respond in the most effective manner. A well-handled crisis can actually leave an organisation in a stronger position eg. Johnson and Johnson's excellent handling of the Tylenol poisoning crisis (when seven people died of cyanide poisoning which had been inserted in their headache tablets) in Chicago in 1982.

MEASURING MEDIA RELATIONS

Free publicity, news coverage or editorial can be monitored, *measured* and analysed. The most basic approach is 'column inches' — how many columns of press coverage refer to a particular organisation, its product or purpose. News clippings can be compiled either in-house, by an agency or by a specialist news clipping company who monitor, cut out, paste up and deliver the clippings daily, weekly or however regularly the client wants.

Similar media monitoring services are also available for television and radio. The size of file, number of references, quantity of space or time devoted to a chosen product, organisation or issue is, again, a simple method of measurement. More detailed analyses give a breakdown of: front page mentions; exclusive mentions; size of mention/cutting; number of beneficial credits; neutral credits adverse credits; opportunities to enquire (includes reach of article, circulation, whether a contact address and/or phone number, enquiry card, coupon, etc was included). Various formulae attempt to calculate the *quality of the coverage instead of the quantity*. These can include photographs/diagrams, position on the page, etc.

A quantified report

When we have a story about a new hotel or product, we identify five key messages we want to put across — it's never more than five — and we're lucky if we get two across in print. We then identify the key target audiences and the most appropriate publications to reach them. This establishes a matrix which ensures the maximum efficiency for our efforts.

Richard Power, Director of Corporate Communications, Forte Hotels

All stories are then monitored on a scale of one to five, according to how favourable they are and how many of the key messages are included. This enables Power to give Rocco Forte and other executive directors a quantified report on just how well they are communicating.

David Churchill, *PR Week*

These forms of analysis measure what gets into the press; they do not measure what gets into the minds of the target audience, ie whether the editorial has changed or reinforced the target audience's attitudes and intentions, or voting patterns, share values, sales levels, etc.

This has to be measured separately by researching attitudes and behaviour patterns. Sales can be measured but it can be difficult to isolate PR from other communications activities when attempting to gauge the effect of any aspect of public relations. The next short case shows how an integrated public relations activity, a conference, can help to open doors which ultimately increase sales.

SHORT CASE

Hewlett-Packard's Alternative Symposium

Situation

Hewlett-Packard has been a long-time player in the minicomputer systems market. The emergence of the UNIX operating system as an industry standard, coupled with increasing demands by customers to protect their huge investments in computer systems, produced a paradigm shift which, many feel, will eventually force all IT (information technology) companies to offer 'open systems', ie hardware, software and systems which would be compatible with other manufacturers' systems. This means suppliers may have to offer service and partnership (see Chapter 10) as a significant USP (unique selling proposition or the supplier's unique advantage).

Problem

Although Hewlett-Packard was the first major player to migrate its products to the UNIX platform, it had done so long before the paradigm shift occurred and was therefore not immediately recognised as an open systems supplier.

Objective

As other major IT companies joined the open systems market, HP realised that it was imperative to establish themselves as not just a player, but as the only credible IT company who could truly be the customer's systems partner. A secondary objective was to generate immediate business opportunities for both direct and indirect sales.

Strategy

A two-pronged communications strategy was developed to position HP as 'the knowledgeable partner' and 'agent of change' for implementing IT solutions while using a creative theme 'think again' (about computer systems) to help undermine a competitor's current advertising approach through a series of top-level conferences.

Target

Executive directors responsible for long-term investments and for management of change:

1) Directors and board level managers in companies with £10–£50 million turnover.
2) Directors and board level management, IT management, and financial management in companies with over £50 million turnover.

Tactics

A series of open systems conferences were designed, using guest speakers from within and without the IT industry, in conjunction with a widespread communications campaign themed 'think again', For each one-day conference, personal invitations were direct mailed to up to 60,000 targets from a number of list sources, and follow-up letters were sent to non-responders in a select 'key contact' target group of 5,000.

montage of Invitation + Press release + FT Advertisement + Mail Shot+ (With invitation in foreground)

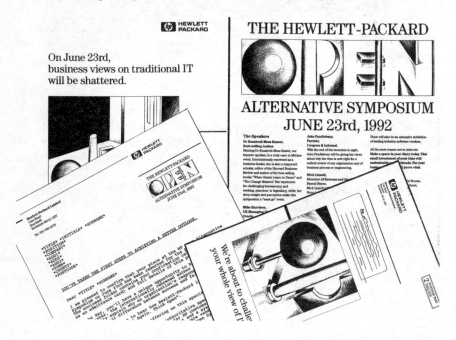

Press releases announcing the events and highlighting the prestigious speakers received editorial coverage in key IT journals. National advertisements were also placed in the *Financial Times*.

Using a TV personality to compere, HP purposely limited itself to a short 'wrap-up' (summary conclusion) by HP's UK managing director. Business and management luminaries were invited to address the conference on such topics as the dynamics of organisational change, competitiveness and speed to market, and protecting IT investments. The speakers were completely at liberty to address their own subjects in their own way and were not instructed to sell HP.

The conferences (with morning and afternoon sessions at a central, desirable venue) included small exhibition areas where HP software partners displayed their solutions. In addition, a major management consultancy and HP offered qualified attendees free consultancy time to evaluate systems needs. A prize draw for HP computers valued at several thousand pounds was conducted at each conference session.

Men and women
The open systems conferences were managed by HP's marketing communications team, working with a number of external agencies responsible for PR, direct marketing, advertising, telesales, event co-ordination, and stage/audio visual production.

Money
Overall budget per conference day, excluding keynote speakers' fees and media advertising, but including mailing, PR, stage set, etc was approximately £140,000. Keynote speakers' fees can range from £2,500 to £25,000 plus expenses. The media spend (advertising costs) brought the average total cost per conference close to one quarter of a million pounds.

Minutes
The whole project took 16 weeks to plan and three conferences were undertaken in the first year.

Measurement
Measurement was based upon the number of applicants registering for the conference, as well as the number of qualified attendees who registered for the free consultancy on the day. In addition, follow-up research was conducted which surveyed attendees and people who were invited and/or confirmed, but who did not attend. The objective of this research was to measure perceptions of HP overall, and as an open systems supplier.

The overall response to the marketing campaigns in terms of attendance at the conference sessions averaged 2 per cent which HP regarded as an above average response. The follow-up research showed 96 per cent indicating a likeliness to consider purchasing HP in the future. Response to the personalised survey (see the questionnaire on page 286) was 56 per cent for attendees and 20% for non-attendees.

"The Open Alternative"
Your Final Chance to Win an HP Palmtop

If you name is incorrect or incomplete, please correct it below:

Mr/Mrs/Miss: _____

Position: _____

Company: _____

Address: _____

_____

_____ Postcode: _____

Telephone: _____

Thank you for attending our recent "Open Alternative" Symposium.

Now we would like to know what *you* think of Open Systems, and, by telling us you could win an HP Palmtop computer.

Complete and return this short questionnaire – it shouldn't take more than five minutes of your time and your completed card will be entered into the prize draw to take place on 17th July 1992.

Which conference session did you find most useful?

- [ ] Dr Rosabeth Moss Kanter
- [ ] Mike Harrison - UK MD of Oracle
- [ ] Tony Fisher - UK MD of Hoskyns
- [ ] John Pendlebury - Partner, Coopers & Lybrand
- [ ] Mick Linsell - Director of Systems and Quality, Parcelforce
- [ ] John Golding - UK MD of Hewlett-Packard Limited

Why? _____

How do you rate the symposium organisation, both beforehand and on the day?

- [ ] Excellent
- [ ] Good
- [ ] Average
- [ ] Poor

CSF 71

What are your views of Open Systems based IT after the symposium?

- [ ] Open IT is now first choice for my business
- [ ] I am prepared to consider a move to Open Systems
- [ ] Open IT is inappropriate for my business

Other: _____

If you are not considering Open Systems IT, why not?

_____

_____

Which computer systems do you use at present?

- [ ] DEC
- [ ] HP
- [ ] IBM
- [ ] ICL

Other: _____

Do you have any UNIX systems installed?

- [ ] Yes
- [ ] No

Which supplier do you perceive as the leading Open Systems IT company? _____

Why? _____

In the left hand column please rank (1 is the most important, 7 the least) the qualities you perceive to be the most important in the Open Systems market place. In the right hand column give HP marks out of 10 for its capability in each area.

'Qualities'		HP 'Score'
	Range of hardware	
	Price	
	Performance	
	Software availability	
	Support capabilities	
	Market profile	
	Standards commitment	
Other: _____		
_____		

Will you consider HP as a supplier for future IT procurements?

- [ ] Yes
- [ ] No

If not, why not? _____

Thank you for your time, now fold and seal by moistening the edges. Once we receive your card it will be entered into the draw, with the winners notified by post during late July.

APPENDIX 1

Video news releases

A video news release (VNR) is conceptually the same as a written press release, except that it is produced on broadcast quality video (BETACAM or BETACAM SP). VNRs keep broadcasters up to date with news items (which they might otherwise have missed). VNRs also save broadcasters from having to send their own busy camera crews out to cover a story.

The VNR consists of two sections: a 90-second 'A' roll which carries a commentary designed to show the editor and/or journalist how the story could run 'on-air', and a three to five minute 'B' roll which is a selection of loosely cut shots ('rushes') designed to be re-edited by broadcasters into their own style, ie the broadcasters use their own commentary, graphics and captions so that as far as the viewers are concerned the story has been originated by the broadcaster. As with a press release, a VNR is paid for by the organisation which is looking for some positive publicity. The TV stations receive them free of charge. Again, as with press releases, there is no guarantee that the material will be used since a bigger story can break at any time. Equally, a VNR can be used negatively, since unlike advertising, there is no control over the message.

A VNR can stretch the impact of communications activities such as sponsored events. For example, a British PLC sponsoring an airshow display team commissioned VISNEWS to produce and distribute a VNR package to run throughout UK airshows during the summer of 1992. As the airshow moved from region to region the local TV broadcasters were offered the VNR as a preview story to be included in the 'things to see at the weekend' section. The VNR was subsequently used (broadcast) on ten different regional television stations reaching a total audience of 4.2 million at a cost of approximately £4,000, giving a cost per thousand of £0.95. (The £4,000 excludes production costs, but these were minimal since the VNR was made mostly from existing corporate library footage).

A VNR can stretch the exposure of advertising campaigns if some behind the scenes shots and/or other previously unseen footage are edited creatively into a newsworthy story. In this way, the OTS's (opportunities to see) a brand can be increased substantially without any above the line media costs (ie no television advertising space has to be bought). Instead of advertising on television, pop band Bananarama used a VNR to get their album publicised on national breakfast television, the six o'clock news and the nine o'clock news. The world's biggest rock band, U2, also used VNRs worldwide to promote their 1992 album *Achtung Baby*.

The revolution

The European television revolution roughly doubled the number of TV stations between 1980 and 1990. There is now eight times more programming with only five times the budgets available. (Independent Programme Producers Association). This means that there are more programmes but less money available for each programme. Here lies the opportunity for organisations to help the programme makers by supplying relevant footage in the form of a timely VNR.

In December 1991 specialists in international broadcast research, Frank N. Magid Associates, were commissioned by VISNEWS to find out exactly how European programme makers felt about VNRs. Here are some of the key findings:

- Seventy-seven per cent had 'very or slightly favourable' attitudes towards VNRs (20 per cent were 'very or slightly unfavourable', 3 per cent were neutral).
- Sixty-three per cent of all broadcasters use VNRs (33 per cent do not and 3 per cent didn't know or were not applicable).

- Seventy-seven per cent wanted to continue receiving VNRs (17 per cent did not and 6 per cent said it 'depends').

Costs

Production costs vary. A camera crew and director can be hired for the day (say, £1,500) to cover an event, an opening, a conference, etc. Editing teams can be hired separately or included as part of the editing requirements of either an advertisement or conference video. Production costs range between £2,500 and £10,000, but some costs can be saved if VNRs are included early in, say, the production of other film footage, eg corporate videos or advertisements. Distribution and monitoring costs can vary according to whether the VNR is used or not, eg £400 for one local station, £5,000 for all stations in the UK, £4,000 for a European-wide service, and to anywhere from £10,000 to £20,000 for worldwide distribution.

APPENDIX 2

Syndicated radio tapes

A syndicated radio tape is, on average, a three-minute recorded interview about an event, a company, a product or service. The tape and script are copied, mailed out (or syndicated) to approximately 25 radio stations in the UK. The same principles as in VNRs apply here – it should be newsworthy and not a blatant plug.

For around £500 the companies that offer a syndicated tape service have a basic package which usually includes:

- Preliminary discussion.
- Interviewer — selecting, booking and briefing.
- Structuring the interview.
- Studio session (one hour).
- Recording (three minutes)
- Editing master tape.
- Two spare copies for client.
- Cue sheet preparation (written introduction to the taped interview).
- Selecting 25 relevant radio stations (only one per area where stations overlap).
- Producing and distributing a boxed, labelled copy to each individual radio station's presenter or producer.
- Monitoring — three to four weeks after despatch a written report giving details of which stations broadcast the information. This is sometimes followed up with a more detailed report.

A 40 per cent take-up of a professionally produced, newsworthy, accurately targeted syndicated radio tape is considered to be an 'average success rate'. There is usually a range of optional extras (eg localised cue sheets or overseas distribution).

Key Points from Chapter 14:

1) PR and marketing are not subsets of each other although they do integrate.
2) Editorial coverage has lower costs, higher message creditability and high risks because of lack of control over the message.
3) Integrated PR contributes to marketing communications synergy.

Further reading

Bernays, E (1923) *Crystallising Public Opinion*, Boni and Livewright Inc, New York

Bernays, E (1955) *The Engineering of Consent*, University of Oklahoma Press, Norman, Oklahoma

Bland, M (1987) *Be Your Own PR Man*, Kogan Page, London

Churchill, D 'The power behind the image', *PR Week*, 15 October 1992, pp. 6 & 7

Cutlip, S Centre, H and Broom M (1985) *Effective Public Relations*, sixth edition, Prentice Hall International, Englewood Cliffs, New Jersey

Hart, N 'Is there a new role for PR in marketing?', *Public Relations*, Volume 11, Number 1, September 1992

Haywood, R (1990) *All About PR*, second edition, McGraw-Hill, London

Jefkins, F (1988) *Public Relations*, third edition, M & E Handbooks, Pitman, London

Murphy, D 'Don't forget the hype', *Creative Review*, October 1992, p.16

Ross, D (1990) *Surviving the Media Jungle*, Mercury Books, London

PRTV (1991) 'Actions speak louder than words' (PR training video), Chartered Institute of Marketing/Institute of Public Relations

White, J (1991) *How to Understand and Manage Public Relations*, Business Books, London

Further contacts

Communications Advertising and Marketing Education Foundation Limited, Abford House, 15 Wilton Road, London SW1V 1NJ. Tel: 0171-828 7506

The Institute of Public Relations, The Old Trading House, 15 Northburgh Street, London EC1V OPR. Tel: 0171-253 5151

The Public Relations Consultants Association, Willow House, Willow Place, Victoria, London SW1P IJH. Tel: 0171-233 6026

SPONSORSHIP

INTRODUCTION

Arts sponsorship is more effective than advertising.

Geoff Shingles, chairman of computer company Digital

We do not sponsor sports. It's a very cluttered market where you can spend millions without getting much return.

David Goldesgeyne, head of sponsorship for Lloyds Bank

So what should be sponsored? How does one choose what to sponsor and what to reject? Maybe arts are good for computers and sports are bad for banks (Barclays would not agree)? If arts sponsorship is so good for Digital why do they bother to advertise at all? Or perhaps their advertising doesn't work, which means any meagre improvement would be deemed to be a success? Do sponsorship funds come out of the above the line budget, ie does it always mean reducing the advertising budget or can it come out of some corporate fund? How much should be spent? How much is too much? When does it become less value for money? How is it measured? Finally, what exactly does sponsorship mean? These are some of the questions which this chapter answers. We will start with the last question first.

WHAT IS SPONSORSHIP?

Sponsorship is more than patronage, altruism or benefaction. It can indeed help others while simultaneously achieving specifically defined communications objectives (see page 294). Some sponsors see sponsorship as a form of *enlightened self interest* where a worthy activity is supported with cash and/or consideration in return for satisfying specific marketing or corporate objectives. As sponsorship matures, its diverse range

of programmes, objectives, advantages and disadvantages require a relatively sophisticated level of management understanding.

Target audiences must be researched in detail, crystal clear qualitative and quantitative objectives must be set, appropriate types of sponsorship vehicles must be
agreed, considered and selected. A programme of integrated communications has to
be planned with precision and sufficient budgets have to be allocated to allow for
'leveraging', stretching or maximising the overall sponsorship impact.

Range and types of sponsorship

All sectors of society can be targeted and reached through sponsorship. Just about
anyone or anything can be sponsored. You can even sponsor *the possibility of an event*
— Granada TV has sponsored Manchester's bid to host the 2000 Olympics. The range
of sponsorship opportunities is only limited by one's imagination. The obvious areas
are *sport, arts, education, community and broadcast.*

Whether the events are large or small (eg blind golf and blind cricket), sport offers
an effective route into the mind of various target markets. Even within a particular
sport there are a range of different sponsorship opportunities. Take soccer for example. It is possible to sponsor a *title* eg the Coca-Cola Cup or the Barclays League, or
a *stadium*, eg the Sunkist Bowl. Perhaps a more interesting example is where Maxwell
House Coffee's Taste of Chicago sponsorship *maximised the off-site potential* by
buying all 37,000 tickets and then giving them away free in return for two empty MH
jars. It is also possible to sponsor: a *club*, eg JVC and Arsenal, Blackdeath Vodka and
Scarborough FC (incidentally, way back in 1987 *Forbes* reported '...of Japan's 12
baseball teams, five are owned by railway companies, four by beverage companies,
two by newspapers and one by an auto company'); a *match* day (eg York City give 12
stand tickets, free buffet, free bar, free ads in the programme, hoardings in the car park
and the opportunity to present the man of the match award and join players in the bar
after the game — all for a cost of between £500 and £800); a *kick-off* (in the US
Anheuser Busch sponsor NFL kickoffs and they are referred to as 'Bud Kick offs'); a
ball, eg Gillingham FC match ball sponsorship costs £100; a *fair play award*, often
tied in with another sponsorship package; a *player* (players receive individual sponsorship and in return they open stores, meet employees and acknowledge the sponsor
in the programme); a *pass*, a *tackle*, a *goal*, a *save* or a *miss* — the Pizza Hut and
American Express examples below show US baseball can create such exciting opportunities.

Fan catches 33,000 pizzas

Pittsburgh Pirates fan Ted Bianucci was picked at random out of a crowd at
Three Rivers Stadium to take the field to try to catch three pop-ups (balls shot
out of a gun used to help catchers practise defence). Sponsors Pizza Hut promised every spectator in the park a free soda at Pizza Hut (just show the ticket
stub), a pitcher of soda or a small pizza if the fan caught one, two or three of the

pop-ups. No one had ever previously caught all three. Bianucci, to the cheers of 33,789 people, caught all three balls. $150,000 worth of pizza is likely to generate a lot of good feeling and probably extra business as 33,000 customers enter Pizza Hut's stores.

Sponsoring a miss

American Express and Best West International Hotels jointly sponsored a programme which donated $300 to children's baseball league every time top baseball pitcher Nolan Ryan bowled or pitched an opposition player out. If Ryan pitched a 'no-hitter' (bowled the whole team out for naught) then a whopping $1.25 million was donated by the sponsors to the league. Amex and Best West also donated three cents every time an Amex card was used to pay for a Best West hotel. In addition, $2 was contributed for every newly approved Amex card member application which came from a 'take-one' box at each Best West Hotel.

Arts sponsorship can be even more diverse — from sponsoring the opening of Euro-Disney, to a film premiere, to a particularly obscure type of a play to gain access to an otherwise difficult target market. *Education* is a sensitive area and sponsorship can come in cash or in kind, eg a computer company donating computers to a school. *Community sponsorship* is becoming increasingly important as businesses recognise the importance of their community and their corporate responsibility. The corporate citizen is alive and well within the 'Percent Club' (in the UK, corporate members of the Percent Club promise to spend one half of one per cent of their profits on community programmes. In the US there are also two per cent and five per cent clubs).

Other types of sponsorship

Here are some other forms of sponsorship which give an indication of the variety and potential available. An organisation can sponsor *an expedition* (Mercury have sponsored a walk to the North Pole). British Aerospace, Memorex and Interflora signed as sponsors for *a voyage into space* (the package was subsequently cancelled). An organisation can also sponsor *a species* (Systematics Association, a scientific group involved in classifying organisms, recently named seven wasps after the directors of Solomon Brothers after they waived a $300,000 debt arrangement). The '*Ugly Bartender*' contest sponsored by the Multiple Sclerosis Society is its second biggest revenue generator. Some years ago *cows* wearing Vladivar Vodka jackets in a field near the London to Brighton railway line were sponsored during the Brighton festival. Akai are sponsoring *bullfights* at £10,000 a fight. BP sponsored Eugene Ionesco's play, *Journeys Among The Dead*. Sponsoring *a war*? It is possible to sponsor sections of the US Army (eg the Medical Corps). On the other hand, sponsoring *peace* initiatives is also possible. For example, during the height of the cold war, the *Irish Times* sponsored an official televised arms debate between Soviet and US diplomats. It is even possible to sponsor an Amnesty International Tour.

Broadcast sponsorship offers possibilities ranging from sponsoring other people's advertisements (Midland Bank's £50,000 and Cancer Research), to *the weather*, specific *programmes* and *themed weeks on cable television* (see the ITC sponsorship code in the appendix).

Advantages of sponsorship

Sponsorship can be *cost effective* (compared to advertising) in terms of reaching a particular audience. It does allow access to very specific types of audiences that otherwise might be difficult to reach. Sponsorship can achieve many different objectives (see 'Objectives' pages 294–5) including: increased awareness; image enhancement; improved relationships with many different 'publics'; increased sales, sampling and database building; creating a platform for new promotional material; beating advertising bans, etc. It also offers creative oportunities including the engagement of an audience in a relaxed atmosphere of goodwill. Sponsorship lends itself to integrated communications and the cost effectiveness of integrated activities. Finally, the effects of a sponsorship programme are also measurable.

Disadvantages of sponsorship

Some say that sponsorship is insidious and that it undermines artistic integrity. In areas such as health and education, some feel that the issues involved are too important to be left to the whim of a corporation. Although sponsorship can deliver extremely cost effective benefits, it can be misunderstood as an excessive indulgence by employees if they are kept in the dark about it and if there are redundancies occurring at the same time. In both cases, sponsorship, particularly high profile sponsorship, needs to be presented to the employees as a cost effective business tool which can help the business to survive and thrive in the future (see page 294). Sponsorship of a competitive activity, such as a football club, can alienate the company or product from the opposition fans, eg a national audience if the teams are involved in an international competition, or an even larger audience if the team or player behaves despicably. Today's footballers are arguably the modern-day sandwich-man (man carrying two advertising boards up and down a street). TSB got round this potential problem with an innovative sponsorship programme which is explained in the short case at the end of this chapter.

Global media coverage may not be a good thing if what is being sponsored in one country is unacceptable in another country, eg bull fighting, camel wrestling, dwarf throwing, etc. If the medium is the message (ie the choice of sponsorship reflects the values of the sponsor) the message can become tarnished through its association with a socially unacceptable event. The uncontrollability of so many variables from weather to fans to strikes to riots makes sponsorship more risky than advertising. Finally, ambush marketing allows non-sponsoring competitors to soak up some benefits without paying full sponsorship fees (see 'Ambush Marketing', page 300).

> *Not The Salvation Army*
>
> This is not the Salvation Army, this is business. Our programme is focused and we are able to quantify what has happened. When I am criticised for paying the wages of dancers while staff are losing their jobs, I say that by supporting dancers, I am supporting more jobs at Digital.
>
> Geoff Shingles, chairman, Digital.

RUNNING A SPONSORSHIP PROGRAMME

The SOSTT + 4Ms acronym (See Chapter 2) can be used to develop and manage a sponsorship programme.

SOSTT + 4Ms involves:

1) Analysing and summarising the current sponsorship situation (including competitive review, previous sponsorship experiences, sponsorship strategies, etc.
2) Defining sponsorship objectives.
3) Clarifying strategy (how the sponsorship programme contributes towards the overall corporate mission, marketing objectives, communication objectives, and how it can be leveraged or stretched, exploited and supported by other communication tools).
4) Developing the tactical details of how it all fits together.
5) Defining target audiences.
6) Considering men, money and minutes (the resources required to run a programme).
7) Building in some form of measurement or evaluation to see whether the programme is worth repeating.

SOSTT + 4Ms is not, strictly speaking, a sequence of activities but more a checklist which should be incorporated into a programme or plan.

A more sequential approach for a sponsorship programme could be along the following lines:

1) Define objectives.
2) Define and analyse target audience/s.
3) Sponsorship policy and programme selection.
4) Fix budgets.
6) Sponsorship strategy.
7) Detailed plan of tactics.
8) Test or run a pilot scheme.
9) Implement the (modified) programme.
10) Monitor and measure.

Objectives

Clear objectives help to focus both the spin-off activities (eg sales promotions linked with the core sponsorship programme) and the marketing support activities (eg advertising and publicity which announces the sponsorship programme). A sponsorship programme can satisfy many objectives simultaneously. The range of objectives is varied:

1) Increase *awareness* — eg Cannon used the Football League partly to create a presence, become a familiar household name and generally raise awareness of a previously relatively unknown company in the UK market place.

2) Build an *image* — can help to reposition or strengthen a brand or corporate image through association with particular types of sponsorship activities, eg a caring image through community programmes.

3) Improve or maintain *relations* — with customers, the trade, employees, and even investors through hospitality and entertainment at a sponsored event. Rumbelows department store sponsored English soccer's League Cup. Part of the agreement allowed the sponsor to appoint their own employee of the year to meet the teams and present the cup to the winning captain. In a sense, it allowed their employee to be a Queen for the day. Community relations can also be enhanced by supporting appropriate local activities.

4) *Increase sales and open closed markets* — Coca-Cola was banned in Arab markets because it built an Israeli bottling plant. Sponsorship of the 1989 Arab Youth Football Competition in Riyadh helped to open the door again.

5) *Increase sales (sampling and direct sales)* — action-oriented sampling opportunities abound in a captive market where the buyer is in a relaxed frame of mind, eg buying and drinking Victoria beer at a touch-rugby competition sponsored by Victoria beer. Some market research can also be carried out. Sponsorship can create a dialogue, whereas a lot of advertising is a monologue (although there are some campaigns that engage the customer in more than just a monologue).

6) *Attract distributors/agents* — ECON are sponsoring a radio station's weather forecasts to build awareness and attract enquiries from agents in other markets.

7) *Create promotional material* — some events offer wonderful photo opportunities with scenes, sights and stars. One climbing equipment company sponsors climbs primarily to secure stunning photographs with branded climbing gear featuring prominently.

8) *Circumventing advertising bans* — sponsorship, particularly of televised events, allows sponsors a way around mainstream above the line advertising bans, eg tobacco companies sponsoring sports events such as snooker. Incidentally, the famous Steve Davis v Dennis Taylor snooker final kept one third of the British population glued to their TV sets until 3.00am.

9) *Miscellaneous* — ranging from, for example, the generation of new product ideas (new product educational competitions) to graduate recruitment.

Target audience/s

There are two different audiences. The first is the one immediately involved with the programme, the second the one which can be reached through advertising and media coverage. Although there are many spin-off objectives which offer benefits to different target groups (as in the previous Rumbelows Cup example), the primary objective should be linked clearly with the primary audience. This involves some *research* into the lifestyles, attitudes, behaviour patterns, leisure activities, issues and demographics relevant to the primary target group. Previous research should have identified the current situation, ie how the sponsor is positioned in the target audience's mind. This will reveal the kinds of specific communications objectives that need to be set.

Sponsorship policy and programme selection

A sponsorship policy helps the programme selection process by defining sponsorship parameters such as the preferred types of sponsorship that fit with the overall *mission statement*, the marketing and communication objectives. Questions to ask include the following. Is there any relevance between sponsor and subject, eg does a chess competition and a computer company share values of intelligence? Is there a consistent *message* or objective behind all the organisation's chosen sponsorship programmes? Does the association add value to the company or product? Is the association *internationally acceptable*? Think global, act local (sponsoring bull fighting or camel wrestling is globally unacceptable). Are there certain types or areas of sponsorship that are preferred? It is often felt that it is better to concentrate in certain areas. What is the *ideal time* in terms of seasonality and length of commitment, eg three year minimum? When should a sponsorship programme be dropped, changed or simply reviewed? Are both *solus* or *shared*/joint sponsorship programmes acceptable? Can *staff involvement* be incorporated? Does the sponsorship lend itself to *leverage* by offering potential for spin-off promotions and publicity? Does it lend itself to sales promotions, etc? Is it *unique*? Is it *protectable* from ambush marketing (see page 300)? What is the *competition* doing? Are 'me-too' sponsorship packages (competition follows with a similar sponsorship programme) preferred to unique (and uncopiable) sponsorship programmes? What kind of *budget* is required? What is defined as *value-for-money*?

The sponsoree's promise

In the search for funding, sponsorees may promise the world to potential sponsors. The potential sponsor needs to exercise some caution. Here are some points worth considering:

1) Have the contract checked by an expert. In particular, check the exit clause and exit arrangements since *it may be harder to get out of sponsorship than get into it*. For example, it is easy to start supporting a local theatre but when the sponsor wants to switch into a different type of sponsorship, the eventual withdrawal of funds may prompt the local paper to print a headline which might read 'Company X Pull Plug On Theatre' or 'Company X Leave Theatre In The Dark'.
2) Can they deliver their promises? Can they provide proof? Have they done it before? Have they any references? Are they financially secure?

Budgets

Budget allocation may in fact determine programme choice rather than the other way around. The formulae for determining the sponsorship budget vary but a rough rule of thumb suggests that the basic sponsorship fee should be at least *doubled* to get maximum leverage from the programme. This then leaves a budget for supporting marketing activities such as advertising and publicity, and maybe even some direct marketing. It also allocates some money for other spin-off activities. For example, sponsors of the Olympics will tend to milk the sponsorship to the maximum by running sales promotions offering Olympic prizes and donations in addition to simply carrying the 'official Olympic sponsors' logo. Payment can be *in cash or in kind*. A sponsor's services or facilities are likely to have a much greater value than cost, eg a newspaper sponsoring a boxing match can offer the fight promoter free advertising space in return for exclusive sponsorship rights. The cost may be minimal if the newspaper is not selling all its advertising space while the value to the promoter is, of course, much greater.

There are also various government sponsorship grant programmes which contribute significantly towards the cost (see 'Further Contacts', page 305).

If the 3Ms (men and women, money and minutes) are the three key resources, then they each need to be built into plans or budgeted for. Who is responsible for what, eg the supporting advertising, the spin-off sales promotions, the hospitality tent, the invitations, the publicity, etc? Is it all handled by an agency or controlled and administered by the in-house team? Time can be the greatest constraint to leveraging a sponsorship programme fully, since there may be lots of great ideas for exploiting the opportunities to the full but each one takes time to plan and ultimately put into action. Some estimates suggest *a minimum of nine months* is needed to develop a proper sponsorship strategy and programme plan.

Sponsorship strategy

The strategy statement briefly explains which types of sponsorship programmes are preferred, why a particular sponsorship programme is selected, how it will be exploited and integrated, and at what cost. To maximise the effect, sponsorship must be *integrated* with other elements of the communications mix, eg advertising, sales promotion, direct mail and public relations. It should also be explained internally and sometimes used internally as part of *psychic income* (see page 197, Chapter 10) as a means of improving employee relations.

Tactical plans

Squeeze as many benefits as possible into the programme. Sponsorship does not involve just adding the organisation's name to an event, team or situation and waiting to see if awareness takes off overnight. A well-planned sponsorship programme involves attracting media coverage, corporate entertainment, new client recruitment, miscellaneous spin-off promotions and staff motivation schemes. (See 'Tactics', pages 38–40, Chapter 2 to help develop (a) a whole communications plan around the sponsorship package or (b) integrate the sponsorship programme into the rest of the marketing communications activities.)

The launch is the easy bit. The real work starts then, as years one, two and three need constant attention to detail. A series of checklists and detailed plans (including contingency plans) have to be developed.

Pilot scheme

In an ideal marketing world all risks are reduced by testing and researching everything. Extra research costs resources, primarily time and money. Sometimes the nature of a sponsorship programme does not lend itself to testing, eg sponsoring the English Football League, but customers can be asked what they would think of it (before signing on the dotted line). Alternatively, a local league can be sponsored to allow management to move up the learning curve. Heinz were reported to have jointly sponsored the 1991 rugby World Cup so that they could learn about how sponsorship worked. The cautious or delayed approach arising from testing can also cause opportunities to be lost since the competition may snap up the best sponsorship programmes.

Roll–Out

This is the exciting side that everyone sees without fully realising the amount of work that goes on beforehand. Nevertheless, it is deceptively hard work since even though the sponsors are enjoying entertaining their clients, it is still work. In smaller sponsorship programmes the sponsor has to constantly think on his feet while entertaining, as minute problems inevitably pop up from time to time. In larger sponsorship programmes the constant alertness, attention to detail and readiness to react can be delegated to other members of staff (or consultancy).

Monitor, measure and evaluate

This is where the clearly defined sponsorship objectives make life easy since results can be compared with predetermined targets. Having measured the result, further analysis as to why a programme was particularly successful or unsuccessful will help future sponsorship programmes. The first three objectives listed on page 295, awareness, image and relations would normally require some formal market research activity such as a survey. There is, in addition, an interim method of evaluating sponsorship — by the amount of media coverage or name mentions. There are many monitoring companies that provide such services.

Cornhill Insurance

In 1988 cricket sponsors Cornhill Insurance received:

- 140 hours TV coverage;
- 7,459 banner sightings;
- 1,784 references on radio;
- 659 references in the national press;
- 2,448 references in the provincial press.

Cost: £1 million over five years.
Result: awareness up 17 per cent

Although cricket is on TV for long periods its audience is often quite small. Sponsorship research company AGB divide broadcast time by audience size to give cricket a ranking of 67, less than half that of ice skating. There are other, sometimes simpler, approaches to measuring the effectiveness of sponsorship. For example, Volvo calculated that its $3 million tennis sponsorship generated 1.4 billion impressions (number of mentions/sightings × audience size), worth about $18 million in advertising. It is worth noting that this only measures the amount of media coverage or output. It does not measure the ultimate objectives, of say, increasing awareness, changing attitudes or improving relations with different groups. This is where money may have to be spent on commissioning a piece of research which looks inside, instead of outside, the minds of the target audience.

The other objectives can be relatively easily measured if a system of measurement is set up in the first place, eg everyone is briefed to log or identify the source of any enquiries from customers, agents or distributors . Then again, a common-sense approach may help to identify results, eg new distributors or increased sales emerge without changing any of the other elements of either the marketing or communications mix (and assuming the competition has not had a strike or a factory fire).

Waffles or Lager?

In 1979 Belgium was `better known for its waffles than its lager'. When TV ads were beyond budget, sponsorship of the Queen's tournament beckoned. TV exposure and tennis's `aspirational and achievement' image matched Stella's objectives. Stella rose to no 1 in Britain's premium lager sector. Sales increased by 400 per cent.

(Source: *The Observer*, 1 April 1988)

Frank Jefkins (1990) thinks Canon got good value for their money when they sponsored the Football League for a limited period only: `Hardly an office in Britain without a *Canon* machine. It only took £3 million and three years – peanuts in that sort of business when you think what the sales are valued at.'

AMBUSH MARKETING

Measurement of the 1991 rugby World Cup broadcast sponsorship demonstrated its ability to influence consumers and override the main event sponsors. Spontaneous brand awareness of Sony rose among rugby World Cup watchers by eight points to 61 per cent (between September and November). According to ITVA, despite the recession, 'the company went on to record sales in December...Sony was also invariably the first name mentioned as sponsor of the rugby World Cup and overwhelmingly seen as the main sponsor. However, Sony was not a sponsor of the event itself; it sponsored only the ITV coverage.'

MISCELLANEOUS TIPS

1) Choose sponsorship programmes carefully, separate the initial excitement from the numerical analysis.
2) Think global but act local (today's satellite communications may highlight a sponsorship programme which is acceptable overseas but unacceptable at home and vice-versa).
3) Consider exit strategies (how difficult or easy is it to switch into another programme one, three or ten years down the road?).
4) Remember, it is not like advertising. There is no total control over the message. Have contingency plans for things that go wrong.
5) Budgets should be developed to allow for maximum exploitation through other communication tools.
6) Check for any government subsidies. For example, Business Sponsorship of the Arts shares costs 50:50 for first time sponsors and 33:66 thereafter.
7) Keep employees informed. Sometimes getting them involved increases the leverage. For example, Marks and Spencer sponsor projects which attract staff involvement.
8) Run a small pilot scheme to iron out any teething problems.
9) Beware of ambush marketing.

SHORT CASE

TSB's Roy of the Rovers

This short case demonstrates how careful audience and media research identified a previously untapped sponsorship opportunity which was integrated with PR to gain access to a traditionally difficult target market.

Situation
TSB research identified sport, particularly athletics and soccer, as a key active interest of its young customers. Success in sport demands discipline and control. Young people, research demonstrates, demand control of their money. TSB's youth products offer a mechanism to help control spending (eg, an instantly updated account which prevents young customers from the nightmare of an unwanted and unauthorised over-

draft). The overall marketing strategy for the youth market was therefore founded on sport and financial control, and linked TSB as the bank for, and in touch with, young people. In an Olympic year, the bank became a £5.2 million sponsor of major British athletics meetings.

Account opening incentives, supported by TV and press coverage, focused on money off anything from Nike trainers to Head tennis rackets at Olympus Stores. The media relations campaign focused on money control issues like 'buying a banger', 'getting a holiday job' or 'setting up a home of your own'.

The athletics opportunity had been seized but the soccer opportunity presented a somewhat more difficult challenge. The glamour of football is sometimes tainted by uncontrollable risks such as injuries, foul play, sendings off, disciplinary committees, board-room coups, protesting fans, rotten results (football), on and off the pitch violence and, of course, the weather. What marketing directors, with top brands in their custody, want logos in full colour in a national paper if it is on the shirt of a player just sent off for a vicious and cynical foul, or if it is being worn by a mass of rioting fans? Having said all that, football does attract audiences — intense loyal, largely young, male, with leisure time and money to spend and save.

The dilemma

TSB faced the soccer dilemma at the launch of the Premier League's first season. The bank, a big institution, was ready to act quickly and it set aside a budget to take advantage of any creative media opportunities.

The solution

A canny piece of media analysis revealed a 'perfect' soccer team that pulls 125,000 schoolboy spectators week in, week out regardless of the weather. Its captain is not only best mates with ex-England captain, Garry Lineker, but even more saintly than him. There are no riots, no drink driving, no smashed up hotel bars, no spurned love children. The results can even be found out months ahead, and they usually win.

The star player of this model team, Roy of the Rovers, and his squad, Melchester Rovers, are, of course, mythical. Roy has been Britain's best-loved footballer since his debut, in 1954, on the pages of the boys' comic, the *Tiger*. Since 1976 he has had a comic named after him.

Target
The immediate audience of 125,000 boys aged 7–12 are all targets for the bank's 'FirstSave' account. Banks want to recruit young customers since they normally stay with the same bank for life and because at least 50 per cent of these accounts are opened before the age of 16. Whether this is lethargy or loyalty is unclear but it does reinforce lifetime value.

Objective
To reinforce the link between TSB and one of its youth markets.

Strategy
Sponsorship of Melchester Rovers supported by a media relations campaign.

Tactics
- In the comic TSB logos feature on Melchester's red and yellow strip and on perimeter boards around the ground.
- Storylines around banking and young people are written into the comic.
- Competitions giving away Olympus kit.
- Covermount (sales promotion attached to the comic itself)
- Media relations campaign involving:

  a) The race to sign up a legendary team was leaked to and covered by national TV and newspapers on a quiet Monday in the dog days of August.
  b) Roy and his agent Dave Hunt, in reality his editor, were 'snatched' leaving secret talks at the Tower Hotel.
  c) The leak served two purposes — it put the comic back on the map with the aim of widening the audience for TSB's sponsorship, and it ensured a packed turn out for the press conference/launch.
  d) The press conference to announce the sponsorship was held at the Tower Hotel and was hosted by sports broadaster Danny Baker.

Men and women
PR consultancy the Quentin Bell Organisation worked closely and intensively with the TSB marketing team.

Money
£20,000 sponsorship fee with an additional £12,000 media relations budget.

Minutes
TSB and QBO moved at breakneck speed from concept to launch within three weeks.

Measurement
The sponsorship programme launch gained media coverage on national and local TV, and in the national and regional press. It is too early to say what the effect of all the sponsorship and media effort is, but the early indications at the time of print, show new account openings to be ahead of target. The montage on page 278 shows some of the press coverage.

Real sponsorship of a ficticious team

APPENDIX

ITC sponsorship guidelines

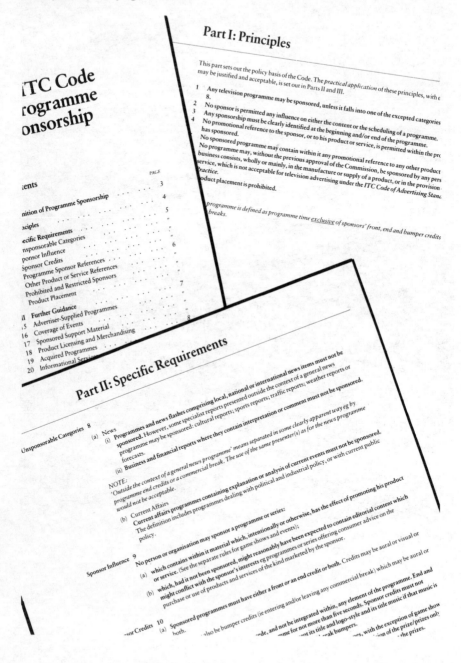

**iTC Code
rogramme
onsorship**

Part I: Principles

This part sets out the policy basis of the Code. The *practical application* of these principles, with e
may be justified and acceptable, is set out in Parts II and III.

1   Any television programme may be sponsored, unless it falls into one of the excepted categories
8.

2   No sponsor is permitted any influence on either the content or the scheduling of a programme.

3   Any sponsorship must be clearly identified at the beginning and/or end of the programme.
    No promotional reference to the sponsor, or to his product or service, is permitted within the pro
    has sponsored.

4   No sponsored programme may contain within it any promotional reference to any other product
    No programme may, without the previous approval of the Commission, be sponsored by any pers
    business consists, wholly or mainly, in the manufacture or supply of a product, or in the provision
    service, which is not acceptable for television advertising under the ITC Code of Advertising Stan
    ractice.
    oduct placement is prohibited.

    programme is defined as programme time *exclusive* of sponsors' front, end and bumper credits
    breaks.

Part II: Specific Requirements

Unsponsorable Categories 8

(a) News
     (i)   Programmes and news flashes comprising local, national or international news items must not be
           sponsored. However, some specialist reports presented outside the context of a general news
           programme *may* be sponsored: cultural reports; sports reports; traffic reports; weather reports or
           forecasts.
     (ii) Business and financial reports where they contain interpretation or comment must not be sponsored.

     NOTE:
     'Outside the context of a general news programme' means separated in some clearly apparent way eg by
     programme end credits or a commercial break. The use of the same presenter(s) as for the news programme
     would not be acceptable.

(b) Current Affairs
     Current affairs programmes containing explanation or analysis of current events must not be sponsored.
     The definition includes programmes dealing with political and industrial policy, or with current public
     policy.

Sponsor Influence 9 No person or organisation may sponsor a programme or series:

(a) which contains within it material which, intentionally or otherwise, has the effect of promoting his product
     or service. (See the separate rules for game shows and events);

(b) which, had it not been sponsored, might reasonably have been expected to contain editorial content which
     might conflict with the sponsor's interests eg programmes or series offering consumer advice on the
     purchase or use of products and services of the kind marketed by the sponsor.

or Credits 10   Sponsored programmes must have either a front or an end credit or both. Credits may be aural or visual or
                      both.
                      also be bumper credits (ie entering and/or leaving any commercial break) which may be aural or
     ede, and not be integrated within, any element of the programme. End and
           me for not more than five seconds. Sponsor credits must not
               nt its title and logo-style and its title music if that music is
                   eak bumpers.
                       es, with the exception of game show
                           ion of the prize/ prizes only.
                               the prizes.

> **Key Points from Chapter 15:**
>
> 1) Almost any target audience can be reached through sponsorship.
> 2) Almost anything can be sponsored.
> 3) Sponsorship can provide a cost effective marketing communications tool, satisfying a range of different objectives.
> 4) Maximum leverage is generated through integrating sponsorship with other communications tools.

Further reading

Head, V (1981) *Sponsorship, the Newest Marketing Skill*, Woodhead-Faulkner, Cambridge
Jefkins, F (1990) *Modern Marketing Communications*, Blackie & Sons, London
Giles, C (1991) *Business Sponsorship*, Butterworth- Heinemann, Oxford
Turner, S (1987) *Practical Sponsorship*, Kogan Page, London

Further contacts

Association for Business Sponsorship of the Arts (ABSA) Nutmeg House, 60 Gainsford Street, Butlers, London SE1 2NY. Tel: 0171-378 8143

Business in the Community, 8 Stratton Street, London W1X 6AH. Tel: 0171-629 1600

European Sponsorship Consultants Association (ESCA), 2 High Street, Chesham, Bucks HP5 1EP. Tel: 01494 791760

The Institute of Sports Sponsorship, Francis House, Francis Street, London SW1P 1DE. Tel: 0171-828 8771

Sponsorship News, CharterHouse Business Publications, PO Box 66, Wokingham, Berkshire RG11 4RQ

EXHIBITIONS

INTRODUCTION

Imagine bringing a whole market together, under one roof for a few days. An exciting idea? An explosive concept?

It happens all the time. Exhibitions are unique in that they are the only medium which brings the whole market together — buyers, sellers and competitors — all under one roof for a few days. Products and services can be seen, demonstrated or tested, and face-to-face contact can be made with a large number of relevant decision-makers in a short period of time.

According to the Incorporated Society of British Advertisers (ISBA), in 1990, in the UK alone, almost ten million visitors attended exhibitions while British companies spent £0.9 billion creating the exhibitions.

European organisations appear to place greater emphasis on exhibitions since they spend a larger proportion (30 per cent of their advertising budget) compared to UK organisations (9 per cent) (National Association of Exhibition Hall Owners). In some UK business to business markets and industrial markets exhibitions can take up to 40 per cent of the marketing budget (Exhibition Industry Federation).

EXHIBITION PLANNING

Exhibition objectives

Exhibitions provide a range of opportunities. Prioritising objectives can vary. Here are some typical objectives:

1) Maintain a presence in the market.
2) Sell to new and existing customers, agents and distributors.
3) Reinforce links with customers by introducing them to managers and directors.
4) Support local distributors/agents.
5) Customer research.

6) Competitor analysis and intelligence gathering.
7) Product testing.
8) Bring staff together. Some exhibitions can be the focal point of the year. They allow staff to come to the show (exhibition) and feel a certain amount of pride in their organisation.
9) Meet new staff or potential recruits.
10) Meet the press.

Exhibitions are a powerful marketing communications tool but they require detailed planning and co-ordination of resources. Much research and analysis, and many decisions have to be made concerning:

1) Developing an exhibition strategy.
2) Selecting the right shows (exhibitions).
3) Agreeing a design strategy.
4) Determining a pre-show promotional strategy.
5) Exhibition plan.
6) Follow-up strategy.
7) Evaluation.

Developing an exhibition strategy

Ideally, exhibitions should not be used as a one-off, ad hoc activity. They can be used more effectively when, (a) they are viewed as a possible series of exhibitions; (b) they are integrated carefully with other communication tools; (c) they are selected and planned well in advance; and (d) their effectiveness is constantly measured.

An exhibition strategy summarises the frequency and types of show selected. It may also summarise the kind of marketing support which is provided and the total level of spending.

Selecting the right shows

As with advertising or any marketing activity, exhibitions need careful targeting. There is an increasing number of exhibitions becoming available. In fact, there are usually more shows available than an organisation can attend. Some of them are better than others. All of them have sales staff dedicated to selling their exhibition space. In *Successful Exhibiting* (1990), James Dudley points out that 'The skill in selection is equal to that of media planners, except that media planners have considerably more audited information available to them.' (See 'Media Selection', Chapter 7). There are various listings which give a diary of exhibitions and events for up to two years in advance.

Selection checklist

1) Type of exhibition: local, national or international; vertical (tight focus of interest for buyers or sellers) or horizontal (wide range of interest for buyers or sellers); general public; trade events; private events; symposia or conferences where a limited amount of exhibiting facilitites are available.

2) Target audience: type and number of visitors — audited figures should be made available, eg ABC (Audit Bureau Circulation) figures are approved by the Association of Exhibition Organisers (the use of ABC figures is also a compulsory requirement of membership of the AEO). This is largely because ABC's figures are reproducible again for checking and testing.

3) Timing: does it meet buyers' purchasing patterns and can the organisation prepare for it in time, eg foreign shows may need to be planned 18 months in advance.

4) Facilities: any limitations or constraints; how the organisers intend to promote the event; supporting contact events, eg dinners, award ceremonies, seminars, breakfast receptions, etc.

5) Costs: comparing 'cost of space' and 'size of audience' ratios between different exhibitions. The space cost is useful for comparison but it only represents a small proportion of the total cost of exhibiting. James Dudley (1990) suggests that the cost of space rental is only 20 per cent of the total cost of exhibiting. The cost of the stand itself plus miscellaneous items (see 'Daily Checklist' on page 311) rapidly escalates costs.

6) How long has the show been running?

7) What official bodies are supporting it?

There are independent surveys which list visitor numbers, visitor quality, sales enquiries and a summary of exhibitors' results (see 'Post-show Evaluation', page 312).

Agreeing a design strategy

The stand design is a key factor in the overall exhibition strategy. It should present the right corporate image (see Chapters 14 and 17), attract interest and look aesthetically pleasing while providing for other functions such as display, demonstration, discussion, hospitality and storage (of spare samples, literature, coats, etc). Identifying measurable exhibition *success criteria* such as sales or orders, number of enquiries, cost per enquiry, cost per order, qualified contact names for a database, visitors' recall or level of awareness of the particular organisation's stand, key message, image or impression made by the stand, etc all help to focus a stand design strategy.

A visitor may have less than *five seconds to scan* and decide whether to enter a particular stand instead of the many other stands competing for that same visitor's attention. Buyers have only got a limited amount of time to visit a limited number of stands (Exhibition Survey's national average suggests that the average visitor attending a show barely calls on 13 stands regardless of the size of exhibition). Buyers have to choose quickly whether to enter or not. Many exhibitions provide a computer print-out of the exhibitors who fall into a particular category of suppliers which is of interest to a particular visitor. The print-out usually includes a map identifying the location of the specific organisations listed in the category. This means that a buyer can pause and decide what route he or she will take, and which stands to visit, before entering the main exhibition hall. Despite a preplanned schedule of visits, an excellent stand design or promotional stunt can still attract an unplanned visit from a busy buyer. A stunt can also attract time-wasting, stand-congesting, non-target market visitors.

Some stunts have been found to deter senior decision-makers as they feel that stunts are aimed at lower level visitors.

> How many exhibition stands explain what business the exhibitor is in?

It is surprising to observe the number of organisations that promote their name first and foremost, perhaps followed by a product name and somewhere, almost hidden, the product and product features are displayed. Product benefits (what buyers really seek) cannot be seen easily. In fact, most buyers have to make the psychological leap and commit themselves by walking on to a stand to engage in discussion which may eventually reveal the hidden product benefits. Larger organisations may feel that they have too many products to highlight individually, or that their name is associated with the product area so strongly that all visitors (including those from overseas) will immediately know what business they are in. Perhaps some exhibitors do not want to reveal their benefits to the competition too readily?

The design should be consistent with the organisation's corporate identity guide-lines (ie logo style, typefaces, primary and secondary colours) yet it should also try to attract visitors. The stand design should facilitate a simple selling sequence of attract-ing a visitor, providing a comfortable space and facilities to demonstrate products, and fostering an environment for detailed discussion and negotiations if appropriate.

The design brief can use the basic *SOSST + 4Ms* discussed in Chapter 6. Essentially the designer needs to know: the situation (exhibition name, exhibition location, stand location, stand size, access and service facilities available, range of competitors, whether the stand is re-usable); objectives (list success criteria and prioritise objec-tives, eg presenting an image, attracting new business, meeting old customers, launch-ing a new product, etc). The designer also needs to know the overall exhibition strategy discussed earlier. Tactics include any promotional ideas, specific numbers of staff and visitors on the stand at any one time, whether any promotional off-stand activities will be attracting visitors on to the stand, whether the stand will be used for photo opportunities, what kind of electronic gadgetry (videos, interactive compact discs), products and sales literature which needs to be displayed. The target audience is arguably the most important information in the design brief.

The designer also needs to know about the 3Ms, the three key resources of men and women, money (budget) and minutes (time). The fourth M, measurement, means that the whole exhibition design should focus on key measurable objectives (are all the elements linked up to and consistent with the overall exhibition strategy, etc?).

Sound, sight, space and even smell can be used creatively by a designer (there are, however, likely to be some constraints imposed by the organisers). Good designers exploit both two-dimensional design (eg graphics) and three-dimensional design (eg the use of space).

Pre-show promotional plan

To maximise effectiveness, many exhibitors do not depend on stand design alone to attract visitors. Careful pre-show promotions can ensure a steady flow of visitors on to a stand. Direct mail, linked with an incentive or sales promotion, free tickets, inserts, advertising, publicity, etc all basically attempt to get visitors to decide to visit a particular stand before they arrive at the exhibition in the first place. Given that the average visitor only visits 13 stands it is important to get on to the appropriate target visitor's *'must visit' list*. Pre-show publicity helps to identify who to expect and who to chase-up. It also provides a fresh opportunity of talking to customers and prospects on the back of the urgency and excitement created by the show.

Given that exhibiting is a resource consuming activity, pre-show activity aims to maximise the effectiveness of the investment. Some types of show, like conferences and seminars, are almost totally dependent on pre-event activity as attendees will not walk in off the street (see the Hewlett-Packard short case, page 283, Chapter 14).

Advertising and editorial opportunities range from the usual trade, professional and domestic press, local and regional media, transport (cabs, trains, buses, stations to the exhibition) through to the exhibition catalogue itself. Sponsorship of guides, maps, promotions, teaser promotions, free gifts, and competitions can all be offered to the target visitor through advertising, editorial, inserts, mailings or even telemarketing. Good exhibition planning can integrate with other communication activities at an early stage. This means that the costs of sales promotions and incentives can be reduced significantly by increasing the organisation's buying power when sourcing many different sales promotion gifts simultaneously. Delivery and invoicing can also be staggered or delayed so that cash flow bottlenecks do not occur.

Exhibition operating plan

Everything — from staffing to samples and sales promotions — has to be meticulously planned. Never underestimate the importance of attention to detail. Even contingencies should be allowed for. Exhibitions are hard work. A staffing roster schedules staff so that they can have a break and a chance to have a look around the exhibition (and report back on their observations). More importantly, the roster ensures that the stand is never undermanned or overmanned with inexperienced staff. *Staff briefing* for exhibitions helps everyone to focus on common objectives and learn how to man a stand (position their badge, approach visitors, qualify enquirers, etc). This in turn boosts everyone's performance. Individual performance on the stand can also be measured against pre-set criteria (number and quality of enquiries, etc).

Sod's law runs rampant in exhibitions — what can go wrong will go wrong. Contingency planning reduces risks but inevitably something unforeseen still emerges. The author has had two such experiences, both of which occurred at international shows: the first in Birmingham, where a new electrical product set itself on fire while being exhibited, the second in New York, where the freight company lost all the samples and display units. Sam Black's book on exhibitions and conferences (1989) highlights a stunning array of errors in exhibitions, ranging from a stand that was built upside down (because the architect read the plans upside down) to neighbouring stands encroaching on each other's area (sometimes by accident).

Daily checklist

The checklist below needs to be checked at the end of each day so that everything is in place for the next day.

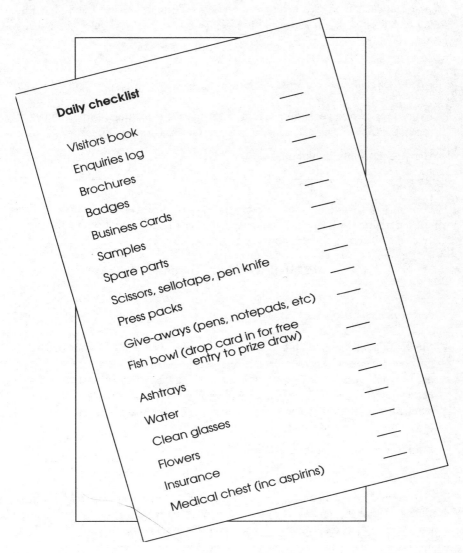

Follow-up plan

The exhibition is not an end in itself, although by the end of the show the exhausted staff probably feel like it is. Careful follow-up work must start almost immediately. This is where the organisation can earn its return from the exhibition. Leads, enquiries, quotations, sales and after-sales discussions need to be followed up in a professional manner. This requires a follow-up meeting where all the staff go through the cards they collected, the people they talked to and the projects or jobs which were discussed.

This prevents the duplication, contradiction and conflict which can arise where two different people from the same prospect organisation have asked two different members of staff for a quotation for the same job. Or two different enquiries have emerged for the same job from two different prospects. The manager can determine who follows up what with a report back meeting date set to see what sales are actually generated.

Eighty per cent make the same old mistakes

Every four or five years 80 per cent of companies exhibiting at trade shows repeat the same old mistakes, because a new man has been appointed.

Harry McDermott, Exhibition Surveys

More detailed evaluation of the true exhibition results can be carried out so that future efforts are improved. It is worth formalising the evaluation process so that the trend, individual, and competitor performance can all be measured.

POST-SHOW EVALUATION

Ninety per cent inefficient

Marketing men feel in their bones that they should exhibit at important events but sometimes don't seem to be able to make them work properly. *Often they are satisfied with inferior results* without realising they are only contacting 10 per cent of the show's potential...a performance that is 90 per cent inefficient mainly through lack of the right information. It is evident that a detailed analysis of visitors to the stand is not enough.

Harry McDermott, Exhibition Surveys.

Post-show evaluation measures performance against the preset objectives. It also examines whether the objectives were realistic, whether the show was the right show, and what was good and what was bad about the organisation's performance? A competitor's performance can also be evaluated to a certain degree. How can the performance be improved? Should the exhibition be run again next year? Was it value for money?

Some post-show questions:

1) What percentage of the potential number of visitors to the whole exhibition (that fit the target market profile) visited our stand?
2) What percentage stopped, but did not visit our stand?

3) What percentage saw but did not stop at our stand?
4) How many leads/enquiries/ were created?
5) What was the cost per contact/visitor?
6) What percentage of contact visitors planned to buy the product or service?
7) What was the cost per 'serious' visitor?
8) What was the cost per order?
9) How effective was each staff member's performance? (According to Harry Mc-Dermott of Exhibition Surveys, 'Stand staff should indoctrinate every visitor they meet on a stand. When those visitors think of the types of product shown they should think of the exhibitor. Research can get visitors to rate individual staff because the visitors' comments can be linked back to the stand record of contacts.')
10) Did we overspend or underspend (too large or too small a stand/too many or too few staff)?

Exhibition value analysis

Exhibition value analysis is a type of survey which includes both a multi-client survey and a confidential private survey so that comparisons can be made between the client company and its competitors's performance. The survey covers visitor potential, the percentage that saw, stopped or visited a particular stand, visitors' peceptions, intentions to buy, and the stand's strengths and weaknesses based on a sample of known visitors to the stand (supplied by the company). See Appendices 1 and 2 at the end of this chapter.

Some research findings suggest that companies do not attend trade exhibitions to sell, but rather to build corporate and brand awareness.

Cost per enquiry

Cost per enquiry averages at £18 and £28 for UK and overseas exhibitions respectively (Exhibition Industry Federation (EJF) 1990). However, the bottom line for many organisations is still 'how much business did it generate?'

$$\frac{\text{Total exhibition costs}}{\text{Number of 'serious' enquiries}} = \text{Cost per enquiry}$$

Cost per order

Total exhibition costs can be divided by the number of orders taken to find the cost per order. There are some difficulties here, however. First there is the timescale (some orders instigated by contact at a trade show/exhibition can take several months or longer before they are finally confirmed). Second, the regular orders (which would have been brought in by the normal salesforce visits anyway), should, ideally, be separated from those incremental orders generated solely by attending the show. Third, there is also a school of thought which suggests that exhibitions do not generate sales; they only allow the exhibitor to meet a useful target market, but whether they buy depends on a number of factors totally divorced from the show (eg the product, competitors' products, prices, etc).

An average of averages shows a cost per order in UK and overseas exhibitions of £70 and £113 respectively (EIF 1990). The UK range appears to be anywhere from £60 (tourism), £215 (engineering) to £323 (marketing services). This, of course, ignores the size of the orders and the profitability of the orders. The size of the orders could be expressed as a percentage figure in the same way as a marketing communications budget is sometimes expressed, ie marketing expenses as a percentage of sales. In this case, exhibition costs as a percentage of sales generated can be calculated as:

$$\frac{\text{Total exhibition cost}}{\text{Number of orders}} = \text{Cost per order}$$

Percentage of sales

As we have said, the difficulty here lies in isolating the sales generated exclusively through the exhibition, ie ignoring sales that would have been taken by the salesforce regardless of the exhibition. Nevertheless the cost of taking the same number of enquiries or sales by routine sales visits should be compared to the costs of enquiries or sales taken during the exhibition.

$$\frac{\text{Total exhibition costs}}{\text{Sales resulting the exhibition}} = \% \text{ of sales method}$$

Return on investment (ROI)

The long-term profitability of the sales is probably the most important of all the criteria. This is difficult to calculate because the lifetime value of a customer (see Chapter 13) is often difficult to calculate, particularly in industrial markets. However, the short-term *return on investment* (ROI) can be calculated by dividing the profit or contribution made from the orders by the total cost of the exhibition.

$$\frac{\text{Contribution}}{\text{Total exhibition cost investment}} = \text{ROI}$$

For example, if the orders taken during a show amounted to £200,000 and the total cost of or investment in the exhibition was £20,000, the calculation would be as follows:

Sales	£200,000
Less cost of sales (say 50%)	£100,000
Contribution	£100,000
Less cost/investment in the exhibition	£20,000
Return or profit on the investment	£80,000

This can then be expressed in percentage terms:

$$\frac{80,000}{£20,000} = 400\% \; ROI$$

The real ROI should in fact only be calculated from additional or new sales which were generated by the exhibition. Say it only generated five new customers who, in total, bought £50,000. The real ROI (on new business) would be 25 per cent. The word investment is a bit misleading since if the exhibition stand cannot be used again it is not an investment but rather an expense. If the exhibition only produced one new customer who bought £10,000 worth then the ROI would be negative.

Experimental non-attendance

Some organisations decide to stop exhibiting and use the opportunity to measure the *impact of non-attendance* on their sales and on their competitors' exhibition results.

The many other functions which exhibitions provide are not included in the costs or revenues used in the previous calculations. Other, non-selling exhibition activities such as maintaining a presence, projecting an image, entertaining customers, marketing research, competitor analysis, product testing, etc, all, in a sense, save costs which would have been incurred if they were commissioned outside the exhibition. Arguably, these 'saved costs' could be subtracted from the other costs in these calculations.

Real costs can certainly be saved by careful co-ordination throughout the whole exhibition planning cycle. As we have seen, the planning cycle includes developing the exhibition strategy, selecting the right shows, agreeing a design strategy, determining the pre-show promotional strategy, drawing up an operating plan, carrying out an accurate post-show evaluation.

TWELVE REASONS FOR POOR PERFORMANCE

James Dudley (1990) highlights research findings which indicate the twelve main reasons for poor performance:

1) Inadequate statements of purpose and objectives — nobody quite knows what they are supposed to do.
2) Poor quality visitors.
3) Bad location of the stand.
4) Ineffective quality and design of the stand.
5) Undistinguished performance of personnel running the stand, because of poor selection, training, motivation or management.
6) Lack of follow-up of leads and enquiries.
7) Ignoring the competition and letting them steal your prospective visitors.
8) Poor recognition of company by buyers.
9) Poor corporate identity leading to low recall of your stand by visitors.
10) Breakdown in organisation and control, leading to last-minute panics, such as an unfinished stand on the opening day of the show or late arrival of literature, give aways and so on.
11) Inadequate arrangements made for staff working on the stand, such as locating

their accommodation too far from the event, failing to obtain car park permits or not organising meal vouchers, etc.

12) Inadequate control of costs and budgets, leading to over-expenditure and consequently a poor return on investment.

SHORT CASE

Sedgwick at RIMS Monte Carlo

This short case demonstrates the kind of detailed planning required to run a successful exhibition.

Situation

The Sedgwick group had a worldwide income of £685 million in 1991. With 60 European offices, Sedgwick is the largest European based insurance broker and risk management consultancy (and ranked third in the world). Although Sedgwick is well respected, the similarity of competitor products and services make professionalism, quality and expertise vital in adding value to the 'invisible' service. The credibility of the whole company is largely dependent on the credibility of the sales and support staff. Exhibitions literally provide a platform for staff visibility and customer contact. RIMS Monte Carlo (Risk and Insurance Management Society) is a focal point for the European risk and insurance market. It takes place every two years and comprises a three-day, high-level conference and exhibition which attracts all major companies and buyers in the sector. It is therefore essential for Sedgwick to be there.

Objectives
Marketing

- To introduce the new European client service network.
- To introduce several pan-European products (including the multilingual service and the eastern Europe network).

- To create an opportunity for cross-selling (new products to existing customers).
- To attract 100 visitors to the stand per day.

Communications

- To reinforce Sedgwick's position as the foremost European based broker with the best European network (including eastern Europe).
- To demonstrate true pan-European expertise (eg multilingual). To project a visibly European image (and not UK dominated). To create a totally cohesive 'one company' image (single European company) in a clear visual statement.
- To improve internal communications by creating a focal point for the meeting of staff from across the contintent to break down barriers between divisions/trading companies.

Strategy

The above objectives would be achieved in a cost competitive manner by developing an outstanding pan-European exhibition involving: a press conference and a press lunch; senior speakers at the main conference dinner; hosting a major dinner; and an innovative exhibition crowd-pulling concept, all integrated into the creative theme 'One Europe, 1st in Europe'.

Targets

Risk managers of medium-sized to large companies and managers responsible for buying insurance (finance directors, company secretaries and heads of administration) across Europe.

Tactics

Given that most of the RIMS exhibition visitors fell into the target group it was essential to create a hub of activitiy around the Sedgwick stand. A new product demonstration was placed alongside a crowd-pulling cartoonist who sketched visitors on pre-printed, branded paper, giving full service and address details on the back. This allowed both client and prospect visitors to take away something that was personal to them but was also Sedgwick branded. The same artist drew European cameos of many countries for a competition. The production of Sedgwick's European magazine, *ERA 2*, (published in six languages) was carefully planned so that it was available for the exhibition. The first article in *ERA* focused on Sedgwick's eastern European operations.

Stand design

The nature of the industry and the economic environment were such that lavishly designed stands could create a worry in the minds of clients that 'we are paying for all this'. For these reasons the stand looked smart, professional and European but was not a luxurious extravaganza. Visually, the stand took its style from the *ERA* magazine to create a cohesive look. All graphics were in French and English. The stand was manned by an international team at all times.

Men and women

The entire project was planned by an in-house exhibition team with both international

and exhibition expertise. Senior management support and commitment to the exhibition was evident by the constant presence and involvement of the managing director of the French operation (the local host). The UK based European PR manager controlled the overall plan and execution.

Money
A basic 3m × 3m unit of exhibition floorspace costs between £2,000 and £8,000 depending on the exhibition. At RIMS the 3m × 6m (two units) cost £5,500. An additional £5,500 was budgeted for all other items such as the cartoonist, contractor, transport, graphics, telephone lines, etc. The high-quality lightweight, flexible, re-usable exhibition kit was tailored for the RIMS exhibition and subsequently built into the 18 square metres of rented space. The standard shell scheme option was rejected ('too bland') as was the purpose-built stand option ('too expensive' — cost anywhere from £10,000 to £30,000). The budget did not cover travel and accommodation which, as is customary in a large organisation, was paid for by each individual trading company.

Minutes
RIMS is a bi-annual event. Sedgwick's planning started 18 months in advance. Early commitment and good relationships with the exhibition organisers helped to secure the best stand location (and choice of halls), speaker opportunities and details of attendees, especially the press. Quarterly meetings were held with French colleagues. Planning meetings immediately before the exhibition were held on site. Daily planning meetings for all staff members (circa 70) were held early *each morning* to agree the day's strategy before the exhibition doors were opened to the public.

Measurement
A post-exhibition meeting was held to arrange a follow-up schedule for all enquiries and to evaluate the overall exhibition performance. The new products and services helped to develop existing clients and attract new clients. One indicator of the stand's success was the front-page coverage of the stand and Sedgwick's keynote conference

speaker in a magazine sponsored by a direct competitor. All stand members felt that the exhibition was a morale booster and it helped them to feel more confident with their clients. The staff began to feel part of one European company. In fact, a subsequent pan-European slogan competition received 400 entries from company staff (nearly 20 per cent of the European workforce). Arguably, the winning slogan was born out of the new post-exhibition mood: 'One Europe, one broker. Sedgwick.'

APPENDIX 1

Exhibition value analysis

The synopsis shown below indicates the type of information which the evaluation should include:

EXHIBITION EVALUATION

Synopsis of

CONFIDENTIAL PRIVATE CLIENT REPORT

CONTENTS			USES
PERFORMANCE SUMMARY	Compares performance with objectives, with exhibition potential, and to your competitors. A factual measurement of achievement	]]]]]	Use as a synopsis for debriefing, in structuring the next exhibition presence.
COMMENTS ON PERFORMANCE	Conclusions and advice	]]]	Use the recommendations for consideration, implementation and discussions with staff or with
ACTION RECOMMENDATIONS	For future developments, changes or corrections	]]	Exhibition Surveys
YOUR POTENTIAL AUDIENCE	The number of exhibition visitors interested in your company's products	]]]]	Use to set budgets, allocate resources, measure results. Factual independent data of your company's exhibition potential
STAND ATTRACTION RATING	Your stand's success in being seen by your target audience	]]]	Measure your designer's performance in creating an attention-getter for your market
STAND EFFICIENCY RATING	Your sales staff's success in contacting your target audience	]]	Measure your stand and your staff's performance in processing visitors
COST PERFORMANCE	Your achieved cost per interested visitor	]]]	Use to evaluate and improve cost-effective competitive performance and to compare with your normal cost per sales call.

YOUR VISITORS, THEIR REACTIONS AND OPINIONS

Visitor quality, product interest and plans to buy	] Specific] evaluations	Use to evaluate performance and make future decisions in the context
Recall of visiting your stand	] against potential	of exhibition potential
Impact of your presentation on visitors	] of your company's	
Performance of stand personnel	] achievements in	
Marketing communications (Association Question)	] these critical areas	

PERFORMANCE COMPARISON WITH COMPETITORS

Number of visitors to specific named stands	] Tabular presenta-] tions of performance	Use to evaluate performance and make future decisions in
Most memorable stands	] across the show,	competitive context
Most impressive demonstrations/ presentations	] including client] companies and] competitors	

APPENDIX
The questionnaire

Exhibition Surveys Ltd,
22 Digby Drive, Melton Mowbray, LE13 0RQ

Exhibition Surveys

APPENDIX 2

Exhibition Survey's Questionnaire

Exhibition Surveys

THE 1992 CADCAM EXHIBITION SURVEY

1. Please tick all previous years you have visited the Exhibition.

1-1( )1991   -2( )1990   -3( )1989   -4( )1988   -5( )First time this year

2. Why did you visit the exhibition this year?

2-1( )To see new products & developments   3-1( )General interest
   -2( )To see a specific company or product   -2( )To make business contacts
   -3( )To buy   -3( )To evaluate the show before exhibiting
   -4( )To obtain technical or product information   -4( )Other..................
   -5( )To help select future suppliers   (specify)

3. Please name any other computer exhibitions that you have visited in the past 2 years.........................
.... 4-1( ) I visit no other exhibitions

4. How many hours did you actually spend at the exhibition? ....hours spread over ....day(s)
                                                5   6

5. How did you learn that the exhibition was to take place?

7-1( )Organisers' direct mail   -2( )Exhibitors' direct mail   -3( )My company
   -4( )Trade/technical press   -5( )Exhibitors' representative   -6( )Friend/associate   -7( )Other..................(state)

6. Try to name three companies whose stands attracted your attention the most.

Company name	Saw demon-stration	Interested in products	Obtained literature	Design of stand	Other reasons (please specify)
....	( )	( )	( )	( )	....
....	( )	( )	( )	( )	....
....	( )	( )	( )	( )	....

7. Tick the products and services that you found of interest at the exhibition. Also tick those that you plan to buy or recommend to buy **as a result of what you saw at the Show. (Tick all appropriate boxes).**

Interested	Recommend/Plan to buy		Interested	Recommend/Plan to buy	
8-1( )	8-1( )	2D Drafting & Design	10-1( )	10-1( )	Manufacturing Control Systems
-2( )	-2( )	3D Solid Modelling	-2( )	-2( )	Networking
-3( )	-3( )	3D Surface Modelling	-3( )	-3( )	Numerical Control
-4( )	-4( )	Architectural CAD	-4( )	-4( )	PC CAD
-5( )	-5( )	Business Software	-5( )	-5( )	Plastics
-6( )	-6( )	Civil Engineering Design	-6( )	-6( )	Plotters
-7( )	-7( )	Computer-Aided Manufacturing	-7( )	-7( )	Printers
-8( )	-8( )	Drawing Office Equipment	-8( )	-8( )	Process Planning Systems
9-1( )	9-1( )	Electrical CAD	11-1( )	11-1( )	Scanning Systems
-2( )	-2( )	Electronic CAD	-2( )	-2( )	Structural Analysis
-3( )	-3( )	Finite Elements Analysis	-3( )	-3( )	Techncial Documentation
			-4( )	-4( )	Workstation CAD

8. What role(s) do you play in the purchase of the following?

Product Category	Final Say -1	Specify -2	Recom-mend -3	No-Role -4	Product Category	Final Say -1	Specify -2	Recom-mend -3	No-Role -4
Personal Computers	12( )	{ }	{ }	{ }	Plotters	14( )	{ }	{ }	{ }
Networking Products	13( )	{ }	{ }	{ }	Printers	15( )	{ }	{ }	{ }

9A. Are you a user (or a manager of users) of **Plotters**?   16-1( )Yes   -2( )No (Goto Q10)

9B. Which company **first** comes to mind when you think of **plotter** manufacturers?   (Please enter below)

9C. Which other manufacturers of **plotters** can you think of?   (Please enter below).

	Manufacturers' names	Number of plotters
FIRST CHOICE	....	( )
OTHER CHOICES	....	( )
" "	....	( )
" "	....	( )
" "	....	( )
" "	....	( )
" "	....	( )
	TOTAL	10

9D. Thinking about all these brands, imagine a hypothetical purchase situation: if you had a budget of 10 units, how would you allocate these 10 units amongst each brand?   (Enter above in right-hand column).

(c) EXHIBITION SURVEYS 1992   ...continued

10. How useful was this year's exhibition?

17-1( )Very useful   -2( )Useful   -3( )Moderately useful   -4( )Hardly useful at all   -5( )Not useful

What features of the Show did you particularly like? ....

What was negative, disappointing or missing? ....

....

11. Of all the exhibitors seen at the exhibition, which one impressed you the most? and Why?

Company.. Reason.. ( )None was impressive

12. Were you employed on your company's stand during the Show?   ( )YES   ( )NO

13. Did you stop to look at, or talk to, or to acquire literature from any of these companies at the Show? (Tick all appropriate boxes). If you talked to any of these companies, please indicate the degree of helpfulness of the person you talked to by placing the following code in the 'Helpfulness of personnel' column below: (4) If Good; (5) If Fair; (6) If Poor and (7) If Stand too crowded - no one to talk to. If a sales person from any of these Companies has called on you in the past year, please tick 'Sales Person Called' column.

	Looked -1	Talked -2	Literature -3	Helpfulness of personnel	Sales Person called -8		Looked -1	Talked -2	Literature -3	Helpfulness of personnel	Sales Person called -8
Calcomp	18( )	( )	( )	( )	( )	Oce	22( )	( )	( )	( )	( )
Canon	19( )	( )	( )	( )	( )	Roland	23( )	( )	( )	( )	( )
Graphtec	20( )	( )	( )	( )	( )	Tektronix	24( )	( )	( )	( )	( )
Hewlett-Packard	21( )	( )	( )	( )	( )	Versatec	25( )	( )	( )	( )	( )

14. Altogether, at approximately how many stands did you stop for a discussion or to obtain literature? ....

15A. Did you visit any of the following companies' stands? Please tick column A.

15B. May we have your views about those companies that you visited?
(Please rate Columns B, C, D, E in terms of: 1 very good, 2 good, 3 satisfactory, 4 not very satisfactory, and 5 unsatisfactory)

Visited A		Stand Quality B	Presentation of Products C	Overall professionalism of staff on duty D	Demonstrations seen E
26( )	Calcomp	35( )	44( )	53( )	62( )
27( )	Canon	36( )	45( )	54( )	63( )
28( )	Graphtec	37( )	46( )	55( )	64( )
29( )	Hewlett-Packard	38( )	47( )	56( )	65( )
30( )	Oce	39( )	48( )	57( )	66( )
31( )	Roland	40( )	49( )	58( )	67( )
32( )	Tektronix	41( )	50( )	59( )	68( )
33( )	Versatec	42( )	51( )	60( )	69( )
34( )	Others............. (please state)	43( )	52( )	61( )	70( )

16. Which 3 companies new products or developments did you see at the exhibition?

Companies   1. .... 2. .... 3.................................

New Product 1. .... 2. .... 3.................................

To help classify your answers, may we have some information about yourself?

17. What is your job title? ....

18. What is your job function? ....71-1( )Trainee
                                              -2( )Full-time student

19. What are the major products or services of the organisation with which you are employed?

....

....

20. What is the approximate number of employees in your organisation (at your location)?

72-1( )1-9 -2( )10-49 -3( )50-99 -4( )100-249 -5( )250-499 -6( )500-999 -7( )1,000 and over

21. Please name three computer magazines that you read regularly ....

....

....

May we have your name to validate our survey? ....

THANK YOU FOR YOUR HELP

> **Key Points from Chapter 16:**
> 1) Exhibitions are hard work. Exhibitions can work hard for the exhibitor if they are planned and integrated with the other marketing communication tools.
> 2) Every element of the exhibition performance can be monitored and measured with a view to making improvements in the next exhibition.

Further reading

Black, S (1989) *Exhibitions and Conferences, from A to Z*, The Modino Press Limited, London
Dudley, J W (1990) *Successful Exhibiting*, Kogan Page, London
Exhibition Industry Federation, *The UK Exhibition Industry — The Facts*, Volume Three, 1991
Northover, J (1990) *The Exhibitor's Handbook*, Kogan Page, London
Talbot, J (1989) *How to Make Exhibitions Work for your Business*, The Daily Telegraph/Kogan Page, London
Walden, R (1985) *Exhibiting for the Small Business*, Nat West Small Business Digest

Further contacts

Association of Exhibition Organisers, 26 Chapter Street, London SW1P 4ND. Tel: 0171-932 0252

British Exhibition Contractors Association, Kingsmere House, Graham Road, Wimbledon, London SW19 3SR. Tel: 0181-543 3888

British Exhibitors Venues Association, Mallards, Five Ashes, Mayfield, East Sussex TN20 6NN. Tel: 01435 872244

Exhibition Industry Federation, 115 Hartington Road, London SW8 2HB. Tel: 0171-498 3306

National Association of Exhibition Hall Owners (NAEHO), for further information contact Peter Bramich, Chairman of the NAEHO at: Brighton Metropole Hotel, King's Road, Brighton, East Sussex BN1 2FU. Tel: 01273 775432

National Exhibitors Association, 29A Market Square, Biggleswade, Bedfordshire SG18 8AQ. Tel: 01767 316255

17

CORPORATE IDENTITY AND CORPORATE IMAGE

WHAT IS CORPORATE IDENTITY?

Corporate identity is what it says — it is a visual means of identifying a corporation, company or organisation. Logos and names are only a part, albeit a very obvious part, of an organisation's identity. Corporate identity is a strategic asset which helps to achieve the longer-term communication goals. It cannot therefore be used as a short-term tactical tool like advertising or PR, which can change from day to day (if required). As with any fixed asset, the corporate identity asset needs to be checked and maintained to keep it in good working order. If allowed to fall into disarray or disrepair, it can, like other assets, eventually become a liability by projecting an inappropriate image.

Corporate identity is a symbolic uniform which acts as a flag expressing everything about the organisation. It is a visual system which uses *all the points of public contact*. This includes the 'permanent media' or buildings (exterior and interior), signage, vehicles, uniforms, business forms (invoices, cheques, letterhead, etc), literature (product brochures, annual reports), exhibitions, etc. Some companies stamp their logos on to their individual brands' advertising, packaging and point-of-sale material, eg Dulux Paints carry the ICI name and logo.

Wally Olins (1989) of the Wolf Olins corporate identity design consultancy suggests that corporate identity makes the corporate strategy visible through design and that it can specifically project three things:

1) Who you are.
2) What you do.
3) How you do it.

'Everything an organisation does, owns and produces should give a clear idea of its aims and standards', says Olins. Corporate identity should also reflect the personalities, core values and direction of a company. It is one way of communicating the values it wants to express. Philip Kotler (1988) says that 'designers identify *the essence of the company* and turn it into a concept backed by strong visual symbols and logos'.

The corporate identity mix

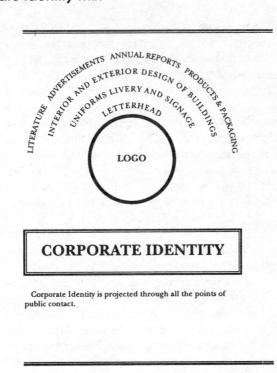

Corporate Identity is projected through all the points of public contact.

Figure 17.1 The corporate identity mix
Reproduced from PRTV's `Corporate image' training video notes.

More than a logo

As can be seen from Figure 17.1, a corporate identity programme is more than just a logo or a lick of paint. Although a logo is a rallying point, it is only, in corporate identity specialist John Sorrell's words `the tip of the iceberg'.

A new letterhead and a new logo is no substitute for a new board of directors.
Rodney Fitch

Painting the lavatory door won't cure the plumbing.
David Bernstein

If you take a lousy low-profile company and give it a major corporate revamp, you end up with a lousy high-profile company. *Wally Olins*

You can put on an Arsenal shirt but if you don't perform like an Arsenal player you have not accomplished very much.
Nick Chaloner

Even if you paint out a skunk's stripes it will smell extremely nasty.
Source: unknown

Logos

The crucifix, the hammer and sickle, the swastika, the red cross or a national flag immediately arouse emotions, feelings, images or interpretations of some kind. Logos are a language (sometimes international) of emotional response. Symbols, shapes and colour all have conscious and unconscious meanings (see Chapter 18). Visual symbols or devices can also be powerful as a means of increasing awareness by facilitating easy recognition. On the other hand, a logo cannot read like a graphic sign, eg 'Ladies'. A logo can act as a focal point to summarise or encapsulate an organisation, although it should not be too complex. Tim King of Siegle and Gale feels that 'If an identity needs too much explaining then it isn't working'.

A logo should be *distinctive, easily recognisable, memorable and reduceable* (can work when reduced on to a business card or postage stamp). It should also *work in black and white* as well as colour, since many corporate images appear in black and white in the press). Ideally, the logo should also be *symbolic* but this is rarely the case.

At first a logo has little or no value because it has no franchise. First, it must be associated with the right kind of images and then its recognition levels can be developed (eg, Lloyds Bank's Black Horse and McDonalds' yellow arches). This takes time since initial reactions to change or anything new is often quite negative. Sometimes the initial reaction is one of upset, dislike or disgust as the new logo does not fit in with the previous set of cognitions (and thereby creates 'cognitive dissonance', tension and possibly even dislike and disgust). The value of the logo eventually starts to increase as the years roll on and as it becomes better understood. In 1992, the Guinness name and logo was estimated to be worth over US$2 billion according to US business magazine *Financial World*.

Logo designs as visual devices

In the 1970s corporate images hardened. The 1980s saw them becoming soft and decorative. Some cynics say that if you wanted to make an abstract organisation look purposeful in the late 1980s, you quite literally gave it a face — preferably a neo-classical one. The Woolworths group, on the other hand, changed its name, logo and total identity to Kingfisher, which was certainly distinctive, easily recognisable, memorable and symbolic of its progressive leadership expansion and growth potential (although some argued that the bird has only got a life expectancy of one year and that robins and blue tits are more popular anyway). Bovis construction company chose a humming bird, which again fitted the above criteria. Others suggest that there is a trend towards *humanising* logos since organisations are all about people (eg the Prudential — see below).

The British Home Stores updated logo has the 'B' and the 'S' in capital letters (commensurate with such an institution). The 'H', on the other hand, is a soft swoosh of blended colours

> 'a dancing kaleidoscope of colour. Red ascender, red tipped blue/green base, all a-shimmer and a sparkle, matching the typographical style. British Home Stores are thus semiotically flanking, presenting and supporting a home that is an exciting, bright, adventurous place to be'.

It is certainly a *unique visual device* which aids recognition and conjures up positive feelings.

Don King's hair

World boxing promoter Don King's elevated hair style (brushed up six inches or more into the sky) makes him stand out amid a crowded post-fight boxing ring. His 'unique visual symbol' helps to ensure that he is easily recognised and seen to be involved with the big fights.

US logos

Late 1980s US research into the *Fortune 500* industrial and service companies revealed that:

* Fifty-one per cent used symbols with their names. Of these:
    — 13 per cent were literal (eg Shell).
    — 27 per cent were company initials.
    — 11 per cent were purely abstract.
* Thirty-five per cent had logo types that were stylised treatments of the company name with no additional symbol (eg Kellogs).
* Fourteen per cent had word marks which integrate a graphic element into the name.

Whether the trend is towards humanisation, swooshes or sharp-edged internationally understood symbols, the corporate identity demands careful management across all the points of public contact. The next part of this chapter looks at how to manage the corporate identity.

MANAGING THE CORPORATE IDENTITY

There are a series of stages in the management of corporate identity:

1) Gain board-level support.
2) Assess current situation and determine ideal image.
3) Brief and select a designer.
4) Develop design concepts.
5) Research, select and test concepts.
6) Explain internally.
7) Implement and initiate a design manual.
8) Review and update.

Gain board-level support

Ideally, the commitment must start at the top. An effective corporate identity pro-gramme needs support and commitment from the board of directors.

Assess the current situation

The key areas for design should be identified, eg for a bank it would be the retail environment design and for a car manufacturer it would be the product design. A *communications audit* examines how the organisation is perceived internally by its own employees and externally by a host of different audiences. As soon as the ideal image is determined the gap between ideal and existing image can be addressed. This paves the way for a brief to improve, modify or design a new corporate identity and, in addition, to address other non-visual areas that affect the corporate image (eg product quality, customer care and employee care — see 'Total Quality Management', page 379, Chapter 20).

Brief and select a designer

The brief should incorporate the SOSTT + 4Ms formula (see Chapter 2 for a full explanation of the formula). Essentially, the brief must include basic information like the situation, objectives, strategy, targets and the resources of men, money and min-utes. The strategy can give an outline of the range of communications tools which use the corporate identity. The last 'M', measurement, is sometimes discussed with a view to developing a system of monitoring the proper use of an identity around the world. The design consultancy selection process is similar to the agency selection process described on page 116, Chapter 6).

Develop design concepts

The next step is the development of rough design concepts that match the brief. It is possible to score the concepts according to specific criteria in the brief. At the end of the day it also comes down to judgement or gut feelings about the early concepts.

Having said that, many articulate and confident design agencies can justify an array of different concepts in a persuasive manner. Rejection fees (payment for rejected or unused concepts) should be clarified in advance of any concepts being presented. The BP's recent global update of their corporate identity involved two agencies, Siegel & Gale and Addison, who initially produced hundreds of concepts.

Select, research and test

A few designs are then selected and checked for registerability. They are then further researched in focus groups and refined or rejected accordingly. This gradual process of elimination eventually presents a preferred name, logo, colours, typeface and style. The new identity emerges and final artwork is prepared for the printer.

In the case of BP five designs were chosen (some with the shield and all on a green background). According to British Airways *Life* magazine (September 1991):

> The prototype designs were erected in mock petrol stations housed within a London warehouse. On their way to work senior executives and board directors were diverted to the warehouse to experience the new designs. The doors were opened to create daylight and then shut for a night-time effect. Another mock-up was built in Oxfordshire to test petrol buyers' reactions. Despite additional consumer research showing a strong preference for a logo without the shield, the shield was kept because executives were convinced that tradition should persist.

Explain internally

As mentioned previously, there is an inherent resistance to change. A new identity can create conflict, particularly if it is not understood. So any new identity will be resented if it is not presented and explained to the employees as 'their' new identity. They need to be fully briefed, firstly, so that they will not be embarrassed by others if asked what the new design represents, and secondly, so that they can use the new design in a careful and consistent manner.

BP wanted to make the colour green an integral part of the brand equity. They wanted to own the colour green in the same way that Coca-Cola own red. Green's environmental connotations suited BP's commitment to improving its environmental performance. In order to convince BP managers that green was good for BP and to help them 'fall in love with green', they showed managers pictures of fresh green peas busrting from their pods, fresh mint, green apples and green fields. After winning over this level of managers, the next level could be educated through newsletters, manuals and meetings to ensure that all employees felt part of, and understood, the corporate identity change.

Implement and maintain

The identity now needs to be placed at all the visual points of public contact. Although it is difficult, it can be done overnight or on a gradual replacement basis. The implementation stage is usually the most expensive and time consuming stage. BP were reported to have spent under £1 million on design and research and £171 million on implementation. By specifying exactly the pantone colours, typeface, positioning of symbols, etc, the *design manual* allows managers in different divisions or in different countries to commission their own marketing communication tools such as brochures, exhibition stands or even advertisements, while adhering to strict corporate identity specifications. This maintains the consistency of the identity wherever it is used. There are other problems, often outside the scope of the design manual, which affect corporate identity, eg a purchasing department may clash with the design manager when buying the cheapest light bulbs or the cheapest stationery.

Ensuring that the identity is protected through constant policing indicates the survival of Drucker's first law: 'Everything degenerates into work.' It is possible to work with the personnel director to develop a reward system which can be built into the salary so that those who maintain the design standards benefit.

The need for cohesion

If an organisation's identity is not co-ordinated or managed precisely, confusing signals about the organisation go out to different audiences around the world. A splintered identity fragments the corporate image which, in turn, dilutes the corporate presence among key audiences. The potential corporate asset (the identity) depreciates to the point where it becomes a liability — the organisation not only has no presence but it also has an unco-ordinated image. This sends out unorganised messages which weaken the initial or final impression left by the organisation.

Air travel worries?

Attention to detailed design manangement can unconsciously influence air travellers. The same logo, typeface, primary and secondary colours, and trim on all visual points of contact help to reassure the traveller while reinforcing the airline's identity. The check-in desk logo, signs, colours and trims should be co-ordinated with the uniform (and badge), ticket holder, baggage tag, departure lounge carpets right through to the plane's exterior graphics, interior carpet and even the trim on the china and linen. Without this co-ordinated corporate identity cognitive dissonance can set in. There is a unconscious unease or discomfort created by the inconsistent messages. A co-ordinated identity reduces this often unconscious tension, which in turn creates a more satisfied passeneger. The cohesive identity does not make the traveller leap off the plane and scream for joy when arriving after a pleasant and soothing flight. But it might make the unconscious difference next time around when choosing between two mutually exclusive airline companies.

Detailed consistency
A logo displayed prominently in an office or on a letterhead makes a good strong

statement, but it is the consistent 'echoing' of the logo, its exact primary and secondary colours, the specific typeface and overall design style on the 'secondary format' of products, packages, business forms and employee uniforms that provides the all important, if subtle, consistent reinforcement.

There is a need to think it through in detail and then to police the usage of all visual points of contact. This is where a design manual guides managers in different buildings and in different countries to specify, in a consistent manner, the *exact* graphic requirement for *every* point of visual contact.

In corporate identity terms, attention to detail needs to spread beyond just graphics. The *1990 US Hall of Shame* reported the following:

> To upgrade its image in 1982 AT&T told its repair people to wear dress shirts and ties, gave them attaché cases for their tools, and renamed them 'system technicians'. But Ma Bell didn't install air conditioning in its cars. So during the summer, the technicians arrived on the job looking like they had just stepped out of a sauna. Said a union official, 'It's hard to have corporate appeal if your shirt is wringing wet'.

The importance of consistency applies right across the communications spectrum. In John Murphy's book on branding, (1987) Klaus Morwind Henkel points to consumer research which 'has indicated that a lack of consistency between the brand name, the packaging and the advertising is subconsciously recognised by the consumer and leads to a feeling of detachment, ultimately resulting in brandswitching.'

So it is important to be consistent and reinforce the identity through all the appropriate points of public contact. Many feel that this should include advertising. In fact, several years ago the UK advertising trade magazine *Campaign* (3 September 1988) suggested that advertising that isn't integrated into an identity programme 'is like a rogue elephant'.

Review and update

When does a corporate identity become out of date? Can the business environment change and move away from the organisation and its values, leaving behind an obsolete, irrelevant and even damaging corporate identity? When do the staff and other audiences get tired with it? Mergers and acquisitions sometimes necessitate a new corporate identity. Occasionally, legal reasons force a change. Sometimes overseas ambitions are restricted by the use of a home-grown logo (eg BT's old logo clashed with overseas companies). Alternatively new identities are developed simply because old management wants to say something new or new management wants to announce its arrival. As Olins (1989) says: 'In a complex and changing company the corporate identity bears a great strain, twisting and turning to fit every new requirement. But a good corporate identity should last a generation.'

Hand-held torch of learning

The National Union of Teachers' twenty-five-year-old 'hand- held torch of learning' was considered to have become 'too strident, aggressive and uncaring, with none too desirable connotations of the conservative party and the Greek fascist party.' Although it was designed in the 1960s it had a 1930s' look. It appeared that the time was right to move the logo on but keep it relevant and maintain the link with the union's heritage. The updated design shows an out-stretched hand embraced by the spelt out words of the NUT tying the symbol together as one cohesive form, either male/female, adult/child to avoid alienation.

Global markets are constantly moving and changing, so much so that some organisations fear that they are being left behind by the 'global update'. A review and redesign helps to keep abreast of trends and avoids being left isolated by a redundant identity. Approximately every 12 years Shell review and update their corporate identity. The shell device has served them well despite their being a petrol company with a 'high explosive' name.

The shell logo moving with the times

Having examined corporate identity, we will now consider corporate image. What is the difference? Is one part of the other? The next part of this chapter looks at how corporate identity is a part of overall corporate image which every organisation has (whether it wants it or not).

WHAT IS CORPORATE IMAGE?

Every company has an image. Whether it is messy, muddled, fragmented and confused, or a clear, strong, positive and unique image depends on management's ability to harness this often underutilised resource.

Corporate image is perception. Corporate identity is the reality of the tangible points of public contact, eg the buildings, the vehicles, the uniforms, the business forms and so on. Corporate image, on the other hand, is the sum of people's perceptions of an organisation. Images and perceptions are created through all the senses: sight, sound, smell, touch, taste, and feelings experienced through product usage, customer service, the commercial environment and corporate communications.

Corporate image embraces everything from the visual impression of a corporate logo, letterhead, uniform, livery, leaflet or advertisement, the aroma in the shop, reception, canteen or offices, to the pleasant feeling of a soft carpet, attractive wallpaper and airconditioned rooms, and the atmosphere created by both the interior and exterior design of a building, to the experiences enjoyed or suffered with product

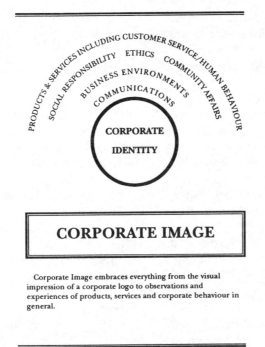

Corporate Image embraces everything from the visual impression of a corporate logo to observations and experiences of products, services and corporate behaviour in general.

Figure 17.2 The corporate image mix
Reproduced from PRTV's `Corporate image' training video notes.

334 / THE MARKETING COMMUNICATION TOOLS

quality and customer service. Corporate image is a result of everything a company does (or does not do).

Corporate image is formed from four areas:

1) Products/services (including product quality and customer care — see Chapter 20).
2) Social responsibility, corporate citizenship, ethical behaviour and community affairs.
3) Environments (offices, showrooms, factories).
4) Communications (advertising, PR, personal communications, brochures and corporate identity programmes — see Figure 17.2).

The corporate image mix

Figure 17.2 shows the corporate image mix.

Advantages of a good corporate image

Corporate image (including the corporate identity) can create competitive advantage, particularly when there is little or no difference between competitors. It can help to:

1) Improve sales.
2) Support new product development.
3) Strengthen financial relations.
4) Harmonise employee relations.
5) Boost recruitment.
6) Manage crises.

Improve sales

1) A unique and easily recognisable identity projects or *raises corporate profile* above the mass of other corporations. Many customers will not buy from a company that they have never heard of because they can have no confidence without knowledge and awareness. A well-known company usually has an advantage over an unknown company.
2) A well-managed corporate identity unconsciously *reassures customers*. Their confidence and trust can be increased by designing an identity which has a tone of planned cohesiveness which subtly presents a reassuring sense of order. As Olins (1989) says: 'A co-ordinated design policy across product, environment and communication makes company products seem more desirable.' (See the airline example on page 330).
3) A strong corporate identity tied to the right corporate image *adds value* to a product or brand. In a sense it is a corporate endorsement.
4) Corporate identity can *reposition, reinforce or sharpen the position* (or perceived image) of the organisation and its products or services. 'Younger', 'friendlier', 'high tech', 'traditional' or 'family firm' positions can be expressed through an identity. Some identities can persuade customers to make 'emotional rather than rational decisions, particularly in the 'indistinguishable financial services sector'.

Support new product development

The image can help new product development by providing a positive corporate platform for launching new products. For example, it is easier for Heinz to launch a new food product than it would be for an unidentified/unknown company. A strong corporate identity tied in with a positive corporate image makes it easier to introduce new products to the market place.

Strengthen financial relations

Carefully co-ordinated corporate identity helps to raise the corporate profile and to make the organisation's *presence known* to influential players within financial circles. In this way it increases awareness, understanding and support. A well-managed corporate identity also increases confidence, suggests a sense of order (good management) and reinforces a desired image. In addition, corporate design can create a strong visual platform for corporate communications, press releases, annual reports, television inteviews, etc.

During a *takeover*, organisations that have ignored the potential of their identity asset often recognise too late their lack of visibility among key audiences such as shareholders, financial analysts, employees, customers, the business community and so on. Corporate identity cannot, on its own, solve these problems, but over time and together with other resources such as communication tools like corporate advertising and PR, it can work to close the vulnerability gap created by a lack of identity.

A strong, cohesive, unified identity can also *strengthen* a company during a takeover. Woolworths' new Kingfisher identity was designed partly to end the confusion between the holding company and the Woolworths retail chain. This was considered to be significant during the Woolworths v Dixons takeover bid. Dixons were reported to have skilfully concentrated attention on Woolworths, which made it difficult to shift attention away from the relatively weak image of the Woolworths retail chain division. The new logo did, however, make a statement: Woolworths is changing, Woolworths' futuristic and progressive management is moving with the times.

Harmonise employee relations

Employees can become lost in an organisation as it grows, diversifies or develops. A properly managed corporate identity can enhance employee harmony by creating a *sense of common purpose* which brings everyone on board the same corporate ship moving in the same corporate direction. A good identity programme clarifies divisional and subsidiary participation. The identity should, if managed properly, boost morale among the employees. This new sense of purpose can contribute towards improvement in everyone's performance. PIMS (Profit Impact of Marketing Strategy, see Chapter 1) have found that high investment in corporate image correlates with a high ROI (return on investment). Caution needs to be exercised because of the inherent dislike of change. A new corporate identity needs to be communicated and managed carefully from within (rather than insulting staff by letting them find out secondhand by reading about it in the press).

Boost recruitment

An identity presents a company's image to many different audiences. Corporate identity helps recruitment by strengthening an organisation's ability to attract (and keep) the best people. Who wants to be associated with an organisation that has a tatty, run down, worn out image? A clear, strong and cohesive identity communicates positive messages to potential employees.

Help during a crisis

Corporate identity contributes towards the corporate image. In times of crisis, a company with a good corporate image enjoys a presumption of innocence.

To sum up, a corporate identity programme or any corporate communications programme provides an opportunity for an analysis of the organisation's corporate strategy and its corporate culture. This, in turn, provides a forum for review, analysis and change if necessary. A new corporate identity programme must be *supported by real changes* in the organisation including the cultural and physical environment, the quality of products and the level of customer services. A new corporate identity can have the effect of raising everyone's expectations. A corporate identity programme cannot paper over the cracks in an organisation. An attempt to do so can rebound negatively after a period of time. This can be partly explained by the theory of raised expectations.

The theory of raised expectations

This theory is derived from the field of political science and is usually applied to the area of popular revolutions. The basic tenet of the theory is that, contrary to intuition, the most likely time for a revolution to occur is not when economic and social conditions are at their worst, but when the situation has improved following a depressed period. The amelioration of conditions induces a greatly heightened sense of expectation...so when launching a campaign to improve and match a new image, they will be much more critical than before, anticipating improvements in standards that the company may not be able to deliver. 'Truth' makes the difference.

(Source: Hooker S, 1991)

SHORT CASE

Cooneen Textiles' passport to Europe

This short case demonstrates how a new corporate identity programme acted as a passport into the European textiles market.

Overall situation

Cooneen Textiles was established in 1966 as a manufacturer of quality baby and children's clothing. Twenty years later Cooneen's quality, reliability and service generated a turnover of £4.5 million. The young, professionally-trained management team doubled the sales by 1989 with £9 million turnover, making Cooneen one of the largest, if not the largest, independent manufacturer in their sector. The company does not market branded ranges of merchandise but supplies directly to multiple chain stores in the UK and Ireland.

COONEEN

Overall objectives

The three-year plan highlighted three main objectives:

1) Broaden the company's product range.
2) Spread its customer base.
3) Widen its market areas.

Overall strategy

Get into Europe before 1992 with a direct mail, telesales and personal sales campaign.

Tactics

Set up a team to investigate the European opportunity with the help of government support funds available to companies seeking to enter the European market. The team's findings highlighted an identity problem which restricted them both at home and from European expansion. They did not have the right image to pursue their objectives. The strategy now required a new corporate identity design to act as a 'passport' and platform for the European marketing campaign.

Now that we have identified the corporate identity problem the rest of the *SOSTT* approach can be applied specifically to the design challenge that lay ahead for Cooneen Textiles.

The old identity (situation)

Research revealed that UK customers perceived the company as a reliable dress manufacturer but did not fully appreciate the depth of its service and product range.

The company did not come across as being dynamic and progressive or as looking for substantial growth. Even Cooneen's staff and the local community did not see the company as a leading light in the clothing industry. Its profile as a privately owned company was considered traditional and low key. The chosen corporate identity design consultants, Conran Design, undertook a review of the competition, both British and European. They examined the identities of rival companies and it became clear that European child's wear manufacturers had a stronger image than most British and Irish companies — often using a well- known adult brand to add value to their products.

The original identity, in green Gaelic script, said the company was old-fashioned in outlook rather than offering traditional quality. It said it was provincial rather than in touch and creative — not a good image with which to enter Europe. Above all, it said nothing about Cooneen's function as manufacturers of children's wear.

The design objective
Initially Cooneen wanted to be seen as a `serious player in the international childrens wear market and to convey' an image of `modern creativity coupled with traditional quality'. The `tone of voice' (or design execution) was to be `young and dynamic yet with a heritage' (RSCG Conran Design, 1990).

The design (identity) strategy
Only a radical departure from the message of the original identity could fulfil the requirements that Cooneen now had.

Target
Major European children's wear retailers (initially focusing in Germany).

Men
A two-man panel (led by Cooneen's managing director) was responsible for the design consultancy selection process. Three consultants were invited to pitch. Conran were selected and they allocated a team of two designers, one researcher and an account director/team leader to Cooneen.

Money
£15,000 was budgeted for the design proposals but not the implementation.

Minutes

December 1987: strategic review identified EC opportunity. December 1988: Conran Design were appointed to develop a new identity. Summer 1989: the new identity was launched.

The design process

Stage	Month
Three-year corporate review	0
Brief design consultancies	8
Consultants pitch	11
Conran selected	12
Further research	12
Concepts	13
Research concepts	13
Select the 'Peter' concept	14
Refine and approve	14
Final artwork	15
Implement	16
European launch	18

Concept research and generation

The first design point that Conran considered was the company's name. Several options were brainstormed before settling on Cooneen Childrens' Wear, which not only expressed the company's function but also translated easily into any European language. Finding a typeface which expressed the nature of a company offering traditional quality with modern creativity was the next challenge. The idea of expressing Cooneen by its character and not just by its name alone was explored. A number of characters were generated; among those considered were rabbits (the meaning of the word cooneen) and clowns. Both of these were rejected as being too childish and not sufficiently flexible.

The design solution

Further development led to 'Peter', a lively new symbol. He is brightly coloured and energetic. He is reminiscent of childhood without being childish, important for representing a new marketing initiative for a serious company. Peter is also flexible, being redrawn to represent different parts of the company — holding a globe to symbolise distribution, a pencil to demonstrate design expertise, a bobbin to illustrate sewing skills and a tape measure to illustrate tailoring. He is accompanied by elegant, classic typography for the logotype, creating a stable base for Peter's energetic gymnastics.

Measurement

Cooneen is now perceived to be a progressive company among customers and staff. The local community are now more conscious of Cooneen. Cooneen's launch into West Germany was accompanied by a new corporate brochure through which Peter moved carrying a tape measure, a bobbin, scissors and a designer's pencil. Twenty-five major German buying groups were mailed. The brochure with its new corporate identity, helped to achieve a 90 per cent success rate (22 appointments were made through the telephone follow-up). The buyers spontaneously remembered the

brochure and kept in their files. This is significant given that German buyers, being the biggest market, are contacted daily by numerous suppliers from all over the world. Furthermore, during the follow-up visits most buyers spontaneously expressed favourable attitudes towards the brochures.

> **Key Points from Chapter 17:**
> 1) Corporate identity can create competitive advantage.
> 2) Creditibility has to be developed before raising visibility.
> 3) The corporate identity can raise visibility.
> 4) Attention to detail is vital.

Further reading

Bernstein, D (1984) *Company Image and Reality: A Critique of Corporate Communications*, Holt, Rinehart and Winston, London

Hooker, S (1991), 'Applying psychology to market research: the theory of raised expectations', Market Research Society Newsletter, January 1991

Jenkins, N (1991) *The Business of Image*, Kogan Page, London

Murphy, J (ed.) (1987) *Branding: A Key Marketing Tool*, Macmillan Press, London

Nash and Zull Products Inc (1989) *1990 US Hall of Shame*, Universal Press Syndicate Co, Kansas City

Olins, W (1989) *Corporate Identity: Making Business Strategy Visible Through Design*, Thames and Hudson, London

Valentine, V (1988) *Signs and Symbols* (survey), Market Research Society, London

Further contacts

The Chartered Society of Designers (CSD), 29 Bedford Square, London WC1B 3EG. Tel: 0171-631 1510

The Design Business Association (DBA), 29 Bedford Square, London WC1B 3EG. Tel: 0171-631 1510

The Department of Trade and Industry (DTI) (The DTI's Enterprise Initiative give grants for design, marketing and quality.) To contact your local DTI office, use the free phone number 0800 500 200

International Council of Graphic Design Associations (ICOGRADA), PO Box 398, London W11 4UG. Tel 0171-603 8494

The Institute of Public Relations (IPR), The Old Trading House, 15 Northburgh Street, London EC1V OPR. Tel: 0171-253 5151

The Public Relations Consultants Association (PRCA), Willow House, Willow Place, Victoria, London SW1P 1JH. Tel: 0171-233 6026

18

PACKAGING

THE IMPORTANCE OF PACKAGING

Since many sales assistants have been replaced by self-service systems, packaging today often has to act as a *silent salesman* helping customers by bringing a particular brand to their attention, highlighting USPs (unique selling propositions/unique benefits), giving friendly tips on usage and, ultimately, helping them to break through the *misery of choice* created by the increasingly vast range of seemingly similar brands. The plethora of 'me-toos' (similar products and brands) and the relentless fragmentation of markets (see page 249, Chapter 13) means that pack designs have to work very hard in these highly competitive, shorter life cycle markets of today.

The design of the pack can create *competitive advantage* by adding value, improving the product (eg improving the freshness or making it easier to pour, etc), developing stronger shelf presence, positioning a brand in a particular way, and creating or strengthening the brand's relationship with the buyer. The pack should be what top designer Michael Peters calls 'a visual magnet' which entices the customer to purchase and ultimately, become loyal to a particular brand. Packaging can also be an *extraordinarily effective advertising medium*, particularly in terms of cost and penetration, and reach or cover of a target audience. On the shelf and in the home, it continues to work day in, day out for 52 weeks of the year. It is also a *free medium*. The JET short case at the end of this chapter demonstrates how pack design can create a sustainable competitive advantage.

No single element of the communications mix comes under as much *environmental* scrutiny as packaging. In a sense, we will see less and less packaging as oversized cartons and unneccessary layers of packaging are stripped away by environmental pressures. Good pack design also pleases the distributor/retailer by helping to make distribution, warehousing and use of shelf space more efficient. In fact, many warehouses are becoming fully automated distribution centres, demanding packs of a size which suits the warehouse handling equipment. Good pack design also *saves manufacturing costs*.

Falling in love with a pack

Packaging *facilitates choice*. Choice is rarely made on a rational basis. In fact the consumer is faced with several thousand packs screaming 'buy me'. A well-designed pack offers *relief from the misery of choice*. Ernest Dichter (1964) suggests that 'this relief may be derived through being permitted to like a product, almost to *love it indiscriminately and irrationally*.' A well-designed pack can offer this permission and so assist in the choice.

THE THREE BASIC FUNCTIONS OF PACKAGING

The three basic functions of packaging are to:

1) Protect (and contain).
2) Offer Convenience.
3) Communicate.

First and foremost, a pack must *protect* its contents during storage, transport and usage. Some packs have to protect the user from the contents (as in the case of children with weed killers, medicine and chemicals, etc). Sadly, some packaging today must also protect the contents from tampering. Six people died in Chicago when Johnson and Johnson's Tylenol pain relievers were laced with cyanide. The development of tamper-proof packaging may follow tamper-evident packaging.

Second, the pack must offer *convenience* in pouring, squeezing, storing, stacking and consuming (in cars, the garden, the beach, the home and one day in space). Sugar and milk have yet to be mastered in terms of truly convenient packaging. Even a minute improvement in convenience can create competitive advantage, as demonstrated by Schlitz beer's Pop-Top can which helped to boost sales from 5.7m in 1961 to 15.1m in 1970. On the other hand, some pack designs are so poor that they cause their own problems. In 1985 the Norwegian company Elopack used TV advertising to try to explain how to open Elopak cartons.

Third, the pack must *communicate*. Before concentrating on the communications aspects of packaging, it is worth mentioning that all three packaging functions are interdependent. The first two functions, protection and convenience, both communicate indirectly. For example, if the product is damaged, tarnished or stale then a negative image is what remains, despite advertising, publicity and sales promotions which claim otherwise. Equally, if the instructions for storage or pouring are not communicated clearly then the pack loses its protective and convenience capabilities.

Some products prioritise some functions over others. Some design solutions (or redesigned packs) cannot optimise all three functions simultaneously because of constraints such as cost or overall pack size limitations. *Trade-offs*, or compromises, between functions will then occur. Surprisingly, some optimum functions can be forfeited for other reasons.

OVERPROTECTIVE PACKAGING

There is a balance between protective packaging, sales, returns and overall costs incurred. Here are three examples from James Pilditch's outstanding book on packaging design, *The Silent Salesman* (1973). They demonstrate how overpackaging can be identified, reduced and subsequently used to boost sales and/or profits.

An electrical light bulb company had a breakage rate so low that it prompted the question — were the bulbs overpackaged and too well protected? They subsequently reduced the grade of cardboard and returns (of damaged bulbs) went up. The overall saving in packaging costs was greater than the increased costs of breakage/returns.

A detergent company used stronger boxes than its competitors. The distributors were aware of this and liked the better boxes because they were able to put these boxes on the bottom of the pile without their collapsing. The product was hidden at the bottom instead of being at eye level, which is the optimum 'buy level'. So the box weight was reduced. The boxes started to collapse and the detergent was soon freed from the bottom of the pile. Sales soon increased.

A London discount house was concerned over the lack of stealing. They thought: 'Maybe we make our goods too hard for people to get at.' So the packs were redesigned.

THE LONG-TERM COMMITMENT

The pack design needs to develop and change as markets constantly move away from existing products (and their packs). The pack may have to reflect changes in the customers' aspirations, incorporate demographic shifts such as an ageing population, exploit new technologically driven opportunities (such as microwaves, which require new food packaging), or simply highlight a new improvement in the product itself. There needs to be a constant review of customers, their perceptions, motivations and aspirations and, of course, a constant review also of competitive packs. Sometimes customers simply get tired of a design.

One of the problems with packaging design is that it never shows up in a normal media budget. A major redesign involving a change of shape as well as a change in graphics can cost anywhere from £10,000 to £100,000 for the design stages. The tooling cost (the machine part/s which the production line needs to produce the new pack shape) will probably double the cost. Packaging design is an *evolutionary rather than revolutionary process*. But not all designs involve three-dimensional changes; often it is simply a two-dimensional change of graphics. Sometimes this is so subtle (a 'design tweak') that the consumer is not even aware of the change yet the new design will be working harder for the manufacturer. Packaging design often does not sit comfortably in the marketing budget at all, but failure to get a pack right is tantamount to possibly wasting millions of pounds worth of above the line advertising.

A constant design analysis looks at ways in which design can help to strengthen a brand's position. Heinz had maintained market share, but only at the expense of margin. Pack design gave it a lift. Turquoise is rarely associated with food except for Heinz. Subtle alterations have been made to make the product 'more appealing' and give it a 'stronger image for the future.' The Heinz lettering was changed from a 'thin typeface to a fuller more generous style; the keystone was broadened and a white

Spot the difference: subtle design tweaks increase shelf presence

in-line used to sharpen its impact; the lettering of "oven" and "with tomato sauce" was changed from turquoise to gold and the tone of the turquoise backround was enriched to create added warmth'(Michael Peters report, 1989).

Packs cannot afford to stay static, because markets and moods change. Rowntree's successful *After Eight* mint chocolate was becoming tired and beginning to look dated. The current pack probably doesn't appear to have changed much. It is the fruit of 18 months of detailed research and development. Five hundred design concepts and 50 dummy packs were considered before agreeing on the new look for the 1990s.

It is possible, as Dichter (1964) suggests, to fall in love with a pack. It is also possible to form extremely strong trusting relationships with a pack, even when it comes to babies.

The result of 500 design concepts

Would you pour a pile of white powder over your new baby?

Would you have the confidence to pour an unknown pile of white powder over your new baby?

Put the powder inside a pack called Johnson's, and emotions are immediately evoked of the caring mother-child relationship. You would certainly trust the product with your baby. You would not be willing to pay much, if anything, for the powder alone. You would be willing to pay a premium for a brand you trust and believe in.

(Source: Lewis M, 1991)

The relationship-enhancing pack can also help to strengthen branding and even the corporate profile of the manufacturer or distributor who controls it. The next part of this chapter suggests how.

BRANDS, PACKS AND CORPORATE IDENTITIES

Some brands, and their packs, are inextricably linked with the corporation which owns or makes the brands (eg Heinz, Honda or BP). Others keep a lower profile with a more subtle form of corporate endorsement (like ICI's Crown Paints). Others still prefer to keep the freestanding brand/pack identity very separate from the corporation, which remains anonymously behind the scenes (eg After Eight chocolates and Rowntree/Nestlé). There are advantages and disadvantages to all three approaches.

The *corporate culture* and *diversity of products and markets* can determine the specific approach. For example, a few years ago Allied Lyons were reported not to see the need for corporate advertising which linked the company to the brand. Financial analysts were not necessarily aware that the much-loved brands that were seen to be successful (and which they or their families bought every day) came from the same company that was under threat from a takeover bid. Somehow the success of the brand management was divorced from the image of the company's management. The shareholders had to decide whether they had faith in the ability of the existing management (and therefore retain it by not selling or swapping their shares) or allow new management (new owners) to take over and run the company. The corporate advertising established the link between the brands and the company and, arguably, saved the company. Today, Allied advertise their brands along with a corporate endorsement. Packs can work in exactly the same way — linking the brand to the parent company. However, this may be restricted by the diversity of products and markets. For example, think of Esso ice cream, Lada Airlines and Beecham's Beer. If any of these products existed the corporate link would not support the brand proposition; in fact, it would, arguably, detract from it.

The strengthening of the link between a company and its brands/packs can help the company by facilitating new product launches and brand stretching or brand extension (eg Heinz Weight Watchers). It can also reinforce corporate presence and, in turn, reassure different audiences, eg existing customers, new customers, investors and even employees (see 'Advantages of a Good Corporate Image', page 334, Chapter 17). On the other hand, the link can create a design strait-jacket which, as Mary Lewis (1991) points out 'inhibits the active development of sub-brands aimed at different target markets.' Since different target markets often require radically different images, these images may pull in different directions thereby detracting from the consistency of the overall corporate identity and image. In addition, if a particular brand has a problem (like product tampering or a faulty production batch) it is immediately associated with the parent company. This negative reflection can, if the link between brand and parent company is clearly established, affect all the other brands operating under the same corporate umbrella. As James Pilditch (1973) says: 'The pack can contribute to instant consumer recognition of the company or the brand.' Now let us consider the other communication functions of the pack.

THE COMMUNICATION FUNCTIONS OF THE PACK

The communication function breaks down into several different mini-functions:

1) *Grab the attention* of the passing shopper.
2) *Persuade* and convince the viewer that the contents match the promise made by advertising or the pack itself. The pack should say 'buy me'.
3) *Build brand personality* and forge links with the buyer.
4) *Build loyalty* with a pack that:
   a) looks nicer on the table;
   b) is easy to find in the garden shed or in the warehouse;
   c) is distinctive and easily recognisable in a shop carrying 9,000 separate items;
   d) is easier to use than the competition's.
5) *Instruct* the user about how to use the product to optimum benefit.
6) *Inform* the user of mandatory requirements such as warnings, source of manufacture or ingredients, etc. Buyers tend to want more information today.

THE SILENT SALESMAN

The pack is the last and sometimes the only opportunity to communicate with and sell to a customer. All the other elements of the communications mix can get lost in the competitive and noisy jungle of commercial messages where each appeals for your attention. The pack is the *silent salesman*. Initially it has to shout boldly to grab attention and then fade into the background and let the product benefits come forward. A well-designed pack can stop customers dead in their tracks, invite them to have a look, pick it up, and pause for a few valuable moments while they are engaged at the point-of-sale. It is here that the pack can *develop a dialogue* by attracting, intriguing, arousing unconscious aspirations, informing, reminding, involving, entertaining and, above all, persuading.

The pack can arouse, or trigger, stored images from a television advertisement which have been lying dormant in the memory bank if either the advertisement includes a 'pack shot' (close-up of the pack) or the pack includes some of the images from the advertisement. The brand can reflect images and aspirations. The pack can help the customer to recall those aspirations and to develop associations between the aspirations and the brand. The hand lifts the pack off the shelf, allowing the customer, his aspirations and the brand to move closer together.

Packs like Heinz are sometimes called '*trigger packs*' because there is little dialogue other than the announcement of a strong, confident tone. The pack design concentrates on being recognised through its unique visual identifiers, the colours, keystone, name and lettering, while heavy advertising communicates the brand values and aspirations. It is interesting to see Campbell's Soups dispense with Andy Warhol's legendary red and white livery and replace it with another aspirational soup setting. The Campbell's graphics portray product values which are arguably less protectable from the inevitable 'me-toos' sometimes produced by the retail stores' own labels. The Heinz image is unique and therefore more protectable.

THE DESIGNER'S TOOLS

The six variables or tools which a designer can use are:

1) Shape
2) Size
3) Colour
4) Graphics
5) Materials
6) Smell.

Shape

Some brands have such distinctive pack shapes that the brand is recognisable from the shape alone (eg Baileys, Mateus Rosé, Perrier and Jif Lemon). Other pack shapes communicate conscious and unconscious meanings.

Ask a group to draw the first image, abstract or otherwise, that comes into their minds when the word 'love' is mentioned. If they struggle with this ask them to imagine they are a design consultancy whose job is to design a logo for a new political party called 'The Love Party'. After a minute ask them to do the same for 'hate'. (Close your eyes or make a doodle yourself before reading on). Over 95 per cent of the drawings tend to conform to the same perceptions about shape. The love image usually has softer edges, curves and maybe heart shapes while the hate image tends to have jagged edges and sharper shapes like swastikas and daggers, etc. We may not consciously associate these meanings with shapes but they are there. During the Second World War US *paratroopers* were tested to find whether they were *shape-oriented* or *colour-oriented* by being shown a film of abstract shapes and patterns. The shapes moved from right to left and the colours moved from left to right. The paratroopers were then asked which way the design was moving. Shape-oriented men are supposed to be more intelligent, stable and less emotional. The *Thurstone test* can be used for packaging design also. It has revealed that younger children respond to colour more than form while adults, and men in particular, react more to form.

Pilditch (1973) suggested that a *rectangular box* created images of sharpness, neatness and cleanliness while a *round box* had associations of security, plentifulness and generosity. Go into a chemist's shop and observe the different packaging shapes used for adult and children's bubble baths. Some shapes give the product a value much greater than its contents. Shapes can also be *masculine or feminine*. Whisky bottles tend to be masculine in shape while some perfume bottles are feminine.

Shape affects the protection and convenience functions in *holding, pouring* and *storing*. How a pack fits into the hand is part of the study of *ergonomics*. A well designed pack fits the hand more comfortably and creates what Coca-Cola proudly call `in-hand embellishment' (it feels good in the hand). *False ergonomics* communicate unreal values to customers. For example, dimples (for fingers to grip) are sometimes placed down the side of a bottle when in fact the bottle is rarely held by the two dimpled sides; instead, it is held by the two flat front and back sides of the pack. The subtle impression created by these false ergonomics is one of `this pack looks slightly better or friendlier'. Customers do not consciously choose one brand instead of another. Ergonomics can help to express that one brand is nicer to use than another. Real ergonomics help the user to have a more pleasant experience with the pack and therefore encourage repeat purchasing.

Can recognise the brand even by feeling it in the dark

Back in 1910 part of the packaging design brief for the now famous Coca-Cola bottle read:

> We need a new bottle — a distinctive package that will help us fight substitution...we need a bottle which a person will recognise as a Coca-Cola bottle *even when he feels it in the dark*. The Coca-Cola bottle should be so shaped that even if broken, a person could tell what it was...

Some shapes *reinforce product values* by designing product features into the pack, as with the honeycomb effect on the base of a honey jar or the dimpled plastic two-litre beer bottles associating the product with a dimpled beer mug. Other shapes *reinforce brand values*, eg the unique Monk's Liqueur bottle designed in the shape of a monk. The ultimate *brand shape* is arguably Jif Lemon's lemon-shaped pack. The Law Lords granted Reckitt and Colman exclusive rights to this shape, ie only Jif can use this unique get-up or shape to package lemon juice. Some other brands can be recognised from their package shape alone (eg Baileys, Mateus Rosé, Perrier).

Can manufacturers own monopoly rights to a pack shape? The test, it seems, is 'whether the shape serves mainly to distinguish a product from its rivals and whether

An immediately recognisable shape

a competitor using the shape is seeking to mislead purchasers' (Warden, 1990). There are an infinite *number* of shapes. Pack shape can form a valuable property of the brand. It can become part of the brand or become part of the brand equity. The shape of Sheridan's new double liqueur bottle certainly helps it to stand out from the crowd.

A pack shape that stands out from the crowd

Size

Size communicates. Would you give your loved one a *perfume packed in a two-litre bottle*? The corollary, ie large pack communicates better quality, is also true in other product sectors such as breakfast cereals. Consumer perceptions about cornflakes have been found to change according to size of pack. Large cereal packs build feelings of plentiful, expansive, energy-giving food whereas a smaller pack may make the cornflakes seem heavy, solid and no good. Size can be used to communicate in different ways. For example, a 33cl bottle of premium beer cannot be fully poured into a half-pint glass. This forces the drinker, after filling a glass, to carry the bottle away from the bar and over to the table where the unemptied bottle continues to work both as a badge and an advertisement.

Different sizes are aimed at different segments, eg the family pack. Pack *size can determine target markets* or is it that target markets can determine pack size? This may be similar to Ehrenberg's philosophy of marketing which states that marketing means excluding many customers from a particular product (target marketing excludes the mass). Certain segments exclude certain sizes as Coca-Cola discovered when it had to withdraw its two litre bottle from the Spanish market after they discovered few Spaniards owned fridges large enough. If the colour was changed would the pack then fit the fridge? Warm colours like red and yellow seem to advance or make the pack appear larger while cold colours like blue recede and make the pack appear smaller. Although a change of colour would not have saved Coca-Cola's large bottle in Spain, colour does communicate in many different ways.

Colour

Colour communicates. In fact, Albert Kner, former design chief of the Container Corporation of America said, 'Colour is the *quickest path to the emotions*'. Words have to be translated into images in the mind. These images, in turn, have to be assembled, organised and categorised to give them meaning. This may be followed by an emotional response, which may subsequently trigger a physical response. Colour skips all this and goes straight into the emotions, often creating a physiological response. *Colour is physical.* Russia's Pedagogical Institute have found that most people can *feel colours*. Eyeless sight or 'bio-introscopy' suggests that all one's skin has seeing power. Red, green and dark blue have been found to be sticky. This may have something to do with electromagnetic fields. There have been claims that the Chinese can teach children to see with their elbows. Forgive the digression. Many years ago the US Colour Research Institute found that the colour of walls in an office could make people feel sleepy, excited or healthy. More recently, a British police force has experimented with pink cells for prisoners. Red increased blood pressure and pulse while blue had the opposite effect.

The Luscher colour test uses colour cards to analyse the reader's psychological, and specifically emotional, state. The choice of green suggests a 'desire of the ego, and ... self- assertion and a certain degree of self-sufficiency'. Green today has another international meaning — environmentalism.

Colour codes

Some product sectors, particularly food, appear to have colour codes. For example, within the carbonated drinks sector, red is cola and yellow is tonic. Freezer meat is red, fish is blue and anything low calorie/diet is white. Pilditch (1973) has suggested that in the wake of health scares many of the world's cigarette packs now emphasise white: 'They hope white is associated with cleanliness and purity.'

Colours have meaning for people. Many people associate colours with images, eg 'garden fresh', 'mountain cool' or 'rugged manliness'. There was a group of people for whom 7-UP's green bottle had almost medicinal links and therapeutic overtones: '...the thing to take when you had the flu and the doctor told you to take a lot of liquid...' Whether it is an annual report, a reception area, some sales literature or a piece of packaging, colour communicates. This applies to products and services in both consumer and industrial markets.

Colour affects perception. This is probably best demonstrated by Ernest Dichter's research (1964) into how packaging colour affects people's perceptions of taste. Unknown to the respondent, the same coffee was put into four cups. One of four different coloured coffee cans was placed beside each cup. Respondents were then asked to match the statements below with each cup tasted. The research revealed strong perceptions linked with specific colours.

- Dark brown can: 73% 'Too strong aroma or flavour'.
- Red can: 84% 'Richer flavour or aroma'.
- Blue can: 79% 'Milder flavour or aroma'.
- Yellow can: 87% 'Too weak flavour or aroma'.

More recent research into packaging colour and perceptions of washing machine powder provided even stranger results. The same powder was put into three different coloured packs. The housewives tried them on delicate clothing for a few weeks and were then asked which was best for delicate clothing. Respondents thought the performance (of the same powder) was vastly different. Statements below demonstrate the striking finding:

- Largely yellow pack: 'too strong...ruined their clothes'.
- Largely blue pack: 'did not work...clothes were dirty looking'.
- Blue and yellow pack: 'fine' and 'wonderful'.

This differs from previous US research reported by Terrell Williams (1982) which tested identical washing powders in three different coloured boxes, yellow, blue and red. The yellow detergent was 'mild, too mild really'. The blue detergent was 'a good all-round laundry product'. The red detergent was 'good for stains and the like'.

Colours may not be international since different colours have different meanings in different cultures. For example, white is life, purity and diet here in the UK but it means death in Japan, as does purple in South America and blue in Iran. Softer pastel colours and brighter colours are perceived differently around the world. In China bright colours symbolise quality. Scott entered the Taiwan market with their American blend of pastel-coloured toilet tissues; the launch flopped. Sales took off when they changed the colours to bright red, yellow and gold. Can you imagine UK toilets with bright red toilet paper? Pilditch (1973) remarked that 'Not only do simpler folk like stronger colours, but people who live under bright sun have different values from those whose outlook is dimmed, say, by England's "leaden" skies. Think of this when designing packs to sell to Italian winegrowers, or Glaswegian dockers.' This is important because cross-border packaging may become more common than cross-border advertising.

The cost of colour

Four colours obviously cost more to print than two colours. Can one be economic with the use of colour, the number of colours and the kind of inks? Is single colour too down-market? Are four colours really needed? Has anyone tested a change in colours?

Graphics

Graphics communicate on different levels. The two-dimensional design on a label can help to *create and protect individuality/uniqueness*, *reinforce a brand name or image*, help to reposition, increase shelf presence, etc. The use of graphics is arguably the easiest of the designer's tools to analyse as marketing managers are reasonably design-literate as far as graphics are concerned. A naked body on a the label of a bottle of beer will attract attention. However, not every brand manager wants this kind of attention. Graphics can use other images to make a pack stand out from the crowd. In terms of branding the visual image should be distinctive and should make the pack *immediately and easily recognisable*. Even an ordinary tin box can become a valued item once some attractive graphics have been applied. Graphics *add value* by adding *aesthetic quality*. This creates '*stay after value*' which allows the branding to keep working inside the home for many years, sometimes generations. Graphics are sometimes used as a kind of *sales promotion* by becoming *a limited edition/collector's item*, as in the case of the Guinness centenary Christmas label. Graphics can add value by offering, for example: additional features such as games (eg a box of matches with matchstick puzzles); intrigue (eg the label below positions the ancient drink, mead, as a bottle of history rather than just a bottle of alcohol); a room-enhancing, stimulating plaything rather than just a dull necessity (baby lotion with colourful children's toys); or simply creating quality associations with images of far-off places (coffee with palm trees).

Repositioned as a bottle of history rather than just a bottle of alcohol

A room-enhancing, stimulating plaything rather than a dull lotion

Quality associations with far off distant places

Good graphics can create a mood or trigger *lifestyle aspirations* which reflect the often latent desires of the target market, eg a shampoo label showing an English country scene for one target market and a rugged desert for another aspiring lifestyle segment.

Attention to detail combined with an understanding of the cues and symbols which are relevant to a particular target market allow the designer to *play with the unconscious meaning of symbols and images*. In the case of a cooking fat, according to the psychologists, the positioning of a *wooden spoon* made it 'possible for the housewife to rehearse the use of the product while it was still on the shelf.' Pilditch (1973) explained that 'the spoon also served to inject the product with some of the reliability of grandmother's honest-to-goodness, my doesn't that smell good, old-fashioned kitchen.' In a separate piece of research the analysts turned to the number and layout of *biscuits* on a package. A picture showing biscuits scattered all over created psychological discomfort, or dissonance, because it suggested gaeity, disorganisation, permissiveness and irresponsibility ('never know how many were eaten by the kids'). A different picture showing the biscuits in a neat line triggered associations with orderliness, parsimony, and fear of disrupting the line by taking a biscuit, which again resulted in unconscious psychological tension or discomfort. The third image of just a few biscuits on a plate cut out the chaos and the irresponsibility and invited the the viewer to feel free to take a biscuit. The number of biscuits was, however, limited to demonstrate authority and control.

Graphics affect taste

In the same way as colour, graphics also affect taste perceptions. In fact, packaging designers can test different label graphics by asking focus groups or consumer panels to give their opinions on the taste of (unknown to them) the same product. The more elegant bottle will tend to have a refined taste, the macho label might have a stronger flavour, etc.

Graphics integrate with other packaging variables to create effective communications. Mary Lewis (1991) suggests that 'if the form (shape and size of the pack) makes the statement then the graphics should step back'. The Lewis Moberly consultancy worked on Yves Rocher Aromatherapy Oils and created a *tactile experience* prompted by graphics 'by running the typography (letters) right round the bottle to encourage the viewer to turn it, touch it and begin to experience the product through the pack.'

Typography creating a tactile experience

Many years ago Coca-Cola discovered that their dynamic white contour curve (the flowing white ribbon underlining the Coca-Cola and Coke logo) 'reminded observers of the famous profile of the hobble skirted contour bottle'.

The graphics should be developed only after some other key questions have been asked. These include: does the pack use the *logo* effectively? Can the graphics make space for future *on-pack promotions*? Do the graphics leave space for international copy translation (usually requires more space than English)? Will the graphics lend themselves or at least link with point-of-sale *materials*? Are the graphic images unique and *protectable* or can someone else design something similar, leaving customers confused and unaware of their own brand-switching decision?

The other pack functions are also helped by good graphics, eg a blend of visual and verbal instructions can make a product and pack much easier to use and store (*convenience and protection*).

Spreadable graphics

A new spreadable butter was reportedly the same as the old butter except that the graphic instructions read 'do not put in fridge'.

Graphics can also indicate production processes or corporate caring values such as 'recycled' or 'free from animal testing'. There is some confusion currently because of the lack of central agreement on appropriate logos.

AGAINST ANIMAL TESTING

Packaging that expresses caring corporate values

Finally, *bar codes* linked with *EPOS* (electronic point-of-sale) scanners at retail store check-outs help internal communications between the retailer and supplier by updating stock levels, re-order information and other sales analysis (eg by product, by store, by day, etc).

Bar codses provide useful marketing information

Materials

Materials communicate. Certain materials, like glass or metal, have an intrinsic value. Glass still seems to be associated with higher quality. Many wine drinkers would be suspicious of a supposedly top quality wine if it was presented to them in a plastic bottle. Having said that, the packaging of wine has gone through the most radical of shake-ups. Twenty years ago, if someone had forecast that an individual would be drinking wine out of cardboard boxes within 20 years it is likely that the comment would have been taken as an insult — with hints of socially unacceptable behaviour. Yet today the wine box is arguably packaging's greatest innovation, with a nation happily drinking from cardboard boxes.

The materials used in packaging *affect perceptions of product quality*. A good example of this was discovered in the USA, in 1977 where, ironically, the better product was perceived to be the more difficult to open package. Crisps of equal freshness were packaged in wax paper bags and polyvinyl bags. The crisps in the polyvinyl bag were perceived (by 87 per cent) to be 'superior in taste and freshness' despite being more difficult to open.

Guinness found that packaging materials, and tins in particular, affected taste perceptions. There were comments like 'too gassy, it taints the flavour and it tastes of tin' (Nicholas, 1991). Prelaunch research of the *Guinness draught can* showed that in blind taste tests equal numbers preferred the pure draught Guinness and canned draught Guinness. Subsequent sight tests (showing the source, ie can or tap) revealed the hidden associations of tin cans: there was a 70:30 split in favour of the draught Guinness.

Certain overseas markets have different packaging material expectations than what is considered to be the norm in the UK. For example, in *Europe*, meats, fruit, vegetables, pet foods and fruit juices are packed in glass. This means that if UK manufacturers want to enter these markets, they will have to work with a new packaging medium, which may well be glass. In the UK tin has an emotional quality. It can become even more emotional when mixed with shape and colour, eg a red-heart-shaped, tin box of chocolates for St Valentine's Day. Today, tin box packs are used for boxer shorts and children's clothes as well as food.

Technological developments allow relatively sophisticated printing techniques to be used on almost any kind of surface, as demonstrated by the attractive graphics used on today's cardboard wine boxes and tin boxes.

Some packaging materials have to work very hard. For example, microwave packs have to be able to protect and store the food at temperatures below zero and then have to offer convenience cooking by being able to be put into a microwave at very high temperatures. Some packs are then used to eat out of. *Self-heating* and *self-cooling* cans offer new levels of convenience. Apart from the *convenience and communications* implications of packaging materials, the final materials choice is integrated with a host of other factors such as optimum size, weight, strength, cost, filling speed, overlaying with other features such as colour, closure, secondary packaging, shelf life, barrier properties, tactile characteristics and shelf impact.

Finally, material is the variable which is affected directly by *environmental pressure groups*. New legislation is putting pressure on manufacturers and retailers to use more environmentally-friendly packaging. The US *garbologist* now probes land fill sites to determine the state of decay of various materials. In Europe, Germany leads the way in environmental legislation. A company's overseas growth may be stifled by packaging and materials which do not meet legislative criteria. Despite the *logistical nightmare*, the refillable pack is here to stay. The environmental factor has a direct impact on packaging and, in particular, on packaging materials. Warner-Lambert is developing a new *disposable plastic* made almost entirely out of biodegradeable starch derived from potatos, corn, rice and wheat.

Smell

Smells can change shopping behaviour. In a Philadelphia jewellery store last year, casual shoppers lingered longer than usual because, claim the Monell Chemical Sense Centre, scents change shoppers moods. In this particular case, it was a fruity floral scent. Mood-changing odours change people's brain patterns. The *Chicago Tribune* reported Alan Hursch, neurological director of the Smell and Taste Treatment and Research Foundation in Chicago, as saying 'Eventually we will be able to influence in a much more powerful way. By making people more relaxed or more trusting you could sell them more.' Scented packaging is becoming more popular.

WHAT IS A BRAND?

As Mary Lewis (1991) says: The brand is the aura of beliefs and expectations about a product (or service) which make it relevant and distinctive. It stretches beyond the physical and into the psychological and is extremely powerful.

WHY REDESIGN?

'If ain't broke, don't fix it'. Perhaps, but some pack designs can become tired, dated or the market simply moves away, making the pack's current position a liability. On the other hand, valuable brand equities or properties like names and logos are assets worth maintaining. They may need 'tweaking' from time to time, but rarely need to be disposed of. Perhaps a creative brand manager and a professional printer can produce an updated or even new graphic design for a pack. Jan Hall of Coley Porter

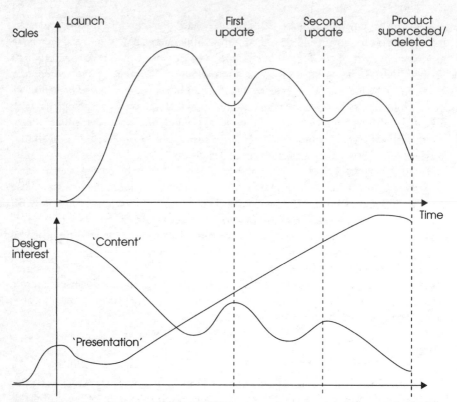

Figure 18.1 How design attention shifts between content and presentation as a product progresses through its life cycle

Bell says this would be like 'putting together the *Pope and a paint company* to paint the Sistine Chapel'. Alan Topalian (1984) suggests that the designer's interest (or input) into the pack increases progressively during the course of the product's life cycle (see Figure 18.1). In other words, the pack design has an increasingly important role as competition becomes more intense.

A PACKAGING DESIGN BRIEF

The SOSST + 4Ms can be used as a checklist when writing a design brief. See how it is modified for a corporate identity design brief (page 328, Chapter 17) and an advertising brief (page 118, Chapter 6).

Situation/background

- Company (history, production facilities).
- Product (range, features and benefits, material properties, eg liquids, gases, chemicals, etc).
- Market (size, growth, competitive structure, positioning, specific requirements such as pallet configuration, etc).

- Reason for design (eg pressure from retailers' own labels).
- Brand factors and personality, key design elements.

Objectives

What packaging functions are prioritised (protection, convenience, communication)? If communication, state specifically, eg repositioning from what to what? Or is the new pack design primarily aimed at shouting louder or creating a stronger shelf presence, etc?

Strategy

How the pack fits in with the rest of the communications mix strategy (the communications objectives and communications mix). The brief may also state whether the pack design is a low risk (new unit load, new material, temporary sales promotion, secondary panel changes, new ingredients, etc) or a high risk design project (new name, new colour, new image, new logo, new shape, etc).

Tactics

Details not always required here.

Targets

Segments, targets, decision-making units (this is particularly tricky with gift products, eg at whom do you target the design — the giver or receiver?).

Men

Contact names for technical discussions (eg production manager) and for marketing discussions. Clarify who makes the key decisions, and who can provide answers to miscellaneous questions. Names of any other agencies who may be working on other marketing communications aspects such as advertising or sales promotion, etc.

Money

Means design fee, rejection fee (some designers charge a rejection fee for presenting ideas or concepts even during a pitch), changeover costs (this may incur capital expenditure if a change of shape requires a new machine tool) and, ideally, an indication of maximum unit cost of new pack (the designer will need to know size of production runs, etc).

Minutes

The time-scale. What are the launch deadlines? When must concepts be presented, agreed, researched, refined and approved? When must the final artwork be delivered?

Packaging Design Process

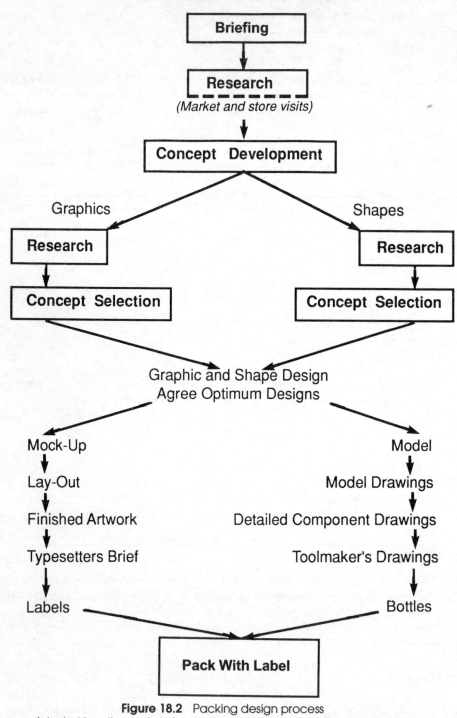

Figure 18.2 Packing design process
Adapted from the pack design management video 'From Dream to Reality'

How long has been allowed for tooling (can take up to 50 per cent of the total design time, eg three months).

Measurement

What kind of research will be carried out to monitor the effectiveness of the new pack design?

Miscellaneous

Design constraints, eg size, shapes, colours, images or materials to be used or avoided because of technical, legislative and corporate restrictions on materials, warnings/warranties, and logos respectively.

THE PACKAGING DESIGN PROCESS

The brief may emerge after an initial review of the pack design. The designer/s (whether in-house or an external consultancy) often take the brief away, interpret it and rewrite it. Then they present this to the marketing team to ensure that everyone agrees with each other before embarking on any further creative work or research. This may be followed by further research and eventually a range of concepts (two-dimensional labels and three-dimensional-pack shapes, sizes and mechanisms) are developed for further research. This guides the selection of a concept for ultimate development into the new pack. Figure 18.2 shows the standard stages of a design project (this was the process used in the JET short case at the end of this chapter).

INDUSTRIAL PACKAGING

The design resource is not exclusively reserved for FMCG goods. There is always room for design, creativity and innovation in industrial markets also. Electric cable manufacturer BICC used pack design to stand out from the competition in the commodity cable market and to offer USPs to a traditionally conservative market. They moved from the traditional reel of cable to a newly designed box of cable. This helped the electrical wholesaler by making stacking, storage and identifying (holes in the pack allowed the different colours of cable to be seen) a lot easier. The pack, however, was not allowed to look too up-market as the conservative buyers assumed it would be more expensive. Before phasing out the old cable packs (reels), they were used to advertise the imminent arrival of the new packs — the box of cable.

THE PACKAGING OPPORTUNITY

A recent Mintel report revealed that packaging is an area of opportunity since consumers revealed high levels of dissatisfaction with packaging in general. 'Impenetrable packs, inadequate labelling, messy packets and overpackaging' were common complaints. In short, packaging, by and large, is not user-friendly. Boxes of tea leak tea dust, sugar packs spill everywhere, bottles dribble after pouring and so on. In a market where pack design is weak, new design can steal the advantage. It is worth remembering that although pack design, at worst, is just a recognition symbol, at best it can offer so much more. As the cost of advertising rises, product life cycles shorten and competition becomes fiercer, marketers need to get more from their packaging. Creative packaging can create competitive advantage. Even dull and seemingly staid pack designs can be redesigned to create a competitive, cost effective edge.

There is a whole lifestyle wrapped up in a package. The combination of the size, shape, name, graphics, colours, materials, contents and the supporting communications, ie advertising, point-of-sale, PR and promotions all create the brand.

Will milk eventually be delivered in easy-to-open, bio-degradeable, pan-European, udder shaped cartons?

SHORT CASE

JET's new oil pack

Situation

Conoco distributes petrol and oil throughout the UK under the JET brand name. Research showed that as an oil brand JET was perceived to be of a lower quality and performance than the major brands such as Castrol and Duckhams, despite having comparable specification. Consumers were seven times more likely to reject JET than a major competitor. The JET brand was clearly underperforming but had substantial potential if the communication to the consumer could be corrected.

Objectives

1) To reposition JET oil as a quality 'good value' product with a unique identity.
2) To increase sales by 15 per cent from a base of 1.5 million litres per annum within 12 months of launch.
3) To increase margin by 10 per cent relative to 1991 prices.

Strategy

The unique identity and product repositioning would be achieved through a new structural pack design, in addition to the national programme of petrol station redesign which was being undertaken during the same period and without the aid of extensive advertising support.

The design brief

Part of the brief explained that the key criterion for the repositioning was defined as the JET brand personality. This personality profile was developed as a whole and used to steer the development of all aspects of the brand. The specific objective given to the design consultancy was to define the personality as the new direction for the JET oil brand for the 1990s through the use of packaging design. The personality details were made up of target consumer, target consumer needs, brand personality, the consumer take out.

1) Target consumer: 52 per cent of petrol/oil buyers are price conscious inasmuch as they rank price as the first or second requirement when choosing to buy petrol.

2) Target consumer needs: a brand of petrol/oil that is a legitimate alternative to the other full petrol brands of oil.
3) Brand personality: a smart buy for the savvy motorist.
4) Consumer take out (or how the consumer feels about the new JET Oil before, during and after buying it): 'Choosing JET makes me a smart buyer'.

The pack had to offer clarity of communication through the pack form (shape and function), and a substantial simplification of product use (eg opening, closing, pouring, carrying, etc). The marketing and commercial targets had to be achieved without the aid of extensive advertising.

The brief required the packaging design consultancy, PI Design Consultants, to design and develop the packaging to the prototype stage, including any tooling development, and also to provide a solution that contained intellectual property, ie something new and so unique that it was protectable (through design registration and patents) and which would allow Conoco to gain long-term advantage from the design work.

The design solution

A pack that communicates clearly while making product usage easier through the unique swivelling closure that transforms the shape from an oil pack into a pouring jug. The pack has a series of ergonomically refined details to support ease of use, eg the extended handle that allows optimum hand position for carrying and pouring, including two-handled use for women. The handle curve ensures that at any holding angle the weight of the pack is below the holding point maximising comfort and control, a feature unique to this design. The pack also has a unique single piece cap that provides an exceptional degree of control when pouring. This feature was critical to the design. Most devices of this type are two-piece components, which are costly to manufacture and inferior ergonomically.

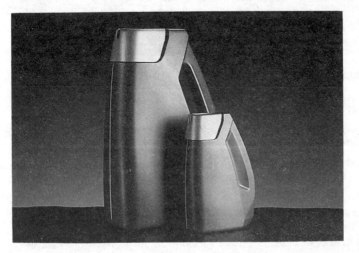

Jet's award winning new pack design

JET schedule

Briefing	Oct 88
Concepts	Nov 88
Visit to filling plant	Nov 88
Feasibility study	Jan 89
Jet weekend (including clients, sales and marketing advertising agency and packaging consultants)	Apr 89
Liaison with market research agency	
Design development and presentation	Jan 90
Detailing and refining pack	Feb 90
Market research	Feb 90
Qualitative research results	Feb 90
Decision to proceed with design	Mar 90
Visit to production site	Apr 90
Detailed component drawings	May 90
Tooling and component progression	Jun 90
Tool trials –prototypes produced for evaluation	Aug 90
Production tooling and patent progression	Oct 90
Project signed off	Oct 90
Product launch	Apr 91

Results

The design consultancy was briefed in October 1988 and the redesigned pack was launched in May 1991. Distribution to all JET stations was completed by May 1991. Distribution to independent dealers (under the JET brand) was improved by 50 per cent by October 1991. Sales volume for the 12 months to April 1992 was 2.1m litres representing a 33 per cent year-on-year increase. The increased margins were sustained and overall profit increased by 43 per cent. The design cost of the project, including tooling costs, was around £120,000 and payback has been achieved. Current sales data indicates that repeat sales are achieving a satisfactory level and a long-term change in the consumer's perception of the JET brand is reported. The pack design also won the Institute of Packaging's Gold Star Pack Award in 1992.

Key Points from Chapter 18:

1) Packaging has three functions, one of which is to communicate.
2) Packaging design can create competitive advantage.

Further reading

Coca-Cola (1986) *Coke! Coca-Cola 1886-1986: Designing a Megabrand*, The Conran Foundation

Dichter, E (1964) *Handbook of Consumer Motivations: The Psychology Of The World Of Objects*

Lewis, M (1991) in Cowley D (ed.) *Understanding Brands*, Kogan Page, London

Milton, H (1991), *Packaging Design*, The Design Council, London

Nicholas, R `Come home to a real beer', *Marketing Week*, 15 February 1991

Opie, R (1987) *The Art of the Label*, Quatro

Pilditch, J (1973) *The Silent Salesman*, second edition, Business Books, London (soon to be reprinted – contact the Institute of Packaging below)

Smith, P R (1991) `From Dream to Reality', Media Services, Guildhall University, London

Williams, T G (1982) *Consumer Behaviour*, research report, West Publishing, St Paul, Minnesota

Topalian, A (1984) *Management of Design Projects*, Alto Design, London

Warden, J `White paper gives shade to trademarks', *Marketing*, 27 September 1990

Further contacts

The Chartered Society of Designers (CSD), 29 Bedford Square, London WC1B 3EG. Tel: 0171-631 1510

The Design Business Association (DBA), 29 Bedford Square, London WC1B 3EG. Tel: 0171-631 1510

The Institute of Packaging, Sysonby Lodge, Nottingham Road, Melton Mowbray, Leicestershire, LE13 ONU. Tel: 01664 500055

19

MERCHANDISING

INTRODUCTION

There was a time when below the line point-of-sale (POS) materials were considered to be relevant only to cosmetics, perfumery, confectionery or other impulse purchases. Today merchandising techniques apply to a broader spectrum of markets from consumer to industrial. Although vast budgets can be spent above the line on advertising to gain the customer's attention or change an attitude, fewer resources are sometimes allocated to the crucial moment in the buying process — the point in the buying cycle where the customer is physically in front of the product and is about to make a decision whether to buy or pass by — the point-of-sale.

Shopping for happiness

Going shopping is claimed to be Britain's second most popular leisure activity after watching TV. This is also evident in the USA, where retailers almost double as leisure centres. `Mall-walking` is now a significant activity in the US. In the north of England customers are transported in by the coach load to spend a day at Europe's largest retail centre, Gateshead's Metro Centre.

In many consumer markets, the consumer's *final decision to buy is often made inside*, and not outside, the store. Merchandising techniques such as display and store design are therefore vital communication tools which can guide a buyer towards making a purchase. They are often the last chance to communicate with the buyer. Merchandising does not just apply to the traditional retail outlets of supermarkets, garages and department stores but also to DIY stores, brown goods retailers (stereos and TVs), corner shops, office equipment showrooms and cash and carry wholesalers.

The merchandising opportunity lies relatively untapped in industrial wholesale outlets such as electrical wholesalers or builders' suppliers, where a lot of merchandising tends to look dusty, dirty and uninteresting. There is room here for creative, intelligent and effective merchandising. It does require a delicate balance since a hard-working electrician who is in search of some 2-core 3mm cable might assume a distributor to be too expensive if it looked too glitzy and comfortable. On the other hand, merchandising here can provide customers with useful information, eg reminding the buyer about other relevant products and any special offers.

MERCHANDISING TOOLS

In addition to store design, layout, and merchandise ranges and policies, there are a number of in-store merchandising tools:

1) Leaflets and leaflet dispensers ('take one' boxes)
2) Stickers
3) Posters
4) Showcards and cardboard cutouts
5) Branded racks or display units
6) Dump bins
7) Three-dimensional
   — injection moulded characters (note: the tool-making process required takes too long for some campaigns)
   — holograms
   — free standing floor displays
8) Electronic gadgetry
   — spotlighting systems
   — video walls
   — illuminated display systems with fibre optics
   — magic mirrors
   — interactive POS systems, eg product advice systems and personal consultation systems
9) Shelf space (number of facings, colour blocking — see page 370, integrated pack design — how all the packs look beside each other on the shelf)
10) Shelf positioning (premium locations, cross-merchandising, etc)
11) In-store sampling
12) Window displays

McEnroe's service

Imagine walking into a high street department store and being greeted by a three-dimensional lifelike copy of John McEnroe's head. As you walk past, it starts to move and even speaks to you...pointing out the features of a tennis racket suspended in mid-air in front of you with no apparent means of support. Then a giant pair of moving lips — mounted on a glass display — suddenly start talking to you, inviting you to try on the store's winter fashions without even undressing. All you have to do, say the lips, is stand in front of a 'magic mirror' select an item of clothing and, before you can say 'Bruce Oldfield', your reflection is wearing it.

Brian Oliver, *Marketing Magazine*, 10 September 1987

These systems have been available for many years now. One possible problem with high tech POS is that customers end up admiring the POS material instead of buying the product. On the other hand, products can benefit from POS support as many products can get lost, eg among 16,000 items of food which a superstore displays. An innovative POS attracts attention — a key stage in the AIDA communication model discussed on page 71, Chapter 4. Although it is important to present fresh images to repeat visit customers to maintain their interest and loyalty, many retailers' obsession with product density and profit per square foot means they instantly dismiss most of a supplier's branded merchandising tools. In fact the majority of stores do not have the flexibility or the luxury of space to dedicate to one-off 'stunts' with in-built novelty obsolesence.

DISTRIBUTOR EMPATHY

Skilful supplier merchandising requires an ability to empathise with both the customer and the retailer/wholesaler (distributor). Understanding customers is one thing. Understanding distributors and their perspectives, goals, strategies and tactics is another. It is easy to grasp the importance of maintaining the theme of an advertising campaign inside a store with carefully designed point-of-sale displays. It is not so easy to understand when, why and how a retailer will allow its space to be used for such in-store promotions and display, ie what its merchandising policies are and how to operate within that framework.

This *'distributor empathy'* helps a supplier to make his product or service (and the relevant marketing communications) fit in with the retailer's plans. The retailer relationship is even more important in today's UK retail market since *market power* has moved from the manufacturer into the hands of a few major retail chains. It is therefore necessary to understand the various distributor strategies and their approach to merchandising techniques.

Many UK retailers do not enter into any merchandising arrangements with suppliers as they (the retailers) prefer to control all aspects of product presentation centrally to ensure commonality and consistency in all their stores. This is managed by carefully supervised store personnel and/or a roving display management and merchandising team. This does not mean that the supplier can have no involvement in the merchandising. Many stores encourage pro-active contributions from their suppliers. Some suppliers gain permission to use their own display teams to ensure that their particular products or services have optimum display on their allocated shelf at all times (see the Thomson Tour Operators short case at the end of this chapter).

RETAIL STRATEGIES

Every retailer has its *own marketing mix*. This fits in with its retailing strategy, which should, in turn, exploit its source of *competitive advantage* (eg exclusive products, lower prices, location or image). A department store exploits location, its quality of service and its quality range of products. A small independent grocery cannot compete on product range or price but can compete on its convenient location, opening hours and friendly relationship/rapport. A take-away restaurant may promote its unique home delivery service. Competitive advantage is relative to competitors' USPs (unique selling propositions) and customer needs. A constant monitoring of the uncontrollable variables which affect markets reveals how competitive advantage can emerge or erode over relatively short periods of time (see Chapter 8). Merchandising strategies are also affected by corporate cultures. For example, some distributors/ retailers are more profit-oriented than turnover-oriented. This, in turn, affects their pricing policies, promotion policies, merchandising policies, and in general, their merchandising strategies. Merchandising tools are now summarised and discussed under six key headings.

KEY MERCHANDISING TOOLS

1) Store image (external and internal).
2) Store layout (customer traffic flows).
3) Merchandise ranges.
4) Colour blocking.
5) Point-of-sale displays/retail sales promotions.
6) Miscellaneous.

Store image

The human eye is more sensitive than is sometimes imagined. Clues about a shop are absorbed, often sometimes without our knowing it. Psychologists call these '*cue patterns*'. These help shoppers to decide what kind of a shop it is before actually entering (if entering at all). The store's exterior offers an opportunity to communicate with the customer, eg to invite them into the store or to reinforce a desired corporate image. Inside the shop, the concept of the '*retail theatre*' becomes evident. It has been suggested that a retail design concept lasts only three to five years and hence the need for the adaptable retail theatre which allows the store's interior layout and design to be changed easily. It is worth remembering that *products, service and store design* all contribute towards the overall store image, but if a customer has no prior experience of a particular store nor any word-of-mouth reference from peers, then the decision to enter or not to enter may be made solely from the store's visual image (or simply the way it looks). The store's exterior is a bundle of cues. Even the psychological barrier or obstacle, the door, is removed or minimised wherever possible, thereby facilitating an even easier store entry.

Layout and traffic flow

Customer traffic flow can be directed around a store through detailed attention to layout. For example, nine out of ten people are right-handed and naturally prefer turning to the right so most supermarkets have the primary doors on the left-hand side so the shopping is done to the right in a sort of clockwise manner. *Flow-modelling time-lapse photos* analyse which people go where in the store (and at what times, days, weeks or months). Further analysis reveals where the *high density areas* are and whether they match the high turnover areas. Customer movements can be predicted by model questions like. 'If a customer were here (in the store) where would he/she go next?'. This is important because, as a general rule, if the goods are in the wrong place they won't sell: 'Out of sight out of mind'. *Primary and secondary visual points* (as opposed to clutter) are used to pull the customer around the store or to 'shop the full shop'. Lighting, signage, photographs, software packages and even popular products like KVIs (known value items) in a food supermarket help the customer to shop the full shop (or visit every part of the store ('the more you see the more you buy'). It is estimated that out of 16,000 food items on display in a superstore only approximately 200 are essentials (KVIs) such as tea, coffee, bread, etc.

Merchandise ranges

Once inside the store, the customer is faced with a bundle of retail cues which are never neutral. Fruit or perfume is positioned at the front of a store (supermarket and department store respectively). This helps to create images and feelings of freshness and luxury respectively. Impulse products are placed at key positions. Cross-merchandising reminds the customer of related end-use products, which are carefully positioned beside each other, eg shirts and ties together, pasta and pasta sauce. The maxim *'full shelves sell best'* is valid for FMCG retailers but not necessarily so for some clothes boutiques. Although *eye-level is buy-level*, shelf positioning can reflect the current *product life cycle* stage. The larger retail chains use *merchandising display software* packages to determine the right allocation of space to a particular product or brand. An 'optimum shelf lay-out' print-out (see Figure 19.1) shows what mix and quantities of packs on a shelf maximises a store's objectives (eg maximise sales, minimise over and under stocking maximise profitability, etc). It even gives a colour print-out of what the recommended shelf layout would look like. Some retailers like to have their own brands placed alongside the main brands, often on the left-hand side (since the western eye reads from left to right and therefore spots the own brand first).

Colour blocking

A supermarket customer scans shelves at the rate of four feet per second from a distance of eight feet away. Packaging, therefore, has to work very hard to attract the customer's eye. Retailers and packaging designers sometimes use colour blocking to attract attention by placing similarly coloured items close to each other to create a stronger shelf presence by means of a block of colour. Colour blocking can also link colours to product use associations, eg blue, green and white can be associated with stimulating and refreshing surf. This in turn might be built in to the shower gel section.

Point-of-sale displays/sales promotion

This includes displays, sampling points, dump displays and so on. Many retailers will not allow suppliers this free space since every square foot of retail generates a certain amount of revenue. Engel (1991) suggests that the manufacturer's response to a store's non-use of its POS materials is to double the quantity made available. This demonstrates the suppiers' lack of empathy with the retailers' merchandising policies,

(optimum display printout)

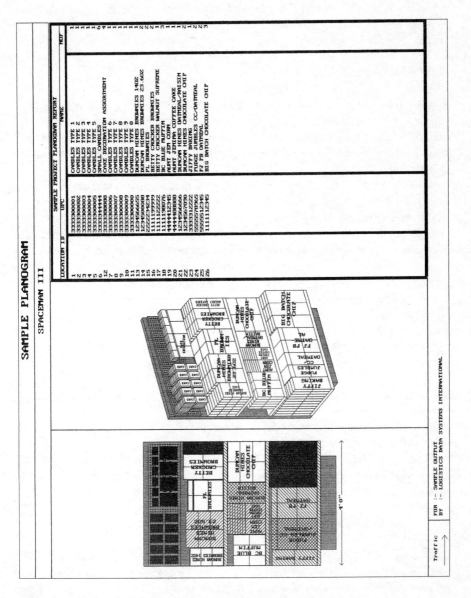

Figure 19.1 Optimum shelf printout shown from two angles

which is a waste of time and money as well as being a nuisance. On occasions, and in the appropriate store space, a retailer may allow the supplier the privilege of using extra space. Prime selling space can be bought by suppliers. A product's sales can be boosted depending on its location and shelf positioning. In-store *sales promotion* can *tie in with advertising, co-operative advertising, publicity* and perhaps even trade discounts and rebates. It should be designed to boost sales but without creating any conflict with overall store image. Balance, proportion, lighting, colour and display units should be used to create the optimum impact on a consistent basis (perhaps across many hundred stores). Once the store grants permission, field marketing agencies can then provide merchandising teams to maintain proper POS displays or shelf facings (see the Thomson short case at the end of this chapter).

Miscellaneous

In-store *sound* effects can be used to make announcements (eg to direct shoppers' attention to a special offer), to add atmosphere (crowd applause in sports shop video walls), to relax the buyer or to stimulate the buyer to move faster (eg varying the types of music) and so on. Some POS tools engage customers in a dialogue by asking questions.

Scents are also used inside a store to change shoppers' moods and buying behaviour. The Monell Chemical Sense Centre in Philadelphia has found its pilot projects highlight how the use of smell affects sales. For example, certain scents (in this case, a fruity floral scent) caused casual shoppers at a jewellery store to linger longer. An individual's brainwaves and moods (eg relaxed and trusting) can be changed by extremely low levels of certain scents. In the UK, a particular home furnishings retailer uses a bakery/cafe to entice customers into the store to buy non-food related products, eg clothing and lighting.

In supermarkets it is interesting to note how the smell from the fish counter is not as strong as the wafting smell of freshly baked bread at the bread counter.

London based Marketing Aromatics offer to create 'a particular atmosphere in a retail store, relax patients in a waiting room, perk up your sales team, or evoke associations in your customers' minds' through a variety of dispersion techniques 'from central ventilation systems to hand held sprays, in liquids, granules, gels or powder. Even pressure sensitive micro-encapsulated strips. These produce specific moods, neutralising unpleasant odours, impregnating product or corporate literature, endorsing a company's corporate identity — an aromatic logo.'

Finally, '*mindshare*' (discussed in Chapter 10) combined with merchandising techniques provides an extremely potent communications package as the store's sales staff, space and display promote a particular supplier's goods.

MEASURING MERCHANDISING EFFECTIVENESS

The bar code scanner at the checkout records what is being sold instantaneously. It can record the sales effect of allowing a product more shelf space, different shelf location, special displays and so on. EPOS (electronic point-of-sale) scanners also measure sales responses to new advertising campaigns and price changes, as well as providing operational stock control data to central warehouses. As suppliers and distributors work more closely together and become strategic partners, some suppliers are given access to a selection of EPOS data which measures sales results, store by store around the country, on a daily, weekly or even hourly basis.

SHORT CASE

Thomson Tour Operators

This short case demonstrates how vital merchandising is and how a field marketing agency manages the whole operation.

Racking is crucial to tour operators

Situation
Major travel operator Thomson Tours enjoys a dominant market share and offers a wide range of long and short-haul holidays to prospective customers via the travel agent in the competitive, and currently economically vulnerable, travel sector. 'Racking' (the display of a brochure in travel agents) is crucial to the success of all tour operators. Holidays are rarely booked without a comparison of the product offering from several competitors. Over 75 per cent of holidays are booked from a brochure that has been picked up and read. Few consumers ask counter staff for a brochure. It is therefore essential to ensure that the 30 different types of Thomson brochures are positioned in the right store, on the right shelf at the right time of year. Stock of replacement supplies has to be ready so that the appropriate brochure is available at the point-of-sale at the right time. The several thousand travel agents mean that this is too big a requirement to be handled by Thomson's in-house marketing and sales team.

Objective
To ensure that the right brochures are available to the 3,000 nominated travel agents at all times.

Strategy

A comprehensive brochure management and merchandising support programme was developed and contracted out to the a field marketing agency.

Tactics

- Stamping, racking and ordering brochures as required and where stocks allow. This includes use of BOBCAT — a computerised brochure ordering system based on Psion technology developed by Thomson with CPM Field Marketing. The system allows the merchandiser to transmit daily via a handheld computer to the brochure distribution house, thereby ensuring a speedy, accurate and effective stock control and delivery system.
- Carrying out short sales presentations, highlighting key selling points to counter staff.
- Supporting brochure launches with additional tactical activity during key periods. Blitz operations such as these involve the team making 3,000 calls in two days, with the final results presented to Thomson three weeks later.
- Three thousand agents are visited, normally every two weeks.

Targets

Three thousand nominated UK travel agencies.

Men

The field marketing agency, CPM, allocated a team of 65 field staff, eight supervisors, and one account manager to the on-going field marketing activity. This team is increased to 150 merchandisers and eight supervisors to support blitz operations at key times such as brochure launches. Both teams are headed by a national field manager who reports to Thomson's marketing department.

Money

Comprehensive field marketing activities range from £50,000 to £1,000,000 annually, depending upon the size and scope of the operation.

Minutes

All field marketing staff attend a fortnightly half-day briefing. This is supplemented by six-monthly one-day sales conferences where major briefing and reviews are presented. The normal call cycle which covers every one of the three thousand travel agents is two weeks. This means that every targeted travel agent gets visited and updated once a fortnight. Alternatively, a faster blitz can be completed within two days by using an extra 150 merchandisers.

Measurement

Thomsons previously sent off batches of brochures to travel agents without really knowing which agents were running out, which agents placed them on which shelves and which agents had them thrown in a pile in the store room. The new merchandising system gives them on-line data, which reduces wastage as the team ensures the right brochures are on the right shelf at the right time. This has helped to increase sales by ensuring that the brochures are available at all the targeted agents. At the same time, it has helped to reduce costs incurred by inappropriate print runs, unnecessary deliveries, etc.

Key Points from Chapter 19:

1) Merchandising techniques offer a last chance to communicate with the buyer.
2) Manufacturers need to empathise with their distributors' strategies and merchandising policies.

Further reading

Danger, P (1968) *Using Colour To Sell*, Gower, Aldershot

Engel, J, Warshaw, M and Kinnear, T (1991) *Promotional Strategy: Managing the Marketing Communications Process*, seventh edition, Irwin, Homewood, Illinois

Erlichman, J 'How hidden persuasion makes shoppers spend', *Guardian*, 11 August 1992

Further contacts

British Merchandising Association, Suite 12, 4th Floor, Parkway House, Sheen Lane, East Sheen, London SW14 8LS. Tel: 0181-878 0825/0738

Institute of Sales Promotion, Arena House, 66–68 Pentonville Road, London N1 9HS. Tel: 0171-837 5340

Sales Promotion Consultants Association (SPCA), Arena House, 66–68 Pentonville Road, London N1 9HS. Tel: 0171-702-8567

WORD OF MOUTH

WORD OF MOUTH

People talk about organisations, their products, their services and their staff. Whether it is a complaint, admiration or an endorsement, products and services are often a source of conversation. Today, it is not just the products themselves but their marketing communications including advertising campaigns, editorial stories, stunts and special offers which are also discussed. The multi-stage communications model on pages 60–1, Chapter 3 shows how word-of-mouth (WOM) can work for both advertisements and products.

Of all the elements of the communications mix, WOM is by far the *most potent* on a one-to-one basis. No amount of advertising or expert selling could compete with a colleague or friend recommending or criticising a particular product or service. Similarly, it is unlikely that a teaser advertisement could motivate a viewer to actively watch out for the next advertisement in a campaign in the way that WOM could. For example, a previous discussion about a particular advertisement among friends can arouse interest in and increase observation of subsequent television advertisements.

Communication tools themselves can be used to generate WOM. Publicity stunts, clever mailings, creative promotions and challenging advertising campaigns stimulate conversation among buyers and potential buyers, either because of their shock, humour and entertainment, or because of their abstract ideas.

There are other devices which encourage the WOM process such as postcards, T-shirts, photographs, awards and certificates (issued to visitors, customers and enquirers). NGN ('neighbour get neighbour') promotions (discussed in Chapter 3), referrals and networking all create opportunities for some form of dialogue about a particular product, service or organisation. This personal WOM medium can be budgeted for, planned and integrated into the marketing communications mix.

Marketing managers obviously want to ensure that first, people always say nice things about their products and second, that people never say bad things about their products. The most influential and controllable aspect of WOM communication is, of course, an individual's own direct experience of an organisation's products or services. This chapter therefore focuses on the two key factors which affect this experience: quality and customer care. But we first consider why and how WOM occurs.

Why and how word of mouth occurs

Why do people bother to talk about products and services in the first place? What exactly do they talk about? Do some people talk more than others? Are other people listened to more than others? Who are these *opinion leaders/opinion formers*? In industrial markets, the opinion leaders are relatively easy to identify, whereas in consumer markets careful research is usually required to identify the opinion leaders, their aspirations, lifestyles, media usage, etc. See how *style leaders* are fed specific messages on pages 61–2, Chapter 3.

Research suggests that *dissatisfied customers* talk about their bad experience to two or three times more people than *satisfied customers*. A dissatisfied customer can tell up to 11 other people about the bad experience they suffered with a particular product or service. Often the company never gets to hear about the complaint but the complaint is allowed to continue rampaging through a market. Bad news travels fast. As Philip Kotler (1988) says: 'Bad word of mouth travels further and faster than good word of mouth and can easily poison opinion about the company.' Satisfied customers, on the other hand, tend not to tell so many other people. They are, however, more likely to be retained as loyal customers since they enjoyed the experience in the first place.

Higher standards and higher levels of expectation among buyers are partly responsible for today's more vociferous customers. They are better informed and are less willing to make do with shoddy service or a faulty product. The consumer magazine *Which* publishes a leaflet called 'How to Complain'. Despite the higher standards and levels of expectancy, and greater customer confidence and knowledge about complaining, few dissatisfied customers actually bother to complain. Many organisations today try to get their customers to talk to them and tell them what is wrong (and also what is right) by asking them to fill in questionnaires (see Appendices 1 and 2 at the end of this chapter, pages 391 and 392) or by inviting them to phone free of charge on a free-phone (0800) number. Those who do phone in are generally invaluable to the company's future. Some organisations are so keen on developing a dialogue with their customers that they will operate outbound telemarketing campaigns as well as inbound (0800 numbers).

Welcome complaints

Only one in every 24 dissatisfied customers bother to complain (source: Technical Assistance Research Programme (TARP), USA). Rather than facing an unknown enemy of bitter, disappointed and dissatisfied customers, a complaint offers a chance to sort out the previously unknown problem. It gives the organisation the opportunity to find the enemy within (internal problems such as quality control, demotivated staff, etc). One company chairman takes time to listen to the taped telephone complaints while driving home in his car. Many service companies actually ask their customers to fill in a form about levels of satisfaction or dissatisfaction.

Solutions are relatively easy. Identifying the problem is the difficult part. Complaints are generally helpful. Philip Kotler (1988) suggests that companies should 'set up suggestion and other systems *to maximise the customer's opportunity to complain*'. He points out that the 3M company claim that 'over two thirds of its innovation ideas come from listening to customer complaints'. Listening is just the beginning. It is vital to have a system that enables a constructive response.

Stopping complaints before they happen

Telemarketing provides a low-cost method of keeping in touch with customers. Some customers may occasionally have the odd question which does not merit them making a telephone call but nevertheless they would like it answered. If left unanswered, the question can fester into a source of dissatisfaction. Frequent outbound telephone contact (where the company calls the customer) in the form of after-sales service (eg simply checking to see if everything is all right or whether any stocks need replenishing) can be used to support the field salesorce schedule of personal visits. Inbound (0800 and freephone) customer service lines can also reassure customers if they are made aware of the facility. ICL computer company has a team of *telephone diagnosticians* who handle fault reports from customers. Linked to a sophisticated computerised diagnostic kit, they can identify whether the fault really exists or not. Many problems arise from the user's lack of knowledge, which means many potential problems or frustrations can be sorted out over the phone. If a fault is identified, the diagnosis informs the engineer in advance so that he or she arrives with the right spare part.

The 1 – 10 – 100 rule

In *Customer Care* (Sarah Cook, 1992) points out that it has been proven that by actively listening to customers (and their complaints) companies can save, rather than spend, money. Federal Express's 1 – 10 – 100 rule illustrates the point. This says:

> For every pound your company might spend on preventing a quality problem, it will spend ten to inspect and correct the mistake after it occurs. In the worst case, the quality failure goes unanswered or unnoticed until after your customer has taken delivery. To fix the problem at this stage, you probably pay about 100 times what you could have paid to prevent it from happening at all.

Influencing word of mouth

In addition to the other WOM tools discussed at the beginning of this chapter, WOM is, as already mentioned, directly affected by levels of customer satisfaction. This experience is, in turn, directly affected by two key controllable factors:

1) Quality
2) Customer care.

The new importance of quality and customer care

Quality and customer care have become an important element in differentiating one company from another. Managed properly, they can create competitive advantage. Talking about quality and customer service, Tom Peters (1992) recently said that they were 'very commonplace words that had slipped out of the business lexicon in favour of a whole bunch of jargony words which ten or fifteen years ago were dominating America and coming to dominate the thinking patterns in Great Britain.' He continued: 'at the time everyone was involved in their portfolio strategy models, and their optimisation and their regression analysis and their linear programmes and so on.' These are useful but the message is clear — do not forget about customers, who are ultimately the centre of the universe for the corporation. Peters added: 'Ten years ago you would not have had a conference with that title ("Conference on Customers") in Manhattan, London, Milan or Frankfurt. Ten years ago, we would have had "marketing strategies for the 90s" or something like that and would have gotten out the next ten obscure theories.'

QUALITY

During the 1950s Dr Joseph Juran's 'managerial breakthrough' programmes in Japan helped to create and consolidate quality systems in Japanese business through his 'breakthrough and prevention' versus 'control and inspection' approach. The design profession has developed a similar approach to product and manufacturing design. The design maxim 'design quality in, instead of, inspecting faults out' speaks for itself.

Forty years later Tom Peters spoke to top British managers about quality and said 'Quality — one of the better-kept secrets — secrets well known to people such as the Germans and the Japanese — not so well known, unfortunately, to the Americans and British! Quality has always paid.'

Quality guru John Humble reasserted the importance of quality by highlighting its impact on financial performance when he said that 'research demonstrates that sustained financial performance is determined by the relative perceived quality of an organisation's products and services.' (Euromonitor Conference on Quality, London, May 1989.)

Total quality management

Today, total quality management (TQM) is becoming better understood. The British Standard BS 5750* gives companies an opportunity to set targets and formally measure quality standards throughout the organisation. TQM has three elements:

1) A documented system which defines quality standards.

---

* BS 5750 is identical to both EN2 9000 (Euro Norm) and ISO 9000 (International Standards Organisation)

2) Organisational processes to ensure quality is focused on customers.
3) A system of measurement which helps to monitor and control.

TQM is not a bureaucratic quagmire creating mini-empires, but rather a visionary management system of improving both customer and employee levels of satisfaction, communication and motivation. There are many methods of measuring whether TQM is worthwhile or not. One simple criterion is the level of *customer retention* (how many existing customers come back again). In 1984, Rank Xerox had a customer retention value of 52 (52 per cent came back and 48 per cent went elsewhere). They launched their TQM programme in the same year. By 1990 customer retention was up to 92 while return on investment just about doubled. Today they measure (a) new customer satisfaction within 48 hours of installation, (b) all customers and their levels of satisfaction every month (see questionnaire on page 392), (c) levels of customer satisfaction compared against competition (called 'benchmarking') once a year, and (d) employee satisfaction.

The McGregor Cory short case at the end of this chapter demonstrates the improvements in customer communications that can come about through innovative TQM.

Partnership sourcing

Partnership sourcing encourages open communications and close co-operation between customer and supplier. In a sense it is the *ultimate in marketing communications*.

When John Egan became chairman of Jaguar he systematically questioned Jaguar owners, analysed warranty claims, etc and found 150 recurring faults. Sixty per cent originated with bought-in components, so Egan raised the suppliers' standards by initiating joint studies and quality audits. Suppliers had to sign an agreement accepting responsibility for warranty costs caused by failure of their part/s. Partnership sourcing creates even closer involvement between suppliers and buyers by encouraging both parties to work together more closely on everything from specifying manufacturing systems, investment in machinery, delivery schedules, repeat orders and exclusivity. Price is only one element in the total cost negotiations. These can cover many other aspects which ultimately affect costs and sales (eg delivery size and frequency of deliveries, quality levels, materials and design specifications, etc).

The short case at the end of this chapter demonstrates how partnership sourcing and customer care integrate successfully.

CUSTOMER CARE

A gentle mind and a Disney smile

The motto of one department store in the Ginza district of Tokyo reads: 'leading store in courtesy and kindness'. Employees make a written commitment to increase customer service called a 'kindness declaration'. The president's own proclamation is to 'treat customers with gentle eyes, gentle face, gentle words, gentle behaviour and a gentle mind.' Two examples from the employees' declarations read: 'I will never get upset' and 'I will keep a Disney smile'.

(Source: Open University, 1990)

Customer care is more than an isolated 'smile campaign'. In fact it has to be sustainable and *internally marketed* or promoted so that all staff believe in, and are happy about, the customer care programme. The Mariott Hotel chief, Mr Mariott, once summarised the issue when he said 'How can we make customers happy with unhappy staff?' So staff have to be happy and trained in customer care. Involvement, reward and recognition can create forms of psychic income (see page 196, Chapter 10) which motivate staff. Research findings from the Harvard Business School suggest that organisations should now refocus equally on their employees, their customers and their investors (as opposed to investors first, customers second and employees last). The idea is that happy employees generate happy customers, who generate repeat business plus positive WOM references, which, in turn, boosts sales, profits and ROI.

Tom Peters (1992) says that managers need to be trained to 'allow people to use their heads as well as their arm muscles'. It has been suggested that 85 per cent of problems are created by managers. Empowerment is a great motivator, eg ideas or solutions generated by staff are more likely to be imlemented. Some supervision is, of course, needed. Everyone cannot implement their own idea. Even cost saving/revenue generating suggestions need resources to manage them. In one year alone Matsushita Electric had 6,446,935 suggestions or 79.6 suggestions per employee (Japanese Human Relations Association). It requires resources to deal with and respond to suggestions. A suggestion scheme without feedback defeats the purpose since it can create disillusionment, demotivation and even distrust. Feedback in customer care terms is also vital. A measurable customer care programme which is communicated to the staff helps them to understand the direct effect of their input.

The first generation

The first generation customer care programmes dealt with the customer interface. This can be difficult enough. Dealing with customers who have had a bad experience, or who are sometimes irritable, tired, confused, ripped off, lonely, greedy, demanding and occasionally downright dishonest, is, in itself, demanding. Nevertheless, a plastic smile supported by the 'have a nice day' syndrome may eventually make both staff and customers even more weary, as the Ed McLachlan cartoon overleaf demonstrates.

The ability not just to be sympathetic but to solve problems is worth developing. *The second generation* customer care programme goes beyond simply trying constantly to improve the first generation results. The second phase programme goes behind the customer interface and into the back room where organisation structures, operational systems and management styles exist. The steps in the process from customer enquiry or complaint through to customer satisfaction have to be analysed for duplication and inefficiencies.

Arthur Daly

Customer care is the antithesis of the Arthur Daly school of used car salesmen, who, after making a sale, fall on their knees and pray that they never see the customer again.

The 'have a nice day' syndrome may eventually make staff and customers even more weary

Perhaps chairmen and directors are as guilty of the Arthur Daly syndrome as anyone else. After all, how many of them actually spend time with customers instead of just spending time with shareholders, bankers, other directors and staff? David Jackson of Digital (1992) suggested that it is worth checking the director's diary to see what, if any, time is reserved for customers. He went on to ask these potentially embarassing questions:

> Do reports about customer satisfaction regularly appear on the agenda of senior managers' meetings?

> Is impact on customer satisfaction considered when new investments are being appraised?

> How many policies and rules introduced last year relate directly to improving life for the customer?

Fortune magazine recently reported that the NCR company makes every corporate officer, including the chief executive officer, personally responsible for a couple of big customers.

Ten stages of developing a customer care programme

Sarah Cook's *Customer Care* (1992) identifies ten stages of developing a customer care programme:

1) Gain management commitment.
2) Develop TQM.
3) Listen to customers.
4) Establish a customer care programme.
5) Engender ownership.
6) Understand internal customers (employees).
7) Train.
8) Communicate.
9) Recognise and reward good service.
10) Sustain a customer focus.

Listening to customers is a basic requirement of marketing. Yet how many organisations really listen to customers, let alone prospects? Effective listening is action oriented, ie feedback is not an end in itself. It facilitates improvement through better behaviour and actions.

Customer care — over-commitment

Roy Hill reported that some years ago when Japan Airlines' passengers on a flight to Europe suffered severe food poisoning, the man in charge of catering in Japan committed suicide.

Eight ways to lose a customer

This list could be expanded to a hundred ways but here are a few classics:

1) Poor quality product or service.
2) Making it difficult to buy (complex order or enquiry forms).
3) Poor internal communications (playing 'pass the customer' until somebody eventually decides to deal with the customer).
4) Slow response to enquiries, orders, problems or complaints.
5) Slow phone answering.
6) Inadequate information (no brochures, no prices, unknowledgeable salespeople, etc).
7) Rash promises (the product/service doesn't match the promise).
8) Arrogance.

Customer kindness

Philanthropists might see customer kindness simply as a nice way to work and live with other people. Some companies see it as a means of developing a competitive advantage. As mentioned previously, the Open University highlights a leading department store which sees courtesy and kindness as tools which sharpen their competitive edge. A store where the employees sign a 'kindness declaration' and the store's president makes 'gentleness policies' ('with gentle eyes, gentle face, gentle words, gentle behaviour and a gentle mind') may seem dream like, a land where shops aim to be 'kind and courteous, smiling, careful, friendly, gentle and warm'. A land where employees repeat 'I will never get upset. I will keep a Disney Smile'.

Service while you queue

A Japanese store minimises queuing as an obstacle to happy shopping by handing out towels (hot in winter and cold in summer) to motorists queuing for parking.

MANAGING QUALITY AND CUSTOMER CARE

Many organisations realise that their future survival lies in their customers' current levels of satisfaction. New customers can be won at a much higher cost (five times) than retaining old ones. The everlasting customer can come back again and again if satisified ('marketing is the selling of goods that don't come back to those that *do*'). Quality programmes and customer care programmes require resources, including the 3 Ms. Some argue that certain markets, depending on the stage in their life cyle, require less service than others. How expensive are the trappings of service? What is the cost of TQM? Does it have a direct effect on return on investment? Can it be sustained? Is customer care a gigantic task? The final part of this chapter attempts to answer some of these questions, and finishes with a look at the manager of the future.

The trappings of service

Managers are constantly facing the question 'can costs be significantly cut by reducing the trappings of extra service?' This, of course, can affect the rest of the marketing mix since reduced cost can allow prices to be cut or the savings enjoyed (from the reduced cost) to be spent on extra promotion, extra product improvements, or kept in reserve for short term profits. On the other hand, would a lack of service create a competitive disadvantage? Or perhaps there is a segment of customers who don't want the frills but would welcome a more cost effective basic product or service? Can extra service create competitive advantage and for how long? Shiv Mathur (1981) has written some interesting papers addressing what he calls 'transaction costs'. He suggests that there are at least four different ways of making transactions and competing, by mixing different levels of customer service with different types of products in different markets. Some transactional mixes are more appropriate than others at various stages in the product life cycle.

The cost of total quality management

Companies like Rank Xerox consider the cost of quality to consist of three components: 1) cost of conformance; 2) cost of non-conformance; and 3) cost of lost opportunity. The cost of conformance means the cost of conforming exactly to a customer's specific requirements. In other words, what it costs to get it right first time every time so that the customer gets exactly what he wants every time instead of most of the time. If conformance does not occur (or it is not right first time) then the mistake, or non-conformance, has to be fixed. This second component costs money, time and efforts. Since the money spent on fixing the problem is no longer available for investment in the market then an additional forfeited opportunity or 'cost of lost opportunity' arises. This is the third component. They estimate that the cost of non-conformance plus the cost of lost opportunities is typically 20 – 25 per cent of the revenue of a company. For some companies that means one out of every four or five employees go to work every day to fix yesterday's mistakes.

Federal Express's 1 – 10 – 100 rule on page 378 might calculate the cost as even higher. If the customer is lost the cost could perhaps be boosted by the lifetime value or forfeited repeat sales.

Return on investment

Customer kindness and efficient service can help to retain customers by building customer satisfaction and, ultimately, customer loyalty. The cost of retaining customers is conservatively estimated at one fifth of the cost of acquiring a new customer. Existing customers generate bigger margins and profits (per customer) than new ones. A customer retention level of 94 per cent yields profitability of just 50 per cent of what it would be at 98 per cent retention level (American Managment Centre, Europe). Customer satisfaction makes the difference between short-term success and long-term growth and prosperity. Higher customer retention generates higher ROI (as we saw in the Rank Xerox example on page 380).

If profits increase while customer satisfaction is falling then poor financial results are on the horizon. Kotler (1988) makes the point:

> Profits could go up or down in a particular year for many reasons, including rising costs, falling prices, major investments, and so on, but the ultimate sign of a healthy company is that its customer satisfaction index is high and keeps rising. *Customer satisfaction is the best indicator of the company's future profits.*

Having said that, the company has to understand that customer care may incur immediate or short-term costs while some of the financial benefits may sometimes only emerge in the medium to long-term. Japan's world-class management guru, Kenichi Ohmae (1982), sees management time horizons as a fundamental difference between eastern and western strategies. Western companies plan for short-term profits while Japanese companies plan for long-term profits.

However, some western companies are waking up to the value of investing in customer satisfaction, customer care and overall quality of product. Quantified objectives can be set that can translate directly into turnover or bottom line profits.

One per cent customer satisfaction = $500m

IBM calculate that each percentage point improvement in customer service satisfaction translates into $500 million more revenue over five years.

Sustained performance

After the initial enthusiasm dies down, the real management task begins — sustaining and even improving the levels of customer care, satisfaction and retention. Competitive advantage may erode as other companies develop their own TQM systems. In the long term, customer service is not just about customer care or product quality. According to Professor John Murray of Trinity College, Dublin (1991), it is about 'serving customers by creating and leveraging distinctive company capabilities in a manner that outperforms competing companies in a sustainable form'. In a sense this also requires clear communications with the customer so that they are fully aware, at all times, of just how good the company is, how much it tries and succeeds, and how much it cares.

Customer care — a gigantic task

Customer care is considered by some to be difficult to manage as staff often encounter customers in an unsupervised situation. Large organisations can find the customer care concept difficult to spread throughout the organisation. It seems sometimes that everyone loves to hate someone some of the time. *Marketing Week*'s resident cynic, Iain Murray (1990) once commented:

> Few things can be more foolish than British Rail's continuing attempts to inculcate some small measure of charm in its employees. Even if it could be achieved, which, given the raw material to hand, it could not, it would never work in practice since railway staff have no vested interest in the satisfaction of customers and therefore see not the slightest need to be nice to them.

Nevertheless, there lies the challenge. Before King Hassan of Morocco made a visit to Britain the *Independent* newspaper reported that:

> the King has been known to close airports and entire cities when visiting. The king is accustomed to high standards of personal service. At home, he walks in his eight palaces preceded by his chamberlain carrying a mace while the courtiers cry 'May Allah preserve our Lord and Master'. It is hoped that British rail staff will meet the challenge.

Caring for customers, employees and stockholders

The challenges of customer care, product quality and employee satisfaction are worth meeting as Harvard Business School professors John Ketter and James Heskett (1992) point out: Their 11 year study examined the effects of prioritising three stakeholders: customers, employees and stockholders. They found that highly profitable companies serve the interests of all three stakeholders while less profitable companies only satisfy one or two of these stakeholders (eg good customer care scores but low employee satisfaction). Over 200 major US companies were extensively surveyed. Those who successfuly satisfied the three interests increased sales (over the 11 year period) by an average of 682 per cent compared with 166 per cent for those companies that only satisfied one or two of these stakeholders. Differences in stock performance were even more extreme: up 901 per cent and 74 per cent respectively.

Tomorrow's manager

Tomorrow's successful companies will be leaner, flatter (less hierarchical) and more flexible. This means that tomorrow's marketing manager will have to be multi-skilled and fully understand people management, programme management, customer care programmes and quality management programmes.

SHORT CASE

McGregor Cory's Partners

This short case demonstrates how customer care and product quality come together to create the ultimate communications tool.

Situation
Increasingly, manufacturers and retailers are realising the benefits of contracting their

distribution requirements to a professional third-party operator whose sole business is distribution. In this way, valuable resources such as capital, labour and time can be released for re-investment. The company can focus fully on its core activities.

McGregor Cory is a contract distribution services company operating in the UK and mainland Europe. With an annual turnover rapidly approaching £100 million, they are one of the top five UK players in a highly competitive market where word of mouth is sovereign.

Objective
To become an outstanding player in European contract distribution.

Strategy
Establish and develop long-term strategic partnerships with customers, through the provision of a total quality service.

Tactics
In the autumn of 1990 the total quality management (TQM) system was formally set up. It required a company commitment to the staff and to the customers. By winter of 1990 things were already beginning to change — for the better. The TQM programme was designed to improve the quality of employment, the quality of product (actual delivery service) and the quality of customer care. It encompassed the following key areas:

1) Staff motivation, training and consultation.
2) Customer awareness and responsiveness programmes
3) Partnership documents (including multi-level channels of communication/man-for-man marketing).
4) A system of measuring effectiveness.

Staff motivation, training and consultation
Since winter of 1990 staff are invited to *team briefing sessions* which allow a regular, two-way, direct dialogue with management. There is no restriction on the subject matter during these discussions and, rather than providing a forum for mutual verbal abuse and accusation, they have proved invaluable in identifying new ways of improving McGregor Cory's service to its customers. Through group discussion and evaluation of operational systems, a genuine sense of ownership is generated in individual employees. This, in turn, encourages greater employee commitment, especially when employers know that their suggestions will not go unheeded and, where valid, are actually 'actioned'. Through the team briefing system, individual concerns are initially addressed to management and, if the matter cannot be resolved at this stage, it will be referred upwards, if necessary to the chief executive.

Personal recognition is also important in terms of motivation. Certificates of Merit are awarded for long service, or for an outstanding idea that measurably improves efficiency. Both the achievement and the presentation ceremony are reported extensively in the company newsletter — one of many invaluable uses of this popular communications tool. As well as to increasing self-esteem and a sense of pride in one's work, the awards also tend to bring out the natural competitive spirit in the workforce, thereby promoting staff morale and improved service levels on a wider scale.

Exchange visits to and from the customer's workplace and open days for employees families are ongoing activites aimed at developing the potential of the individual and at the same time optimising employee commitment to the corporate aim of outstanding customer service. The customers also appreciate it as both parties are able to put faces to names. They also get to understand how the other works and, in particular, what the customer really needs.

Customer awareness and responsiveness programme

Here, the importance of the customer is explained in a way that clearly shares the responsibility of all staff towards customers, the company, their jobs and their future. The concept goes beyond 'the customer is king' to ' the customer is a partner', where their business is part of McGregor Cory's business and McGregor Cory's business is considered to be an extension of the customer's operations. The continued importance of addressing customer needs swiftly and efficiently is reinforced by ensuring that key customer messages permeate every level of the organisation. Specially commissioned posters, calendars, pens, mugs, coasters, notice boards, quality bulletins and the in-house newsletter constantly carry messages such as the cartoon calendar below.

The cartoon calendar format was originally suggested by a member of the UK staff. The 1993 concept has come from staff in Holland.

Customer responsiveness is measured across a range of pre-set objectives (eg maximum number of rings of the telephone is three). Individual targets are set for each customer, as explained in the partnership document.

The partnership document

These non-legally-binding documents operate alongside the main contract of service and seek to quantify the key aspects critical to establishing a long and succesful partnership. The document includes (a) mutual responsibilities and expectations; (b) clearly defined performance criteria and measurement; and (c) agrees multi-level channels of communication. This 'man-for-man marketing' ensures that each individual from managing director to contract manager at both companies is appropriately matched to discuss relevant aspects of the operation. For each management level, regular opportunities to meet, review and forward plan for future needs are mutually agreed in advance, thereby ensuring a regular dialogue between both parties. It also helps to take doubt out of the relationship.

Written and signed by both parties, key sections of the document are then placed on permanent display at the distribution centre concerned. In this way, all those involved in the business are made constantly aware of their repsonsibilities and how their performance will be judged. The document remains subject to regular review and adaptation to meet the evolving nature of the operation.

A system of measurement

Without measurent and feedback the whole TQM system falls apart.

Customer satisfaction is measured at least twice annually, using critical success factors (CSFs) decided by the customer. These CSFs cover aspects such as handling, accuracy, delivery and housekeeping. Surveys may be conducted by post, telephone or face to face, whichever method is preferred by the customer. The surveys consist of a series of prompted and unprompted questions. The results enable McGregor Cory to measure with reasonable accuracy the company's progress in raising customer service levels, as well as to pinpoint any further areas for improvement.

In this way customer trust is gained at the outset, and customer satisfaction and loyalty is generated, which generally manifests itself in repeat business or extended business. The new TQM system has already boosted customer retention while employee turnover and absenteeism are down.

A detailed survey of the Institute of Transport Management's 17,500 members — drawn from all areas of transport and distribution — asked respondents to identify one company they would entrust their distribution requirements to, taking account of key service considerations such as quality and reliability. McGregor Cory proved to be first choice. In the same year they won the *Motor Transport* award for customer care.

In an industry where word of mouth is sovereign the ultimate accolade comes from the customers themselves: 'We cannot speak too highly of the full co-operation and identification of McGregor Cory with our aims objectives' (taken from a letter to McGregor Cory from one of its major customers).

APPENDIX 1

Nissan customer questionnaire

PLEASE TELL US WHAT YOU THINK.

1. Which ONE of the following statements BEST describes the way you feel about the action taken by our Customer Care Department and dealer network to respond to your request for assistance?

   ☐ I was completely satisfied.

   ☐ I was not completely satisfied but the action taken was acceptable.

   ☐ I was not completely satisfied ·but some action was taken.

   ☐ I was dissatisfied with the action taken.

   ☐ I was very dissatisfied - I don't consider any action was taken at all.

2. How satisfied were you with our Customer Care Department in *each* of the following areas?

	Very Satisfied	Quite Satisfied	Neither Satisfied nor Dissatisfied	Quite Dissatisfied	Very Dissatisfied
RESPONSE:					
Promptness	☐	☐	☐	☐	☐
Clarity	☐	☐	☐	☐	☐
Helpfulness	☐	☐	☐	☐	☐
Follow-through on promised action	☐	☐	☐	☐	☐

   Please answer the rest of the items in Question 2 only if you PHONED our Customer Care Department:

	Very Satisfied	Quite Satisfied	Neither Satisfied nor Dissatisfied	Quite Dissatisfied	Very Dissatisfied
EASE OF CONTACT:					
Ability to get through on the first call	☐	☐	☐	☐	☐
Length of time on hold	☐	☐	☐	☐	☐
PERSONNEL:					
Courtesy	☐	☐	☐	☐	☐
Professionalism	☐	☐	☐	☐	☐
Knowledge	☐	☐	☐	☐	☐

3. How many times did you have to contact our Customer Care Department before your question/problem was answered?

1	2	3	4	5+	Final Action Still Not Taken
☐	☐	☐	☐	☐	☐

4. Please rate your overall satisfaction with our Customer Care Department.

Very Satisfied	Quite Satisfied	Neither Satisfied nor Dissatisfied	Quite Dissatisfied	Very Dissatisfied
☐	☐	☐	☐	☐

5. How likely is it that that you would recommend Nissan vehicles to a friend or colleague?

I definitely will	I probably will	I might or might not	I probably will not	I definitely will not
☐	☐	☐	☐	☐

APPENDIX 2

Rank Xerox customer questionnaire

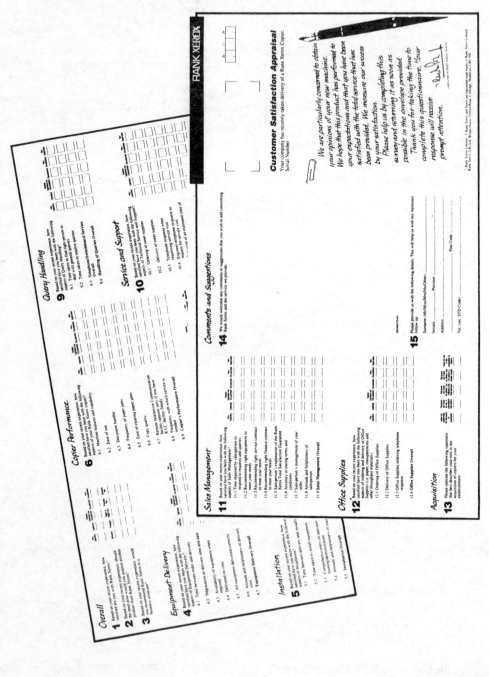

Key Points from Chapter 20:

1) Customer experiences of product/service quality and customer service have a bigger impact on individual customers than any other communications tool.
2) Customer retention boosts sales, profits and return on investment.

Further reading

Barwick, S 'King Hassan's bed and breakfast in Brighton', *The Independent*, 11 July 1987

Christopher, M, Payne, A and Ballantyne, D (1991) *Relationship Marketing*, Butterworth-Heinemann, Oxford

Clutterbuck, D 'Counsel of care', *Marketing Magazine* 18 May 1989

Cook, S (1992) *Customer Care*, Kogan Page, London

Crosby, P (1984) *Quality Without Tears*, McGraw Hill, New York

Jackson, D 'The art and science of service', *Marketing Business* July/August 1992, p.32

Kotter, J and Heskett, J (1992) *Corporate Culture and Performance*, Free Press

Kotler, P (1988) *Marketing Management Analysis, Planning, Implementation and Control*, sixth edtition, Prentice Hall, Englewood Cliffs, New Jersey

The Marketing Institute News, 'Competitive advantages versus customer care', Marketing Institute of Ireland, vol 4, no 9, December 1991

Mathur, S (1981) 'Strategic industrial marketing: transaction shifts and competitive response', City University, Working Paper No.33

Murray, I, 'Civil servant without a smile', *Marketing Week*, 21 September 1990

Ohmae, K (1982) *The Mind of the Strategist*, Penguin Business Library

Open University (1990) *Retail Management: Policy and Merchandising*

Peters, T (1992) *In Conversation With*, BBC Training Videos

Stevens M (1992) *The Handbook of Telemarketing*, Kogan Page, London

Wilson, J (1991) *Word of Mouth Marketing*, John Wiley & Sons, Chichester

Further contacts

Institute of Customer Care, St John's House, Chapel Lane, Wescott, Surrey RH4 3PJ. Tel: 01306 876210

The British Quality Foundation, 215 Vauxhall Bridge Road, London SW1V 1EN. Tel: 0171-931 0607

British Standards Institute, 389 Chiswick High road, London W4 4AL. Tel: 0181-996 9000

The National Quality Information Centre, PO Box 712, 61 Southwark Street, London SE1 1SB. Tel: 0171-401 7227

Technical Assistance Research Programme (TARP), 6 Spring Gardens, Citadel Place, Tinwort Street, London SE11 5EH. Tel: 0171-793 1866

CONCLUSION

Repeat business is the name of the game. Reasonable quality products and services, supported by solid customer care, creates a platform for successful marketing communications. Just as the tools of the marketing communications mix are integrated, so too are the other elements of the marketing mix, namely product, price and place.

Marketing is not an isolated discipline. It has to integrate with finance, production, personnel, administration and many more areas within the organisation (see the profile below). In fact, the longer-term corporate strategies should feed into various marketing activities, from new product launches and corporate identity development to advertising end lines. The longer term and corporate perspective (which, in turn, drives the marketing strategies) has over the last few decades given eastern companies the advantage over their western counterparts, who suffer from the competitive disadvantage created by the over-emphasis on short-term profits. The knock-on effect of an eventual change in corporate cultures will affect all marketing activities. Similarly, constant changes in the business environment will require constant review and probable changes in marketing communications.

Finally, may skills are required in marketing. The profile opposite is taken from a recruitment advertisement placed by Colgate Palmolive.

Today's marketing professional requires more than just a knowledge of marketing communications. The challenge is yours.

If you have any comments, criticisms or suggestions for improvements in the next edition, please write to me at Kogan Page Publishers.

Paul R Smith

- **STRATEGIC BUSINESS UNDERSTANDING**
  CONCEPTUAL
  TAKES BROAD, LONG TERM VIEW
  CONSIDERS ALL PERSPECTIVES
  EVALUATES ALL FACTORS
- **CREATIVITY AND FLEXIBILITY**
  INNOVATIVE
  QUESTIONS STATUS QUO
  ANTICIPATES AND INITIATES CHANGE
  MULTI-DISCIPLINARY INTERESTS
  CHAMPIONS NEW IDEAS
- **ANALYSIS AND DECISION MAKING**
  CLARIFIES OBJECTIVES
  IDENTIFIES KEY ISSUES
  EVALUATES OPTIONS
  CONSIDERS IMPLICATIONS
  ACTION ORIENTATED
- **NUMERACY AND FINANCIAL UNDERSTANDING**
  UNDERSTANDS FINANCIAL ACCOUNTS
  PROFIT CONSCIOUS
  COSTS OUT ALL OPTIONS
  BACKS RECOMMENDATIONS WITH QUANTITIVE DATA
- **RESULTS ORIENTATION**
  CAREFUL ORGANISER AND PLANNER
  PROACTIVE
  EXPLOITS AVAILABLE RESOURCES
  OVERCOMES OBJECTIONS
  DELIVERS PROMISE
- **MANAGEMENT OF RELATIONSHIPS**
  TEAMWORKER
  LISTENS TO OTHERS
  DIRECT AND OPEN
  PERSUASIVE
  CONFIDENT IN VIEWS
  PROMOTES EFFECTIVE WORKING
  RELATIONSHIPS
- **COMPUTER LITERACY**
  APPLIES NEW TECHNOLOGY
  READILY ACCESSES DATA
  ANALYSES PERFORMANCE

© Nucleus Advertising, London, 1991.

The Integrated Marketer

INDEX